# Rethinking Media Change

**Media In Transition**

David Thorburn, *series editor*

Edward Barrett, Henry Jenkins, *associate editors*

# Rethinking Media Change

The Aesthetics of Transition

*Edited by David Thorburn and Henry Jenkins*
*Associate Editor: Brad Seawell*

The MIT Press
Cambridge, Massachusetts
London, England

First MIT Press paperback edition, 2004

This book was set in Perpetua by Graphic Composition, Inc.
Printed and bound in the United States of America.

Library of Congress Cataloging-in-Publication Data
Rethinking media change : the aesthetics of transition / edited by David Thorburn and Henry
    Jenkins ; associate editor, Brad Seawell.
        p. cm. — (Media in transition)
    Includes bibliographical references and index.
    ISBN 13: 978-0-262-20146-9 (hc. : alk. paper), 978-0-262-70107-5 (pb.)
    ISBN 10: 0-262-20146-1 (hc. : alk. paper), 0-262-70107-3 (pb.)
        1. Mass media—History.  I. Thorburn, David. II. Jenkins, Henry, 1958–  III. Seawell, Brad.
    IV. Series.
    P90.R38 2003
    302.23'09—dc21
                                                                                    2002044447

10 9 8 7 6 5 4 3

# Contents

## Series Foreword

David Thorburn, *editor*
Edward Barrett, Henry Jenkins, *associate editors*

New media technologies and new linkages and alliances across older media are generating profound changes in our political, social, and aesthetic experience. But the media systems of our own era are unique neither in their instability nor in their complex, ongoing transformations. The Media in Transition series will explore older periods of media change as well as our own digital age. The series hopes to nourish a pragmatic, historically informed discourse that maps a middle ground between the extremes of euphoria and panic that define so much current discussion about emerging media—a discourse that recognizes the place of economic, political, legal, social, and cultural institutions in mediating and partly shaping technological change.

   Although it will be open to many theories and methods, three principles will define the series.

- It will be historical—grounded in an awareness of the past, of continuities and discontinuities among contemporary media and their ancestors.
- It will be comparative—open especially to studies that juxtapose older and contemporary media, or that examine continuities across different media and historical eras, or that compare the media systems of different societies.
- It will be accessible—suspicious of specialized terminologies, a forum for humanists and social scientists who wish to speak not only across academic disciplines but also to policymakers, to media and corporate practitioners, and to their fellow citizens.

*Rethinking Media Change: The Aesthetics of Transition*
**edited by David Thorburn and Henry Jenkins**

Challenging the assumption that new technologies displace older systems with decisive suddenness and have a revolutionary impact on society, the essays in this book see media change as an accretive, gradual process, always a mix of tradition and innovation, in which emerging and established systems interact, shift, and collude with one another.

The editors' introduction sketches an aesthetics of media transition, patterns of development and social dispersion that may operate across eras, media forms, and cultures. Some of the essays that follow are case studies of such earlier technologies as the printed book, the phonograph, early cinema, and television, while others examine contemporaray digital forms and explore something of their promise and strangeness. A final section probes aspects of visual culture in such environments as the evolving museum, movie spectaculars, and "the virtual window."

The editors wish to thank Barbara Thorburn for her rigorous editorial help.

Many of the essays originated in conferences and forums on the topic of media in transition funded by the Markle Foundation to mark the retirement of its visionary president *Lloyd Morrisett, to whom this book is dedicated.*

# Rethinking Media Change

# 1 Introduction: Toward an Aesthetics of Transition

David Thorburn and Henry Jenkins

## Against Apocalypse

*A change has taken place in the human mind. . . . The conviction is already not very far from being universal, that the times are pregnant with change; and that [our era] . . . will be known to posterity as the era of one of the greatest revolutions . . . in the human mind, and in the whole constitution of human society. . . . The first of the leading peculiarities of the present age is, that it is an age of transition.*
—John Stuart Mill, "The Spirit of the Age" (1831)[1]

Set aside the nineteenth-century tonalities, and this passage could belong to our own era. Its apocalyptic rhetoric and its self-conscious awareness of change closely mirror the discourse of the so-called digital revolution. Mill is responding to the vast transformations that define the nascent Victorian age—the introduction of the railroads, the emergence of powerful new manufacturing technologies, fundamental alterations in the economic and political order of English society, the expansion of a global empire.[2] The advent of the computer also has generated visions of apocalyptic transformation. In one recurring scenario, we stand on the cusp of a technological utopia where emerging communications systems foster participatory democracy and give all citizens access to an infinite range of commercial services, audio-visual texts, job training, libraries, and universities. The reverse of such optimism envisions an on-line culture of chaos, instability and greed in which pornographic images corrupt children and challenge parental authority; information is commodified and available only to those who can pay; political discourse is balkanized by extremist special interests; and human experience itself is "denatured" or displaced by the virtual reality of the computer screen.[3]

Similar utopian and dystopian visions were a notable feature of earlier moments of cultural and technological transition—the advent of the printing press, the development of still photography, the mass media of the nineteenth century, the telegraph, the telephone, the motion picture, broadcast television.[4] In these and other instances of media in transition, the actual relations between emerging technologies and their ancestor systems proved to be more complex, often more congenial, and always less suddenly disruptive than was dreamt of in the apocalyptic philosophies that heralded their appearance.[5] Across a range of examples, including the introduction of the compass in the middle ages, the telegraph, radio, satellite television, software, and digital music, Debora L. Spar argues that technological change follows a cycle of innovation and experimentation, commercialization and diffusion, creative anarchy and institutionalization.[6] During each phase, discourses proclaiming radical change may locate stress points where emerging forms of wealth and power appear to threaten established institutions.

In our current moment of conceptual uncertainty and technological transition, there is an urgent need for a pragmatic, historically informed perspective that maps a sensible middle ground between the euphoria and the panic surrounding new media, a perspective that aims to understand the place of economic, political, legal, social and cultural institutions in mediating and partly shaping technological change.[7] The essays in this book represent an effort to achieve such an understanding of emerging communication technologies. At once skeptical and moderate, they conceive media change as an accretive, gradual process, challenging the idea that new technologies displace older systems with decisive suddenness.[8]

Some contemporary doomsayers warn that the digital revolution signals the death of the book and the end of cinema. In such simplified models of media in transition, the new system essentially obliterates its predecessors, taking on the functions of its ancestors, and consigning the older form to the museum and the ash heap. The science fiction writer Bruce Sterling, for example, has established a website devoted to "dead media," old technologies that have outlived their usefulness.[9] But this seems a narrowly technical idea of media. Specific delivery technologies (the eight-track cassette, say, or the wax cylinder) may become moribund, but the medium of recorded sound survives. As many studies of older and recent periods attest, the emergence of new media sets in motion a complicated, unpredictable process in which established and infant systems may co-exist for an extended period or in which older media may develop new functions and find new audiences as the emerging technology begins to occupy the cultural space of its ancestors. Thus, traditional oral forms and practices outlast the advent of writing and even the culture of print; the illuminated manuscript survives for a time into the Gutenberg era; theater and the novel co-exist with movies and television; radio reinvents itself after TV displaces its entertainment and news-reporting role in the national culture. Moreover, in many cases apparently competing media may strengthen or reinforce one another, as books inspire movies which in turn stimulate renewed book sales, as television serves as a virtual museum for the history of film, as newspapers, television and movies today are discovering a variety of strategies for extending and redefining themselves on the World Wide Web.

As these instances suggest, to focus exclusively on competition or tension between media systems may impair our recognition of significant hybrid or collaborative forms that often emerge during times of media transition. For example, the Bayeux tapestry (c. 1067–1077) combined both text and images, and was explicated in spoken sermons—a multimedia bridge between the oral culture of the peasants and the learned culture of the monasteries.[10] Or consider the nineteenth-century practice of the painted photograph, an aberrant oddity to recent generations who take for granted the representational accuracy of mechanical reproduction in relation to images drawn by hand. In its day, though, the painted photograph—correcting photography's monochromy and its tendency to fade over time—was understood within the centuries-old tradition of portrait painting.[11] As a final example, contemporary experiments in story-telling are crossing and combining several media, exploiting computer games or web-based environments that offer immersive and interactive experiences that mobilize our familiarity with traditional narrative genres drawn from books, movies and television.

Current discussion about media convergence often implies a singular process with a fixed end point: All media will converge; the problem is simply to predict which media conglomerate or which specific delivery system will emerge triumphant.[12] But if we understand media convergence as a process instead of a static termination, then we can recognize that such convergences occur regularly in the history of communications and that they are especially likely to occur when an emerging technology has temporarily destabilized the relations among existing media. On this view, convergence can be understood as a way to bridge or join old and new technologies, formats and audiences. Such cross-media joinings and borrowings may feel disruptive if we assume that each medium has a defined range of characteristics or predetermined mission. Medium-specific approaches risk simplifying technological change to a zero-sum game in which one medium gains at the expense of its rivals. A less reductive, comparative approach would recognize the complex synergies that always prevail among media systems, particularly during periods shaped by the birth of a new medium of expression.

## Self-conscious Media

As our contemporary experience demonstrates, a crucial, distinguishing feature of periods of media change is an acute self-consciousness. McLuhan argues that "media are often put out before they are thought out."[13] Yet the introduction of a new technology always seems to provoke thoughtfulness, reflection, and self-examination in the culture seeking to absorb it. Sometimes this self-awareness takes the form of a reassessment of established media forms, whose basic elements may now achieve a new visibility, may become a source of historical research and renewed theoretical speculation. What is felt to be endangered and precarious becomes more visible and more highly valued. In our time the most decisive instance of this process is the multi-national scholarship devoted to the history of the book.[14] As William Mitchell's suggestive essay in this volume implies, the promise or threat of electronic books engenders a renewed consciousness of the rare and durable qualities of printed books, not least of which is their portability and their stability across time. Compared to the short life of various electronic and digital systems, including the operating systems of computers, the printed book is a "platform" reassuringly stable and secure.

Moreover, a deep and even consuming self-consciousness is often a central aspect of emerging media themselves. Aware of their novelty, they engage in a process of self-discovery that seeks to define and foreground the apparently unique attributes that distinguish them from existing media forms.

Consider this definitive instance of the profound self-reflexiveness of which a new medium is capable. In the third chapter of Part II of *Don Quixote* (Part I, 1605; Part II, 1615) the hero consults with his squire Sancho Panza and the learned scholar Sampson Carrasco, who is to report on the mysterious publication of Part I of the novel. This volume has appeared as if "by magic art," and much to Quixote's discomfort, even while

> the blood of the enemies he had slain was scarcely dry on his own sword-blade. . . . [I]f it were true that there was such a history, since it was about a knight errant it must perforce be grandiloquent, lofty, remarkable, magnificent and true. With this he was somewhat consoled; but it disturbed him to think that its author was a Moor, as that name of Cide suggested. For he could hope for no truth of the Moors, since they are all cheats, forgers, and schemers. He was afraid too that his love affairs might have been treated with indelicacy. (J. M. Cohen translation; Penguin Books, 1954)

The complex unease suggested here—Quixote's doubts about his chivalric enterprise encouraging the defensive suspicion that Moors are untrustworthy—continues through the whole of this chapter and the next, and makes a comic and aesthetically complex contrast with Sancho's confident, even aggressive loquaciousness. Repeatedly interrupting his learned betters, Sancho directs our attention toward those elements of their past adventures that are least Quixotic and most congruent with the pragmatic earthiness of his sense of the world. Some readers, Carrasco says, "would have been glad if the authors had left out a few of the countless beatings" endured by Quixote and his squire. The hero agrees, of course, but his squire does not. "That's where the truth of the story comes in," Sancho insists. This wonderful mixture of comic energy and philosophic/aesthetic argument is further enriched when Carrasco inquires into an apparent inconsistency in the history. "I don't know how to answer that," said Sancho. "All I can say is that perhaps the history-writer was wrong, or it may have been an error of the printer's."

This characteristic moment is, of course, a disconcertingly bold way of reminding us that the book we are reading is a physical object, a commodity produced and perhaps altered by technicians who know nothing of Dulcinea and probably do not care to know. It is appropriate, even deeply significant that Quixote actually visits a printing plant late in Part II, where he studies the physical processes by which books are made and where he discourses on the difficulties of translation, finally seeing a proofreader at work on the spurious second part of the *Quixote* itself.

This insistence on the limits of the book we hold in our hands, and especially Cervantes' recurring tactic of allowing the novel's several narrators to intrude into Quixote's story and to interrupt it, deflects attention toward what has been called *the drama of the telling,* a drama concerned not with the protagonist's adventures themselves but with the problems and difficulties of writing about them. The *Quixote* is, among other things, then, a book about the making of books and the nature of story telling. Its daring self-reflexive comedy is also a systematic exploration of the special properties of the infant medium of the novel.[15]

As the example of *Don Quixote* implies, often the most powerful explorations of the features of a new medium occur in comedy.[16] Many forms of self-reflexiveness are inherently skeptical, self-mocking, hostile to pretension. The early television comedian Ernie Kovacs regularly toyed with audience's expectations about the visual bias of television, creating anarchic comedy in absurd synchronizations of classical music with mundane activities (such as cracking open eggs to the *1812 Overture*). In one segment, Kovacs places a portable radio in front of the camera while the radio announcer's voice describes a woman in a revealing bathing suit. Here as elsewhere Kovacs seems to wink at the audience, as if to suggest that there are some things best enjoyed on television. In another skit, Kovacs makes the soundtrack visible on screen, exploring the possibility that even audio may have an arresting

6 David Thorburn and Henry Jenkins

visual component. Kovacs assumes that his viewers actively *watch* television, fixated on the novelty of the image, in contrast to some more recent television producers who have assumed that spectators divide their attention between television and other household tasks.

Early movies, of course, are another immensely fertile space for experimentation. Many early motion picture exhibitors, for example, used the camera and projection technology to dramatize the shift from still to moving pictures—either opening with a still image before setting it into motion or projecting footage backwards to reverse the sequence of action we've just seen, so that a wall that had been destroyed as we watched is now magically rebuilt before our eyes. As Tom Gunning has written, early cinema "directly solicits spectator attention, inciting visual curiosity, and supplying pleasure through exciting spectacle."[17] This cinema emphasized its "visibility," often calling attention to its grand illusion by toying with the possibility of transgressing the boundary between the audience and the world projected on the screen. A similar degree of self-consciousness emerged in the early sound era. Al Jolson's proclamation in *The Jazz Singer*—"You ain't heard nothing yet!"—dramatically emphasizes the spoken word, but not nearly so powerfully as the sudden shift back to the conventions of silent cinema when his father, the cantor, appears and demands "Silence!"[18]

In some instances the earliest phase of a medium's life may be its most artistically rich, as pioneering artists enjoy a freedom to experiment that may be constrained by the conventions and routines imposed when production methods are established. It is widely argued, for example, that the most creative era in the history of the American comic strip was its first decades, a period in which artists controlled the layout of their own pages. Winsor McCay's *Dreams of the Rarebit Fiend* and *Little Nemo in Slumberland* contained bold, surrealistic images of topsy-turvy worlds and of figures stretched imaginatively out of proportion. These strips also manipulated the shape and proportion of the frame itself and even created frames within a frame, such that characters inside the comic panel would read picture books that in turn contained panels. Another early comic artist, George Herriman, drew characters who interacted with the panels below them and created images that burst free of the confines of the frame, releasing havoc across the page. One of Herriman's early strips included a second row of panels depicting the experiences of mice beneath the floorboards of the depicted space. When comic strips came to be distributed by national syndicates, rigid formulas were imposed to insure that the panels could be slotted into any newspaper page. Since the comic strip had to have a preset number of panels in a fixed relationship to each other, artists ceased to explore the complex formal properties of this popular medium.[19]

## Imitation, Discovery, Remediation

If emerging media are often experimental and self-reflexive, they are also inevitably and centrally imitative, rooted in the past, in the practices, formats and deep assumptions of their predecessors. The first printed book, the Gutenberg Bible (c. 1455), contains a stunning emblem of this unvarying law of media evolution. For in what seems today a perverse failure to exploit the defining feature of print as against scribal texts, Gutenberg's landmark book has been elaborately and painstakingly illustrated by hand-artisans in the established style of the medieval illuminated manuscript. The striking if perverse continuity thus created was dramatized in a recent exhibition by the Huntington Library, which juxtaposed a copy of the Gutenberg, open to a richly illuminated page, with the famous Ellesmere manuscript of Chaucer's *Canterbury Tales* (c. 1400), also beautifully illustrated by a scribal artist (see fig. 1.1). The print revolution—the power to reproduce a large number of identical texts—is latent but invisible here, suppressed or ignored by an impulse of continuity, a need to experience this new medium under the aspect of established ways of reverence and of art.[20]

Such holdovers of old practices and assumptions have shaped the introduction of many new technologies and may be best illustrated by examples from outside the realm of media history. The physical design of early automobiles, as many have noted, embodied a version of the same continuity principle. Why do the first cars look like horse-drawn buggies, many of them preserving for as long as twenty years such nostalgic and nonfunctional features as dashboard whip sockets? Nothing in the technology of the internal combustion engine requires these forms of obeisance to older models of transportation. But, of course, invention itself is shaped and constrained by history, by inherited forms of thought and experience.

Yet another instructive version of the power of traditional practices to channel our understanding and use of new technologies is available in Harold L. Platt's *The Electric City,* an account of the emergence of the electric utility industry in Chicago at the turn of the twentieth century.[21] The key transition here is not technological so much as cognitive or psychological, for according to this fascinating history, a sustained campaign of political lobbying and consumer marketing was needed to persuade home-owners and businesses to abandon their individual power-generating systems and purchase their energy from a central station or power plant. The idea that energy supplies could be "outsourced" more efficiently and economically than self-generation ran counter to centuries of practice in which homes, farms, mills, businesses and factories maintained their own systems of

Figure 1.1    A page from the Ellesmere manuscript of Chaucer's *Canterbury Tales* (above) and a page from the first printed book, the Gutenberg Bible, demonstrate the power of continuity and tradition in media history. After being printed, the Bible was illustrated by hand so as to resemble its ancestral medium, the illuminated manuscript. Reprinted with permission of the Huntington Library, San Marino, California.

energy production. Does that history of an earlier turning from reliance on privately owned, home-based systems to centralized power-nodes anticipate contemporary shifts, already discernible in much corporate computer use and among many individual web surfers, from autonomous desk-top computing to forms of data-sharing and outsourcing?

These examples—Gutenberg, the horseless buggy, the electric city—and many others we've not mentioned illustrate how inherited forms and traditions limit and inhibit, at least at the start, a full understanding of the intrinsic or unique potential of emerging technologies. But this continuity principle must not be conceived as merely or essentially an impediment to the development of new media. In Jay David Bolter and Richard Grusin's influential formulation, all media engage in a complex and ongoing process of "remediation," in which the tactics, styles and content of rival media are rehearsed, displayed, mimicked, extended, critiqued.[22] We should be clear that not all forms of self-consciousness are profound—some are simply trivial novelties, and not all forms of continuity are constraining—some may quicken latent possibilities in the emerging medium, while others, more simply, may aim to help confused or disoriented consumers make the transition into the unfamiliar terrain opened by the new medium. Self-reflexivity and imitation are contrasting aspects of the same process by which the new medium maps its emergent properties and defines a space for itself in relation to its ancestors.

The novel, for example, is born as an amalgam of older forms, which it explicitly invokes and imitates—the romance, the picaresque tale, certain forms of religious narrative such as Puritan autobiography, and various forms of journalism and historical writing. At first it combines these elements haphazardly and crudely. Then, nourished by an enlarging audience that makes novel writing profitable, this central story-form of the age of print begins to distinguish itself clearly from its ancestors, to combine its inherited elements more harmoniously, and to exploit the possibilities for narrative that are uniquely available in the medium of print.[23]

As many have argued, something of the same principle can be seen in the history of the movies, which begin in a borrowing and restaging of styles, formats and performances taken from a range of older media such as theater, still photography, visual art, and prose fiction. A second powerful source for early cinema was such public attractions as carnivals, the circus, amusement parks, vaudeville. Some film historians have argued that the defining attribute of the birth of the movies was the contention between a self-reflexive and populist "cinema of attractions," (to use Tom Gunning's helpful term) and a more respectable, even middle-class tendency toward narrative as inspired by theater and print.[24]

Such perspectives remind us that the forms achieved by a "mature" medium do not comprise some perfect fulfillment of its intrinsic potential but represent instead both a range of limited possibilities and promises unexplored, roads not taken.

Recent scholarship has even suggested that the movies assumed and more fully achieved some of the prime ambitions of its ancestors. The time of the birth of a new medium, these histories remind us, is often ripe with anticipation. Vanessa R. Schwartz, for example, suggests that fin-de-siècle Paris was awash in visual spectacles such as panoramas and wax museums offering an immersive reproduction of the world that would be realized truly only by the movies.[25] Lauren Rabinovitz has studied how the cinema took shape in the context of amusement-park attractions.[26] Erik Barnouw has shown how magicians prepared the ground for the movies by introducing their technical marvels to the public.[27] And in some cases, these expectations were frustrated by the new medium: William Uricchio suggests, for example, that some early critics were disappointed when cinema failed to realize their expectation of simultaneous transmission of distance events.[28] The story is not merely one of imitation and self-discovery, then, but something more complicated. If movies were in some sense replicating earlier media, those ancestor systems were also aiming imperfectly and incompletely to satisfy expectations that would ultimately give rise to the cinema.

As we suggested earlier and as these examples indicate, medium-specific perspectives may limit our understanding of the ways in which media interact, shift and collude with one another. The evolution of new communications systems is always immensely complicated by the rivalry of competing media and by the economic structures that shape and support them. In some cases, such as broadcasting where the same networks dominated both radio and television, existing institutions simply expand to absorb and appropriate emerging technologies.[29] In other cases, as in the competition between nickelodeons and legitimate theaters, emerging media may offer opportunities for investment and upward mobility prohibited by the rigid infrastructure of established systems.

To comprehend the aesthetics of transition, we must resist notions of media purity, recognizing that each medium is touched by and in turn touches its neighbors and rivals. And we must also reject static definitions of media, resisting the idea that a communications system may adhere to a definitive form once the initial process of experimentation and innovation yields to institutionalization and standardization. In fact, as the history of cinema shows, decisive changes follow upon improvements in technology (such as the advent of sound, the development of lighter, more mobile cameras and more sensitive film stock, the introduction of digital special effects and editing systems); and seismic shifts in the very nature of film, in its relation to its audience and its society, occur with the birth of television.

## No Elegies for Gutenberg[30]

As the foregoing implies, these processes of imitation, self-discovery, remediation and transformation are recurring and inevitable, part of the way in which cultures define and renew themselves. Old media rarely die; their original functions are adapted and absorbed by newer media, and they themselves may mutate into new cultural niches and new purposes. The process of media transition is always a mix of tradition and innovation, always declaring for evolution, not revolution.

We citizens and scholars do well to recognize such continuity principles and to remain skeptical of apocalyptic projections of gloom or glory. Is the printed book obsolete? Almost certainly not. Will many of its noblest and most valuable functions—most forms of scholarship and research, dictionaries, encyclopedias—migrate to the computer? Yes, absolutely. This has already begun to happen. But—as the poet Milton says—nothing is here for tears. The crucial continuity involves not books but language itself. Language is migratory across communications media and will endure.

## Notes

1. Rpt. in George Levine, ed., *The Emergence of Victorian Consciousness: The Spirit of the Age* (New York: Free Press, 1967), 71.

2. The nineteenth century as the site of the emergence of a new information culture and as a parallel to our own age of transitions has received extensive consideration in recent years. See, for example, James W. Carey and John J. Quirk, "The Mythos of the Electronic Revolution," in James W. Carey, *Communication as Culture: Essays on Media and Society* (New York: Routledge, 1989); Tom Standage, *The Victorian Internet: The Remarkable Story of the Telegraph and the Nineteenth Century's On-Line Pioneers* (Berkeley: Berkeley Publications, 1999); Thomas Richards, *The Imperial Archive: Knowledge and the Fantasy of Empire* (London: Verso, 1996); Doron Swade, *The Difference Engine: Charles Babbage and the Quest to Build the First Computer* (New York: Viking, 2001); Daniel R. Hendrick, *When Information Came of Age: Technologies of Knowledge in the Age of Reason and Revolution, 1700–1850* (New York: Oxford University Press, 2000); James W. Cortada, *Before the Computer* (Trenton: Princeton University Press, 2000). For a fictional response to this same topic, see William Gibson and Bruce Sterling, *The Difference Engine* (New York: Spectra, 1992).

3. On the competing visions of the computer, see, for example, Mark Stefik, *Internet Dreams: Archetypes, Myths and Metaphors* (Cambridge, MA: MIT Press, 1996).

4. On the rise of nineteenth-century technologies, see, in addition to texts cited above, Carolyn Marvin, *When Old Technologies Were New: Thinking About Electronic Communications in the Late Nineteenth Century* (Oxford: Oxford University Press, 1990); Lisa Gitelman, *Scripts, Grooves and Writing Machines: Representing Technology in Edison's Era* (Stanford: Stanford University Press, 2000); Daniel Czitron, *Media and the American Mind: From Morse to McLuhan* (Chapel Hill: University of North Carolina Press, 1983); Stephen Kern, *The Culture of Time and Space, 1880–1918* (Cambridge, MA: Harvard University Press, 1983); Wolfgang Schivelbusch, *Disenchanted Night: The Industrialization of Light in the Nineteenth Century* (Berkeley: University of California Press, 1995); Wolfgang Schivelbusch, *The Railroad Journey: The Industrialization of Time in the Nineteenth Century* (Berkeley: University of California Press, 1997); Friedrich A. Kittler, *Gramophone, Film, Typewriter* (Stanford: Stanford University Press, 1999); Friedrich A. Kittler, *Discourse Networks, 1800/1900* (Stanford: Stanford University Press, 1992); David E. Nye, *The Technological Sublime* (Cambridge, MA: MIT Press, 1996); David E. Nye, *Electrifying America* (Cambridge, MA: MIT Press, 1992); Claude S. Fischer, *America Calling: A Social History of the Telephone to 1940* (Berkeley: University of California Press, 1994); M. Susan Barger and William B. White, *The Daguerreotype: Nineteenth-Century Technology and Modern Science* (Baltimore: Johns Hopkins University Press, 2000); Jonathan Crary, *Techniques of the Observer* (Cambridge, MA: MIT Press, 1992).

5. Much of what follows has been inspired by Raymond Williams, *Television: Technology and Cultural Form* (New York: Schocken, 1977). There is also a growing body of literature on media transitions or information revolutions. See, for example, Brian Wilson, *Media Technology and Society: From the Telegraph to the Internet* (New York: Routledge, 1998); Irving Fang, *A History of Mass Communications: Six Information Revolutions* (New York: Focal, 1997); Alfred D. Chandler and James W. Cortada, eds., *A Nation Transformed By Information: How Information Has Shaped the United States from Colonial Times to the Present* (Oxford: Oxford University Press, 2000); Wiebe Bijker, *Of Bicycles, Bakelites, and Bulbs: Toward a Theory of Sociotechnical Change* (Cambridge, MA: MIT Press, 1995); Michael E. Hobart and Zachary S. Schiffman, *Information Ages: Literacy, Numeracy, and the Computer Revolution* (Baltimore: Johns Hopkins University Press, 2000); Neil Rhodes and Jonathan Sawday, eds., *The Renaissance Computer: Knowledge Technology in the First Age of Print* (New York: Routledge, 2000); Steven Johnson, *Interface Culture: How New Technology Transforms the Way We Create and Communicate* (New York: Basic, 1999); Lev Manovich, *The Language of New Media* (Cambridge, MA: MIT Press, 2001).

6. Debora L. Spar, *Ruling the Waves: Cycles of Discovery, Chaos, and Wealth from the Compass to the Internet* (New York: Harcourt, 2001).

7. One possible model for such a discourse is represented by the technological realists. See, for example, <http://www.technorealism.org/>.

8. Paul Duguid, "Material Matters: Aspects of the Past and Futurology of the Book" in *The Future of the Book,* ed. Geoffrey Nunberg (Berkeley: University of California Press, 1996). For other significant work on the impact of digital media on the culture of print, see Roger Chartier, *Forms and Meanings: Texts, Performances, and Audiences from Codex to Computers* (Philadelphia: University of Pennsylvania Press, 1995); James Joseph O'Donnell, *Avatars of the Word: From Papyrus to Cyberspace* (Cambridge, MA: Harvard University Press, 2000); John Seely Brown and Paul Duguid, *The Social Life of Information* (Cambridge, MA: Harvard Business School Press, 2000); David M. Levy, *Scrolling Forward: Making Sense of Documents in The Digital Age* (New York: Arcade, 2001); Sven Birkerts, *Tolstoy's Dictaphone: Technology and the Muse* (St. Paul: Graywolf Press, 1996); Janet Murray, *Hamlet on the Holodeck: The Future of Narrative in Cyberspace* (Cambridge, MA: MIT Press, 1999).

9. Bruce Sterling, Dead Media Project, <http://www.deadmedia.org>.

10. See Wolfgang Grape, *The Bayeux Tapestry: Monument to a Norman Triumph* (Munich: Prestel, 1994); Richard Gameson, ed., *The Study of the Bayeux Tapestry* (Rochester, NY: Boydell Press, 1997); Suzanne Lewis, *The Rhetoric of Power in the Bayeux Tapestry* (New York: Cambridge University Press, 1999).

11. Heinz K. Henisch, *The Painted Photograph 1839–1914: Origins, Techniques, Aspirations* (Philadelphia: University of Pennsylvania Press, 1996).

12. For a fuller discussion of media convergence, see Henry Jenkins, "Convergence? I Diverge," *Technology Review* (June 2001); "Quentin Tarantino's *Star Wars*?: Digital Cinema, Media Convergence, and Participatory Culture," in this volume; Thomas Elsaesser and Kay Hoffman, eds., *Cinema Futures: Cain, Abel, or Cabel* (Amsterdam: Amsterdam University Press, 1998); Dan Harries, ed., *The New Media Book* (London: BFI, 2002).

13. Marshall McLuhan, "The Playboy Interview," in *The Essential McLuhan,* ed. Eric McLuhan and Frank Zingrone (New York: Harper Collins, 1996).

14. See, for example, David Hall, *Cultures of Print: Essays on the History of the Book* (Amherst: University of Massachusetts Press, 1996); Robert Darnton, *Literary Underground of the Old Regime* (Cambridge, MA: Harvard University Press, 1985); Robert Darnton, *The Forbidden Best Sellers of Pre-Revolutionary France* (New York: W. W. Norton, 1996); Roger Chartier, *Order of Books* (Stanford: Stanford University Press, 1994); Lucien Febvre, *The Coming of the Book: The Impact of Printing, 1450–1800* (London: Verso, 1997); Elizabeth L. Eisenstein, *The Printing Press as an Agent of Change: Communications and Cultural Transformations in Early Modern Europe* (Cambridge: Cambridge University Press, 1980); Frederick G. Kilgour, *The Evolution of the Book* (Oxford: Oxford University Press, 1998); Natalie Zemon Davis, *Society and Culture in Early Modern France: Eight Essays* (Stanford: Stanford University Press, 1977).

15. This material draws on David Thorburn, "Fiction and Imagination in *Don Quixote,*" *Partisan Review* XLII, no. 3 (1975): 431–443. See also Robert Alter, *Partial Magic: The Novel as a Self-Conscious Genre* (Berkeley: University of California Press, 1975).

16. On comic self-reflexivity, see J. Hoberman, *Vulgar Modernism: Writings on Movies and Other Media* (Philadelphia: Temple University Press, 1991).

17. Tom Gunning, "The Cinema of Attractions: Early Film, Its Spectator and the Avant Garde" in *Early Cinema: Space, Frame, Narrative,* ed. Thomas Elsaesser and Adam Barker (London: BFI, 1990). For other influential discussions of early cinema (beyond those found in Elsaesser and Barker), see Charles Musser, *The Emergence of Cinema: The American Screen to 1907* (Berkeley: University of California Press, 1994); Charles Musser, *Before the Nickelodeon: Edwin S. Porter and The Edison Manufacturing Company* (Berkeley: University of California Press, 1991); Charlie Keil, *Early American Cinema in Transition: Story, Style and Filmmaking, 1907–1913* (Madison: University of Wisconsin Press, 2002); Ben Brewster and Lea Jacobs, *Theater to Cinema: Stage Pictorialism and the Early Feature Film* (Oxford: Oxford University Press, 1998); John L. Fell, *Film Before Griffith* (Berkeley: University of California Press, 1983); Yuri Tsivian *Early Cinema in Russia and Its Cultural Reception* (Chicago: University of Chicago Press, 1998).

18. For discussion of the coming of sound, see Donald Crafton, *Talkies: America Cinema's Transition to Sound, 1926–1931* (Berkeley: University of California Press, 1999); Henry Jenkins, *What Made Pistachio Nuts?: Early Sound Comedy and the Vaudeville Aesthetic* (New York: Columbia University Press, 1991).

19. On the richness of early comics, see Bill Waterson, "The Cheapening of the Comics," *The Comics Journal* (October 27, 1989). On the emergence of comics, Robert C. Harvey, *The Art of the Funnies: An Aesthetic History* (Jackson: University Press of Mississippi, 1994); John Canemaker, *Winsor McCay: His Life and Art* (New York: Abbeville Press, 1987); Richard Marschall, ed., *Dreams and Nightmares: The Fantastic Art of Winsor McCay* (Westlake Village, CA: Fantagraphics Books, 1988); David Kunzle, *History of the Comic Strip* (Berkeley: University of California Press, 1973).

20. Scott D. N. Cook, "Technological Revolutions and the Gutenberg Myth," in Mark Stefik, *Internet Dreams: Archetypes, Myths and Metaphors* (Cambridge, MA: MIT Press, 1996): "The same standards of craftsmanship and aesthetics associated with manuscripts were applied to printed books for at least two generations beyond the Gutenberg Bible" (71).

21. Harold L. Platt, *The Electric City: Energy and Growth Of the Chicago Area, 1880–1930* (Chicago: University of Chicago Press, 1991).

22. Jay David Bolter and Richard Grusin, *Remediation* (Cambridge, MA: MIT Press, 2000).

23. Ian P. Watt, *The Rise of the Novel* (Berkeley: University of California Press, 1957); Michael McKeon, *The Origins of the English Novel, 1600–1740* (Baltimore: Johns Hopkins University Press, 1988); Nancy Armstrong, *Desire and Domestic Fiction: A Political History of the Novel* (Cambridge: Oxford University Press, 1995); Ruth Perry, *Women, Letters, and the Novel* (New York: AMS Press, 1980). This paragraph and later sections of this introduction draw

extensively on David Thorburn, "Television As an Aesthetic Medium," *Critical Studies in Mass Communication* 4 (1987): 168–169.

24. Tom Gunning, *D. W. Griffith and The Origins of American Narrative Film* (Chicago: University of Illinois Press, 1994); David Bordwell, Janet Staiger, and Kristin Thompson, *Classical Hollywood Cinema* (New York: Columbia University Press, 1985); Ben Singer, *Melodrama and Modernity: Early Sensational Cinema and Its Contexts* (New York: Columbia University Press, 2001); Roberta Pearson, *Eloquent Gestures: The Transformation of Performance Style in the Griffith Biograph Films* (Berkeley: University of California Press, 1992); William Uricchio and Roberta E. Pearson, *Reframing Culture* (Trenton: Princeton University Press, 1993).

25. Vanessa R. Schwartz, *Spectacular Realities: Early Mass Culture in Fin-de-Siècle Paris* (Berkeley: University of California Press, 1999).

26. Rabinovitz, *For the Love of Pleasure: Women, Movies, and Culture in Turn-of-the-Century Chicago* (New Brunswick: Rutgers University Press, 1998)

27. Erik Barnouw, *The Magician and the Cinema* (Cambridge: Oxford University Press, 1981).

28. William Uricchio, "Technologies of Time," in *Allegories of Communication: Intermedial Concerns from Cinema to the Digital,* ed. J. Olsson (Berkeley: University of California Press, 2002).

29. On the evolution of radio broadcasting, see Susan Douglas, *Inventing American Broadcasting 1899–1922* (Baltimore: Johns Hopkins University Press, 1997); Michele Hilmes, *Radio Reader: Essays in the Cultural History of Radio* (New York: Routledge, 2001); Susan Smulyan, *Selling Radio: The Commercialization of American Broadcasting, 1920–1934* (Washington, DC: Smithsonian Institute Press, 1994). For considerations of cultural responses to the introduction of television, see Lynn Spigel, *Make Room For TV: Television and the Family Ideal in Postwar America* (Chicago: University of Chicago, 1992); Lynn Spigel, *Welcome to the Dreamhouse: Popular Media and Postwar Suburbs* (Durham: Duke University Press, 2001); Cecelia Tichi, *Electronic Hearth: Creating an American Television Culture* (Oxford: Oxford University Press, 1992); Jeffrey Sconce, *Haunted Media: Electronic Presence From Telegraphy to Television* (Durham: Duke University Press, 2000); Anna McCarthy, *Ambient Television: Visual Culture and Public Space* (Durham: Duke University Press, 2001).

30. Sven Birkerts's *The Gutenberg Elegies: The Fate of Reading in an Electronic Age* (New York: Fawcett, 1995) seeks to defend the culture of the book against the emerging digital culture.

# I  *Media Changes*

# 2 *Web of Paradox*

David Thorburn

---

The World Wide Web is more than technology, more than modems, bandwidth, computers. It is a thing made of language and of history, a Web of Metaphor.

Of course, we view all new technologies through perspectives or metaphors that limit our understanding and obscure intrinsic qualities and possibilities. Nothing inherent in the internal combustion engine required that the first cars resemble horse-drawn carriages. That beginning was dictated by metaphor, by inherited notions of conveyance, centuries of carts and wagons and palanquins, by how we imagine human transport by land. (My father, 92, remembers driving an early Ford whose elaborate leather dashboard was fitted with a socket for the handle of a buggy whip.)

So, too, though more dangerously, the dominant metaphors deployed to describe our experience of things digital constrain our understanding, limit and channel our inventions and even our speculations. We need more discussion of such rich but also limiting descriptors as cyberspace, highway (or the bilingual neologism infobahn), market, space, site, frontier.

Am I wrong to think that these are especially American and capitalist metaphors, carrying an undersong of adventure, of risk and speed and danger, of entrepreneurs or Starfleet commanders or homesteaders braving the wilderness? Like the early popular Nintendo computer games, discussed in a 1995 essay by Henry Jenkins and Mary Fuller, such figures implicitly celebrate motion, activity, acquisition, the conquest of space. Odd at first thought, but deeply instructive on reflection: that such swashbuckling metaphors should define the essentially sedentary experience of sitting at a computer terminal with mouse and keyboard at the ready.

Think of the acerbic point, made a decade ago by the cultural critic Gerald Graff, that if the self-preening metaphors of peril, subversion and ideological danger in the literary theorists' account of their work were taken seriously, their insurance costs would match those for firefighters, Grand Prix drivers, and war correspondents. In this same spirit of skeptical realism, might we recognize a resemblance between computer users and long-haul truck drivers, strapped in behind the wheel from LA to Memphis, listening to country-and-western songs of cowboy truckers, the great American highway, faithful wives? Are the drivers who buy into the sentimental mystifications of such songs victims or eager and sometimes creative collaborators in a mythology that converts the actual confinement and the tedium of long-distance truck driving to an experience of freedom and masculine fulfillment?

Marx and de Certeau would supply alternative answers. But they would agree on the paradox.

Just so, we might say, do computer users and Web surfers navigate or maneuver across (or down or through) a superhighway, a teeming marketplace, a frontier, the vasty deep of cyberspace—yet all the while situated physically in safe domestic or professional cubicles, tethered to the computer screen, perhaps in the dark, maybe tracked and surveilled by their bosses or by the merchants and other strangers whose sites they have visited.

This awareness of contradiction or dissonance between our celebratory, heroic metaphors and the physical—and moral and intellectual—actualities of computer use grows still more paradoxical when we consider the computer or the Internet in explicitly political ways. We use words such as support group, interest group, news group, chat room, market, subculture, community, society to designate some of the ways people link together on the Internet. These and similar terms try to name the web's participatory, activist potential, its power to create new communities and theoretically to permit isolated minorities to find one another across geographic and political boundaries.

But we clarify and complicate this sense of the web's powers when we add the necessary adjective "virtual." As many have noted, this is a deep paradox, fundamental to our experience of computers: virtual environment, virtual community, virtual reality.

These puzzling tropes point toward something of the immense promise but also the immense peril of the Web: its apparent power to gratify vastly divergent tendencies and yearnings. The Web is kind to impulses often at war in our selves and in the social world. It allows us to traverse the globe, to convene for many causes, to converse intimately or publicly with many persons. Yet to accomplish these interactions we must sit, solitary, at the computer keyboard, interfacing deeply not with a human other but with Windows XP.

The computer encourages joining, interaction, sharing, the creation of communities of interest; yet it is also congenial to our uncivic preferences for isolation, the avoidance of human contact, solipsism, "lurking," voyeurism. Through its power to confer anonymity, it feeds instincts for scandal, revenge, name-calling, surveillance, pornography.

It is the best of Webs, the worst of Webs. It promises, simultaneously, to become the Agora or True Democracy, but also Big Brother. "Do I contradict myself?" asks the American poet. "Very well then I contradict myself. I am large, I contain multitudes."

It is easy to misconceive the import of such discourse about the Web's contradictory nature, and especially its power to threaten such vital conceptual and psychological boundaries as "near" and "far," "presence" and "absence," "body" and "self," "real" and "artificial." Prompted by the adventure myths embedded in our vocabulary for cyberspace and also by the futurist, technological aura of the whole enterprise of computing, we may be led to see these profound paradoxes as part of the future, uniquely modern, uniquely ours. But of course, and of course paradoxically, the reverse is true. The new grows out of the old, repeats the old, embraces, reimagines and extends the old. To understand the Web, I'm saying—to understand our emerging digital culture—we need a continuity not a discontinuity principle.

From the aspect of the continuity of history, then, it becomes possible to recognize that this supposedly unique and certainly central aspect of our experience of the Web reenacts a distinctive joining or blurring of "real" and "false," of "connection" yet "isolation," "public" and yet "private" that is also at the root of our experience of the movies, of television—yes, even the book. (Reading this, my son, 33, a historian, insisted rightly that these formulations are excessively literary and leave implicit such equally relevant precursors as the telegraph and the telephone, collapsing space and time by enabling instantaneous communication over any distance.)

From this angle, then, as from many others, this World Wide Web of paradox is not at all new, at least in some of its defining powers, but instead undertakes and carries forward the cultural work of its predecessors and ancestors.

This is no quibble, some minor casuistry. I'm saying the experience of hearing stories, reading novels and poems, attending plays, looking at paintings, watching movies—all are in a fundamental way virtual experiences, where actuality is re-presented, tested by hypotheses, experienced vicariously as metaphor and spectacle and make-believe.

Dr. Johnson's retort to complaints against Shakespeare's failure to observe the neoclassical unities of place and time is a famous crystallizing of this durable idea of art as a site of "play," of "let's pretend." It is absurd, Johnson says, a breach of our contract with the very idea of theater, to credit the objection that it is implausible for successive scenes to take place in Rome and then half-way round the world in Egypt (or for ten years to elapse in a play instead of a few hours) but then to think that the entirety of sets, costumes, actors, audience—the whole environment of artifice—is not a far stronger cause for disbelief. We do not rush from our seats like Don Quixote to save the puppet-heroine because we understand and embrace the enabling convention of all drama: that its world is imaginary, a virtual site.

I find it instructive, I find it consoling to think about Jules Verne's Captain Nemo and *Star Trek's* Captain Kirk—of course they are also emblems for their audience, for bookreaders and TV watchers—navigating unexplored and perilous universes even as they sit in the familiar confining safety of the captain's chair, on the captain's bridge, joystick ready, watching the screen.

# 3 Historicizing Media in Transition

William Uricchio

## Introduction

In Book Two of *The Histories,* Herodotus digresses from his tale of Greece's struggle to defeat Persian aggression in order to describe his visit to Egypt.[1] His encounter with Egypt, its history, customs, and inhabitants, produced an epistemological vertigo of sorts. Herodotus, called by Cicero the "father of history," was confronted by the inescapable realization that not only was Greece not the center of the civilized world, but that Egyptian civilization, evidently thousands of years older, had provided the Greeks with the elements which they took to be identifying marks of their own civilization. Beyond serving to balance his larger narrative of the triumph Greek culture in the face of the marauding threat from the east, Book Two is striking for the manner in which it relativizes the author's assumptions regarding his own culture—the culture, after all, through which he perceived the world around him and told his tale.

I open this essay on writing media histories with reference to Herodotus' *The Histories* because his situation in Book Two speaks directly to our current predicament in media studies. My starting point is that the shift from medium-specific histories—film's history in particular—to media history, has induced something like the epistemological vertigo experienced by Herodotus. Familiar reference points, long-held assumptions, and the self-assurance that comes with an apparent monopoly on the truth have all been challenged, recontextualized, shaken. Film's own history and developmental trajectory, and its assumed agency with regard to "derivative" media such as television, have been recast in the light of an array of precedent technologies, practices, and notions of mediation. Given, for example, film's somewhat precarious position within the academy (not to mention the perception by many in the industry and academy alike of the looming threat posed by digital culture), this reordering of the taken-for-granted has created a sense of disorder, anxiety, and reaction. While these symptoms are not necessarily productive, we should nevertheless remember that it was thanks to film scholars (among others) that this reorientation occurred in the first place. As we shall see, the paradigm shifts associated with the re-writing of cinema's early history in the 1980s, and the consequent efforts of a number of scholars who have continued to interrogate long-held truths, have been fundamental to the project of rewriting media histories generally.

Herodotus, both in Book Two and throughout his text, offers a second relevant entry point: central to his mode of historical inquiry is an insistence upon multiple causalities and co-existing interpretations. His own observations as a historian are usually seen as but one of several possibilities. This insistence upon the partiality of truth, upon its refracted and often contradictory nature, no doubt accounts for why generations of historians have parted ways with Cicero and dubbed Herodotus the "father of lies," but it also helps to explain his resonance (if not relevance) to the post-structuralist notion of history. I mention this not so much to reveal my own partiality to this brand of historiography, but rather to anticipate the multiple and sometimes contradictory causalities which I take to be characteristic of media's development. For the record, I understand media to be more than mere technologies, institutions, and texts—a statement I would think was obvious were it not for the substantial body of literature that holds otherwise. Instead, I see media as cultural practices which envelop these and other elements within a broader fabric offered by particular social orders, mentalities, and the lived experiences of their producers and users. Such a view is generationally inscribed, with students from different academic generations being apt to respond differently to these issues. As one of many who cut their teeth on Raymond Williams and the like, I have not yet lost my taste for this notion of media.[2] Such an admittedly full definition of media requires an embrace of multiplicity, complexity and even contradiction if sense is to be made of such a pervasive cultural experience. The comments that follow are built around two central points: the first concerns a very brief and somewhat biased history of how we got to the present point in writing media histories (for how better can a historian reflect upon his own trade?); and the second concerns an even more biased set of thoughts on the current construction of media history. Unless otherwise noted, my comments refer to developments within the Anglo-American world.

### The State of Things

A few words are in order regarding the status quo in media historical writing. As an object of the historicizing gaze, the media have, not surprisingly, been subjected to dominant trends in historiography, but with curious institutional results. The long rule of national-political histories and economic histories tended to relegate cultural history in general and media history in particular to the margins of historical study. Culture and media were instead institutionalized as specialized arts or humanities disciplines such as art history, literary studies, and musicology. Although outside the discipline of history proper, this cultural niche found ample support both within the walls of the academy and in strategic alliances with cultural institutions such as museums, galleries, concert halls, publishing houses, etc., helping to define hierarchies of expressive (i.e., aesthetic) media and to maintain, to invoke Bourdieu's phrase, the rules of art.[3] But while important as a means of developing analytic and discursive frames for particular (that is, aesthetic expressions of) media, this constellation of interests tended to fetishize its objects and consequently was generally blind to media forms and texts perceived as popular, commercial, or multiple (thus, the greater part of mass media, often excepting photography—an interesting case unto itself). One of the many paradoxes to arise from this situation was, on one hand, the strict exclusion of mass media from the academic study of "art" media (recorded popular music found as little welcome in musicology as film found in the visual arts), while on the other hand, academics concerned with the study of mass media seized upon the arts as both the justification and critical framework for their study. Film, for example, when it finally entered the mainstream (U.S.) academy in the 1960s, did so as an "art" which generally meant favoring the often intersecting categories of historical, European, and avant-garde production, while at the same time marginalizing contemporary commercial film production. That the study of the film medium would center on the study of texts, and would borrow classification schemes from its sister arts (genre, authorship, style histories) makes perfect sense given the rationale for the film medium's initial inclusion in university curricula as a curious sort of modernist "high art" together with film scholars' own disciplinary aspirations.

While it would be unfair to say that culture was outside the agenda of historians proper (for there is a long history of exceptional and diverse historical voices which have spoken on the matter), it is particularly in the twentieth century with the emergence of the Annales historians[4] and British historians of society and the working class[5] that cultural practice appeared as an object of increasing historical interest. Not coincidentally, a number of historians in both groups showed a general interest in the forces of social cohesion in what might be termed a broadly Gramscian notion of hegemony, in which consensus and the means of its construction were central topics of interest.[6] Culture was seen both as underlining the notion of consensus and as providing the evidence for national identity, values, and aspirations. Significant to these developments in historical approach was the notion of culture as something much larger than the arts, something anthropological in definition. Given the particular functions of culture that were being explored—identity, cohesion, direction—media assumed increasing prominence.

Now, it might be argued that the timing of this interest (post-1930s) owed much to the fact that by the second decade of the twentieth century, three distinct mass media waves had swept across the western world in quick succession, fundamentally altering the exercise of state power, the construction of the citizen, and public memory itself. The cheap rotary press, film, and radio each organized data and the public in distinctive ways, and each was the subject of considerable political wrangling in ordeals that usually demonstrated the principle of "rationalization through regulation."[7] Indeed, one might even argue that the larger historiographic turn towards everyday culture and the life of everyman was a response to the widespread democratization apparent in many western nations by the early to mid twentieth century. Women's successful bid for voting rights and the recognition of labor's right to organize were due in part to these groups' use of the new mass media, and in a larger sense, media occupied an increasingly significant part of the information infrastructure essential to the functioning of democratic governments and the capitalist system (consumer society in particular) upon which they were built. That said, we should not underestimate the incentive to look more closely at culture and media inspired by those nations such as Hitler's Germany or Stalin's Soviet Union which developed anti-democratic mass movements and uncharacteristic levels of state aggression. In the search for causal attribution, the mass media stuck out as an obvious factor, meriting careful study—and pathologization.

These factors, among others, help to account for the turn of mainstream attention to the history of cultural practices (media included) in the twentieth century, and the roughly parallel appearance of mass medium-specific university disciplines such as journalism by the turn-of-the-century and film studies by mid-century. The nexus of interest formed by cultural history and two medium-specific disciplines is worth briefly pursuing, since it helps to account for recent transformations in media historiography. In many of its incarnations, journalism has had a disciplinary status closer to that of law or medicine than to art history or literary studies, in the sense that from its inception, it has tended to function as a professional study, offering training for future journalists and maintaining close relations with the journalistic industry. Its functionalist research orientation (with an interest in effects, policy, etc.) made it instrumental in the definition of the "new" social science discipline of mass communications, where it was joined by radio and television, but not, with a few notable exceptions, film. Rooted in the late nineteenth century development of sociology, mass communications tended to be far more concerned with the 'present' of testable hypotheses than in the precedent of the past (history)—a temporal orientation that continues to characterize the field.

Film studies by contrast, emerged with virtually no contact with the larger professional field. Indeed, in the United States, it initially defined its interests almost in opposition to commercial production, focusing instead upon the medium's history, its aesthetic markers, and the development of a set of academic disciplinary terms and practices. These latter terms relied heavily upon the fields of art history and literary criticism, disciplinary environments where the archive or museum was far more relevant than design or publishing houses. I will not rehearse the history of the discipline, except to point to the moment in the mid 1970s when two very different but ultimately related discursive strands drew together to redefine the study of film, and with it television. One strand was to be found in the history discipline's previously mentioned turn to cultural issues and "bottom-up" history.[8] The other emerged from within literary studies and marked a (roughly parallel) shift from author-dominated or literary expert-dominated notions of textual meaning, to the meanings which literary texts actually encountered in the world of readers.[9] The subsequent move from reader response and reception of the literary canon to the analysis of the full range of literary forms which readers encountered was both logical and profound. Film studies, as usual, took its lead from literary studies, and its shift away from the canon drew it both to popular film and to that moving-image medium most often encountered in the world—television. Television, long the cultural "other" whose mundane reality justified the serious consideration of film as art (at least avant-garde, historical, and "foreign" film), was suddenly rehabilitated by some in the film studies community as a key element of popular culture. Although television texts were approached in much the same way as film and literary texts (style histories, authorship, etc.), the emergence of cultural studies as an autonomous sphere of activity offered new and radical possibilities.[10]

Cultural studies, deriving from the cultural interests of historians, from a fascination with the 'lived reality' of cultural participants on the part of some within literary and film studies, and from redefinitions within the social sciences (anthropology and ethnography in particular), found itself in a position to broker diverse methodologies (from textual analysis to audience ethnographies to history), while at the same time focusing emphatically upon a politicized notion of popular cultural reception.[11] Cultural studies helped scholars in both the social sciences and the humanities to redefine their approaches to the media of film and television, focusing less on text-specific or institution-specific endeavors, and more on the situation of producers, texts and readers in the world and their encounters with one another. Thanks to this confluence of events, television's history as something fuller than institutional history or textual analysis finally appeared on the research agenda.

One might consider this entire transformation from a slightly higher level of abstraction. For example, one might point to such factors as the changed demographics of post-war university attendance, where new populations drawn from a broad class and ethnic spectrum began to dominate higher education, bringing with them new cultural reference points and a broader array of interests than had previously been the case. Or one might point to shifting notions of disciplinarity, as academic fields defined in the mid- to late-nineteenth century began to give way to comparative and trans-disciplinary studies (American studies, women's studies, STS (science-technology-society), as well as new alliances between art history and anthropology, or economics and history, etc.). And, one might in particular point to the pervasive (if yet to be fully acknowledged) influence of post-structuralism that offered an intellectual framework for breaking from long-established taste categories, notions of academic disciplinarity, and explanatory master narratives of various sorts. But for our present purposes, we might also consider one further turn in media historiography since it has specific bearings upon the questions that are currently being asked, and the methods put forward for answering them. I refer to that aspect of the 1970s–1980s ferment in the field most specific to the writing of the film medium's history—research into early cinema.

The 1979 International Federation of Film Archives (FIAF) conference held in Brighton, England, signaled the emergence of a new generation of film historians.[12] Informed by the work of scholars such as Jay Leyda, Robert Sklar, and Garth Jowett, and to some extent reacting against the perceived excess of theory then vogue in the field, these historians focused on that most neglected aspect of the medium: early cinema.[13] The dominant histories of the day described early film in strictly teleological terms as "primitive" cinema—a view fundamentally contested by these new historians. Moreover, traditional research strategies unwittingly tended to reinforce the vision of the film medium long held by dominant cultural institutions—the institutions which sought not only to regulate the medium in various ways, but which were also responsible for producing and saving much of what we have received as the surviving archival record. Thus, for example, the experiences of newspaper reviewers and censors survive, whereas those of ordinary viewers have been lost; the concerns of the fire insurance regulators live on, while those of film projectionists do not, etc.

Post–Brighton scholarship looked into production histories, stylistic trends, the period's reception, and so on, effectively breaking with the teleological trends of the past

by re-positioning this body of films simultaneously as the culmination of various nineteenth century representational efforts, and as a catalogue of unexpected possibilities for
a yet-to-be disciplined medium.[14] In this sense, it effectively embraced the notion of a
media dispositif (a concept which links apparatus, the cultural imagination, and constructions of public), but radicalized the deployment of the notion by standing open to
grounded speculation. This shift in perspective was profound, rupturing the taken-for-
grantedness of the narrative of the medium's progress from simple black and white silent
films, to today's virtual reality systems (or, for that matter, the parallel narrative of ever-
more refined techniques of ideological control). Instead, the medium was positioned
within intertextual and intermedial networks, acquiring meaning and possibility through
grounded historical positioning rather than hindsight.[15] Scholars began to situate cinema
within representational systems with longer histories than the cinema's such as the theater, the magic lantern and photography.[16] Considerations of how publics constructed
themselves around dime museums, fairgrounds, and scientific spectacles offered new insights into cinema's own modes of attraction.[17] And at least one historian focused on the
horizon of expectations that greeted cinema, arguing almost heretically that television (in
the sense of a live or simultaneous moving picture medium) preceded the film medium
by over a decade, rendering film the great compromise (rather than the great wonder) of
the nineteenth century.[18]

   The emergence of this new historical perspective was obviously informed by the developments discussed above (the rise of cultural studies, the turn to cultural history, etc.), but
it included several notable characteristics that bear mentioning. First, it was marked by a
profound shift in viewing position (something akin to Herodotus' insights in Egypt) with
consequences for the whole of cinema history. Second, many scholars felt the need to
re-theorize the process of "doing history." That is to say, since the early cinema evidence
record contained so many gaps (missing films, production records, audience responses)
and deformations (ideologically weighted evidence supporting the views of certain social
groups and suppressing those of others), film historians of necessity had to think through
the consequences of how to account for absences and irregularities in evidence, how to
compensate with creative alternatives, and how to make their cases. The result (enabled
by the paucity of data and the short length of the films) included new techniques of textual
analysis, and new approaches to extra-cinematic evidence (intertextuality, intermediality,
and historical reception studies among them). Third, the development of an elaborate series of collaborations among scholars, film archives, and film festivals, helped to stimulate
and guide the restoration of the cinematic evidence base (restoring films, getting them

back into circulation, providing period documentation, etc.), while at the same time am-plifying new perspectives on the medium's history. In a move not without serious concep-tual dangers, this historical perspective effectively enabled the translation of historical insights and interpretations into historized artifacts (i.e., re-constructed or restored films), closing the loop between interpretation and text. The danger, of course, is that fu-ture historians will only have access to a particular period's notions of historical accuracy in the form of preserved films; but the alternative options for dealing with a perishable medium are few indeed. Whether considering the use of the many early color or sound systems, or the period's distinctions between fiction and fact, or alternate media systems that may have positioned expectations for the film medium, the results of this historical turn are (and will continue to be) profound.

## Constructing Media Histories

The space between theory and practice is always a great one, but it seems particularly pro-found in the case of contemporary media history. Much ink has been spilt critiquing the historiographic efforts of the past, or establishing new parameters for the historians of the future, but rarely do such discourses embrace the mundane specificity of historical prac-tice. Yet the latter realm, complicated by the stubbornness of data and the particularity of argumentation, yields some of the strongest insights. And it is this realm which ac-counts for my insistence on the plural form of history (histories), since historical practice is not unified by the abstractions of theory, no matter how well intended. As the work of such scholars as (among others) Kittler, Gumbrecht, and Zielinski in Germany, Ong, Douglas, and Marvin in the United States, and Flichy, Virilio, and Mattelart in France has shown, we are seeing an increasingly sophisticated (and eclectic) array of considerations of media's complex histories.[19] Since the important work of these and other authors is available, in the remaining space I would like to make a few comments about what seem to me to be several central issues in the construction of media historical practice: focal points for historical investigation; a few central organizing topoi; and finally, a nod in the direction of historical specificity.

The media's transitional status is not only ongoing but multi-faceted. Changes in tech-nology, signifying systems, cultural contexts and cultural practice have been pervasive and complicated by trans-national dimensions (adaptation, recycling, variant cultural meanings) and cross-platform/cross-audience dimensions (representational pressures, identity problems, moral panics). Nevertheless, some moments of change are more revealing than others: the "birth" of media forms, when technological possibility finds systematic deployment as media practice; or the dramatic re-purposing of media systems (e.g., radio's shift from an individuated two-way communication system to a broadcast system); or the intermedial redefinition of media (e.g., digital technology's implications for the media of photography, film, and television). Such moments are usually accompanied by rich discursive evidence regarding perceived media capacities, anticipated use patterns, and intermedial relations.[20] But perhaps most importantly, such moments challenge the "taken for grantedness" that under normal circumstances tends to blind us to the possibilities inherent in a particular medium and the processes by which social practice gradually privileges one vision of the medium over the others. My own work, as but one example, has tended to focus on such periods, including a look at competing models for the medium of television (a case study of German television in 1930s and 1940s); or cinema's balancing act with mass popularity and cultural respectability (case studies centering on representation strategies and on debates over social space); or the post-1876 realization of the camera obscura in a notion of the "televisual" rooted in the telephone and magic lantern.[21] Were I pressed for an explanation as to why these particular moments are of such interest, I would most likely conclude that these moments resonate in a particularly powerful way with a media present that is itself very much in transition . . . that I inhabit a moment of media instability, and that it has shaped my horizon of interests. But at the risk of extrapolating too far beyond my own speaking position, I would go on to assert that these moments of tension and instability offer particularly sharp insights into the construction of media form. While there is much that can be said for the quotidian (particularly if one's interest is in media texts), our understanding of media *as* text benefits greatly from moments of instability.

The notion of media as social practice pertains as much to the development of technological infrastructure and representational capacity (not to mention deployment), as it does to the "user," the human side of the equation. Communication studies have long privileged selected aspects of this situation, for example favoring notions of content transfer ("encoding and decoding" to recall Stuart Hall's formulation[22]), or the extension and organization of social power (from political communication to political economy). The functionalist agenda implicit in these interests has generally favored a focus on the present, relegating historical framing to the margins (or to the critics of these traditions). As well, these functionalist studies have tended to be funded in accordance with the perception of their relevance, with the result that historically oriented work has usually had to content itself with less than a full share. Institutional realpolitik aside, however, one of the greatest consequences of these tendencies has been the marginalization of research on the implications of media for the world of perceptual experience (the malleability of time and space so well chronicled by Stephen Kern[23]), or for our notions of epistemological order, or for our sense of individual and collective memory. These rather broad categories help to highlight various long-term endeavors such as storage (from medieval "tally sticks" to Sony's memory sticks) and liveness (telegraphy, telephony, radio, webcams), and long-term concerns with the audience (from effects and claims of demoralization to critical re-workings and assertions of empowerment). At the same time, these topoi provide a comparative frame, giving coherence to analytic shifts across media forms, historical times, cultural contexts, and levels of analytic specificity.

Obviously the media in question pose significant challenges to any imposition of neat conceptual categories on their development, and the triad perception, epistemology, and memory is but one of many possible ways to tackle the problem. That said, these elements and others like them offer a way to cope with the radical repositioning which seems increasingly apparent in the field. Media studies are very much in motion, despite having entrenched institutional interests. As previously mentioned, the academic repositioning of specific media (e.g., film) into a web of pre-existing, competing, and alternative media practices has done much to resituate the possible meanings that an isolated medium can generate. The ripple effects of the overdetermined "Brighton" moment are continuing to be felt in the ongoing redefinition of media studies disciplinarity. But an equally compelling factor is 'external' to the academic world and apparent from contemporary media practice. Digitization and convergence have redefined our present as a moment of media in transition. The ontological frameworks for various media forms have been challenged and redefined (consider the shifts within a medium such as film, once defined in terms of its photo-chemical base, but now edited on a magnetic medium [video] and displayed in digital formats [DVD]). As so often happens at moments of transition, the divisions between some media forms begin to erode and disappear. Convergence, too, has challenged old certainties. Whether we think in terms of the media corporations which now circulate texts among their various divisions, or in terms of the textual networks created as particular narratives or characters sweep across media forms, or in terms of the audiences constructed around cross-media notions of textuality, it is increasingly clear that old certainties are very much up for grabs.

Together, the efforts of historians to reconsider the taken-for-granted and the demands of the digital and convergent present have compelled a new view of media, one which benefits from considering other moments of media in transition, and one which demands new sorts of conceptual focus.[24] At the same time, more than ever the embrace of the specific, of the detail, is essential if we are to deepen our appreciation of media as social practice. The ideological implications of evidence and argument are particularly compelling when considering mass media experiences that are located at contentious junctures in developmental and social history—like early cinema both defining itself as a functioning medium and as a medium in the midst of the struggle to reaffirm the place of the dominant classes in America (a tool in a larger ideological context).[25] But even if we step back and take a more abstracted look at media history (like history itself), our particular worldview or what we might call our ideological inscription, is always a factor. The difficulty is that this worldview is bound up with particular material practices, and thus much more accessible from the perspective of working history than historical theory. That said, I wish simply to draw on a publication that has recently appeared in German that (in part) takes on the problem of projectionists in the years before 1913, offering something in the way of a cross-platform text.[26] The early definition problems of this occupational category speak to the developmental problems of cinema more generally, and in turn, to the position of popular culture in the first decade or so of the twentieth century—a period of crisis at least in the United States.[27] Yet drawing upon the particularity of the projectionists as a way to understand the competing demands of regulation (both political and professionalization), identity and resistance is rendered difficult thanks to the sad realities of collective memory as reified in the archive (the projectionists' experiences failed to find a place there).

As far as my coauthor on this project, Roberta Pearson, and I know, no projectionist recorded his impressions of his daily routine; the best approximation of the physical realities of the projectionists' lives derives from reading the evidence of dominant institutions "against the grain," that is, looking for unintended traces and evidence in remaining official records. This results in an historical procedure that some readers might dismiss as overly speculative, and while we acknowledge the limits of such speculation, we believe that it produces better historical understanding than a simple replication of the period's own written evidence. Our essay openly acknowledges the fragmentary nature of the evidence that we use (it hardly conforms to the documentation standards taken for granted by many historians) in order to permit glimpses into the lives and motives of individual projectionists. In so doing, we seek to restore some sense of agency to the operators, even though the weight of evidence presented supports a Foucauldian vision of projectionists as subjects produced through disciplinary regimes.[28] Like Herodotus (though perhaps for different reasons), we do not favor one of these interpretations over the other, instead permitting them to oscillate back and forth.

Such oscillation violates some of the fundamental precepts of conventional historiography. Wary as we are of constructing historians as a monolithic category, it seems that many historians are trained to weave evidence from various sources into a coherent narrative that they believe best represents the events and causality of the past. They are trained to believe that there are better and worse interpretations and better and worse stories to be made of the same evidence. As Robert Berkhofer says in *Beyond the Great Story,* "That two or more stories can be told about the same set of events deeply disturbs even sophisticated normal [non-postmodernist] historians."[29] Such historians resist the relativistic chaos precipitated by the oscillation between (among) two or more stories. Yet, as just argued, the evidence available for the study of early cinema history (and for many other potential histories as well), exhibits a pattern of selective survival and filtration that structures the stories that can be told. Historians' training might incline them to accept certain textual forms (city ordinances, records of fact) as solid, hard evidence, while dismissing other forms (the anecdote, the oblique reference or the structured absence) as questionable. The former texts, those endowed with institutional endorsement and "objectivity," seem frequently to represent the forces that reigned dominant within the period; they represent the views articulated by and later archived by dominant institutions. Historians' dependence upon these sources, and thus their tendency to reproduce dominant narratives, stems from several preferences and prejudices regarding the construction of history:

- the desire to establish hierarchies of consistency, preferring the more consistent to the less;
- the desire to avoid contradiction, seeking instead mutually reinforcing data and conclusions;
- the desire to see history as transparent rather than constructed; as an object rather than a text;
- the desire to engage in holistic analyses and construct integrated narratives.

In contrast to conventional historical practices, in our article (and the larger project of which it is a part), we tried to be sensitive to evidence, however scarce or inconsistent, that restores some agency to dominated factions and to construct a narrative that gives the dominated a voice. The nagging question of this approach's general applicability remains, particularly since we have based our argument upon evidence from the geographically specific locale of New York City. But with historical topics that centrally involve socially marginalized subjects at moments of media instability, such an approach offers a means by which the readily available record of the dominant classes can be interrogated and complicated.

## Conclusion

The processes of digitization and convergence together with the post-structuralist Zeitgeist have, I have tried to argue, given rise to something like the situation Herodotus describes in Book Two of his *Histories*. Long-held certainties have been shaken and knowledge frameworks, de-centered. At this profoundly transitional moment in media development, the working agenda for historians can quite productively make use of those earlier transition moments when related forms of instability threw into question media ontologies (and with them, issues of epistemology, perception, and memory). The task of researching and writing new media histories shows signs of invigoration, particularly as debates over appropriate questions and methods grow more forceful. My own work as well as that carried out with Roberta Pearson embraces these debates, and continues to benefit from close attention to the textures of the past informed by a sense of what has been structurally elided, by the "that which has not been said." Moreover, such specificity is a central means of restoring an ideological edge to the historical effort. As just noted, this sort of approach can be at odds with certain notions of traditional historiography, but it remains open to the play of plurality and alterity that so enlivened the historical practice of Herodotus and informs the work of a growing number of historians. We cannot extract ourselves from the cultures into which we are historically embedded, and to be sure, the range of contemporary debate is very much circumscribed by our historical moment. This is a limiting factor that we can ignore, pretending that our intellectual insights are free from this gravity (although even if we believed this, the realpolitik of the publishing business and its synchronicity with the dominant order of the present should give us pause . . . ). Or it is one that we can embrace, using it as a compass in our search for a relevant precedent.

## Notes

I wish to thank Henry Jenkins, Brad Seawell, Frans Jeursen, and the members of the media history seminar at Utrecht University for their comments on this essay. Portions of it have appeared in German as "Medien des übergangs und ihre Historisierung," *Archiv für Mediengeschichte—Mediale Historiographien* (2001): 57–72.

1. Herodotus, *The Histories,* trans. A. R. Burn (New York: Penguin, 1972).

2. See in particular chapter one of Raymond Williams, *Television: Technology and Cultural Form* (New York: Schocken Books, 1974).

3. Pierre Bourdieu, *The Rules of Art: Genesis and Structure of the Literary Field* (Stanford: Stanford University Press, 1996).

4. See, for example, Fernand Braudel's *The Mediterranean and the Mediterranean World in the Age of Philip II* (New York: Harper & Row, 1972).

5. E. P. Thompson's work is here exemplary, as is Raymond Williams's. See, for example, Thompson's *The Making of the English Working Class* (New York: Pantheon Books, 1964); and Williams's *Culture and Society, 1780–1950* (New York: Columbia University Press, 1960).

6. Antonio Gramsci offered the term "hegemony" as a way to describe the broad consensus that helps to move social agendas, contrasting it with "political domination," by which he meant the overt force of the state. Culture plays a key role in the formation of willing consensus. See *The Prison Notebooks* (New York: Columbia University Press, 1992).

7. Social regulatory processes, encouraged by the state, and in the period referenced, capitalist interests, have tended to reduce the radical potentials of media forms through regulatory processes such as the allocation of frequencies or the enforcement of broadcasting practices in the case of radio. Part of film's struggle for respectability was related to this process, described in part by Max Weber's notion of "rationalization."

8. See E. P. Thompson.

9. For an overview of this shift, see Terry Eagleton, *Literary Theory: An Introduction* (Minneapolis: University of Minnesota Press, 1996). For more a more specific overview of reception theory, see Janet Staiger's summary in *Interpreting Films: Studies in the Historical Reception of American Cinema* (Princeton: Princeton University Press, 1992).

10. Now classic texts include Ien Ang's *Watching Dallas: Soap Opera and the Melodramatic Imagination* (London: Methuen, 1985); David Morley's *The Nationwide Television Studies* (London: Routledge, 1999); Henry Jenkins, *Textual Poachers: Television Fans and Participatory Culture* (New York: Routledge, 1992); see also Morley's *Television, Audiences, and Cultural Studies* (New York: Routledge, 1992).

11. Cultural studies, at least as I am using the term, must be credited to the British academic scene. Not only was the humanities/social science divide differently articulated than in the United States, but the strong qualitative tradition in sociology took the lead in studies of popular culture. Moreover, discussions of such concepts as ideology, power, and class interest were possible in Britain in ways that were off limits in the U.S. academy. That "American" cultural studies have tended to embrace the abstractions of post-modernity rather than considering the lived experiences of those that construct culture speaks to this difference.

12. The Brighton meeting of the International Federation of Film Archives was notable for its inclusion of film scholars in a group otherwise dominated by professional archivists. The Brighton Project, more formally a symposium entitled "Fiction Film, 1900–1906," inspired the investigation of the early cinema area. Some articles stemming from this conference may be found in the *Quarterly Review of Film Studies* 4, no. 4 (1979).

13. Jay Leyda's famed Griffith seminars at NYU in the 1970s helped to create a generation of early film scholars; Robert Sklar's *Movie Made America: A Cultural History of American Movies* (New York: Random House, 1974) and Garth Jowett's *Film: The Democratic Art* (New York: Little, Brown, 1976) marked important turns in writing about film history as social/cultural history.

14. Among many others, see Tom Gunning, *D. W. Griffith and the Origins of American Narrative Film* (Urbana: University of Illinois Press, 1991); Charles Musser, *High Class Moving Pictures: Lyman H. Howe and the Forgotten Era of Travelling Exhibition, 1880–1920* (Princeton: Princeton University Press, 1991); William Uricchio and Roberta E. Pearson, *Reframing Culture: The Case of the Vitagraph Quality Films* (Princeton: Princeton University Press, 1993); Richard deCordova, *Picture Personalities: The Emergence of the Star System in America* (Urbana: University of Illinois Press, 1991).

15. For example, Uricchio and Pearson; Miriam Hansen, *Babel and Babylon: Spectatorship in American Silent Film* (Cambridge, MA: Harvard University Press, 1991).

16. For example, Gunning; Roberta Pearson, *Eloquent Gestures: The Transformation of Performance Style in the Griffith Biograph Films* (Berkeley: University of California Press, 1992).

17. For example, Musser; Robert Allen, *Horrible Prettiness: Burlesque and American Culture* (Chapel Hill: University of North Carolina Press, 1991).

18. William Uricchio, "Cinema als Omweg: Een nieuwe kijk op de geschiedenis van het bewegende beeld," *Skrien* 199 (1994): 54–57; with a more developed argument, "Technologies of Time," in J. Olsson, ed., *Allegories of Communication: Intermedial Concerns from Cinema to the Digital* (London: John Libby/Bloomington: Indiana University Press, 2003).

19. Friedrich Kittler, *Discourse Networks 1800/1900* (Stanford: Stanford University Press, 1990); Siegfried Zielinski, *Audiovisions: Cinema and Television as entr'actes in History* (Amsterdam: Amsterdam University Press, 1999); Hans Ulrich Gumbrecht and K. Ludwig Pfeiffer, *Materialities of Communication* (Stanford: Stanford University Press, 1994); Walter J. Ong, *Orality and Literacy: the Technologizing of the Word* (London: Methuen, 1982); Susan Douglas, *Inventing American Broadcasting, 1899–1922,* (Baltimore: Johns Hopkins University Press, 1987); Caroline Marvin, *When Old Technologies Were New: Thinking about Electric Communication in the Late 19th Century* (Oxford: Oxford University Press, 1988) Patrice Flichy, *Dynamics of Modern Communication: The Shaping and Impact of New Communication Technologies,* (London: Sage Publications, 1995); Paul Virilio, *The Vision Machine,* (London: British Film Institute, 1995); Armand Mattelart, *Networking the World, 1794–2000* (Minneapolis: University of Minnesota Press, 2000).

20. Wiebe Bijker, *Of Bicycles, Bakelites, and Bulbs: Toward a Theory of Sociotechnical Change* (Cambridge, MA: MIT Press, 1995).

21. See for example, William Uricchio, "Television as History: Representations of German Television Broadcasting, 1935–1944," in *Framing the Past: The Historiography of German Cinema and Television,* ed. Bruce Murray and Christopher Wickham (Carbondale: Southern Illinois University Press, 1992), 167–196; Uricchio and Pearson (cited above); William Uricchio, "Technologies of Time" (cited above).

22. Stuart Hall, "Encoding, Decoding" in *Culture, Media, Language: Working Papers in Cultural Studies* (London: Routledge, 1992/1980).

23. Stephen Kern, *The Culture of Time and Space 1880–1918* (Cambridge: Harvard University Press, 1983).

24. See for example, Jenkins; the cites mentioned in note 19.

25. The years between 1906 and 1913 in the United States were, for example, formative years for the film industry; yet the young medium found itself situated in a series of struggles over ethnicity, citizenship and class that plagued in particular urban turn-of-the-century America. The dominant classes' association of the film medium with immigrant and working class patrons led in part to a series of repressive strategies (the 1908 closing of over 550 nickelodeons in New York City alone; censorship; audience age and ethnicity restrictions; police supervision, etc.). Some in the film medium sought to ally themselves with the agenda of the dominant class factions, in the process attempting both to reposition film as "respectable" and to serve the cultural interests of those "better" classes. See Uricchio and Pearson, and Pearson and Uricchio,*"The Nickel Madness": The Struggle to Control New York City's Nickelodeons in 1907–1913.* (Berkeley: University of California Press, forthcoming).

26. William Uricchio and R. E. Pearson, "Filmvorführer in New York, 1906–1913," in *KINtop: Jahrbuch zur Erforschung des frühen Films* 9 (2000): 91–108

27. The crisis I refer to was economic (a series of economic crises resulting in unemployment and food shortages), social (reactions to the influx of millions of new immigrants from southern and eastern Europe), and political (a consequence of both). It played out in a series of fundamental debates over culture, citizenship, and the meaning of "America."

28. Michel Foucault's larger project involved understanding the human subject as a creation of particular systems ("disciplinary regimes") that entailed social, behavioral, ideological, and institutional dimensions. A particularly clear instance of his thinking in this regard may be found in *Discipline and Punish: The Birth of the Prison* (New York: Vintage, 1979).

29. Robert Berkhofer, *Beyond the Great Story: History as Text and Discourse* (Cambridge, MA: Harvard University Press, 1995), 24.

# 4 Re-Newing Old Technologies: Astonishment, Second Nature, and the Uncanny in Technology from the Previous Turn-of-the-Century

Tom Gunning

## Old and New: The General Line from Amazement to Habit

What can we learn from a cultural history of technology? Beyond chronicling the development, introduction and proliferation of specific technologies, what can we learn from investigating, to use Carolyn Marvin's revealing phrase, the time "when old technologies were new"?[1] Technology in the modern age has a direct relation to the phenomenon of innovation and novelty, and therefore to what makes the modern age modern. To imagine an old technology as something that was once new means, therefore, to try to recapture a quality it has lost. It means examining a technology or device at the point of introduction, before it has become part of a nearly invisible everyday life of habit and routine. But it also must mean examining this move from dazzling appearance to nearly transparent utility, from the spectacular and astonishing to the convenient and unremarkable. This transformation needs to be interrogated for the cultural myths of modernity it assumes and creates. The move from astonishment to a habitual second nature may be less stable than we think, and this instability may explain our fascination with rediscovering technology at its point of novelty. This essay, then, is perhaps more intimately involved with novelty than with technology, or rather with the intersection between them.

History deals not only with events but, primarily, and some would claim exclusively, with the discourses they generate and which record them. The introduction of new technology in the modern era employs a number of rhetorical tropes and discursive practices that constitute our richest source for excavating what the newness of technology entailed. The Universal Expositions that mark the latter part of the nineteenth and the early part of the twentieth centuries celebrated, represented and explained the agents and effects of the modern world. Their visual displays and verbal proclamations, protocols and practices, announced key aspects of modernity: an overcoming of space and time that allowed a new sense of the global in a world shrunken by new technologies of transportation and communication; a demonstration and, nearly, the deification of new sources of energy and power, especially electricity; a narrative of progress exemplified by a series of new technical devices and goods placed on display in order to launch them into the world of newly created consumers; and last, but not least, a mode of highly stimulated spectatorship in which huge crowds were encouraged to envision a future that would be simultaneously spectacular and convenient.[2] We are all aware of the ambivalence of these official celebrations, the racism inherent in their myths of globalized progress and the exploitation of world-wide laboring populations, camouflaged by a narrative of an irresistible march of mankind towards an exalted future.[3] But there is more to be uncovered in these Expositions than an ideological swindle, if only in their contradictions.

Primary among these is the paradoxical celebration in these festivals of the novel in the guise of the eternal, and of the technological in the form of magic. Expositions primarily presented a conservative face, such as the Columbian Exposition of 1893 in Chicago whose White City imaged an Imperial Utopia considered appropriate to a nation garnering its first colonial possessions overseas, while turning its face away from the smoke wreathed gray city of slums a few miles from the fairgrounds.[4] But every visitor knew that this pastiche of Rome and Venice was made of plaster rather than marble, designed to dissolve and disappear within a year of festivities.[5] Indeed, the ruins and conflagrations left in its wake drew almost as large crowds as its glorious opening. Monuments to progress possess an inherent instability, as the attractions of a consumer society depend on novelty as much as utility, seeking cheaper and more attractive as well as more effective methods and devices. Newness and amazement became a mode of reception for technology at these Expositions.

Novelty in modernity enacts a consistent scenario. Initial reactions express astonishment, which gradually gives way to an acceptance of the new technology as second nature, in both the colloquial meaning of that term—an accustomed familiarity—("it's second nature to me now"), and in the more complex meaning the term acquired in the work of Lukacs and the Frankfort school, of a reified human-made environment which confronts mankind as an alien reality. Astonishment and familiarity contrast strongly, but they form successive stages within modern experience and are therefore interrelated. The appearance of a new technology is celebrated for its novelty and astonishment is the proclaimed response. This is precisely the experience that the Universal Expositions were designed to provoke, the thrill they offered their mass audience. It can be summed up by the response of one visitor to the Philadelphia Centennial Exposition in a postcard home: "Dear Mother: Oh. Oh. ooooooooo!"[6] and by

Owen Wister's description of his entrance to the Columbian Exposition : " . . . my mind was dazzled to a standstill."[7]

But astonishment is inherently an unstable and temporary experience. One finds it difficult to be continually astonished by the same thing. Astonishment gives way to familiarity. Astonishment acts as a sort of threshold experience and for this reason, the actual approach to a World Exposition, as Wister noted, was often the most dazzling experience, one renewed by the visitor's first entrance into the various pavilions. A journalist described entering the Palace of Electricity at the 1904 Louisiana Purchase Exposition by noting, "As you enter the Palace of Electricity you hear uncanny whirrings and snappings; you see electrical lights of hues and intensities that you never saw before; strange machines begin to glide or whirr or glow or click."[8] Such visual and auditory novelty beckons one to enter into a new world. But once within, once past the threshold, astonishment gives way to curiosity and investigation and eventually to familiarity. (This account of the Palace of Electricity continues with the statement, "the meaning of all these things is that electricity is put to more varied uses . . . than ever before."[9]) The narrative of the World Exposition opens with heightened astonishment, gradually fading into understanding as the dazzle of the first encounter yields to knowledge.

Although this arc of reaction exemplifies the response to new technology in modernity, it draws on fairly universal cognitive patterns. John Onians's incisive essay, "I Wonder . . . A Short History of Amazement" offers a cognitive understanding of this cycle, stating, "If we are to write a history of wonder we must write a natural history."[10] In his outline of this process he sees four stages by which amazement leads to learning: (1) a striking experience, usually visual, but sometimes aural; (2) a consequent physical paralysis; and (3) a mental reaction which results in something being learned which may be followed by (4) a new action.[11]

Onians relates his natural history of amazement to Darwin's analysis of the expression of emotions in man and animals. For Darwin, the characteristic expression of amazement involved raising the eyebrows and opening the mouth. The practical aspects of this expression lay in the improvement of vision and the easing of breathing (the "oooooooo" of the Centennial Exposition visitor or "wow!" of a sports fan simply vocalizes this sharp intake of breathe).[12] Modern modifications of this explanation, based on the chemical processes of the brain, still fundamentally describe amazement as an adaptive behavior to new stimulus.[13] The physiognomy of astonishment was well known and employed by painters from Leonardo through Le Brun.[14] Le Brun's mentor, Descartes, describes amazement clearly in *The Passions of the Soul*:

> When our first encounter with some object surprises us and we find it novel, or very different from what we formerly knew of from what we supposed it ought to be, this causes us to wonder and to be astonished at it. Since all this may happen before we know whether or not the object is beneficial to us, I regard wonder as the first of all the passions.[15]

Astonishment may shed light on the cycles of cultural as well as natural history. Onians declares the sixteenth and seventeenth century as a "great period of wonder" due to the mass of new discoveries, technological and territorial, during this period.[16] This period of astonishment "was brought to an end . . . by a wave of explanation and classification."[17] If there are periods of cultural wonder, then the period roughly from the 1870s through to World War I would seem a likely candidate, an era of technological acceleration and transformation of the environment. Onians sees all periods of wonder as marked by the display of novelties (from the collections of Assurnasirpal II of Assyria to the cabinets of curiosity of Rudolph II),[18] and the World Expositions played this role in the modern period, with a global consciousness, industrial context and mass appeal that defined their modern characteristic. However, Onians declares the sixteenth and seventeenth century as the *last* great period of wonder, undoubtedly because of the greater availability of scientific explanations after this period. But even a cursory glance at the World Expositions reveals that the display of curiosities and the fascination caused by them continues and gains power in the modern era. The cycle between amazement and explanation may have become shorter, but one could also claim that the increased pace of modernity supplies a constant stream of environmental changes, sufficient to renew wonder even if in shorter cycles.

What happens in modernity to the initial wonder at a new technology or device when the novelty has faded into the banality of the everyday? One might claim that having gone through Onians's four phases, wonder becomes subsumed in action, then in habitual action and ultimately in the diametric opposite of wonder, automatism. This creates a world of disenchantment. Effects that seemed miraculous or wondrous, through their rational interpretation become banal, and even the astonishing becomes familiar. Although I feel this is an accurate description of one aspect of the cycles of modernity, I am not fully satisfied that it completely explains the modern alternation between astonishment and familiarity that the World Exposition first rehearsed. The contrast between Onians's cognitive description of *individual* astonishment in which astonishment would of necessity be short-lived, and a social and historical concept like a century of wonder should give us pause. As illuminating as the cognitive description of the cycle of astonishment may be, I do not think it offers us an unmediated understanding of the role of astonishment in modernity or of the fascination with "new" technology.

Wonder and curiosity seem to be universal human traits and I believe their investigation provides insight into their historical manifestations. But we are dealing not simply with individual experiences but with social practices and I, for one, am unwilling to enter into a debate about which causes which. Mediation enters into the natural in unexpected ways, as a brief excursus on the illustration Onians borrows from Darwin to portray the typical expression of astonishment reveals. It derives, of course, from G. B. Duchenne de Boulogne's famous photographs of typical expressions of the human face.[19] As a physiologist, Duchenne was primarily interested in the mechanics of facial expressions, which muscles were involved in their creation. He understood facial movement as part of a God-given language of expression. The expression reproduced by Darwin and Onians was not a spontaneous reaction by a human subject, but an already determined expression that Duchenne sculpted on the face of his experimental subject by means of electrodes, to be photographed by Nadar Junior in 1853. I do not dispute the validity of the interpretation of this expression, but merely indicate that even in the center of a naturalist demonstration, ideas of a pre-existent facial language and the play of the then novel technologies of electricity and photography intervene and mediate.

As historical phenomena, human experiences have always already been caught in the net of social discourse. And I believe that the "newness" of new technology, its capacity to dazzle us, is always in some sense the product of discourses surrounding it. Discourse includes more than verbal statements, although these are obviously privileged by historians for the relative clarity of their interpretation. In the World Expositions, the carefully arranged lay-out of space and the logic of form and color in the architecture, evoke cultural associations and determine the temporal and spatial unfolding of vistas and patterns. The stimulus of sound and light, the prose of guidebooks and explanatory signs, make up the discursive positioning of the new technology in the Expositions and cued visitors to experience astonishment. The discourse of modernity, then, is not only one of innovation, but precisely one of novelty, maximizing the dazzling experience of the new.

## *Making It New and Making It Strange: The Uncanny Route of Return*

But what makes the new *new?* Russian formalist Victor Shklovsky discovered the function of this rhetoric of newness when he set out to write a history of the introduction of electric light to Moscow and Petersburg and its transformation of the city nightscape.[20]

He abandoned the project after combing the newspapers of the period and finding no mention of the phenomenon, no recorded astonishment at this major technological transformation. Journalists instead recorded traditional genres of news: gossip, royal visits, politics, but not the new genre of technological innovation. Shklovsky concluded from this discovery that "the new arrives unnoticed."[21] In effect, we must learn to be surprised, at least as recorded in print, astonishment is not simply a natural phenomenon. Now I (and I presume Shklovsky) would not claim no one was astonished by the electrification of Moscow (he indicates, "at that time electricity already functioned in Moscow and some people were even delighted about the fact"[22]). The journalistic silence does not simply reflect a blasé attitude on the part of Moscow's citizens. Rather, journalists lacked a discursive context, or tradition, for the expressing of such astonishment. As Shklovsky puts it, "newspapers are extremely slow in perceiving the new because they lack a method for giving it form."[23] There apparently was not a spectacular and highly ritualized practice such as the nightly lighting of the electric lights at the Chicago Columbian Exposition, or the highly publicized inaugural turning on of electricity in downtown shopping areas so well recorded in U.S. urban history.[24] Undoubtedly, as a social phenomenon and particularly as one that gets officially noted, surprise is learned, fostered and expressed by discursive practices whose implementation brings profit to someone: merchants, policy makers, civic fathers justifying municipal power plants, or any one of a number of interested parties. Modernity must partly be understood as learning to be surprised by certain innovations, a discourse that valorizes and directs our attention to such changes and the excitement they can provoke.

And what of the final phase of Onians's natural history of wonder, its dissolution in knowledge and new practices? While knowledge certainly plays a role here, it may belong more directly to the opening of the cycle, closer to amazement than to habit. It was the educational potential of the World Expositions that organizers lauded, a firm belief that wonder prompted learning about technical innovation. The submerging of innovation into a realm of second nature would seem to have more to do with what Shklovsky elsewhere describes as habituation and automatism.[25] This phase, the opposite of amazement, indicates less a gain in knowledge than a loss of vivid experience. As Shklovsky says, "habitualization devours works, clothes, furniture, one's wife, and the fear of war."[26] Rather than knowledge, the outcome of this habitualization is to render us unconscious of our experience.

As historians searching for the novelty of old technology, we confront a dilemma. Is decline into invisibility irreversible and irresistible? Does the wonder at technology head in the express lane towards either the outmoded and discarded or the practical and un-noticed? Once understood, does technology ever recover something of its original strangeness? I maintain there are several ways that this can happen. Shklovsky describes an aesthetic path back towards heightened perception through the technique he called de-familiarization or "making it strange."[27] For Shklovsky, art takes up the struggle against this loss of sensual awareness. Through techniques of formal play—such as roughened language or unusual perspectives—"art removes objects from the automatism of per-ception."[28] But for Shklovsky defamiliarization deals with perception not knowledge.[29] I think it is an error to believe that we possess a full understanding of technology through a scientific explanation of how it works. There are layers of knowledge that emerge in our dealings with technology that also cause us to wonder anew. Heidegger's early discussion of work in terms of the dynamic of the tool shows that we can suddenly gain a new per-spective on technology through an interruption of habitual actions. His conception of the tool as "the ready to hand" gives us another way to conceive the "unconsciousness" of habit in terms of technology.[30] According to *Being and Time,* it is in the nature of a tool not to assert itself, but rather to withdraw in favor of the project it is supposed to accomplish. When a tool works, we pay it no attention; it seems to disappear. However, if the tool breaks down, if in some way it doesn't function, it suddenly becomes conspicuous.

I would claim, then, a more complex cycle for the cultural introduction of technology than Onians's. A discourse of wonder draws our attention to new technology, not simply as a tool, but precisely as a spectacle, less as something that performs a useful task than as something that astounds us by performing in a way that seemed unlikely or magical be-fore. The discourse highlights and defines this magical nature. This wonder intrigues and attracts us, allowing curiosity to give way to investigation and education, usually carefully channeled by social discourses. However, habituation dulls our attention to technology. But, in different ways, both Heidegger and Shklovsky claim that wonder can be renewed. Shklovsky's de-familiarization employs aesthetic and rhetorical means, refashioning dis-course away from the automatic so that the familiar becomes strange and can be redis-covered in its sensual specificity and vividness. Heidegger's renewal has less of a celebratory thrust. It is the breakdown of equipment that allows us to experience it afresh. The interruption makes the project itself explicit. When a tool is missing "our cir-cumspection comes up against emptiness, and now sees for the first time what the miss-ing article was ready-to-hand with and what it was ready-to-hand for. The environment announces itself afresh."[31]

There are several points that I want to stress in this more complex model. First, the various stages relate to one another dialectically, so that one announces the reversal that the next one achieves. Secondly, neither astonishment nor habit derive simply from individual cognition of single objects, but are triggered by changing relations to the world, guided or distracted by language, practice, representation and aesthetics. Inattention can be transformed into wonder; wonder can be worn down into habit; habit can suddenly, even catastrophically, transform back into a shock of recognition.

Wolfgang Schivelbusch's influential discussion of the railway supplies a specific example of this dialectical interaction.[32] Initial reception of railway travel was shaped by concerns about safety and anxiety about the possibility of railway accidents. Early railway journeys entailed a gnawing fear of death through accident, a fear founded in a very real possibility, and in the novelty of traversing space at unheard-of speeds. But this fear seemed to vanish by the turn of the century, as new practices (such as the introduction of reading during the train journey) created, as Schivelbusch put it, "a new psychic layer that obscures the old fears and allows them to lapse into oblivion."[33] But this psychic buffer zone involves more than the disappearance of wonder through new knowledge, for the possibility of disaster has been camouflaged, not eliminated. A series of cultural practices serve to allay anxieties rather than dispel them, like the nearly sedated voices making announcements in international airports, which, combined with design and color schemes with all-too-evident calming intentions, always make me feel like I have wandered inadvertently into the psycho ward. As Schivelbusch says, "any sudden interruption of that functioning, (which has now become second nature) immediately reawakens the memory of the forgotten danger and potential violence: the repressed material returns with a vengeance."[34] Just as a breakdown in equipment makes the context of the tool suddenly visible for Heidegger, for Schivelbusch a more advanced technological breakdown seems to tear apart acquired familiarity and assurance, creating a disaster within our second nature.

I would like to introduce another term to mediate between the extremes of astonishment and automatism: the uncanny. In contrast to Shklovsky's de-familiarization and Heidegger's glimpses of the total environment of the tool, this phenomenon involves less a new perception understanding than an overriding uncertainty. Rather than clearly coming at the end of a cycle of habitualization, the uncanny seems to permeate the whole cycle, hinted at in the experience of wonder re-emerging just when rational explanation seemed to have triumphed. I rely here on Freud's analysis of the particularly pregnant German term *Das Unheimlich*.[35] Freud, following Schelling, pointed out the essential ambivalence of this word, which literally means "un-home-like." The specific effect of the uncanny comes from the flowering of a sense of unfamiliarity in the midst of the apparently familiar. For Freud, the uncanny signals the emergence of unconscious material from repression, and it can take many forms. We must recognize that repression in Freud's sense should not be equated with the dulling of our awareness sought by nineteenth-century railways or contemporary airlines. "An uncanny experience," Freud states "occurs either when infantile complexes which have been repressed are once more revived by some impression, or when more primitive beliefs which have been surmounted seem once more to be confirmed."[36] "Primitive beliefs" refers to magical and superstitious ideas that Freud as a rationalist felt mankind had properly discarded, but which, as a psychologist, he acknowledged "remained preserved under a thin disguise."[37]

"Primitive beliefs" recall the discourse of wonder that mark the introduction of new technology, picturing them as magical creations and elemental beings. While this rhetoric is nearly always couched in a ironic or at least condescending form—the childish prologue to the true knowledge to be gained—the spectacular stage managing of technological fairylands, such as the World Exposition, do in fact, produce that authentic dazzlement of wonder with which we began our discussion. If the uncanny as understood by Freud also harks back to childhood beliefs of in animism and the omnipotence of thoughts, the fact that many of us as children first encounter technology through the lens of such manufactured folktales, may in fact produce lasting impressions, preserved beneath a later learned rationality. In other words, new technologies evoke not only a short-lived wonder based on unfamiliarity which greater and constant exposure will overcome, but also a possibly less dramatic but more enduring sense of the uncanny, a feeling that they involve magical operations which greater familiarity or habituation might cover over, but not totally destroy. It crouches there beneath a rational cover, ready to spring out again.

Thus the cycle from wonder to habit need not run only one way. The reception of technology allows re-enchantment through aesthetic de-familiarization, the traumatic surfacing of allayed fears and anxieties, as well as the uncanny re-emergence of earlier stages of magical thinking. While this may not exhaust the variety of responses that we find to technology (parody and nostalgia are two other notable responses I won't treat here), it does, I think, provide a relevant model for a cultural history of the reception of technology in the modern era. But we should realize that not all technologies are received in the same ways and that the experiences of wonder and especially of the uncanny are more likely in some technologies than others. While a series of uncanny experiences seem to cluster around technologies of communication like the telephone, or of representation like the photograph, technologies that are arguably equally important in the environment of modernity, such as refrigeration or canned food, don't seem nearly as subject to these responses. I want next to explore those aspects of technologies of reproduction that especially invite uncanny effects.

### Technological Doppelgangers: Modern Memento Mori

Certain associations evoke the technological uncanny. Challenges to basic categories of experience—such as the locomotive's "annihilation of space and time," or the telephone's blurring of the categories of presence and absence—elicit uncanny reactions. The same is true of recording technologies that seem to alter ontological status, techniques of representation which create simulacra so intense they appear as to double the originals. A cluster of nineteenth-century inventions—the photograph, the phonograph and the motion picture—were all greeted as technological responses to the ultimate limit to human life, mortality. The photograph became the means of preserving the memory of family members after their death and it was this practice that Thomas Edison had in mind when he likewise proposed the newly invented phonograph as: "The Family Record—a registry of sayings, reminiscences, etc., by members of a family in their own voices, and of the last words of dying persons."[38] Georges Demeny, an important pioneer in the production of motion pictures, described his Phonoscope as a technological improvement on the family album's hedge against death through the addition of motion, declaring, "How valuable it would be to illuminate the actual and varied expressions of these portraits which are too often mummy-like, and to leave behind us documents of our existence which can be made to live again like actual apparitions."[39] All of these technologies claimed to preserve human traits (expression, movement, voice) after the subject had died. As an objective form of memory, these recording techniques represented man's triumph over death, the ultimate astonishment and wonder of which man was capable.

But the uncanny aspect of these technologies does not reside simply in their apparently miraculous overcoming of fatal oblivion; a deep ambivalence marks these means of reproduction. Each delivers an uncanny foretaste of death, as a peculiarly modern *Memento Mori*. The proclaimed technological defense against death became death's image. The preservation of distinctive human traits divorced from a living individual, produced less an experience of immortality than a phantom, a bodiless transparent, or even invisible, double, who haunts our imagination rather than re-assuring us. As Charles Grivel has put it, "my self would live *without me*—horror of horrors!"[40]

Still photography originally generated grave suspicion due to its seeming uncanny resemblance to its subject and the apparently automatic nature of its production. The new technology allowed a re-animation of the ontological instability of all mimetic representation. The most extreme expression of this uncertainty appears in spirit photography, the belief that this new sensitive medium could pick up the images of invisible spirits of the dead hovering around a posing subject. Photography possessed supernatural associations for writers like Balzac who thought photographs captured a series of emanations from the surfaces of things,[41] or Hawthorne whose daguerrotypist Holgrave in *The House of the Seven Gables* claimed photography brought out the secret character of subjects in a way no painter could match.[42] The ties of these frozen images to death have been widely remarked upon from the beginning, when photographs took on an important role in memorial imagery, to the recent eloquent characterization by Roland Barthes of photographers as the contemporary agents of the image of death.[43]

Do such associations apply to moving pictures? Barthes derives part of photography's connection to death from its suspended temporality: it is death in the future that still photographs convey.[44] Moving images would seem to evoke the very stuff of animation, of life, as one early commentator put it, they "catch life on the fly."[45] Yet this asymptotic approach to the reproduction of life produces the effect of the uncanny and phantasmatic. For Maxim Gorky, viewing Lumière's Cinematographe in 1896, the movement itself seemed only to stress every other aspect of reality these moving pictures lacked: sound, color, three dimensionality.[46] For Gorky, the animated world of Lumière's new invention presented a gray and silent world, a realm of shadows only. Its apparent familiarity intertwined with this fundamental ontological alienation to produce a sense of malaise: "Before you a life is surging, a life deprived of words and shorn of the living spectrum of colors—the gray, soundless, the bleak and dismal life. . . . It is terrifying to see, but it is the movement of shadows, only of shadows."[47]

But if the projection of shadows, of images somehow lifted from the bodies of the living and preserved with all its mimetic resemblance in the immaterial play of darkness and light, seems too easily to partake of the uncanny, what of the other aspect of the modern motion picture, whose lack Gorky felt so strongly, the world of sound and voice? The recording of sound and the recording of images share a similar ambivalence in the face of death. A consideration of the single most famous image of astonished reaction to technology, Francis Barraud's painting "His Master's Voice" helps us unravel the ambivalence surrounding recorded sound. The image provides another illustration for Onians's natural history of amazement, substituting a rather domesticated dog for Darwin's Halloween cat. The dog, Nipper, sits posed before human technology, his clearly readable physiognomy expressing his recognition of "his master's voice" coming over this machine, his curiosity at this phenomenon, and some degree of doggie-style wonder. Animals can be as amazed by technology as humans are; wonder is a natural reaction to an unnatural object. As Michael Taussig had pointed out in his canny discussion of this image, the dog becomes humanized by his legible expression.[48] And yet his animal nature plays a key role in the power of this image. Dogs' ears possess great acuity, reaching beyond the limits of human hearing. And dogs' intense sense of hearing and smell indicate a direct connection to nature, unlikely to be confused by the obfuscation of discourse (they can neither talk, nor see pictures). Therefore Fido becomes the perfect emblem of audio fidelity. Nonetheless, as Taussig points out, the dog *is* being fooled, and our recognition of this deception guarantees our own human position of knowledge in relation to technology.[49] Like the rubes who flourish in comic strips, jokes and motion pictures of the turn of the century, the dog's astonishment and ignorance about technology serves as a foil to our growing familiarity with this second nature.

The global circulation of this image is striking. Not only was this trademark recognized world wide (note the wonderful scene with images of Nipper in Yasujiro Ozu's Japanese gangster film from 1933 *Dragnet Girl*), as Taussig shows, the image became a favored motif of the embroidered Mola blouses of the Cuna Indians of Panama.[50] Beneath the apparent disparity of the adoption of this Western commercial emblem for a Third World handicraft, ( and the delight this conjunction provides Western consumers), Taussig discovers the spell of the modern commodity, its aspiration towards a condition of magic.[51] But if the Cuna blouse shows again the possibility of the re-enchantment of technology (which I feel is the source of its delight for us, the recovery of that slumbering amazement), it is the two homunculi that stand as ministering attendants to the apparatus that highlight its magical nature. Like the little men within machines that populate both a child's vision of technology and advertising's attempt to endow commodities with magical attractions, these minions convert the machine into a ritual act, completing its circuit between animate and inanimate.

But two things should be pointed out in addition. First, the original image was made famous as an advertisement and trade mark, a discourse orienting consumers towards the phonograph, evoking and at the same time disavowing a primal astonishment.[52] Secondly, this image of master/slave discourse possesses an uncanny dimension. According to Taussig, Barraud intended his painting as a memorial image.[53] The master whose voice the dog recognizes was reportedly Barraud's dead brother, whose voice had outlasted his earthly existence. This presumably supplies another level to the dog's confusion, a canine uncanny.

The ultimate uncanny of modern technologies of reproduction lies in the blurring of the frontier between life and death, both as an occult utopia liberation expressed in the spiritualist's embrace of photography and in a much more sober and chilling sense that such apparatuses have flattened out the line between the living and non-living with an endless loop of replayed discourse and information for which a human speaker would be only a contingent factor, like Dixie the Flatliner in William Gibson's novel *Neuromancer,* a computer-generated construct which continues functioning after the death of its human model and whose one repeated request is to be erased.[54] This triumph of an unending stream of discourse may sound like a basic definition of post-modernity and should prompt one to ask whether an essay like mine traces post-modernity to the effects of recent technologies, or whether I simply offer a contemporary reception of technology colored by the fashionable discourse of post-modernity. I would opt, and hope, for another alternative. I believe that technologies and cultural discourses interpenetrate, discourses shaping how we perceive and use technology, while technologies function not simply as convenient devices, but refashion our experience of space, time and human being filtering through our arts works, dreams and fantasies.

Therefore it matters less which end of the process we seize than that we grab hold of the whole dog. But my investigation of the reception of technology at the turn of the last century makes me hesitate about terms like post-modernity. I find the two ends of the Twentieth Century hail each other like long lost twins. Both periods generate inventions revolving around reproduction and communication and, perhaps even more clearly, both mine these new technologies for theoretical and aesthetic implications. Although differences should never be underestimated, I believe that this period of early or pre-modernism has so much continuity with the present day that I can never entirely endorse the post of post modernity. We have been repeating this story for sometime, although periodically everyone seems to forget it. It is the historian's task to recall it.

## The Systematic Derangement of the Senses

If questioning of the unified subject stands as one of the hallmarks of post modernity, doesn't anyone notice that this theme was first sounded in the period from 1871 to the first years of the twentieth century, from the work of Rimbaud through to the work of Freud? If Freud's discovery of the fissure between conscious and unconscious still provides the terrain for most radical speculation about the nature of the subject, Rimbaud's earlier dictum, "I am an other" still supplies, to my mind, the motive for aesthetic practices which challenge both containment and contentment. It is the tradition of the avant-garde that most coherently addresses the question of technology from the viewpoint of the uncanny and de-familiarization. But this is not simply a matter of an inert relation between aesthetic technique and technology as a theme. Avant-Garde discourse on technology responds to transformations of experience technology offers. To specify the concrete nature of this historical mutual interpenetrating, I would like to briefly show how, without direct involvement on his part, the reproduction of sound and motion pictures circulate around the figure of Rimbaud.

The first and most powerful connection comes through the fascinating and ambiguous figure of Charles Cros, an amateur scientist and inventor, symbolist poet and major figure in the turn-of-the-century Parisian bohemian cultural scene. It was Cros who went with Paul Verlaine to pick up Rimbaud at the station on his arrival in Paris. And a few months later Rimbaud, in one of his notorious displays of contempt for Verlaine's friends, apparently put sulfuric acid in Cros's drink. Possibly in retaliation, it was Cros who showed Madame Verlaine Rimbaud's love letters to her husband.[55] And it is Cros that Ronald Gelatt, author of the standard history of the phonograph, declares the first to conceive of a practical phonograph in April 1877, several months previous to Edison's invention, although due to lack of funds Cros did not produce a prototype.[56]

In May of 1871 Rimbaud made his declaration "Je est un autre," "I am an other," or "I am someone else," a declaration against the classical conception of a unified self, in a now famous letter in which he set out the aspirations of an aesthetic Avant-Garde, involved in a dangerous and fundamental exploration of the limits of consciousness and experience.[57] Now referred to as the "Lettre du voyant," the letter of the visionary, this missive was sent by Rimbaud to his friend Paul Demeny, a minor symbolist poet. It is not known if Paul showed this letter to his brother Georges, but as Laurent Mannoni has remarked, it was Georges Demeny who in some sense fulfilled Rimbaud's statement literally through his work in motion pictures, first with Etienne Jules Marey and then independently on a number of extremely important pioneer motion picture machines.[58] These include the Phonoscope, one of the first attempts to interrelate sound and motion pictures and first intended as a tool for the instruction of the deaf in the techniques of speech.[59]

While this fraternal connection between motion pictures and Rimbaud's avant-garde project may indicate nothing more than the contingent crisscrosses of history, the connection between Cros's poetry and his science seems to me quite significant for understanding the cultural roots of the fascination of modern technology. Although most frequently descriptions of Cros as a "poetic" scientist simply refer to his lack of practicality in commercially exploiting his brilliant insights,[60] I believe his nearly systematic engagement with the technology of reproduction derives from the symbolist's belief that they were creating a new art of the senses, what Rimbaud in his *lettre du voyant* describes as "the systematic derangement of the senses."[61] Cros not only discovered the principles of the phonograph ahead of Edison, he also described the basic technology of motion pictures as early as 1867 and labored for years perfecting processes of color photography.[62] The systematic derangement of the senses and their systematic reproduction, I maintain, went hand in hand.

Cros's poetry, however, did not yet envision the actual transcription of sound as an inspiration for poetic effects, as Italian Futurist poet F. T. Marinetti or Russian Futurist poet, soon to be filmmaker, Dziga Vertov did in the first decades of the twentieth century.[63] But the ability of the phonograph to transcribe sound (an issue that fascinated Cros, partly because of his involvement with the education of the deaf)[64] introduced a new model for avant-garde practice. As James Lastra has shown, earlier attempts to reproduce speech drew on a long tradition of automatons, machines that gave the semblance of life and whose form was based on the human body.[65] While investigations of the physiology of speech led to apparatuses whose form no longer mimed the human figure, even the version of Farber's Talking Machine displayed at the Barnum Museum, which used bellows and complex machinery to reproduce speech, still included a human head as a residual emblem of the earlier ambition to recreate the voice as part of the artificial creation of a mechanical human being.[66]

Reportedly, Barnum challenged customers with a rewards of 10,000 dollars if they could match the effects of Farber's device, a proclamation quickly removed when he heard rumors of Edison's phonograph.[67] But neither Edison's phonograph nor Cros's invention resembled a human being. Cros's friend Villiers de l'Isle Adam in his 1886 satirical symbolist novel *The Eve of the Future* portrayed Edison inserting a phonograph into the breast of Hadaly an automaton figure of a woman he had fashioned, in order to comfort his friend Lord Ewald in his disappointment over a faithless lover. This perfect robot woman would be supplied with recordings in order to offer Lord Ewald the delights of witty conversation.[68] But the phonograph, as Theodor Adorno understood, derived from a tradition of inscription rather than simulacrum.[69] Both Edison and Cros were inspired by Chladni's experiments tracing in sand images left by sound vibrations, as well as devices such as the phonautograph which provided a linear inscription of sound patterns.[70]

As Villiers has his fictional Edison proclaim , "the vibrations of sounds around us can be inscribed in tracks that can be fixed like handwriting."[71]

As Thomas Levin has shown in his magisterial essay on Adorno's appreciation of the phonograph, an inscription of sound carried aesthetic possibilities rather different from the immediate resemblance offered by photography and motion pictures.[72] The curving path of the needle offered the possibility of a new language and form of writing. The inscription of sound on the phonograph record simultaneously possessed a direct, causal relation to the sound that made it, and yet translated sound, not simply into its reproduction, but into a form of script, the pitted groove scored by the recording stylus. Without offering film's illusion of an immediate reality, the phonograph record offered, Adorno claimed, borrowing a phrase from Walter Benjamin, "the last remaining universal language since the construction of the tower."[73]

It is this *transcription* of sound, rather than the trick of the reproduction of the voice, that fascinated Adorno. Influenced, as Levin demonstrates, by a long German tradition of the hieroglyphics and signatures of nature concealing encrypted messages of a higher realm within a fallen world, Adorno proposed the record as a harbinger of the apocalypse threatened by technology, with the potential to destroy the world of second nature through its own means.[74] Adorno concluded his essay on the phonograph record with these prophetic and cryptic words:

> What may be announcing itself here, however, is the shock at the transfiguration of all truth of artworks that iridescently discloses itself in the catastrophic technological progress. Ultimately the phonograph records are not artworks but black seals on the missives that are rushing towards us from all sides in the traffic with technology; missives whose formulations capture the sounds of creation, the first and last sounds, judgment upon life and message about that which may come thereafter.[75]

We find in Adorno perhaps the most sophisticated (and enigmatic) formulation of the uncanny of technology, the shock of astonishment transformed into the still sealed message of the future. Recorded sound carries overtones of first and last things, echoes from beyond.

Such a conception shatters the kitsch image of Nipper harking to the voice of his master from beyond the grave, with a deeper sense of catastrophe in which we are all implicated. Technology's ambition to crack open the seals on the mysteries of nature produces not simply knowledge, but a fundamental transformation of the human subject and of representation and calls up obscure glimpses of a brave new world well beyond Barraud's painting. I have a counter image to propose. As a young student, Rainer Maria Rilke constructed a phonograph with his science class. His description of his initial reaction perfectly conveys the astonishment that we have been probing:

> The phenomenon, on every repetition of it, remained astonishing, indeed positively staggering. We were confronting, as it were, a new and infinitely delicate point in the texture of reality, from which something far greater than ourselves, yet indescribably immature, seemed to be appealing to us as if seeking help.[76]

But Rilke finds, like Adorno, that it was not the simple reproduction of sound that most fascinated him, subject as it seemed to be to a growing familiarity and loss of power. Instead, the inscription of sound itself, this runic language promised something beyond the already known:

> At the time and all through the intervening years I believed that that independent sound taken from us and preserved outside of us, would be unforgettable. That it turned out otherwise is the cause of my writing the present account. As will be seen, what impressed itself on my memory most deeply was not the sound from the funnel but the markings traced on the cylinder; these made a most definite impression.[77]

It was the visual qualities of the marking that most impressed Rilke, the translation from sound to a sort of writing. Rilke rediscovered this signature of nature during anatomy lessons years later at the École des Beaux-Arts. Examining a skull he recognized something in the coronal suture:

> . . . a certain similarity to the closely wavy line which the needle of a phonograph engraves on the receiving, rotating cylinder of the apparatus. What if one changed the needle and directed it on its return itself naturally—well: to put it plainly, along the coronal suture, for example. What would happen? A sound would necessarily result, a series of sounds, music . . .
> Feelings—which? Incredulity, timidity, fear, awe -which of all the feelings here possible prevents me from suggesting a name for the primal sound which would then make its appearance in the world . . . [78]

Let us re-imagine Barraud's painting. Nipper sits attentive and amazed as an elaborate apparatus spins a memorial skull, its stylus tracing a path down the coronal suture, operated by the Cuna Indians' little helpers. How does Nipper respond? "Alas poor Rainer, I knew him, Teddy?" What sound issues from this cranium? Is this a collage by Max Ernst or a cartoon by Tex Avery?

These specifically avant-garde receptions of technologies of reproduction reveal another dimension to the astonishment generated by new technology. Part of this astonishment comes not simply from unfamiliarity, an experience easily overcome, but from the prophetic nature of new technologies, their address to a previously unimagined future. Every new technology has a utopian dimension that imagines a future radically transformed by the implications of the device or practice. The sinking of technology into a reified second nature indicates the relative failure of this transformation, its fitting back into the established grooves of power and exploitation. Herein lies the importance of the cultural archeology of technology, the grasping again of the newness of old technologies. As Friedrich Kittler says, "What reached the page of the surprised author between 1880 and 1920 by means of the gramophone, film and typewriter—the very first mechanical media—amounts to a spectral photograph of our present as future."[79] But it is precisely this imagined future, whether catastrophic or utopian or both, that can never completely disappear; it can only be to some degree forgotten. But what can be utterly forgotten in a world where the recording of the ephemeral has become obsessive? Even in the midst of familiarity, within the practices of everyday life, fissures open and the forgotten future reemerges, with uncanny effect. The question is, simply, is any one watching or listening?

## Notes

1. Carolyn Marvin, *When Old Technologies Were New: Thinking about Electric Communication in the Late Nineteenth Century* (Oxford: Oxford University Press, 1988).

2. My sense of the World Expositions has been shaped by James Gilbert, *Perfect Cities: Chicago's Utopias of 1893* (Chicago: University of Chicago Press, 1991); Philippe Hamon, *Expositions: Literature and Architecture in Nineteenth Century France* (Berkeley: University of California Press, 1992); Neil Harris, *Cultural Excursions: Marketing Appetites and Cultural Tastes in Modern America* (Chicago: University of Chicago Press, 1990); Neil Harris, Wim de Wit, James Gilbert, and Robert Rydell, *Grand Illusions: Chicago's World's Fair of 1893* (Chicago: Chicago Historical Society, 1993); John F. Kasson, *Amusing the Million: Coney Island at the Turn of the Century* (New York: Hill & Wang, 1978); Thomas Richards, *The Commodity Culture of Victorian England: Advertising and Spectacle 1851–1914* (Stanford: Stanford University Press, 1990); Robert W. Rydell, *All the World's a Fair: Visions of Empire at American International Expositions, 1876–1916* (Chicago: Chicago University Press, 1984); Alan Trachtenberg, *The Incorporation of America: Culture and Society in the Gilded Age* (New York: Hill and Wang, 1982); Rosalind H. Williams,

*Dream Worlds: Mass Consumption in Late Nineteenth-Century France* (Cambridge, MA: MIT Press, 1982). I have dealt with the World's Fair phenomenon in my article "The World as Object Lesson: Cinema Audiences, Visual Culture and the St. Louis World's Fair," *Film History* 6, no. 4 (Winter 1994): 422–444.

3.  See Rydell in particular.

4.  See Gilbert, 75–130.

5.  See Neil Harris, "Memory and the White City" in *Grand Illusions,* 3–32.

6.  Quoted in Rydell, 13.

7.  Quoted in Trachtenberg, 213.

8.  *The World's Work* viii, no. 4 (August 1904): Special Double Exposition Issue, 5088.

9.  Ibid.

10. John Onians, "'I wonder . . . ' A short history of amazement" in *Sight and Insight: Essays on Art and Culture in Honor of E. H. Gombrich at 85,* ed. John Onians (London: Phaidon Press, 1994), 11.

11. Ibid., 12.

12. Charles Darwin, *The Expression of the Emotions in Man and Animals* (Chicago: University of Chicago Press, 1965), 280–285.

13. Onians, 14.

14. Ibid., 16.

15. Quoted in Ibid., 18.

16. Ibid., 24.

17. Ibid., 26.

18. Ibid., 18–26.

19. G. B. Duchenne de Boulogne, *The Mechanism of Human Facial Expression* (Cambridge: Cambridge University Press, 1990).

20. Victor Shklovsky, "Electricity and the Theme of Old Newspapers," *Podenshchina* (Leningrad: Pisatelej, 1930), 14–15. Another debt owed to Yuri Tsivian who directed me to this discussion and supplied a translation and summary.

21. Ibid., 14.

22. Ibid., 15.

23. Ibid.

24. See David E. Nye, *Electrifying America: Social Meanings of a New Technology* (Cambridge, MA: MIT Press, 1990), 47–73.

25. Victor Shklovsky, "Art as Technique" in *Russian Formalist Criticism: Four Essays,* ed. Lee T. Lemon and Marion J. Reis (Lincoln: University of Nebraska Press, 1965), 3–24.

26. Ibid., 12.

27. Ibid., 12–22.

28. Ibid., 13.

29. Ibid., 18.

30. Martin Heidegger, *Being and Time* (New York: Harpers and Row, 1962), 95–107.

31. Ibid., 105.

32. Wolfgang Schivelbusch, *The Railway Journey: Trains and Travel in the Nineteenth Century* (New York: Urizen Books, 1979).

33. Ibid., 132.

34. Ibid.

35. Sigmund Freud, "The Uncanny," in vol. 17, *The Standard Edition of the Complete Psychological Works of Sigmund Freud* (London: Hogarth Press and the Institute of Psycho-analysis, 1953–1974), 217–256.

36. Ibid., 249.

37. Ibid., 242.

38. Edison quoted in Roland Gelatt, *The Fabulous Phonograph: from Tin Foil to High Fidelity* (Philadelphia: Lippincott, 1955), 29.

39. Demeny quoted in Jacques Deslandes, *Histoire comparee du cinema,* tome 1: 168.

40. Charles Grivel, "The Phonograph's Horned Mouth" in *Wireless Imagination: Sound, Radio, and the Avant-Garde,* ed. Douglas Kahn and Gregory Whitehead (Cambridge, MA: MIT Press, 1992), 35.

41. Honoré de Balzac, *Cousin Pons* (London: Penguin Books, 1978), 131.

42. Nathaniel Hawthorne, *The House of Seven Gables* (New York; New American Library, 1961), 85.

43. Roland Barthes, *Camera Lucida* (New York: Hill and Wang, 1981), 13–15 and passim.

44. Ibid., 89–90.

45. From *La Post* December 30, 1895, quoted in Bernard Chardere, *Le Romans des Lumières* (Paris: Gallimard, 1995), 314.

46. Maxim Gorky, appendix in Jay Leyda, *Kino: A History of the Russian and Soviet Film* (London: Allen & Unwin, 1960), 407–409.

47. Ibid., 407.

48. Michael Taussig, *Mimesis and Alterity: A Particular History of the Senses* (New York: Routledge, 1993), 212–235.

49. Ibid., 224.

50. Ibid., 225.

51. Ibid., 233.

52. Gelatt, 108–109.

53. Taussig, 224.

54. William Gibson, *Neuromancer* (New York: Ace Books, 1984).

55. My main source for biographical information on Cros comes from the Introduction and Chronology, Charles Cros, Tristan Corbiere, *Oeuvres Completes,* ed. Louis Forestier and Pierre-Olivier Walzer (Paris: Gallimard Bibliotheque de la Pleiade, 1970), 3–45.

56. Gelatt, 24.

57. Arthur Rimbaud, À Paul Demeny, May 15, 1871, in *Rimbaud Complete Works, Selected Letters,* ed. Wallace Fowlie (Chicago: University of Chicago Press. 1966), 304–311.

58. Laurent Mannoni, *Georges Demeny: Pioneer du Cinema* (Paris: Cinemathesque Francais/ Pagine, 1997), 12.

59. Ibid., 40–51.

60. Gelatt, 23.

61. Rimbaud, 307.

62. Cros, "Procede d' enregistrement et de reproduction des coleurs, des formes at des mouvements" in *Oeuvres Completes,* 493–498, his writing on color photography can be found on 498–510; 575–591.

63. See F. T. Marinetti, "Destruction of Syntax, Imagination without Strings, Words-in-Freedom," in *Futurist Manifestos,* ed. Umbro Apollonio (New York: Viking Press, 1973), 104; Dziga Vertov early sound experiments are briefly described in Dziga Vertov, "From the Notebooks of Dziga Vertov," in *Film Culture Reader,* ed. P. Adams Sitney (New York: Prager, 1970), 362. Goerges Sadoul discusses Vertov's "Laboratory of the Ear" in relation to the sound experiments of the Italian Futurists, Marinetti and Russolo in *Dziga Vertov* (Paris: Editions Champ Libre, 1971), 15–46.

64. Cros's early work in the education of the deaf can be found in the documents collected in *Inédits et Documents,* ed. Pierre E. Richard (Villelongue d'Aude: Editions Jacques Bremond, 1992), 1955.

65. James Lastra, *Sound Technology and the American Cinema: Perception Representation and Modernity* (New York: Columbia University Press, 2000).

66. See the photograph of Farber's Talking machine on display at the Barnum Museum in Philip B. Kunhardt, Jr., Philip B. Kunhardt III, and Peter W. Kunhardt, *P. T. Barnum: America's Greatest Showman* (New York: Knopf, 1995), 63.

67. Ibid.

68. Villiers de 1'Isle-Adam, *Eve of the Future Eden* (Lawrence, Kansas: Coronado Press, 1981), 149.

69. Theodor Adorno, "The Curves of the Needle," *October* 55 (winter 1990): 49–55.

70. See Thomas Y. Levin's insightful article, "For the Record: Adorno on Music in the Age of Its Technological Reproducibility," *October* 55 (Winter 1990): 39–41. Lastra also discusses Chladni's influence.

71. Villiers, 20.

72. Levin, 24–26 and passim.

73. Theodor Adorno, "The Form of the Phonograph Record," *October* 55 (Winter 1990): 59.

74. Levin, 38–41.

75. Adorno, "Form of the Phonograph Record," 61.

76. Rainer Maria Rilke, "Primal Sound," in *Selected Works: Vol. I, Prose* (New York: New Directions, 1961), 52.

77. Ibid.

78. Ibid., 53.

79. Friedrich A. Kittler, "Gramophone, Film, Typewriter," in *Literature Media Information Systems,* ed. John Johnson (Amsterdam: Overseas Publishers Association, 1997), 29.

# 5 How Users Define New Media: A History of the Amusement Phonograph

Lisa Gitelman

$M$y interest is in posing questions that might bedevil the strict dichotomy of production and consumption, which is so familiar to accounts of the history of media and technology and so characteristic of research on the phonograph to date. The production/consumption dichotomy harbors a particular determinism: within it lurks a tendency to use technology as a sufficient explanation of social and cultural change. It puts production first and has helped orient the history of technology away from the experience of any but white, middle-class men; rendering a history, according to one observer, in which "inventing the telephone is manly; talking on it is womanly."[1] An unreflected reliance on the same dichotomy has led to a history of the phonograph that runs something like what follows:

After Edison invented the phonograph, competition arrived from inventors at Alexander Graham Bell's Volta Laboratory (the "graphophone") and from Emile Berliner (the "gramophone"), prompting Edison's own commercial development of his machine. The phonograph and graphophone were marketed by the North American Phonograph Company, incorporated in 1888, via a network of local companies operating in protected sales territories. The expensive devices were leased and later sold as dictating machines, without much success, since office workers resisted the complicated and still temperamental machinery. But one California entrepreneur cleverly adapted his phonographs into nickel-in-the-slot machines, which both gradually proved the success of recordings as amusements and gradually created a demand for prerecorded musical records. When Emile Berliner started to market his gramophone and disc-shaped records in America in 1894, he faced competition from imitators and from companies like the Columbia Phonograph Company and, in 1896, Edison's National Phonograph Company, both of which sold only cylinder records at first. The market for home machines was created through technological innovation and pricing: Phonographs, gramophones, and graphophones were cleverly adapted to run by spring-motors (you wound them up), rather than by messy batteries or treadle mechanisms, while the musical records were adapted to reproduce loudly through a horn attachment. The cheap home machines sold as the $10 Eagle graphophone and the $40 (later $30) Home phonograph in 1896, the $20 Zon-o-phone in 1898, the $3 Victor Toy in 1900, and so on. Records sold because their fidelity improved, mass production processes were soon developed, advertising worked, and prices dropped from one and two dollars to around 35 cents.[2]

What's missing? Besides the elision of consumption and *buying* (phonographs and records are *played,* after all), such accounts limit the definition of production to the activities of inventors and entrepreneurs. What if that kind of production were only a tiny part of the story, granted its singular importance by the same cultural norms and expectations that construe technology as a male realm? The very meaning of technology might be at stake. The spring motor phonograph "worked" in homes around the world, but would it have been described as "working," if it did not already make sense somehow within the social contexts of its innovation? For that matter, would the nickel-in-the-slot phonograph have worked in just the way it did if the women who were disparaged as "nickel-in-the-slot stenographers" by the North American Phonograph Company executives had embraced rather than resisted the dictation machine? Questions like these get women (and other "end users") back into history. "Recorded sound," burbles one historian, "is surely one of the great conveniences of modern life."[3] Yet we know from Ruth Schwartz Cowan's important *More Work for Mother* and a few other feminist histories of technology just how vested the definition of "convenience" can be within the gendered, social and economic constructs of a time and a place.[4] It must be that homemakers helped make home phonographs to the complicated extent that they "made" "homes," once we acknowledge that technological change is not a laboratory event or a corporate strategy but a fully social practice.

I am suggesting that phonographs and phonograph records had rich symbolic careers, that they acquired and possessed meanings in the circumstances of their apprehension and use, and that those meanings, many and changeable, arose in relation to the social lives of people and of things. Perhaps because they are *media* in addition to being technologies and commodities, phonographs and records seem to have possessed an extraordinary "interpretive flexibility," a range of available meanings wherein neither their inventor nor the reigning authorities on music possessed any special authorial status.[5] Thomas Edison's intention for the machine was largely confounded, while composers and musical publications left the phonograph virtually unnoticed until its immense popularity forced them into addressing its role as a musical instrument. Instead, the machine was authored by the conditions of its sale and use, acquiring its cultural heft as it acquired its range and circulation among human hands and human ears as well as among other media and other goods.[6]

Though largely ignored by cultural theorists and cultural historians who tend to emphasize the *extensive* qualities of mass culture, phonographs and phonograph records suggestively exhibited *intensive* qualities to accompany those extensive ones.[7] While they came to possess extensive, mass appeal and notably to rely upon the consumption of public taste as such—in the form of fads, hits, and stars—phonographs and records also made sense according to intensive uses, at first by customers at public phonograph parlors and later by listeners at home. I will begin by introducing this intensity and by drawing a comparison between phonograph records and another contemporary medium, the mass circulation monthly magazine, which is seen by some as the cardinal form of American mass culture, at least before the nickelodeon. I will then address the discursive definition of the phonograph as a form of mechanical reproduction and as a musical instrument dependent upon women as agents and as subjects. I conclude by alluding to the ways in which the norms and habits of shopping helped to define the home phonograph.

Many Americans first experienced recorded sound as part of public demonstrations or in public parlors. Whether it was seen as more edifying (in the demonstrations) or more amusing (in the parlors), recorded sound from the beginning involved public participation, collective accedence to its existence as one or several among the curious, the remarkable, the novel, the entertaining, and the worth-between-a-nickel-and-a-quarter. Such participation importantly accompanied further, tacit participation in the conventions of recording as a medium, offering ways for the listeners of records to make and remake themselves as moderns, as part of an imagined community that was both familiar with the phonographic mediation of sound and constituted in the availability and circulation of phonograph records. The first nickel-in-the-slot machines were located at train stations, then at hotels and drug stores, where such an imagined community would have been both diffuse and masculine. A few years later brightly lit arcades promoted as "parlors" were located along busy shopping streets, pedestrian thoroughfares where the imagination could dilate, as it must have at country fairs and summer resorts, where showmen plied among women, children, and men. Customers listened to records through ear tubes, so that this public experience was in another sense a profoundly private one. The modest volume of the early records made ear tubes preferable, and so (like the nearly contemporary necessity of watching projected motion pictures in the dark) the medium itself helped divide customers from one another even as it drew them into crowds and helped imagine them as communities. Photographs that survive show phonograph parlor patrons standing together yet listening by themselves, their eyes vacant as their ears enjoy.

Nickel-in-the-slot machines and public phonograph parlors enjoyed great popularity for several years in the mid-1890s without, I think, becoming a genuinely "mass" phenomenon. The number of machines playing in public could usually be easily counted. One source notes 140 machines in Washington, D.C., in 1892, when a best-selling record might mean a sale of 5,000 copies over two years.[8] By contrast print media already enjoyed a mass audience of long standing, though print forms too underwent dramatic change during the mid and late 1890s. In *Selling Culture* Richard Ohmann argues specifically that American mass culture arrived in the pages of magazines like *Munsey's, McClures,* and *Cosmopolitan*. Starting around 1893 a growing number of monthly magazines such as these integrated additional illustrated advertisements into their feature pages and started to profit more on the sale of ad revenue rather than on the sale of issues and subscriptions. Both the timing and the scale of the modern monthlies make them helpful yardsticks. Simply in terms of numbers, the aggregate circulation of monthly magazines shot from 18 million in 1890 to 64 million in 1905. In terms of content, scholars generally agree that the magazines helped map the social spaces of American life in which "women were usually singled out as the trainees for participation in the commodity-laden modern world." Advertisers pitched to women in the women's and the general circulation magazines, so that the vague category of "consumption" itself became gender-typed.[9] Indeed, the National Phonograph Company advertised in *Munsey's* as early at 1900, while the Victor Talking Machine Company had begun its lavish advertising campaigns in *Cosmopolitan* and the *Saturday Evening Post* by 1902. In 1906 the Victor company boasted that its "advertising campaigns reached some 49 million people every month," more than half the U.S. population, while Edison's reputedly less aggressive National Phonograph Company advertised its wares by placing full page ads in more than a dozen national circulation magazines each month, including *Cosmopolitan, Munsey's, Good Housekeeping, Everybody's,* and *Outlook.*[10]

More than simply a platform for advertising home phonographs, the modern monthlies helped enable and were enabled by some of the very social, economic, and cultural conditions that helped make home phonographs a success. If the "big three" phonograph companies, Victor, National, and Columbia, started their meteoric rise roughly three years after the new *Munsey's, McClures,* and *Cosmopolitan,* they nonetheless joined the modern monthlies as, in Ohmann's terms, a "major form of repeated cultural experience for the people of the United States." By 1909 the phonograph industry was producing a steady 27.2 million records a year, still a fraction of the aggregate circulation of the magazines.[11] Yet while monthly issues had a shelf life of one month, phonograph records individually survived on a logic of repetition. Even more than print media of the time, records were *repeated* cultural experiences, literally played again and again and again. This distinction seems central to the meaning of the home phonograph as an element of mass culture: When a woman took down a box of Uneeda or opened a package of Sapolio, the brand name was familiar and the biscuit or the soap was continuous with the contents in previous tins or packages. All Uneeda biscuits looked the same, and that sameness formed part of the magic of standardized mass production. It was "magic" in part because as much as the biscuits looked the same, they really were different. By contrast the phonograph introduced the intensity of true repetition to the performance of mass markets.

When American consumers went mad for the best-selling novel *Trilby,* for example (serialized by *Harpers* in 1894), they entered a world of mass consumption characterized by the apparent seamlessness of connections enacted between fiction, advertising, illustration, drama, and dry goods: Trilby hats, Trilby dolls, Trilby shoes, and more.[12] This was just when the amusement phonograph was earning its appeal and, as the recording engineer Fred Gaisberg recalled: "The thirst for music among the people must have been prodigious to endure the crude and noisy records produced at that time. I remember my own affection for those rough tunes. I seemed never to tire of repeating the record of 'Ben Bolt' from *Trilby.*"[13]

Americans could eat ice-cream versions of the character Trilby's shapely feet (her feet are important in the novel), but they could also, as Gaisberg did, actively reproduce the strains of Trilby's haunting, mournful ballad. Each of these acts of consumption—eating ice-cream feet, wearing your Trilby shoes or wearing down your record of "Ben Bolt"—produces its own meaning, according to the mode, the frequency, and the reproducibility of its experience.

Gaisberg's "Ben Bolt" and his phonograph made sense of each other, over and over again, in the context of Gaisberg's home. Such intensity, such repetition had previously been more a feature of musical education ("practice, practice, practice") than of musical reception. It was reminiscent of the literacy practices surrounding devotional texts, for instance, or literacy in situations of particular scarcity, when a single newspaper or a mail order catalogue got read intensively, again and again, and by many readers. Today we have gotten used to the way in which small children play the same video cassettes over and over again, or the way some idiosyncratic cultural forms seem to elicit idiosyncratic repetitions (*Rocky Horror Picture Show, The Wizard of Oz,* e.g.), but adult American culture consumes and discards, reads and recycles, buys extensively and buys some more. Phonograph records, tapes, CDs, and videocassettes all counter that trend; part of their logic as possessions is repetition and reenactment, rewind and replay.

I will return briefly to this question of repetition and the role that almost ritualized repetition seems to have played in the social construction of the home phonograph, amid the magic and the desires of the modern marketplace. First, however, it is necessary to think more directly about the domestication of mechanical reproduction. The phonograph was a reproductive technology. It is possible to call it this with assurance because one crucial part of every phonograph was its "reproducer" (containing a "diaphragm"), a term which of necessity entered the vocabularies of many phonograph owners at the turn of the century. And if phonographs thus provoked little changes or additions to the semantic lives of Americans, they likewise came to have meaning within and against existing "discourse" more broadly defined. The vocabulary with which the phonograph was introduced and the symbolic terrain it occupied were all part of its definition, its coming into focus, first as a novelty and eventually as a familiar within American homes, right near where the radio and then the TV would sit further on into the century. Like the discursive lives of those later media, the discourses making sense of recorded sound formed a matrix of heterogenous, changing and even contradictory messages. These messages were registered in part within promotional representations—advertising, trade brochures, published accounts, and the habits of retail establishments handling the products. Also like radios and televisions, part of the discursive life of the phonograph emanated from the design and use of machine itself.[14] The japanned surface of an early table-top machine or the mahogany finish of an enclosed-horn Victrola (1906) were each suggestions of the way a machine might fit into home decor, while musical records were also *representations* of music in the home, two-minute versions of a genre, a composition, and a performance, packaged materially and acoustically for domestic consumption. Early Columbia and Edison records started with recorded announcements, and not a few of the earliest records had ended with recorded applause.

What happened in part was the displacement of personification and its gradual replacement with richer figurative identifications of the phonograph within the existing discourses surrounding music and home in American life. Although the earliest phonographs and those promoted for office use were routinely represented according to metaphors of embodiment and gyno/ anthropomorphism, the home phonograph was not. That makes it unusual. Cars and boats remain "she," while many early domestic appliances, including home electrification, were frequently represented in terms of domestic servants or even slaves.

When Edison unveiled his invention at the New York offices of *Scientific American,* he and witnesses alike anthropomorphized the device. A decade later, a program distributed at Worth's Palace Museum in New York City urged novelty seekers, "Before leaving the museum don't fail to interview the wonderful EDISON PHONOGRAPH." Americans stood ready to personify new technology. Among the widely anticipated applications for the machine were talking dolls and talking clocks, cyborgs with mechanical bodies and women's voices. (Both dolls and clocks were attempted, without much commercial success.) Meanwhile the dictation phonograph was promoted as a businessman's "ideal amanuensis," at first gendered male. A few years later, when women made up more of the nation's office workforce, the cover of one National Phonograph pamphlet made a simple equation by picturing a phonograph beside the words "Your Stenographer." In other representations it was the tubular wax record that formed "The Stenographer That's Always Ready," while corporate propaganda assured wives that their businessmen husbands were dictating to a phonograph, "instead of talking to a giddy and unreliable young lady stenographer." Yet somehow these metaphors did not follow the phonograph into American homes. Playback did not elicit the same personifications that recording did.[15]

Instead, catalogues and advertisements for amusement phonographs and related supplies indicate that claims of more literal verisimilitude dominated representations of the machine. As they had in the imagination of talking dolls and clocks, women's voices continued to form a kind of standard, in this case because they were particularly hard to record well. Columbia proved unsuccessful at recording women's voices as late as 1895, when Lilla Coleman's records were admitted in their catalogue to be "suitable only for use with the tubes—NOT ADAPTED FOR HORN REPRODUCTION." The Boswell Company of Chicago offered its "high grade original" records in 1898 with the assurance that "At last we have succeeded in making a true Record of a Lady's voice. No squeak, no blast; but natural, clear, and human." The Bettini Phonograph Laboratory in New York similarly claimed "The only diaphragms that successfully record and reproduce female voices." Just as Boswell records were reputedly "original," Bettini's were "autograph records," the telling expressions of unique human voices. (Bettini was fond of mixing his metaphors; in 1900 his slogan was "A True Mirror of Sound.") Both terms meant to indicate that these records were recorded from human voices rather than duplicated from preexistent recordings, a common practice in 1898. It was a distinction between records that may have confused consumers, who were necessarily more mindful of the broader distinction between live music and recorded sound.

Film theorist Richard Dyer has explained the way that film lighting historically normalized white skins, making the filmic reproduction of non-white complexions the special or "abnormal" case. Recorded sound provides something of a related (if inverted) case, in which recorded music was normalized in relation to women's voices, particularly the soprano. Victor advertisements soon assured readers that "The living voices of the worlds' greatest artists can now be heard, whenever you choose, in your own home." Edison records were "the acme of realism."[16]

Slippage in terms like "original," "true," "natural," "living," and "real," served to emphasize rather than to contradict the apparent power of mechanical reproduction to appeal and entrance: Everywhere Victor's trademark dog, Nipper, sat listening for "his master's voice." The pleasures of that slippage, the contiguity and contestation of imitation and reality, are evident in the mass circulation of Nipper's image as well as in the records themselves. The earliest records were marketed without identifying the recording artists who preformed them. A few years later some of Columbia's recording artists were each sold under many different names. Bettini, who did identify well known bel canto singers of the day, also offered records of "Lady X," coyly represented in his catalogue with her back turned to conceal her identity. Because recordings displaced the visual norms of performance (you couldn't see the stage) they hinted at imitation or ventriloquism in new ways, just as mimicry was becoming so popular in American vaudeville, the particular province of comediennes like Cissie Loftus, Elsie Janis, and Juliet Delf. Their mimicry and its reception helped open "questions about the relationship between self and other, individually and reproducibility" that proved both provocative and timely.[17] As Susan Glenn, Miles Orvell, and others have described, American culture was deeply engaged with questions of authenticity and artifice, realism and illusion, at the turn of the century. There were celebrations of certain imitations as potently "true," while in literature and the other arts, "the real thing" proved an elusive category, pleasurably attended. In the marketplace rhetoric was hardly as nuanced: manufacturers urged us to "Accept no imitations." Even in the music trades, record companies were beset by pirates, and more than half of the pianos sold were reportedly the infamous "stencil" instruments, labeled and sold by companies that had not manufactured them (the particular bugaboo of Steinway, Chickering, and the other famous makers). Of course the preeminent claim of verisimilitude available to phonograph promoters and listeners alike was the surprisingly pliable notion of acoustic fidelity. Recordings sounded exactly like the sounds they recorded, although the quality of sounding "exactly like" has continued to change over time and according to available technology, most recently from the standard of analog to that of digital recording.[18]

In addition to tapping the varied discourses of American realism, home phonographs gradually came to make sense against (and eventually within) the musical practices of the day. To give a complete summary would be impossible, but there are certain "givens" regarding American musical life at the turn of the century, among them the association of home, woman, and piano, and the complimentary though perhaps less portentous association of outdoor public space, man, and band music.—Both were to be tested by the immense popularity of recorded band music for home play.—Music literacy rates were high. Among the middle and upper classes some level of musical literacy was expected of all women, and those talents were freighted with the sanctity of home and family. Hundreds of companies made pianos to feed these expectations, and the industry managed to produce 170,000 pianos in 1899 alone. Meanwhile, there were more than 80,000 bandsmen at the turn of the century, some professionals but most amateurs, their gathering, practicing, and playing evidence of community identities fostered by geographic, ethnic, or institutional association. Towns with populations as small as 2,000 supported amateur bands, composed primarily of lower and middle class male workers. Music of all kinds had recognized social functions, gendered relations, and moral valences. Opera, in particular and somewhat like Shakespeare, was both the subject and the instrument of (high/low) cultural hierarchy. Pianos were both the subject and the instrument of (middle) class aspiration. Ragtime was both the subject and the instrument of quickening markets and (racialized) play.[19]

Clearly the arbiter of musical activity within the home was woman, while the most direct arbiter of musical activity at large tended to be an uncalculated combination of sheet music publishing houses, musical periodicals, instrument makers, urban performance institutions, and an army of roughly 80,000 music teachers of both sexes. Professionalization on the civic and national levels was applauded, while the professionalization of women was usually condemned. Musical periodicals carried chastening stories of popular divas and their harrowing lives, while mass circulation monthlies like *Good Housekeeping* lamented when any young woman, suffering from too much talent or too much ambition, returned from Conservatory and denied "to her father and mother the simple music that they love and understand," ("She has learned that Beethoven and Chopin and Schumann are great, but she has not realized that simpler music has not lost its charm . . .

Perhaps she has caught Wagneritis . . . "). To some observers, women were simply condemned to amateurism. James Huneker, a writer fond of sorting European composers into masculine and feminine types (Bach and Beethoven vs. Haydn, Chopin, and Mendelssohn), summed up, "*Enfin:* the lesson of the years seems to be true that women may play anything written for the piano, and play it well, but not remarkably."[20]

It helped not at all that the most successful popularizer of "good" music in the era, band leader John Philip Sousa, was both prone to a noticeably "feminine" fastidiousness, and explained his often popular repertoire as an act of redeeming the fallen. Played by Sousa and his men, a "common street melody" became a respectable woman:

> I have washed its face, put a clean dress on it, put a frill around its neck, pretty stockings, you can see the turn of the ankle of the street girl. It is now an attractive thing, entirely different from the frowzly-headed thing of the gutter.[21]

Thus Sousa popularized good music and made popular music good. In his several perorations on the "menace of mechanical music" Sousa deployed similar metaphors to equal effect. The pianola and the phonograph, he was sure, would reduce music to "a mathematical system of megaphones, wheels, cogs, disks, cylinders, and all manner of revolving things, which are as like real art as the marble statue of Eve is like her beautiful, living, breathing daughters." To use these devices was to subvert nature in a world where naturalness and womanliness coincided with seeming ease; "The nightingale's song is delightful because the nightingale herself gives it forth." Sousa warned that these machines were like the recent "crazes" for roller skates and bicycles, but that they might do more damage, like the English sparrow, which "introduced and welcomed in all innocence, lost no time in multiplying itself to the dignity of a pest, to the destruction of numberless native song birds." Here were Sousa's metaphors adrift amid gender and national categories in their allusion to birds and description of musical culture. Women amateurs have "made much headway" in music, he wrote approvingly, but the mechanical music will make them lose interest, and "Then what of the national throat? Will it not weaken?" Sousa's American amateur loses some of her gender definition directly in his next question: "What of the national chest? Will it not shrink?" His rhetoric was extreme, but Sousa foresaw the diminishment of amateur music with great perspicacity.

In all of its modalities—performance, instrumentation, composition, education,—the sounds, subjects, and spaces of American music were shot through with assumptions of moral and aesthetic value that remained inseparable from active categories like tradition, class, race, gender, domesticity, and professionalism. What interests me here are the translations that appeared available between categories around 1900, which might indicate points of contestation or of change in the mutual discourses of music and home. Among them there were public, performative translations, of course, like Sousa's play across the Popular and the Good, like the adaptive traditions of blackface, or like the success of a few "lady" orchestras. But there were other translations as well, and the home phonograph became party to many. Victor advertisements asked, "Why don't you get a *Victor* and have theatre and opera in your own home? The *Victor* is easy to play. . . ." (1902), while National Phonograph assured that its product "calls for no musical training on the part of any one, yet gives all that the combined training of the country's greatest artists give" (1906). Both appeals resemble contemporary advertisements for pianolas and player pianos, which stressed ease of play along with salutory musical production, good for the soul, good for the family.[22] At work was a partial translation between amateurism and professionalism that tended to enforce the amateurism of home listeners, not just in the subsequent withering away of live home music making, as Sousa recognized, but also in the celebrated availability of professionally produced music in the home. Records and piano rolls were professional in the dual sense that they reproduced the work of professional, paid musicians, and that they were the standardized, mass products of purposeful corporate concerns with which listeners engaged in commercial relations.

Even as home-based amateurism was enforced, the possibility of professional reproductions in the home seemed empowering. In Britain, where similar conditions pertained, Virginia Woolf recalled, "We opened one little window when we bought the gramophone; now another/ opens with the motor [car]—I was going to say, but stopped." Woolf's image of "one little window" is from her diary, that most private of public documents.[23] Like her hesitant analogy to the automobile, it suggests the role that the home phonograph played as a translation device between private and public spheres. Playing recorded music at home mediated between *at home* and *in public* in ways that seem to have offered its listeners a sense of autonomy, however fleeting, that was greatly in contrast with later, Adorno-like assessments of the media as an instrument of social control or collective torpor.

But the home phonograph was more than just a transparent divide, a pane of glass between public and domestic space, in part because neither the public nor the domestic sphere were homogeneous or unchanging. The middle and upper-class parlor with its piano was becoming a "living room," as American homes became more expressive of the personalities of their inhabitants.[24] Public space evolved as well, as an increasingly urban population and a growing number of women in the workforce helped forge what historian Kathy Peiss calls "the shift from homosocial to heterosocial culture."[25] The shift was evident in the consumption of public amusements, as well as in the tissue of outdoor, public advertising, in changes to the patterns of retail, and in changes to the habits of outdoor recreation.

Consider the chaotic social spaces where people shopped. The Victor Talking Machine Company erected a huge electric sign above Broadway at 37th Street in New York City in 1906. Visible from Madison Square three quarters of a mile away and illuminated at night by 1,000 light bulbs, the sign read "VICTOR" above the usual picture of Nipper. Below the caption, made plural in this instance—"His Masters' Voice,"—the sign continued in seven-foot letters, "The Opera At Home." The company boasted that 800,000 men and women saw the sign each day. The sign loomed two blocks north of the new Macy's at 34th Street and two blocks from the old Metropolitan Opera House on Seventh Avenue at 36th. It is illustrative in several respects. The "Opera" advertised in gigantic letters "At Home" could not but evoke and resemble the more sedate "Opera" between "Metropolitan" and "House" a few steps away. Stars at the Metropolitan were already cutting records, to be sure, yet there was no simple conversion of Opera House into Home Opera, in large part because the terms of such a conversion were contested by the public and commercial nature of its suggestion. "Opera" seen by 800,000 moving people already violated a central precept of opera as a taste category or as a performance of status definition for a comparatively select few. This "Opera" had as much to do with Macy's, which aggressively sold Victor goods, as it did with the Metropolitan. And it had plenty to do with popular music, which remained a staple at all of the record companies, despite commercial paeans to opera and classical. Likewise, the gigantic "Home" could not signify a family abode, a refuge from urban chaos, without calling upon the public spaces which served to inscribe if not to jeopardize that sanctum, among them the workplace, street, and store. Then the image of Nipper, as difficult to parse as it was apparently compelling, loomed all the more confusing in the plurality of his "Masters'" unitary "Voice." Was Nipper at "Home"? Who were his "Masters" there? And how was their one "Voice" reproduced on the record player that sat beside him? These unasked and unanswerable questions at once recall the slippage in descriptive terms like "real" and "live" as they were applied to recorded sound, and demonstrate the extent to which the translation from public to private remained shot through with power relations, indeterminate evocations of taste hierarchies, social superiority, mastery and seduction, all tied intricately to the immense power of mimesis and mechanical reproduction.[26]

The same translation(s) were necessarily evoked inside stores like Macy's, where the "dream world" of mass consumption beckoned.[27] Department stores were not the only stores to sell phonographs and records, however. They were sold in music stores, from the gigantic Lyon & Healy firm in Chicago to small town shops specializing in sheet music, lessons, and instrument repair. And they were also sold in stores where hardware, sporting goods, or dry goods were the main articles of trade. In each of these venues, phonographs and records helped theatricalize the point of sale. Without radio to familiarize listeners with new songs and recordings, phonograph demonstrations were a necessary part of every shopper's curiosity and desire. So called "pluggers" (and payola) tried to influence sheet music sales in music stores and at the music counters of the big department stores. Demonstrations were a recent if familiar part of selling everything from Fuller brushes to cosmetics. Phonographs and records put the two together, helping to ensure that home play was re-play, the repetition of a public and commercial desire and its translation into related, private, personal reenactments. Lyon & Healy offered "concerts" every day, free and open to the public; a live pianist performed, but most of the music came from a Victrola, playing to tired women shoppers and lunch-time idlers in the Loop. Smaller stores sometimes organized "recitals" but were also prepared to play sample records upon request.[28]

Faced with a legal challenge to its sales rights in New York State, Edison's National Phonograph Company did a survey of its upstate dealers in 1906. It was a boom year for cylinder phonographs, and the survey offers a rare look at local sales operations. Out of 133 dealers visited (some of them also wholesale jobbers), it was notable when one, like William Harrison in Utica, devoted his or her business to phonographs and records exclusively.[29] In Watertown (pop. 27,787) there were seven dealers, one specializing in "stoves and household goods," and another in "wallpaper, mouldings, etc." Many music stores carried phonographs, though some were notably discouraged "that it affects the piano and musical end of their business." In Buffalo there was a drug store selling phonographs out of a back room; in Elmira the Elmira Arms Company was doing well; and in Syracuse a furniture store was struggling. In Oneonta one tiny dealership "keeps Edison phonographs and records to accommodate his customers who are mostly farmers"; "He says when they come to his place for records they are liable to purchase other goods that they might require." Most carried very small stocks of machines and records, and all save the one dealer in Cobelskill (pop. 2,800) had competition from other Edison dealers in the same town, plus the dealers pushing Columbia and Victor goods.[30] One common situation was a bicycle or sporting goods store that specialized in phonographs during the winter. There was the Utica Cycle Company, the Rome Cycle Company, as well as George W. Johnson of Rochester, who "May first of each year takes his phonographs from the windows and puts in bicycles and on October first each year he takes his bicycles from the window and puts in phonographs and records." The association of phonographs and these other goods unavoidably suggests context for recorded sound. The seasonal equilibrium between bikes and phonographs, in particular, offers a reminder that such goods circulated amid an economy in a modest sense determined by cultural conversations about New Women and about middle-class domesticity. Ellen Gruber Garvey has demonstrated persuasively the ways in which bicycles became the subjects and the instruments of gender definition, according to which advertisers represented women's bodies and helped construct their roles as consumers.[31] By 1906 the bicycle "craze" had largely subsided, but I wonder just how distant the craze for ragtime and jazz records really was, in social as well as commercial terms.

I have been suggesting that "inventing" or "producing" recorded sound cannot be narrowed to the activities of Thomas Edison or to the efforts of corporate entities invested in the manufacture, advertisement, or sale of phonographs and records at the turn of the twentieth century. To my mind the phonograph provides an exemplary instance of cultural production snatched from the hands of putative producing agents. Understanding its social construction suggestively complicates our notions of technological and media change at the same time that it provides an opportunity to add a little more context to two well studied loci of modern mass culture, the department store and the monthly magazine. In this light, casting mass culture as a shift from a tactile, craft-oriented world to a visual, mass-production one seems simplistic at best. Our readings of cultural history must also include the squeaks and noises of change. We must be prepared to explain the intensity of modern cultural experiences as well as their extensive range and appeal. Far from simply transferring public music into private homes, the popular success of the amusement phonograph formed part of a profound transformation in the public sphere, signaling new subjectivities and continued developments in the categorization of gender, class, as well as other relevant parameters of identity and community.

A bit like newspapers or like photographs and other print media, phonographs relied upon a logic of transparency, of pure mediation, that was as chimerical as it was accessory to the imagination of self and community, to a sense of location amid social spaces and forces. As much as their promoters seemed to invoke the possibility, records could never be transparent windows between musical experiences at the concert hall and in the home. There were differences in sound quality, of course, the lacking "aura" of performative origination, differing commercial and emotional investments, differences in arrangement, instrumentation, and so on, as well as the tacit participation that all such differences required of audiences. This tacit participation is that part of media and mediation that invisibly unites us, even as "we all" want to hear the latest recordings by our favorite artists, even as "everybody" knows who the stars are and have been. In the case of recorded sound, mediation seems clearly to have involved assumptions regarding women and their roles in society. It is not just that women were represented and reproduced (think of the comparable inquiries: blacks *in* radio, gays and lesbians *on* television), rather that modern forms of mediation are in part *defined* by normative constructions of difference, whether gender, racial, or other versions of difference. Women's voices early provided a standard for both the desire and the accomplishment of recorded sound. Gender colored distinctions between work and play, recording and playback, business and amusement. Gender infused contemporary experiences of reality and imitation, performance and mimicry. And gender flavored the pursuits of middle-class self-improvement and self-indulgence. Phonographs only "worked" when they got women's voices right, just as home phonographs only "worked" according to the ways they interlocked with existing tensions surrounding music and home, with ongoing constructions of shopping as something women do, and with the ways in which users of all sorts wanted, heard, and played recorded sounds.

## Notes

1. Carroll Purcell, "Seeing the Invisible: New Perceptions in the History of Technology," *Icon* 1 (1995): 9–15. Purcell's is a recent and cogent critique. See also Rosalind Williams, "The Political and Feminist Dimensions of Technological Determinism" *Does Technology Drive History?: The Dilemma of Technological Determinism,* eds. Merritt Roe Smith and Leo Marx (Cambridge, MA: MIT Press, 1994), 217–235.

2. The most thorough account of the history of the phonograph is still Oliver Read and Walter L. Welch, *Tin Foil to Stereo: Evolution of the Phonograph,* 2nd ed. (Indianapolis: Howard W. Sams & Co., 1976). For a recent version of the story see Leonard DeGraaf, "Thomas Edison and the Origins of the Entertainment Phonograph," *NARAS Journal* 8 (Winter/Spring 1997/8): 43–69, as well as William Howland Kenney's recent and welcome *Recorded Music in American Life: The Phonograph and Popular Memory, 1890–1945* (New York: Oxford University Press, 1999). Much of the technocentric focus of literature on the phonograph (a focus Kenney's cultural history finally shifts) may derive from the interests of collectors, for whom I have the utmost respect.

In the interest of simplicity I am going to use the eventual American generic, "phonograph," for the graphophone and gramophone as well as the phonograph. Of course in Britain and much of the postcolonial world the generic is "gramophone."

3. No gender is specified for these stenographers; *Proceedings of the First Annual Convention of Local Phonograph Companies* (Nashville: Country Music Foundation Press, 1974 [1890]), 57. Andre Millard, *America on Record: A History of Recorded Sound* (Cambridge: Cambridge University Press, 1995), 1.

4. Ruth Schwartz Cowan, *More Work for Mother: The Ironies of Household Technology from the Open Hearth to the Microwave* (New York: Basic Books, 1983). On feminist histories of technology I'm thinking gratefully of a panel at the recent workshop, "Science, Medicine, and Technology in the 20th Century: What Difference Has Feminism Made?" Princeton University, October 2–3, 1998. See also (in chronological order) Judith A. McGaw, "Women and the History of American Technology," *Signs* 7 (1982): 798–828 and "No Passive Victims, No Separate Spheres: A Feminist Perspective on Technology's History," in *In Context, History and the History of Technology: Essays in Honor of Melvin Kranzberg,* eds. Stephen H. Cutcliffe and Robert C. Post (Bethlehem, PA: Lehigh University Press, 1989), 172–191; Judy Wajcman, *Feminism Confronts Technology* (University Park: Penn State University Press, 1991); also *Technology and Culture* 38 (January 1997), a special issue on gender and technology, eds. Nina E. Lerman, Arwen Palmer Mohun, and Ruth Oldenziel, with their introduction, "The Shoulders We Stand On and the View From Here: Historiography and Directions for Research," 9–30.

5. This is a term from the "Social Construction of Technology" program, outlined by Wiebe E. Bijker, among others; see *Of Bicycles, Bakelites, and Bulbs: Toward a Theory of Sociotechnical Change* (Cambridge, MA: MIT Press, 1995).

6. According to anthropologist Mary Douglas, "All goods carry meanings, but none by itself. . . . The meaning is in the relations between all the goods." She writes that "Goods are used for marking in the sense of clarifying categories"; *The World of Goods,* Mary Douglas and Baron Isherwood (New York: Basic Books, 1979), 72, 74.

7. I have adapted this dichotomy of intensive and extensive from both the work of American book historians, where it has been appropriated from R. Englesing, and from the work of anthropologist Sidney W. Mintz in his discussion of *Sweetness and Power: The Place of Sugar in Modern History* (New York: Viking, 1985), 152, passim.

8. On Washington, Katherine K. Preston, "Music for Hire: A Study of Professional Musicians in Washington, 1877–1900"; *Sociology of Music,* No. 6 (Stuyvesant, NY: Pendragon Press, 1992) 239; Tim Brooks, "Columbia Records in the 1890s: Founding the Record Industry," *Association for Recorded Sound Collections Journal* 10 (1979): 5–36.

9. Ohmann's *Selling Culture: Magazines, Markets, and Class at the Turn of the Twentieth Century* (London: Verso, 1996), 29 and passim. "Trainees" is from R. F. Bogardus, "The Reorientation of

Paradise: Modern Mass Media and Narratives of Desire in the Making of American Consumer Culture," *American Literary History* (1998): 508–523, which reviews two books that develop the point, including Ellen Garvey, *Adman in the Parlor: Magazines and the Gendering of Consumer Culture, 1880s–1910s* (New York: Oxford University Press, 1996).

10. On Victor advertising, Frederick O. Barnum III, *"His Master's Voice" in America* (Camden: General Electric Company, 1991), 29; *The Music Trades 31* (April 7, 1906): 46. On Edison, National Phonograph Company Records, "Advertising" folders, 1906 and other years, Edison National Historic Site (ENHS).

11. Notably, print runs for the monthlies were vastly beyond the runs of individual records, which went from several hundred in the late 1890s, to several hundred thousand by 1920. Annual record production topped 60 million in the 1920s before plummeting during the Depression. See U.S. Bureau of the Census, *Census of Manufactures 1914* (GPO, 1919), Vol. 2, p. 825.

12. On *Trilby* as an exemplary fad, see Elaine S. Abelson, *When Ladies Go A-Thieving: Middle-Class Shoplifters in the Victorian Department Store* (New York: Oxford University Press, 1989), 34; see also Edward L. Purcell, "Trilby and Trilby-Mania, The Beginning of the Bestseller System," *Journal of Popular Culture* 11 (1977): 62–-76; and Emily Jenkins, "Trilby: Fads, Photographers, and 'Over-Perfect Feet,'" *Book History* 1 (1998): 221–267. Jenkins's interesting attempt to account for the Trilby fad fails to mention the novel's vicious anti-Semitism, consumed, along with the novel's Parisian setting, just as the Dreyfus case was played out in the press.

13. Frederick W. Gaisberg, *The Music Goes Round* (New York: Macmillan, 1942) 18.

14. See Lynn Spigel's helpful account, "Installing the Television Set: Popular Discourses on Television and Domestic Space, 1948–1955," *Camera Obscura* 16 (1988): 11–46. On radio, see Susan J. Douglas, *Inventing American Broadcasting, 1899–1922* (Baltimore: Johns Hopkins University Press, 1987), chapter 9.

15. *Scientific American* 37 (December 1877): 384. Worth's museum program from the Theater Collection, New York Public Library (elsewhere NYPL). Edward Bellamy managed to work the clocks into a short story in 1889; he imagined a time traveler spending the night "enjoying the society of [his] bodiless companion and the delicious shock of her quarter-hourly remarks"; "With Eyes Shut," *Harper's* (1889). Bellamy was not alone in sexualizing the machine. In Arthur Conan Doyle's, "The Voice of Science" (*Strand* 1 [1891]: 312–317) a recording phonograph foils a caddish suitor who is unknowingly recorded; "Into the slots he thrust virgin [record] plates, all ready to receive impression, and then, bearing the phonograph under his arm, he vanished into his own sanctum. . . . " On the business phonograph, letterhead and advertisements from ENHS; on giddy stenographers, National Phonograph Company, "The Phonograph and How to Use It" (1900), 140. I have written elsewhere about the dolls and clocks. On cyborgs and subjectivity, the manifesto of course, Donna J. Haraway, *Simians, Cyborgs, and Women: The Reinvention of Nature* (New York: Routledge, 1991); see also Felicia

Miller Frank, *The Mechanical Song: Women, Voice, and the Artificial in Nineteenth-Century French Narrative* (Stanford: Stanford University Press, 1995).

16. I am grateful to Ellen Garvey for pointing me towards Dyer's work, *White* (London: Routledge, 1997), chapter 3.

17. On early Columbia records, Tim Brooks; and Fred W. Gaisberg *The Music Goes Round* (New York: Macmillan, 1942), 41. On stage mimicry, see Susan A. Glenn's valuable "'Give and Imitation of Me': Vaudeville Mimics and the Play of the Self" *American Quarterly* 50 (March 1998), 47–76; "The mimetic moment in American comedy coincided with the mimetic moment in American social thought" (48–49).

18. Miles Orvell, *The Real Thing: Imitation and Authenticity in American Culture* (Chapel Hill: University of North Carolina Press, 1989); Jackson Lears in, among other titles, "Beyond Veblen: Rethinking Consumer Culture in America," in *Consuming Visions: Accumulation and Display of Goods in America, 1880–1920,* ed. Simon J. Bronner (New York: W. W. Norton, 1989), 73–98; see also the Henry James short story "The Real Thing."

19. Craig H. Roell, *The Piano in America, 1890–1940* (Chapel Hill: University of North Carolina Press, 1989); US Bureau of the Census, *Census of Manufactures 1914,* Vol. 2, 807–825; Margaret Hindle Hazen and Robert M. Hazen, *The Music Men: An Illustrated History of Brass Bands in America, 1800–1920* (Washington, DC: Smithsonian Institution Press, 1987); Kenneth Kreitner, *Discoursing Sweet Music: Town Bands and Community Life in Turn of the Century Pennsylvania* (Urbana: University of Illinois Press, 1990).

20. "Music in the American Home," *Good Housekeeping* 39 (1904): 292; Huneker's "Women and Music," *Harper's Bazaar* 33 (1900): 1306–1308, and reported in *Current Literature* 39 (1905): 436–437. Sousa's band sometimes had a woman harpist for concerts, but was an all male concern. Records of Sousa's band were really records of a smaller ensemble.

21. "Sousa and His Mission," *Music* 16 (1899): 272–276. The following observations by Sousa are from "The Menace of Mechanical Music," *Appleton's* 8 (1906): 278–284.

22. Roell, 37–45. American music magazines tended to carry advertisements for "automatic" pianos, but not for phonographs. *Etude* magazine, for instance, apparently did not carry Victor Talking Machine ads until around the time of the Copyright Act of 1909, protecting composers against mechanical reproductions. (*Etude* urged its readers to support the bill in Congress.) But piano roll manufacturers were equally culpable. That Victor sought out music publications confirms the more highbrow associations of the company, its machines and records; Edison and Columbia, by comparison, were more lowbrow, despite attempts to market grand opera and classical music.

23. *The Diary of Virginia Woolf,* ed. Anne Olivier Bell, 5 vols. (San Diego: Harcourt Brace, 1980) III, 151.

24. Karen Halttunen, "From Parlor to Living Room, Domestic Space, Interior Decoration, and the Culture of Personality" in *Consuming Visions: Accumulation and Display of Goods in America, 1880–1920,* ed. Simon J. Bronner (New York: W. W. Norton, 1989), 157–190.

25. *Cheap Amusements: Working Women and Leisure in Turn-of-the-Century New York* (Philadelphia: Temple University Press, 1986), 6; see also John F. Kasson, *Amusing the Million: Coney Island at the Turn of the Century* (New York: Hill & Wang, 1978), 41–50.

26. For descriptions and illustrations of the sign see the in-house *Voice of Victor,* July 1906. For one particularly good reading of the Victor trademark, see Michael Taussig's *Mimesis and Alterity: A Particular History of the Senses* (New York: Routledge, 1993). Virginia Woolf proved astute on this point as well; again from the *Diary* (in 1939, about phonograph and radio), "L[eonard] out at Fabians; played gramophone; listened to Our Masters Voice, Hitler less truculent than expected. . . . "

27. There is now a vast literature on department stores. "Dream worlds" is Rosalind Williams's title; see also Abelson; see William Leach, *Land of Desire: Merchants, Power, and the Rise of a New American Culture* (New York: Vintage, 1993).

28. *Everything Known in Music: A Souvenir of the New Home of the World's Foremost Music House* (Chicago: Lyon & Healy, 1916) [NYPL]. On pluggers and payola, Kerry Segrave, *Payola in the Music Industry: A History, 1880–1991* (Jefferson, NC: McFarland, 1994).

29. "Report as to Conditions in the Sale of Edison Phonograph in the State of New York," 66-page manuscript by Joseph McCoy, (June 4, 1906), 20; ENHS. There were a few women dealers and a few couples with dealerships; and one notably "up-to-date Jew."

30. The Cobelskill dealer had only 6 phonographs and 400 records on hand, while the largest dealers, like two in Utica, had around 75 phonographs and 30–40 thousand records in stock. The size of dealership and the number of dealers in each town were neither strictly proportional to population. The National Phonograph Co. had a total of 8,143 retail dealers in the United States and Canada during the week the report was written; see "Report of Jobbers & Retail Dealers Agreements," 1/2-page manuscript by C. H. Wilson, June 18th, 1906; National Phonograph Co. Records, ENHS. Some Edison dealers also handled Columbia goods.

31. Garvey, chapter 4, "Reframing the Bicycle: Magazines and Scorching Women," 106–134.

# 6 Books Are Dead, Long Live Books

Priscilla Coit Murphy

*Tell us how it will be with letters, with literature and books a hundred years hence!*

*If by books you are to be understood as referring to our innumerable collections of paper, printed, sewed, and bound in a cover announcing the title of the work, I own to you frankly that I do not believe (and the progress of electricity and modern mechanism forbids me to believe) that Gutenberg's invention can do otherwise than sooner or later fall into desuetude as a means of current interpretation of our mental products. . . . Our grandchildren will no longer trust their works to this somewhat antiquated process, now become very easy to replace by—*

That statement was written for *Scribner's* magazine in 1894, in enthusiastic response to recent technological developments. Its author, Octave Uzanne, completed his prediction with the word "phonography." For him, the reproduction of sound heralded the end of print mediation between author and audience.

Because "reading . . . soon brings on great weariness,"[1] phonography would ease the physical fatigue (from the positions imposed by reading) and excessive burden on the eyes. Dismissing concern about the expense and weight of phonographs, he was confident that they would soon become quite inexpensive and portable—suitable for taking a "promenade" using "small cylinders as light as celluloid penholders, capable of containing five or six hundred words," (fig. 6.1[2]). The only draw-back—the absence of illustration—would be met by the simultaneous enjoyment of "Mr. Edison's kinetograph," projecting pictures on the living room wall in synchrony with the phonographic narrative (fig. 6.2).[3]

Uzanne did anticipate some attendant social change: "Libraries will be transformed into phonographotecks," and bibliophiles, who would become "phonographiles," "will still surround themselves with rare works . . . bound in morocco cases."[4] Questioned about the elitism of the proposed scheme, Uzanne saw "the people" served through "fountains of literature in the streets," wired for casual listening, along with communal listening in specially wired apartment buildings or train cars (see figs. 6.3 and 6.4).[5]

Phonographic Literature for the Promenade.

Figure 6.1    From A. Uzanne, "The End of Books," p. 228.

The Romance of the Future.
(With Kinetoscopic Illustrations.)

Figure 6.2    From A. Uzanne, "The End of Books," p. 230.

The Author Exploiting his Own Works.

Figure 6.3    From A. Uzanne, "The End of Books," p. 229.

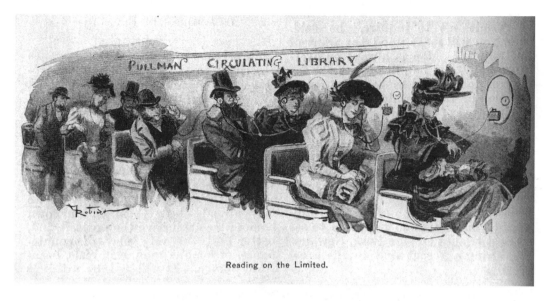

Reading on the Limited.

Figure 6.4    From A. Uzanne, "The End of Books," p. 230.

Above all, the relationship between author and reader was to change. "Readers" would now be able to hear the voice of the author directly. The author, having duly copyrighted his voice and narration, could preserve the benefit of his works for himself, while the nature of the celebrity-author would change:

> Men of letters will not be called Writers . . . but rather, Narrators. . . . The art of utterance will take on un-heard-of importance. . . . The ladies will no longer say in speaking of a successful author, "What a charming writer!" All shuddering with emotion, they will sigh, "Ah, how this 'Teller's' voice thrills you, charms you, moves you."[6]

Were Uzanne writing today, one might expect words like "orality," "interactivity," and "media convergence" to appear, yet the core of his discussion was a trope on novel machinery and a few of the immediate, first-order effects of adoption. However, many of the assumptions underlying his view of the future have been present within later spates of predictions that the book-as-we-know-it would soon disappear. Before embarking on discussion of those assumptions, it is worth examining some of the later waves of—it now seems—premature obituaries for the bound book.

Uzanne's exuberant futurism came with the earliest awareness of what has come to be called the Technological Age. A certain fearlessness, similar to that seen in events like the 1893 World's Exposition, would soon give way to doubts in the face of increasing complexity as mass society employed technology in its pursuits. Just as society became acquainted with one new medium, along would come another. Those most directly affected—other than the audience—found themselves repeatedly challenged to divine what would happen to their own medium as a new one appeared.

In 1919 Rupert Hughes, writing for *Bookman,* discussed another writer who "viewed with alarm" the theft of children's attention, as moving pictures lured them away from books. "The child of today knows more than is good for it. Murder and arson are its daily food."[7] Equally worried about the minds of adults, a 1925 publisher saw the public's attention overwhelmed, to the detriment of books:

> Personally I agree with the pessimists that all these things, especially the overproduction of magazines and newspapers filled with trivial and cheap contents, injure the book business. Human beings have only a certain maximum of leisure, and if they spend an evening reading a sex magazine and listening to the radio there is no time left for a good book.[8]

However, he had faith that books would yet prevail: "Ultimately, I believe all of these so-called obstacles will redound to our advantage, for surely automobiles and radios and movies, yea, even sex magazines, stimulate the mind, and eventually when the mind is sufficiently stimulated and in the right direction we have a new book-reader."[9]

In 1927 the technology of convenience led a journalist to guess that radio would soon steal print media's thunder. He drew the inference from an MIT dinner at a New York hotel, at which the first "radio newspaper" was published. He foresaw an automatic printing machine in each home, radio-operated and able to offer whole pages of newspapers instantaneously as news broke.[10] While he did not make the leap to home printing of book pages, eleven years later another writer was to extrapolate a little further, this time imagining the precursors of microfilm. Arthur Train, writing in 1938 for *Harper's,* predicted that fifty years hence the "man of 1988" would not only receive his newspaper via facsimile machine, but he would possess few books, reading them at home from "tiny reels of film" projected onto the screen of a "reading machine."[11]

As mass culture was becoming a defining characteristic of American society, many commentators on the future of books found themselves looking for a good defense. Richard Mealand, at one time head of the writing and story department of Paramount Pictures, wrote in 1946 for *Publishers Weekly* about the relative worth of books and movies, in a reported argument among a producer, writer, publisher, and a "sensible looking lady with up-turned horn-rimmed glasses." She claimed not to get as much out of movies as she did from a good book, and said she'd "gladly pay three dollars for a good book" but resented "having to pay more than a dollar for even the best picture." The producer pronounced her a "reading-woman" who wouldn't go to movies, anyway. "Some people take to drink, or dope. Others go to movies. Others listen to the radio. Others read books. But they're all trying to experience life without going out and actually experiencing it."[12]

As the great one-eyed monster lumbered over the horizon and began to overrun American culture, *Saturday Review*'s august Bennett Cerf sounded an early alarm in 1948, raising the specter of undermined book sales and deterioration of reading:

> By the end of 1950 . . . the panic will be on in earnest. . . . Publishers and authors can only hope that they will be able to get a small cut of the gravy—and that after the novelty of television has worn off, people again will prefer a good book to the spectacle of two unknown prize-fighters staggering around a ring, or a syrupy-voice huckster proclaiming the virtues of Dinkelspiel's Deodorant.[13]

By 1950 the panic was indeed on. Now it wasn't just books but reading itself that was again feared to be in peril. *Life* magazine publisher Andrew Heiskell asked "Have the Newer Media Made Reading Obsolete?"—specifically addressing the advent of television. No, he said: "On the contrary, they are all, to a large extent, complementary rather than mutually exclusive." In his view, the changes in democracy were demanding increased flow of information to the public and creating even better media consumers: "the habitual book reader also reads more magazines, sees more movies, looks at more newspapers than non-book readers." He welcomed the newer media as forces for democratization and as desperately needed competition for the printed page—whose economics of distribution were, in his mind, severely antiquated.[14]

Nonetheless, even those who believed that television would not entirely eradicate book reading were still deeply concerned by the changes it might impose on reading itself. Once again, hands were wrung over the palpable deterioration in taste, thanks to the vulgarizing influence of television. But the quality of the reading act itself began to be scrutinized. Round-tables and symposia about television and reading sprang up, commonly sponsored by industry groups such as the American Booksellers Association and the American Library Association, or by publishing or library trade publications. One such ABA panelist, educator Florence Brumbaugh, described the effect of television on her pupils, leading them to prefer the liveliness of television to the relative passivity of books: "I believe that the vicarious experiences in the child today are more real than their first-hand experiences." But she saw reason for hope so long as booksellers understood the interactions among media: "Television can interpret books. Books can interpret television. We faced radio. We faced all the other mass media, and we think we won because children are reading more and better than they did in the past."[15]

In one of Frederick Melcher's weekly *Publishers Weekly* commentaries, he quoted another optimistic panelist in 1950, who noted that "the users of TV are to a large extent a new market reaching into homes of many who were never book readers."[16] But five years later, August Frugé, director of the University of California Press, wrote of continuing gloom in the outlook for books, his primary grounds for hope residing in cheaper paperback prices and a marketing effort to make book ownership "fashionable once again."[17]

In a sadly overlooked *Library Quarterly* symposium in 1955 devoted to the future of books, several library professionals looked at social, historical, and technological aspects of the book. Though they had the role of libraries and librarians firmly in sight, they found themselves confronted with the definition of what a book is, information and communication theory of the day, the function of books for individuals and society, and the likely consequences of changes in form and format.[18] They were prepared to imagine a bookless information age, but they wanted to know why and how that would come about.

Finally, perhaps the mid-century's most well-rounded discussion of the future of books was publisher Dan Lacy's, written in 1957. Lacy's discussion flowed from his understanding of the media production and distribution systems, including the profound importance of audience behavior and preference. Able to envision transmission of text as "patterns of electrical energy," he nonetheless discounted wholesale relegation of books to electronics, in part because he could not foresee the miniaturization permitted by transistors and microchips, or the efficiency of search-engine programs. For him, converting the Encyclopedia Britannica entirely to a "coded series of impulses on magnetic wire such as are fed into electronic brains" had a few catches: the prohibitive cost, the lengthy and labor-intensive coding effort, difficulties in retrieving specific pieces of information, and that "the wire would take up fifteen times as much shelf space as the printed version."[19]

Nonetheless, Lacy believed that economic and audience changes were at least as important as technological change in determining the future of book publishing. Distribution, he noted, was intimately related to and dependent on the nature of the entire media system; by implication, changes in other media would therefore have a great impact on books. Readership was a function of increased leisure time, urbanization, and above all higher education; and he wondered about the impact of the baby-boom and expansion of the "educated minority" into a possible majority. Would college education become something different? "Can books be made to serve the non-bookish?"[20] Like many before and since concerned about the future of reading, he worried about issues of attention span, curiosity, and depth.

This brief review is far from exhaustive, and it sidesteps more complete discussions of reading and the definition of a book. But it provides illustrations in which three familiar and basic theories seem to be at work.

First is the simple but compelling assumption that media are rivals of each other, competing for a finite amount of audience resources—time, money, and attention. In this view, one medium's gain is another's loss; the benefits of one medium enable it to replace another less convenient or useful; one medium fixes a problem that another inadequately addresses. While seemingly over-simple, the idea of mutually exclusive rivalry actually forms the underpinning of more sophisticated arguments, for example those from ergonomics and cognitive alteration. Uzanne's Ur–Walkman would replace a book because it was physically more comfortable and communicationally more immediate—literally—than a book. Movies are livelier than books, television is yet more immediate, and sex magazines are certainly more distracting. Once someone has become a consumer of other media, therefore, his or her attention-span and taste are irrevocably altered—such that staying with the content of a good book becomes impossible and a skilled reader is forever lost to television watching. Later discussions of those such as McLuhan,[21] Meadow,[22] and Birkerts[23] hinge in part on this view of audience choice, practice, and habit.

Moreover, until very recently it has been typical of the publishing industry in particular to conceive of the economics of the media system in this zero-sum paradigm—at its most extreme believing that a dollar spent for a movie, a CD, or software is a dollar taken from the bookseller. Yet *Publishers Weekly*'s industry stock index for 1998 rose 116.6% (compared to 16.1% for the Dow-Jones industrials), led of course by distributor Amazon.com's 321% rise—which in itself says something about the relationship between books and new media—but also reflecting healthy increases by publishers Time-Warner, Wiley, McGraw-Hill, and Viacom.

There is, of course, undeniable validity to the idea that audiences do not "use" two media for precisely the same function and that they will discriminate among media in spending time and money. And one must thereby also acknowledge the thought that competition could be "good" if it improves or refines the communication process. Yet as recently as 1998, when William Mitchell offered a text simultaneously on-line and in paperback, he was surprised to find many using cyberspace to order the paper book.

"Why would anyone buy a copy when the online version was right there at no cost?"[24] He declined to answer his own question, but the answer is highly relevant to the future of books. History has thus far shown that no new medium has ever completely replaced an earlier medium, although some have been profoundly altered from their original form.

That alteration relates to the second familiar theory lurking within predictions about the end of books—that of convergence. In this perspective, a new medium will so affect an existing one that the two may converge to meet all prior purposes and perhaps a few new ones. As Lester Asheim wrote for the *Library Quarterly* in 1955, "it is not too illogical to anticipate that out of the thesis, book-reading, and its antithesis, the use of nonbook materials, some synthesis may come which retains the best features of both."[25] This expectation can arise out of a certain tunnel-vision found among technophiles, which assumes that the only reason a new medium has not been completely accepted in preference to an older one is that science just hasn't yet overcome the problem. Once it does, the traits and functions of the older medium will be combined within the newer one—not disappearing but reborn in new and better form—for example, book text on screen.

Uzanne believed that the main obstacle to communication of text through sound was the size of batteries and cylinders. One hears strong echoes in current claims that once electronic paper and ink make electronic readers less cumbersome than bound-paper books,[26] the need for bound-paper books will evaporate except as odd artifacts.

The argument from convergence tends to overlook cultural and economic realities, although there is an element of convergence in the idea of cross-media taste-contamination. Even though Uzanne was able to ponder the rise in status of authors with good voices, he could not anticipate radio's dependence on the automobile for its survival. And cultural attitudes may be much slower to change than technology: "Only Twinkie-charged insomniac dweebs like to read on the screen,"[27] declared one 1992 reader unimpressed by electronic text.

More to the point, Frugé's view of the book as a consumer commodity brings up a substantial area too often ignored by theorists, even those occupied by the ergonomics of new media. What the scientists and theorists may envision as possible, feasible, let alone desirable for the consumer may have little to do with what is actually supported by the economy. Thus, the idea that all household communication devices will eventually be housed in a single unit, with portable, walk-about satellite stations, hinges not only on the eventual acceptance by the consumer but also on industry perceptions of the most lucrative product structure. The unavailability of consumer CD players that can also record is indicative of the force of that mindset. With respect to books, the question may not be whether consumers will continue to buy them; it may be whether media corporations see books as a commodity they are committed to selling.

The third theory underlying many predictions about the future of books is that of complementarity, as Heiskell made explicit. By dint of specialization among media functions and interaction of media within an information and communication system, new media—following a period of shifting and settling—are thought to take on complementary functions with respect to other media. Further, they may even work synergistically to enhance each other's role. In this orientation, each medium has a set of differentiable purposes or uses; and a new medium will only take on those functions it can do better than an existing medium does, leaving some of the original functions to be performed by the tried-and-true, original medium. Closely related media may even stimulate use of both—as for example, the synergistic relationship between filmmaking and television, wherein television operates both as advertising carrier and secondary distributor for movies.

This orientation—reflected in statements about how television can stimulate reading and how reading can interpret television    is grounded in a recognition of the complexities of the media system but also, perhaps, in an over-optimistic view of the audience's receptive capacities. While it may be reassuring that a reader can have Catullus, Swinburne, Carl Hiassen, and Dilbert on the same shelf above a computer on which Mech Warrior can be played, the challenge is to imagine an infinitely segmentable media market. Moreover, as Witcoff suggested, cross-stimulation among media could easily result in a homogenizing of public expectations and standards—at worst a sort of Gresham's Law of mutually induced deterioration.[28] And finally, the idea of complementarity presumes a permanence and orderliness to a media system that has already been demonstrably disturbed by economic, social and—of course—technological changes.

The purpose in identifying these three approaches to the interaction of old media with new—rivalry, convergence, and complementarity—is not to propose any one as definitive but rather to note their existence, and the relevance and flaws in each. When confronted with a pronouncement that books are nigh unto death, one would do well to look first at the eager prophet or worried eulogist. A few are apologists for the glossy, brand new, improved, and patentable. But a great number have been either theoreticians inclined to follow the trajectory of technology to the furthest imaginable conclusion or else those whose professional lives as practitioners are at stake. Those practitioners—in publishing, librarianship, bookselling, even education—may have identified grounds for "doom" or "hope" that may not yet have occurred to the theoreticians. Looking at the technological possibilities is not the same as identifying corporate priorities, school board politics, teenagers' habits, or advertisers' whims. Books are, finally, intricately interrelated to the rest of the media system—economically, socially, intellectually, even symbolically; and those who have envisioned or feared their wholesale removal from the system have generally underestimated that involvement. If one would predict the death of books, one must understand how they live.

## Notes

1. Octave Uzanne, "The End of Books," *Scribner's* 16 (August 1894): 224.

2. Illustrations for Uzanne's article were by A. Robida.

3. Uzanne, 225.

4. Uzanne, 226.

5. Uzanne, 227.

6. Uzanne, 225.

7. Rupert Hughes, "Viewing with Alarm," *Bookman* 49 (May 1919): 263.

8. "Book Production Is Not Increasing," *Current Opinion* (March 1925): 305.

9. Ibid.

10. Silas Bent, "Radio Steals the Press's Thunder," *Independent* 119 (9 July 1926): 33.

11. Arthur Train, "Catching Up with the Inventors," *Harper's* 176 (March 1938): 369–370.

12. Richard Mealand, "What's a Book Got?" *Publishers Weekly* 150 (9 November 1946).

13. Bennett Cerf, "Trade Winds," *Saturday Review* 31 (5 June 1948): 6.

14. Andrew Heiskell, "Have the Newer Media Made Reading Obsolete?" *Library Journal* (1 October 1950): 1577–1578.

15. "Books and TV," *Publishers Weekly* 157 (17 June 1950): 2639.

16. Frederick W. Melcher, *Publishers Weekly* 157 (10 June 1950): 2561.

17. August Frugé, "Books Are Still for Sale," *Saturday Review* (16 Jul. 1955): 22.

18. See *Library Quarterly* 25 (October 1995), especially articles by Lester Asheim, Howard W. Winger, Thompson Webb, and Raymond H. Wittcoff.

19. Dan Lacy, "Books and the Future: A Speculation," *Bowker Lectures on Book Publishing* (New York: R. R. Bowker, 1957), 341.

20. Lacy, 354–56.

21. Marshall McLuhan, *Understanding Media: The Extensions of Man* (New York: McGraw-Hill, 1964); and *Gutenberg Galaxy: Making of Typographic Man* (Toronto: University of Toronto Press, 1962).

22. Charles T. Meadow, *Ink into Bits: A Web of Converging Media* (Lanham, MD: Scarecrow, 1998); and "On the Future of the Book, or Does It Have a Future" (unpublished article, January 1995).

23. Sven Birkerts, *The Gutenberg Elegies: The Fate of Reading in an Electronic Age* (New York: Fawcett Columbine, 1994).

24. William T. Mitchell, "Homer to Home-Page: Designing Digital Books." Electronic document at "Transformations of the Book," Media-in-Transition site, <http://media-in-transition.mit.edu/conferences/book/mitchell.html>.

25. Lester Asheim, "New Problems in Plotting the Future of the Book," *Library Quarterly* 25 (October 1955): 292.

26. See for example, Leander Kahney, "Microsoft: Paper Is Dead," *Wired News* (1 Sept. 1999), <http://www.wired.com/news/news/technology/story/21499.html>; and Jennifer Sullivan and Leander Kahney, "E-Books: Read 'em and Keep," *Wired News* (2 Sept. 1999), <http://www.wired.com/news/news/technology/story/21533.html>.

27. Eliot Weinberger, "Symposium: Twelve Visions," compiled by Charles Barber, *Media Studies Journal* 6 (Summer 1992): 41–43.

28. Raymond H. Wittcoff, "Developments in Mass Communication," *Library Quarterly* 25 (October 1955).

# 7 Help or Hindrance? The History of the Book and Electronic Media

Paul Erickson

The late D. F. McKenzie, in his Panizzi Lecture at the British Library in 1985, defined bibliography as "the discipline that studies texts as recorded forms, and the processes of their transmission, including their production and reception." He went on to define texts to include "verbal, visual, oral, and numeric data, in the form of maps, prints, and music, of archives of recorded sound, of films, videos, and any computer-stored information, everything in fact from epigraphy to the latest forms of discography. There is no evading the challenge which those new forms have created."[1] This essay will discuss the ways in which bibliography and its sibling discipline, the history of the book–the study of the physical, technological, economic, and cultural conditions of reading, authorship, and publishing—have in many respects evaded the very challenges for the discipline that McKenzie raised over sixteen years ago.

Scholars on both sides of the issue regularly proclaim that the appearance of new electronic media represents "the most fundamental change in textual culture since Gutenberg," often proclaiming that it heralds the "end of books."[2] Yet despite McKenzie's call for a broadening of the field of inquiry of the history of the book to constitute a "sociology of texts," the discipline, which takes as its focus the study of textual culture in all its permutations, is for several reasons ill-suited to address the challenges posed to the study of texts by new electronic media.[3] The history of the book is one of the up-and-coming fields of inquiry in the humanities, with its interdisciplinary approach and relative freedom from jargon earning it widespread interest.[4] Within the field, as in almost all others, much discussion has taken place in recent years about the impact of new media on the status of the book, reading, and authorship. The embrace has not been entirely unilateral— the call for papers for these MIT conferences on Media in Transition appeared in the newsletter of SHARP, the Society for the History of Authorship, Reading, and Publishing, the main international professional association in book history. Certainly, the history of the book, with its emphasis on the material form of texts and the impact this has on their meaning, has many valuable contributions to make to our understanding of the role new electronic media will play in our society. But I would argue that, at least in the limited instance of the history of the book as done in America, with its reliance on two major models of the "circuit of print," the models on which the discipline has traditionally relied are of relatively little use to forming an understanding of electronic media. The discipline's most conspicuous failure has been in the lack of analysis of the ways in which readers read electronic media, the least understood aspect of textual history in general.[5] Using a brief example from my own work on the dime novel, one of many "print revolutions" to have taken place in nineteenth-century America, I hope to illuminate both some of the shortcomings of the history of the book in analyzing the role of new electronic media, and some of its potential strengths.

A 1993 article in the *Chronicle of Higher Education* about the rise of book history posited that, "To some extent, the ferment is related to the rise of electronic media, whose growing strength is casting print culture in sharp relief."[6] While it may be the case that the rise of electronic media has begun to force historians of print toward taking a more comparative perspective, this perspective has all too rarely been employed in the other direction. Part of this is no doubt due to the difficulty, both intellectual and professional, of doing truly interdisciplinary work; save for rare exceptions, such as the Media in Transition project, book historians do not mix terribly often with historians of other media forms, especially since so many historians of the book come from literature departments. But it may also be due to the reliance of print historians on models for media culture that, while very well suited to book history, are of limited utility in analyzing other media. The two main models for print culture employed by historians of the book in America are those of William Charvat and Robert Darnton. Charvat, in his pioneering work *The Profession of Authorship in America,* posited a triangular model for print culture, with the author, the book trade, and the reader making up the three corners. This model was an attempt to give all three players, not just the author, a dynamic role in the production of the meanings derived from texts.[7] Given his background as a literary scholar, however, it is not surprising that for Charvat the author remained the focus of attention. As he wrote, this triangular model can offer a "better understanding of the ways in which writers have produced and communicated."[8] Darnton's model, which is more recent and more widely known, given the widespread popularity of his works, is essentially identical to Charvat's, except it is envisioned as a circuit rather than as a triangle. As Darnton describes it, this communication circuit can be understood as beginning with authors and publishers, filtering through printers, shippers, reviewers, and booksellers, to the reader, and from there back to the author.[9] Darnton's model, like Charvat's, has the virtue of allowing intervention at every stage of the circuit, by all actors, instead of employing a linear, top-down model of cultural diffusion. But given Darnton's background as a social historian, and the difficulty of studying the responses of readers, his work and that of many other scholars in the field tends to focus on the book trade elements of the circuit—how publishers interacted with authors, with their printers, suppliers, and shippers; how books were produced, marketed, and distributed. What has only recently begun to draw equal attention, due to the rise of reader-response criticism in literary studies, is the third corner of the triangle—the reader.

These models raise many of the right questions when trying to understand the explosion of print in nineteenth-century America. The expansion of cheap popular reading material in this period, especially beginning in the 1830s with the penny newspaper, has been the subject of a great deal of scholarly attention. Books and newspapers, however, were by no means "new media" in this period, when various technological innovations, most importantly stereotyping and the advent of the steam press, so drastically changed the face of American print culture. These innovations were critical to achieving the closest thing the period can offer to universal media saturation—the cheap newspaper—but the key element in saturation is distribution, a field of technology that, in nineteenth-century America, lagged far behind the rate of advance in printing technology. In a country characterized by a sparsely distributed rural population, the difficulty of distributing printed matter blunted to a certain extent the impact of the revolutions in printing. Additionally, in an America undergoing profound economic shifts that have been lumped together under the term "market revolution," and with no established tradition of artistic patronage, American authors had to make their way in a cultural marketplace that held no models for how to make a living as a professional writer. The elements that we think of today as constituting "authorship"—some system of copyright protection, a cultural system that is able to create name recognition for authors, the prestige attached to being a writer—for the most part did not exist in antebellum America. Given these conditions, Charvat's attention to the economic position of authors in the marketplace of culture and Darnton's emphasis on the modalities of publishing and distribution as businesses,[10] and the stress both place on the impact of the materiality of texts on the meanings they create, seem to pose the right questions for gaining a fuller understanding of print culture in the period.

One example, which I will discuss briefly to illustrate these points, is that of the dime novel, the signature cheap fiction phenomenon of nineteenth-century America. The firm of Beadle and Adams published the first dime novel, *Malaeska; the Indian Wife of the White Hunter,* in June of 1860, and by October were already being copied by competing firms. This story had first been published in a magazine in 1839, illustrating Russel Nye's observation that, "Beadle and Adams' contribution to publishing was one of merchandising, not content. They organized production, standardized the product, and did some shrewd guessing about the nature and extent of the market."[11] The extent of the market proved to be enormous; by 1864, Beadle and Adams had a standing order from the newly formed American News Company for 60,000 copies of each number, and their books, along with those of the competition, flooded the market. Dime novel publishers soon figured out that different types of textual presentation, such as different sizes and styles of binding and illustration, could be applied to the same texts in order to reach different segments of the market, and began issuing their works in endless numbers of different "series," each with a different look and feel. These changes in format, and the accompanying shifts in distribution, helped to construct a readership for the genre and carried a complex set of cultural messages about its influence and content, messages that ironically may have hastened the genre's demise. These texts illustrate quite clearly McKenzie's emphasis on the importance of the physical reality of books in creating their meaning, at times quite independently of the words their pages bear.

The standard dime novel format at its inception was a paper-covered (usually yellow, orange, or salmon), stab-sewn book of around 100 pages, roughly four by seven inches in size. In efforts to stay ahead of postal regulations that charged much higher rates for letters and books than for newspapers or "periodical literature," dime novel publishers started a cat-and-mouse game with the postal system to package their works as some form of periodical, appearing at regular intervals, rather than as books, especially after 1852, when the postal rate for periodicals (a different category) was made the same as that for newspapers.[12] The end result was to make "book material," as Richard Kielbowicz has labeled such marginal print products, look more like newspapers, which tended to be purchased at newsstands instead of delivered to the home. Thus the crucial consumption act of acquiring dime novel texts was removed from under the watchful eye of parents, and situated instead in the liminal, dangerous world of the street, a world that in Gilded Age America was associated with nothing so much as hordes of unruly, potentially criminal boys. This shift is also made apparent by the rise of "illuminated covers," bearing colored illustrations, which began to appear in the mid-1870s, an innovation which only made sense if the product with the colored cover could be seen at the point of purchase and compared to other products without colored covers, i.e., at a newsstand or bookstore. Many cultural critics did not view such changes in format and distribution as morally neutral. Increasing concerns about city streets made newsstands suspect, and the popularity of publications such as the *Police Gazette* heightened the attention paid by at least some concerned citizens to the physical appearance of reading materials, just as the signature bindings of "quality" fiction houses such as Ticknor and Fields became automatic signifiers of acceptability. As the tireless reformer Anthony Comstock noted, "We assimilate what we read. The pages of printed matter become our companions." This vision of the connection between books as material objects and their moral impact, heightened by the long term analogy of reading books as "eating" or "devouring" them, fed logically into Comstock's attacks in the 1880s on dime novels.

An examination of the covers of several dime novel titles illustrates the extent to which dime novel publishers recycled the same texts, often using the same stereotype plates, while trying to conceal the fact of their recycling by issuing them in different formats in different series. I will briefly mention only two examples of what is a much larger and more general phenomenon. Beadle published Ned Buntline's dime novel *Stella Delorme* five times between 1869 and 1900, and their competitor, George Munro, published Buntline's *Old Nick of the Swamp* at least twice, although probably more often. Over the years, the stories were not changed at all—they did not become more sensational, or more violent, or less puritanical over the years, as the standard narrative of the degeneration of the dime novel genre would have it. What did change was the format in which they were published, how much they cost, and where they were purchased. The early incarnations of both stories were in the traditional, pocket-sized format. Over time, however, with their appearances in different series (most notably *Stella Delorme*'s appearances in Beadle's Half-Dime Library) the format of the texts was altered in ways that make it clear that they were being distributed and purchased in different ways; the Half–Dime Library numbers were in 8-page tabloid format, roughly the same size as a modern magazine. Tellingly, the price had also gone down to a nickel, placing the text within the financial reach of even more readers. The final edition of *Old Nick of the Swamp*, published in 1908 shortly before the demise of the M. J. Ivers firm, has a cover with garish colors and a lurid image of an Indian being shot clearly meant to attract the eye at the point of purchase, and ads that clearly construct a readership for the novel as young and male.

Without going into excessive detail, it is clear from the material appearance of these texts, along with a reading of the ads that various editions contain, that the readership constructed by the various incarnations of these stories changed over time. This fact is borne out by the reminiscences of dime novel readers collected in Edmund Lester Pearson's history of the genre *Dime Novels; or Following an Old Trail in Popular Literature,* published in 1929, only seventeen years after the last dime novel series stopped publication. It is also borne out by the things cultural critics had to say about the genre and its readership. In 1864, William Everett was able to describe the early dime novels, which were still appearing in the standard format, as "unexceptionable morally. . . . They do not even obscurely pander to vice or excite the passions."[13] A change in perception, however, based on changes in format and distribution, was clearly evident only fifteen years later. W. H. Bishop, writing in the *Atlantic* in 1879, expressed the predominant view of dime novels at the time, saying that dime novels were "written almost exclusively for the use of the lower classes of society." He described the traffic at an urban newsstand on publication day, saying that "a middle-aged woman . . . a shop girl . . . [and] a servant" stopped by to buy dime novels, "but with them, before them, and after them come boys. . . . The most ardent class of patron . . . are boys."[14]

It is no coincidence that the 1870s, when the bulk of the readership of dime novels was considered to consist of boys, and when advertising for dime novels became more directly focused on attracting boys as consumers, was when dime novels began to be seen as dangerous influences on young people. As soon as they came to be seen as age-specific reading material, instead of shared family pleasures, these books could be used to explain the perennially awful behavior of children. Brander Matthews wrote in 1883 that, "The dreadful damage wrought to-day in every city, town, and village . . . by the horrible and hideous stuff set before the boys and girls of America by the villainous sheets which pander greedily and viciously to the natural taste of young readers for excitement, the irreparable wrong done by these vile publications, is hidden from no one."[15] Yet, forty years later, it would be hidden from Mr. Matthews himself, as he reminisced, "The saffron-backed Dime Novels of the late Mr. Beadle, ill-famed among the ignorant who are unaware of their ultra-Puritan purity . . . began to appear in the early years of the Civil War; and when I was a boy in a dismal boarding school at Sing Sing, . . . I reveled in their thrilling and innocuous record of innocent and imminent danger."[16] These widely varying responses over time to what were, in many cases, the same *texts,* but very different *books,* underlines the importance of issues of format and distribution in the meanings made from texts, crucial links in the communications circuits outlined by both Darnton and Charvat. Equally fruitful information could be gleaned from the study of the dime novel about the rise of authorship as a viable profession in America, filling in another link in the chain, but that is another story. The point remains that the format, distribution, and price of dime novels helped to construct (and, I would argue, engender) an audience, while at the same time offering a narrative of generic degeneration to non-readers.

Fine. But as my dissertation adviser would ask at this point, "So what?" What does this have to tell us about electronic media? I would argue that comparing the evolution of popular print media such as the dime novel with the mechanisms of electronic media can offer insights into both the ways that book history has failed to address this cultural shift in meaningful ways, and potentially fruitful avenues for future work. One critical difference between print media and electronic media, which most models of book history are structurally ill-prepared to address, is that whereas print culture was for most of its history a known medium in search of a distribution system, modern electronic media, especially those involving the Web, tend to be distribution systems in search of content, of a commodity to distribute (television and radio were, at their inception, similar examples, as the stories of early television owners watching test patterns indicate). This is not to say that there is any shortage of content on the Web, but that organizing it in such a way that it can be made comprehensible to consumers/readers is a problem.[17] Thus Robert Darnton, book historian and former president of the American Historical Association, spearheaded an initiative to publish prize-winning dissertations electronically through the Gutenberg-E project with Columbia University Press. It would be the easiest thing in the world to simply post the full text of one's dissertation on the Web, but obtaining the imprimatur of a major scholarly organization and a prestigious university press is a way of "branding" the content in a comprehensible way, since all web sites look pretty much the same and there are fewer extratextual signifiers such as format, binding, or paper stock to provide clues to readers as to the text's reliability.[18] A distribution network like the Web, no longer limited even to the existence of telephone lines, is a wonderful thing, but as Sumner Redstone said when Viacom bought Paramount in 1994, "Software is king, was king and always will be king." In other words, content matters, and part of successful content is its "legibility," which is aided by linking electronic texts with the names of prestigious organizations from the academic and print worlds. Such attempts are crucial for the future of scholarly publishing, but they also represent a certain kind of "editorial fantasy," a desire to control content and erect boundaries between good and bad in a medium that is most notable for its boundarylessness.[19] As Darnton has written elsewhere, "Instead of turning our backs on cyberspace, we need to take control of it—to set standards, develop quality controls and direct traffic. Our students will learn to navigate the Internet successfully if we set up warning signals and *teach them to obey*."[20] Such quasi-authoritarian desires for clarity and control are perhaps grounded, not in the world of texts, which is unruly and infinite, but in the regimented world of academic and elite trade publishing, which is both the main focus of book history and the world in which most academics live.[21]

Book historians need to come up with new models of textual circulation and consumption in which distribution and the market are understood very differently than in the traditional print model, since the whole system of compensation for text produced, copyright and textual ownership, and authorial control operates very differently in electronic media. Very often with electronic texts, there is no "market," no "publisher," since many writers of electronic texts are not paid for their work and publish it on the Web themselves. Thus, the communications circuit is often a direct link between the writer (who is also the publisher and bookseller) and the reader. The medium is itself the distribution system, so the many individuals who are allowed agency in the models provided by Charvat and Darnton simply do not appear in the circuit. The ways in which electronic texts are "distributed" on the Web, if distribution can be understood to be the mechanism by which reader and text are brought together, is often through the random, impersonal agency of the search function.[22] Certainly such a drastic shift in the way in which readers meet texts must have some implications for our understanding of electronic texts, given the importance of distribution in the Charvat triangle and the Darnton circuit. These models can be said to be "flexible" enough to still work for many electronic texts, and certainly this is true for media such as film and television. But if such flexibility is bought at the price of disregarding the very stages of the models that makes them so powerful for understanding the world of print, then perhaps the time for new models more specifically tailored to current conditions has come.

Perhaps a more fundamental failure on the part of book historians is the tendency to view all texts, especially electronic texts, in the terms of the book.[23] The nomenclature of much electronic media has not helped in this regard—we speak of Web "pages,"[24] which we can "bookmark," the many manufacturers of electronic book readers are in a race to see whose appliance can be most "book-like," and companies such as E-Ink are trying to develop electronic paper.[25] This tendency to view electronic media not on their own terms, but as "bad books," is especially pronounced in the alarmists who are forever wringing their hands about the "death of books," goaded on by technological visionaries who gleefully predict print's demise such as Barry Richman, who wrote in *PC Magazine* as far back as 1984, "Surprising, isn't it, how hard it is to kill off a nice little technology like print."[26] This view of the book as the "natural" form for information flies in the face of one of the key insights of book history—the mutable, contingent, and, overall, recent role of print in society and history. Richard Lanham characterizes this naturalized view of the book thus: "The book itself is sacred. Let's protect it. The codex book creates the vital central self. The codex book defines human reason. Our cultural vitals are isomorphic with the codex book. Its very feel and heft and look and smell are talismanic. We must have an agency of the federal government to protect it." Yet even advocates of the possibilities of hypertext such as Lanham confess to having, at one point, shared a naturalized view of books as "the natural and only vehicle for written text" (evidently such humanists never read the newspaper, or street signs, or cereal boxes).[27] Jason Epstein calls movable type a "vector of civilization" that has been "unceremoniously replaced in the last dozen years" after half a millennium by new information technologies.[28] Sven Birkerts claims that the linear quality of print so loathed by hypertext enthusiasts is in fact one of its most salient qualities, that "the physical arrangements of print are in accord with our traditional sense of history."[29] He even goes so far as to claim that our "neural systems" have "evolved . . . to certain capacities" based on the qualities of printed books, a hair-trigger view of evolution that utterly neglects the very recent nature of widespread literacy and book ownership.[30] Epstein reaches the extreme of this view of the printed book as an utterly natural phenomenon rather than a technology when he claims that a culture requires not only books, but bookstores, and not only bookstores, but retail bookstores, to be rightly called civilized.[31]

A further obstacle to a clearer understanding of how readers read and use new electronic media is the sense, coming from both sides of the debate, that the intense, private, emotionally involved way we read prose fiction is the normative reading experience.[32] The archetypal reader is held to be Jane Eyre, huddled in her window seat with the red curtains drawn, shut off from the world and lost in a book (undoubtedly, a cat and tea are involved as well).[33] David Miall argues that this sort of "literary reading," by which he means reading a "lengthy George Eliot novel" or a "complex Sylvia Plath poem," is "rendered incomprehensible by the model of reading put forth in hypertext theory."[34] Birkerts, the best-known spokesman for the "sky is falling" view of electronic media, is exemplary for his assumption that the way that we read contemporary fiction is the scale by which all reading should be measured, by which standards, of course, electronic media fail miserably. He writes, in *The Gutenberg Elegies:* "I will confine myself to the literary novel because that, for me, represents reading in its purest form."[35] Almost inevitably, he later compares reading text on the Web to reading *The Catcher in the Rye,* the archetypal emotionally charged reading experience for Americans of a certain age that confirms in flattering ways the reader's suspicions of his own ineffable individuality and uniqueness. Even scholars who are more enthusiastic about the possibilities of electronic media, such as Jay David Bolter, George Landow, Stuart Moulthrop and J. Yellowlees Douglas, in their analyses of the electronic reading experience, only give attention to how readers read works of prose fiction in an interactive environment. And if the bibliophiles' invocation of Salinger, Eliot, Plath, and Wordsworth as examples of texts with which readers engage emotionally is all-too predictable, the roster of "interactive" texts referred to by hypertext theorists is even more constantly repeated, and just as exclusively reliant on works of fiction (it consists almost exclusively of Laurence Sterne's *Tristram Shandy,* Jorge Luis Borges' *The Garden of Forking Paths,* Julio Cortázar's *Hopscotch,* and Michael Joyce's *Afternoon*).

Despite this incessant attention by theorists to the implications of reading fiction in a hypertextual environment, I do not know anyone who has ever read a novel in its entirety off of a computer screen, unless it was a class assignment (literary historians, who are often forced to read whole novels off of microfilm readers, can attest that it is not an experience to be sought after). But I am even more confident that everybody who has used a computer once has "read" something—plane fares, addresses of old friends, parts numbers for food processor blades, the locations of books in libraries. Many writers have noted that the world of print does not consist solely of literary novels, and that vast numbers of texts exist, such as encyclopedias, directories, manuals, that will be better served by being converted to electronic formats, but the point bears repeating. As Umberto Eco has written, "There are too many books. . . . If the computer network succeeds in reducing the quantity of published books, this would be a paramount cultural improvement."[36] Writing elegies about the "death of the heavy reference book" is not very sexy, and not likely to win one a Guggenheim Fellowship. Such books are likely to disappear, however slowly, although it is likely that Nicholson Baker will find someone to sue over it. But other forms of print reading will persist, and it is likely that new ones will emerge.

The Buggles told us, in 1981, on MTV's first broadcast, that "Video Killed the Radio Star," but since then Rush Limbaugh, Don Imus, Howard Stern, and Dr. Laura, to name a few, have, at least temporarily, disproved their prediction by changing our definition of what "radio star" means. Book history, not just in the instance of electronic media but in general, needs to broaden its definition of what a "text" is that makes it deserving of study, and what "reading" is, if it is to have useful things to say about the ways in which electronic texts are used. Book historians (understandably, given their roots in literary studies) know little about the experience of reading texts other than prose fiction. But it is precisely these other forms of reading that make up the bulk of most people's everyday interaction with printed words.[37] David Miall dismisses the linked nodes of hypertext as tending to "promote superordinate connections and to elicit an analytical response more appropriate to expository prose than to literary texts," as if reading expository prose is not really reading.[38] He objects that the electronic model of textuality implies that reading is simply information processing, which, quantitatively, is precisely what the vast majority of our reading is. I do not seek for meaning when I read "Welcome to South Boston" or "No Turn on Red" or "My Child is an Honor Student at Thornwood Middle School"— I process the information. And I read a lot more words in that manner on a daily basis than I do Sylvia Plath. Alberto Manguel, the historian of reading, notes that, "There never was 'pure reading,'" that the act of reading is always confused with something else.[39] But these everyday textual practices, I would argue, come closer to "pure reading" in the sense of being automatic and relatively unmediated rather than participating in a highly structured ritual of private fiction reading. Birkerts contemptuously speaks of "raw urban scurf—billboard signs for appliances and the glare of the liquor mart," unwilling to consider these textual products as "texts."[40] David Henkin, in his study of public textuality in antebellum New York, writes that a focus on texts encountered in media other than books offers a glimpse of how "acts of reading and textual interpretation figured in a set of broadly inclusive practices that were embedded in the everyday life of the growing city."[41] Book historians must pay more attention to such non-codex forms of textuality if we are to begin to understand the ways in which electronic media are fostering a more intensive "textualization" of the home and work environments.

If book historians tend to view electronic media too much in the terms of the book, at least from the perspective of reading, in another instance, that of the materiality of the reading experience, we take too much for granted. Book history is allegedly primarily concerned with the material conditions of the transmission and dissemination of texts, and how these conditions influence the meaning taken from texts. Yet book historians, along with other scholars, have paid virtually no attention to how the physical means of transmitting electronic texts influences their meaning. In fact, one of the standard claims about electronic texts is that they are "disembodied," that they consist only of "virtual texts" flickering briefly on a screen, transmitted only by electromagnetic impulses and existing physically only on a hidden, mysterious piece of magnetic media or frighteningly futuristic CD-ROM. Yet, for the time that words are on a screen, they are not "virtual texts," a mere "configuration of impulses on a screen . . . an indeterminate entity both particle and wave, an ectoplasmic arrival and departure"; they are texts, words on a surface that you can touch, just as words on a page are.[42] If they go away when a reader clicks on a link, so do the words on a page go away when a reader turns to the next. David Miall writes that, "The principal difficulty lies in the disembodied nature of electronic reading. The presence of the body during ordinary reading makes available types of response that are less available if not absent from the electronic medium. . . . while we can endow the computer with bodily properties, we can do so only figuratively. . . . The metaphor of the Net as space masks the disassociation of Netters from their bodies, masks the fact that the bodies are elsewhere, real, material. . . . "[43] Yet my body is present now, and all-too material, as I read off my laptop screen. And my computer is not at all disembodied; on the contrary, it makes noise, it gives off light, it is heavy when I carry it around. As I write this, in the jet-cooled bowels of Widener Library, I can use my laptop, which gives off a good deal of heat, to keep my legs warm. If I could fit the screens of the three computers I currently own onto a photocopier, most book historians would say that they are just screens, whereas they would immediately be able to interpret the meanings transmitted by the different covers of the dime novels I discussed earlier. But why neglect the materiality and variability of the encounter with electronic texts? All three of my screens are Mac screens, which in itself delivers a whole complex set of signals about their use and the conditions under which texts are likely to be consumed, just as carrying a book with a fine morocco binding would do.[44]

Much has been made of the commodity fetishism of the opposing sides in the books vs. computers debate—the dean of MIT's School of Architecture wrote in 1995 that books will only matter to those "addicted to the look and feel of tree flakes encased in dead cow," while bibliophiles continually rail against the impassivity of the screen, the coldness of the computer, the clumsiness of the mouse.[45] Book history is perhaps most notable for the insights it has gained by, in I. A. Richards' terms, thinking of a book as "a machine to think with," yet the tendency to either think of computers as just machines or as invisible carriers of text plagues the discipline.[46] Given the prominence in the discipline granted to the shift from public to private reading, it is striking that no attention has been paid to the new sites of reading that electronic media engender. What are the differences between reading a text at a public terminal in a library, standing up, or in a quasi-public space such as an office cubicle, as opposed to sitting down at home? What does it do to the textual encounter if you always have to sit near a wall, close to an outlet, because your laptop battery is dead, instead of anywhere you like, as one can with a book? Alberto Manguel has written of the materiality of his computer, aligning it more with the Greek tradition that required textual monuments in stone than with the book-centered Hebrew tradition, stressing how the physicality and locatedness of his computer influences his readings of texts from its screen.[47] Richard Grusin astutely notes that the "ephemeral, evanescent" words of electronic writing are "dependent upon extremely material hardware, software, communication networks, institutional and corporate structures, and so on," and that by avoiding any consideration of these factors as they apply to electronic media, scholars avoid the demands of critical social theory. Further attention needs to be paid to such issues, but book historians cannot do it alone. [48]

There is no question that consuming electronic media texts is a very different experience from reading a book; on this technophiles and bibliophiles agree.[49] There may be some question as to whether or not some of such media experiences should be called "reading" in the traditional sense, or if some new category is required. As Manguel notes, "The CD-ROM (and whatever else will take its place in the imminent future) is like Wagner's *Gesamtkunstwerk,* a sort of mini-opera in which all the senses must come into play in order to re-create a text."[50] This comparison is apt, but also daunting, because we have no theory and no history of how the consumption of *Gesamtkunstwerke* works. But perhaps "reading" is no longer the most useful phylum in which to place such textual encounters. Book historians must work with historians of other media to come up with such a synthesis: with scholars of film and television, to gain a clearer sense of what happens in the experience of receiving texts from a screen instead of a page; with students of radio and the phonograph, to gain insights into the impact of the presence of a strange new machine, a material presence that dispenses texts, in the home; with cognitive theorists, to better understand the interaction between word and image so characteristic of electronic media, where words often become images, and vice versa; and with theorists of everyday life, such as Michel de Certeau and David Henkin.

Especially productive avenues for increasing our understanding of the electronic reading experience lie in collaborations with scholars of television, a medium that is needlessly seen as the "enemy" by many bibliophiles.[51] Not only does television mimic the way in which most people throughout history have received printed texts—by being read to—its physical qualities offer valuable parallels as well. Both computer reading and television watching involve looking at an electronic screen, and "navigating" through its offerings with a small, hand-held extension of the body (the mouse and the remote control). As W. J. T. Mitchell has noted, the tendency of literary study is to view any genre combining text and visual images with either suspicion or disdain, yet this mixture of word and image is one of the most salient features of both television and computer technologies (if you question whether or not television involves "reading," notice how many words appear in almost all television programming).[52] It may be worth considering whether most people think of what they are doing when they are navigating the Web as "reading" or "watching," or some hybrid of the two. Scholars have been paying attention to the role of images in text as far back as Wordsworth, but what do we know about the role of words in primarily visual media, such as subtitles in movies? Enthusiasts of hypertext seem to instinctively grasp the similarity between it and television watching, in their haste to differentiate hypertext from the "narcotizing of American society" wrought by television, which is not to be confused with "the mixture of word, image, and sound emerging now through digital multimedia techniques.[53]

Critics of hypertextuality are especially leery of the effects of electronic linking, which disrupts narrative flow, undermines the authority of the singular author, and defers textual closure. Yet almost everybody engages in a much less coherent form of "electronic linking" every day, when they change television channels using a remote control, and the resultant narrative dislocations have not yet destroyed society.[54] Craig Stroupe's call for developing an approach he calls "visualized English," which would describe the "dialogically constitutive relations between words and images—in a larger sense, between the literacies of verbal and visual cultures," is virtually unique in the field. Scholars of literature, and especially book historians, must seek out collaborations with scholars of visual media if we are to understand how readers actually use electronic media.[55] Perhaps such collaborations will lead us to Walter Ong's conclusion, that we are becoming simultaneously more textual and more oral: "The electronic transformation of verbal expression has both deepened the commitment of the word to space initiated by writing and intensified by print and has brought consciousness to a new age of secondary orality."[56]

My concern here, and in general, is less with theories of how we generate meaning or what our expectations of narrative are than with how people, in their everyday lives, use texts.[57] When people, in significant numbers, start reading entire texts on computer screens, rather than printing them up and reading them on paper, then we should study the phenomenon seriously. Until then, however people use electronic media—whether we choose to call it "reading" or something else—is deserving of the attention of book historians.[58] David Miall writes that it is possible that some electronic literary texts might be able to provide the transformative experience of reading print, but that "the experience of reading is too important for us to allow its fate to be decided by hypertext theorists."[59] Instead of letting the ideas of theorists—any theorists—determine what is and is not possible for electronic media, I would argue that, if we are to take a truly reader-centered approach, we should look at how people use the texts, which is rarely determined by anyone's theory. The need of some literary scholars to "accept and control" cyberspace, embodied in the sentiment that "cyberspace, like the economy, needs to be regulated," constitutes a willful disinterest in the ways real readers read texts.[60] If reading encounters require "making sense" of texts through an interactive engagement with their repertoires of codes and references, rather than a simple "unlocking" of the latent meaning of a text, then it is vital to come to an understanding of how these engagements are structured. Richard Lanham claims that the reader of the electronic word is the responsive reader par excellence: "They can genuflect before the text or spit on its altar, add to a text or subtract from it, rearrange it, revise it, suffuse it with commentary."[61] None of this, of course, is new, as Anthony Grafton's work on Budé's commonplace book has shown. Any reader of a book can choose to skip certain parts, cross others out, write in the margins, or throw the book away. David Dobrin argues that "hypertext is not a new text form. It is not an evolutionary advance. It forces no reconsiderations. It has no potential for fundamental change in how we read or write. Hypertext is simply one text structure among many, made unique by the text conventions it has, conventions that guide the reader's attention and allow him or her to navigate through the text."[62] Indeed, hypertext may not offer the reader any more "choices" than a newspaper does. In his *Hypertext 2.0,* one of the foundational texts for hypertext scholars, George Landow includes the chapters "Reconfiguring the Text," "Reconfiguring the Author," "Reconfiguring Writing," "Reconfiguring Narrative," and "Reconfiguring Literary Education." The only thing that does not get reconfigured is the reader. That may be because the experience of reading is too ineffable to get at, given that the only reading experience we can ever know is our own. Or it may be that the differences between "reading" a text and "reading" electronic media are not as great as most writers on the subject would have us believe. People raised in a literate culture are constantly surrounded by texts of all kinds, in all forms. It may be that our ability to make a coherent narrative out of the many texts we see every day, instead of being paralyzed by their multiplicity, means that the textuality of new electronic media will be more easily assimilated into daily life than many scholars think (especially if the trend continues to use computers to browse for what we want, then to print out the longer items).

To conclude, then, will the history of the book be a help or a hindrance in understanding the impact of new electronic media? I have only very briefly sketched out some ways in which the discipline has perhaps hindered an understanding of how electronic media really work, as well as some potential contributions book historians can make to the debate. Robert Darnton was quoted in 1993 as saying that the history of the book "has the potential to take its place beside the history of art and the history of science."[63] But many book historians, in their insistence on viewing electronic media, especially the Web, as a large book, rather than something else entirely (a library? a conversation? a gigantic movie with lots of subtitles? a poorly-organized warehouse?) run the risk instead of placing the history of the book alongside the history of sculpture or the history of chemistry—that is, an interesting but marginal field subsumed under a much larger discipline, the history of media. But if we view the field of textuality according to D. F. McKenzie's metaphor of the text as the uniting principle, the trunk of the tree, with the different branches making up the different media in which texts are stored and transmitted, perhaps historians of the book are positioned to play a more central role. The failure of book historians to live up to McKenzie's clarion call for a comprehensive "sociology of texts" is understandable; the field of book history itself is new, and electronic media change so fast that it is impossible to keep up.

Perhaps the most important contribution book historians can make, however, is to reinforce an awareness of the mutability, contingency, and the relative historical youth of printed forms, so that the rise of electronic media can be seen perhaps less as a frightening epochal shift and more as what it is—just another change, albeit a big one, in how we communicate. Self-appointed defenders of the book, such as Birkerts, who wish to naturalize the culture of print by linking it to "age-old ways of being," both do the book a grave disservice and hinder our understanding of how the book can shape our understanding of, instead of fear of, electronic media.[64] Since print is only a brief phase in the history of textual transmission, and oral text and visual images rose to new levels of prominence in the twentieth century with the appearance of radio and film, bibliography can ill afford to shut itself off from other fields of media scholarship; as McKenzie noted, "at this time it seems more needful than ever to recover the unity in their otherwise disabling diversity."[65] There is no medium of communication about whose production and consumption we know more than books; book historians are poised to make tremendous contributions to our understanding of new electronic media. And if we are to understand anything about how people read electronic media in the future, it is crucial that we try to understand it now, since almost all the forms of evidence historians of the book rely on to learn about reading in the past—marginalia, borrowing records from libraries, diary entries—do not and will not exist for most electronic media. But book historians must also remain aware of the fact that a very small percentage of all the textual encounters, the interactions of people with printed words, that happen in the world every day involve books, especially works of prose fiction. The history of the book and the history of reading and writing are thus very different things, and an awareness of the fact that reading books is not the same as reading other texts is crucial to the approach to new textual forms. McKenzie admonished us to remember how marginal, in historical terms, the book is to the history of textual communication, and how mutable the physical form of the text can be. A continued attention to the materiality, and therefore the contingency, of the interaction with print, combined with new attention to the materiality of the experience of electronic text, is one direction in which book historians can both continue to expand our knowledge of print culture and contribute to our understanding of electronic culture.

## Notes

1.  D. F. McKenzie, *Bibliography and the Sociology of Texts* (London: The British Library, 1986), 4.

2.  George P. Landow and Paul Delany, eds., *The Digital Word: Text-Based Computing in the Humanities* (Cambridge, MA: MIT Press, 1993), 5.

3.  And there can be little question that it is a challenge. One of the unfortunate characteristics of the discussion regarding the rise of electronic media has been a tendency on both sides, the "book people" and the "computer people," to view the relationship between the two as a zero-sum game, with one side the victor and the other the vanquished. Jay David Bolter, one of the more enthusiastic avatars of electronic text, wrote over ten years ago that, "Until recently it was possible to believe that the computer could coexist with the printed book," and celebrates hypertext as the embodiment of the goals of deconstructionist literary criticism, which, according to Bolter, "envisions its adversary in the form of the printed book" (Jay David Bolter, *Writing Space: The Computer, Hypertext, and the History of Writing* [Hillsdale, NJ: Erlbaum, 1991], 2, 164). Similarly apocalyptic language can be heard often from bibliophiles, who regularly declare that, due to the advent of computers, "we are living in a society and culture that is in dissolution," and excoriate hypertext theorists for the unforgivable sin of "relentless rejection of Romantic poetics" (Sven Birkerts, *The Gutenberg Elegies: The Fate of Reading in an Electronic Age* [Winchester, MA: Faber & Faber, 1994], 20; David S. Miall, "Trivializing or Liberating? The Limitations of Hypertext Theorizing," in *Mosaic* 32, no. 2 [1999]: 163). Not only is such rhetoric counterproductive, it is historically obtuse; print as a medium of communication will not disappear any more than speech did when writing was invented. The debate is not over the future of print, but over the form print takes.

4.  As Anthony Grafton has noted, one of the key signs that book history has "arrived" is the presence of internecine conflict within the field. Anthony Grafton, "Is the History of Reading a Marginal Enterprise? Guillaume Budé and His Books," *Papers of the Bibliographical Society of America,* 91, no. 2 (June 1997): 139.

5.  One reason for this may be the too-literal embrace of the term "history" in the history of the book; many scholars in a field as archive-centered as this is are likely not comfortable doing research involving subjects that are still alive, and in fact may tend to view such work as not being "real history." (Certain exceptions, such as Janice Radway's *Reading the Romance,* can of

course be found.) The result has been that virtually all the research produced on how readers read electronic texts has come from scholars either of curriculum development, composition, or cognitive theory, or publishing insiders and intellectual property experts.

6. Karen Winkler, "In Electronic Age, Scholars are Drawn to the Study of Print," *Chronicle of Higher Education,* July 14, 1993.

7. William Charvat, *The Profession of Authorship in America, 1800–1870* (New York: Columbia University Press, 1992), 284.

8. Charvat, 285, emphasis added.

9. Darnton, *The Forbidden Best-Sellers of Pre-Revolutionary France* (New York: W. W. Norton, 1996), 181–189.

10. Contrary to much theorizing of electronic text, which claims that the "author function" vanishes as a by-product of the interactive reading process and tends to ascribe agency to the technology itself, all electronic text has an "author," and in fact the tendency to attach a name to most electronic text has proven quite resilient. It is precisely these elements, however—the distribution-oriented parts of the circuit—that are removed or utterly changed by the rise of new electronic media such as electronic books and the Internet. As Roger Chartier has noted, the most significant achievement of electronic media is to annul "the heretofore insoluble distinction between the place of the text and the place of the reader . . . " (Roger Chartier, *Forms and Meanings: Texts, Performances, and Audiences from Codex to Computer* [Philadelphia: University of Pennsylvania Press, 1995]).

    For an intriguing analysis of the potential impact on consumers of such developments, which would involve consumers becoming "dependent subcontractors" to retailers because of the costs of establishing relationships with those retailers, see Wilfred Dolfsma, "Consumers as Subcontractors in Electronic Markets," <http://www.firstmonday.dk/issues/issue4_3/dolfsma/>.

11. Russel Nye, *The Unembarrassed Muse: The Popular Arts in America* (New York: Dial Press, 1970), 201.

12. For more specific discussion of these issues, see Richard John, *Spreading the News: The American Postal System from Franklin to Morse* (Cambridge, MA: Harvard University Press, 1995) and Richard Kielbowicz, *News in the Mail: The Press, Post Office, and Public Information, 1700–1860s* (Westport, CT: Greenwood Press, 1989).

13. Nye, 203.

14. Michael Denning, *Mechanic Accents: Dime Novels and Working Class Culture in America* (New York: Verso, 1987), 29–30.

15. Quoted in Denning, 9.

16. Quoted in Denning, 9.

17. Hypertext theorists have long been aware of the need to create links in hypertext in such a way that will not so disorient the reader that they give up on a text. See especially George Landow, "The Rhetoric of Hypermedia: Some Rules for Authors," in *Hypermedia and Literary Studies,* ed. George Landow (Cambridge, MA: MIT Press, 1991), 81–103.

18. Jason Epstein, formerly of Random House, has also argued for the importance of "branding" electronic texts: "Distinguished websites, like good bookstores, will attract readers accordingly. The filter that distinguishes value is a function of human nature, not of particular technologies" (Epstein, *Two Essays on Digital Books,* 14, available at <www.nyrev.com>, originally published on April 27, 2000 and October 16, 2000 in the *New York Review of Books*).

19. It is arguable that the current crisis in scholarly publishing, frequently attributed to a diminished audience for academic books, which in turn forces presses to raise prices, is not a demand problem at all, but rather one of supply. Given the vast numbers of embattled adjunct professors, temporary instructors, not to mention tenure-track junior faculty, all of whom need to find publishers for their books in order to keep their jobs, there is no way that the allegedly larger, more attentive audience for academic books that previously existed could provide sufficient demand to justify university presses in publishing all the books that academics need to get published.

20. Robert Darnton, "No Computer Can Hold the Past," *New York Times,* June 12, 1999. Emphasis added.

21. It is no coincidence that it is this world, that of the academic presses and elite fiction houses, that has produced the bulk of the most over-wrought lamentations about the death of the book and the demise of genteel publishing, where offices had parquet floors and gentlemanly patrons ran publishing houses without bothering to care if they lost money or not. See, for example, virtually anything by Jason Epstein, especially his recent memoir.

22. One important side effect of the removal of the traditional distribution elements from the circuit is that, for the first time, retailers of texts are in a position to track the behavior of their consumers, given the drastic decrease in the number of cash transactions that such a market implies. See Clifford Lynch, "The Battle to Define the Future of the Book in the Digital World," <http://www.firstmonday.dk/issues/issue6_6/lynch/>.

23. Certain book historians have made notable efforts in correcting this and other problems in the field that I address here, and I do not wish to ignore the significance of their work—John O'Donnell, Carla Hesse, Geoffrey Nunberg, and John Feather would head what I am sure should be a much longer list.

24. In a strangely atavistic turn, the most common term for navigating texts on screen— "scrolling"—precedes even the codex book.

25. For a thorough examination of the legal and economic implications of this attempt to make electronic reading material as "book-like" as possible, see Lynch.

26. Barry Richman, "The Death of Print?" *PC Magazine,* May 1, 1984. As Geoffrey Nunberg notes, bibliophiles inevitably rise to such bait, "because their fetishism makes them susceptible to the same technological Darwinism the visionaries trade in: once the old artifacts are given a foothold they will move with remorseless logic to displace the old" (Nunberg, "The Places of Books in the Age of Electronic Reproduction," *Representations* 42 [1993] 13–14).

27. Richard Lanham, *The Electronic Word: Democracy, Technology, and the Arts* (Chicago: University of Chicago Press, 1993), 8.

28. Epstein, 4.

29. Birkerts, 122. Birkerts here evidently is willing to write out of the world of print the many cultures and religious traditions that do not share a linear sense of history.

30. Birkerts, 139.

31. Epstein, 18.

32. See Grafton for a useful counterpoint. In his reading of Guillaume Budé's commonplace book, he finds that Budé read in a way very similar to the way we might browse the Web, copying down pieces he liked and organizing them in his own systematic way.

33. See Patricia Meyer Spacks, "The Privacy of the Novel," *Novel* 31, no. 3 (Summer 1998): 304–316.

34. Miall, 165, 158.

35. Birkerts, 79.

36. Umberto Eco, "Afterword," in Geoffrey Nunberg, ed., *The Future of the Book* (Berkeley: University of California Press, 1996), 301.

37. A useful experiment is to try to keep track, even for ten minutes during a normal day, of everything that you "read"—that is, every word that your eye takes in.

38. Miall, 166. Interestingly, I found Miall's example of expository prose through a hypertext link, perhaps proving his point, although I did not read it on the screen. Like most people, I printed it out.

39. Alberto Manguel, "How those plastic stones speak," *Times Literary Supplement,* July 4, 1997. See also Alberto Manguel, *A History of Reading* (New York: Viking Press, 1996).

40. Birkerts, 142.

41. David Henkin, *City Reading: Written Words and Public Spaces in Antebellum New York* (New York: Columbia University Press, 1998), 7.

42. Birkerts, 154–155. I am not enough of a physicist to belabor the point, but those who are

would be easily able to discuss the fact that the atoms making up printed letters on a page are no more "immutable" than letters on a computer screen.

43. Miall, 164–165.

44. David Dobrin has written of the importance of teaching illiterate adults the conventions of text forms, which I would extend to the physical forms of media, as part of the process of teaching them to read. See David Dobrin, "Hype and Hypertext," in *Literacy and Computers: The Complications of Teaching and Learning with Technology,* ed. Cynthia L. Selfe and Susan Hilligoss (New York: Modern Language Association of America, 1994), 306.

45. Quoted in Nunberg, 65.

46. As is so often the case, Roger Chartier is a welcome exception. He observes that, "Our current revolution is obviously more extensive than Gutenberg's. It modifies not only the technology for the reproduction of the text, but even the materiality of the object that communicates the text to readers" (Chartier, *Forms and Meanings,* 15).

47. Manguel, "How Those Plastic Stones Speak."

48. Richard Grusin, "What Is an Electronic Author? Theory and the Technological Fallacy," in *Virtual Realities and Their Discontents,* ed. Robert Markley (Baltimore: Johns Hopkins University Press, 1996), 46.

49. In particular, research has shown that reading from screens is slower, less accurate, and more tiring. For a summary of this research, see Andrew Dillon, "Reading from Paper versus Screens: A Critical Review of the Empirical Literature," in *Ergonomics: Third Special Issue on Cognitive Ergonomics* 35, no. 10, 1297–1326.

50. Manguel, "How Those Plastic Stones Speak."

51. The pride many bookish people take in either not owning a television or in not taking them seriously as conveyors of information illustrates the extent of the split.

52. See W. J. T. Mitchell, *Iconology: Image, Text, Ideology* (Chicago: University of Chicago Press, 1986).

53. Lanham, 201. Jay David Bolter has gone so far as to describe hypermedia as "the revenge of text upon television," celebrating hypermedia's incorporation of the image into the text instead of television's incorporation of text into the image (Bolter, 26). This reader is unable to tell the difference.

54. Not to mention the fact, which has been noted by many scholars of hypertext, that the ways in which readers use many printed texts—encyclopedias, books with endnotes or tables, catalogs—mimic the modes of reading linked hypertext.

55. Stroupe is especially perceptive regarding the political stakes in English departments that

would be involved in making such gestures. Craig Stroupe, "Visualizing English: Recognizing the Hybrid Literacy of Visual and Verbal Authorship on the Web," in *College English* 62, no. 5 (May 2000): 609.

56. Walter Ong, *Orality & Literacy: The Technologizing of the Word* (New York: Routledge, 1982), 135.

57. Those interested in the other issues, especially those surrounding narrative, should see J. Yellowlees Douglas, *The End of Books—Or Books without End? Reading Interactive Narratives* (Ann Arbor: University of Michigan Press, 2000).

58. Since I define "reading" as a process of gathering up signs—not exclusively letters and words—and making sense of them, that is the term I would choose.

59. Miall, 170.

60. Miall, 170; Darnton, "The New Age of the Book." Craig Stroupe notes that one source of suspicion of electronic media on the part of some literary scholars may be the association of computers with the Cold War military-industrial complex and its politics (Stroupe, 610); George Landow offers the more plausible argument that scholars of literature, as well as authors, feel that new information technology "threatens . . . their power and position" (Landow, *Hypertext 2.0: The Convergence of Contemporary Critical Theory and Technology* [Baltimore: Johns Hopkins University Press, 1997]).

61. Lanham, 6.

62. Dobrin, 308.

63. In Winkler.

64. Birkerts, 3, 15, 139. Such critics are most often embattled professional writers more fearful of losing the prerogatives of their profession in a world where the modalities of remunerative authorship on the Web is not yet clear than impassioned defenders of the print experience. As ever, Birkerts is exemplary for demonstrating the extent to which anxiety over "the death of the book" is so often misplaced anxiety over "the death of how I want to make a living": "These large-scale changes bode ill for authorship, at least of the kind I would pursue. There are, we know this, fewer and fewer readers for serious works. Publishers are increasingly reluctant to underwrite the publication of a book that will sell only a few thousand copies. But very few works of any artistic importance sell more than that" (28).

65. McKenzie, 43.

# 8 Historical Perspectives on the Book and Information Technology

Gregory Crane

Classicists have an unusual perspective on many of the arguments about the history of the book. Many critics who lament the passing of the literate world into which they were born often frame their concerns in such narrow historical terms that they can unintentionally trivialize the changes that they fear are overwhelming us.

Clifford Stoll's *Silicon Snake Oil* fiercely critiques the virtual existence offered by the brave new electronic world, but almost all of these criticisms were leveled at book culture as well. Sven Birkerts's *Gutenberg Elegies* has established itself as a focal point for resistance but, telling as many of his points may be and sympathetic as I find many of his intellectual values, his work seems to delight in its limitations.

The intellectual world upon which he draws scarcely extends beyond the lifetime of a single human being. The earliest book that he cites in this collection of essays was published in 1929—not a single publication was old enough to have forced its way into the public domain. *The Gutenberg Elegies* laments the putative end of an intellectual world that is anchored in the past two generations—precisely that period in which film, radio and television have savagely eroded the culture of the book and in which book culture has attracted many who enjoy the position of marginalized intellectuals surrounded by the barbarian hordes of "mall culture."

Those who have most closely studied both new technology and the broader history of intellectual life seem, for the most part, less fretful about the future. Richard Lanham rightly traces modern debates about the role of technology back to the arguments of rhetoric vs. truth that centered around Isocrates and Plato in the fourth century BC. George Landow and Janet Murray, trained as experts in Victorian literature and immersed in the textuality of the nineteenth century, have emerged among the most sympathetic and serious analysts of hypertext. Jerome McGann, an eminent textual critic and thus expert in the most genuinely (and constructively) conservative practice of the humanities, has found in the new medium both a way to publish the works of Dante Gabriel Rossetti more

effectively than he could in print and a challenge to the ways in which we conceive of textuality itself. Jerome McGann's colleague at the University of Virginia, John Unsworth,
the founding editor of *Post-Modern Culture,* is, as director of the Institute for Advanced
Technology in the Humanities, actively supporting a range of humanistic research projects that range from classical antiquity to modern culture.

As a specialist in classical Greek literature and especially as a classicist at a university
largely dominated by engineers, MD–Ph.D.s, social scientists and "humanists" deeply
suspicious of the label "humanism" and of all traditional culture, I understand the position of marginalized intellectual all too well, but I am, in many ways, more interested in
the general public than I am in my professional colleagues. Those of us who have been so
fortunate as to win permanent jobs depend for our continued existence upon a consensus among non-professionals that what we do matters. The National Endowment for the
Humanities almost vanished, in large measure because many American citizens believed,
and not wholly without reason, that humanists had little interest in, and even disdain for,
those outside of the academy. Decimated, the NEH survived, but its troubles suggested
that we in the humanities must reestablish the relationship between our work and society
at large. Whatever the fate of the NEH and whether or not we depend upon the NEH's
support for our research, the NEH drew fire that was aimed squarely at all of us in the
humanities. Electronic media—whether self-standing artifacts like CD-ROMs and Digital Video Disks or distributed hypertexts like the World Wide Web—constitute a new
vernacular, much as Italian or Chaucer's English. It is our responsibility, as humanists, not
only to master this vernacular but to foster its development. The greatest challenge that
we face over the coming years is the need to adapt ourselves to the new media and the
new media to those intellectual and cultural values that we cherish.

Classicists as a group certainly have their share of techno-angst and the achievements
of our discipline in adapting digital tools to our use have not assuaged the fears that many
of our colleagues still share. Nevertheless, those trained in classics who have thought
seriously about the technology often seem much less anxious than many of their postmodern colleagues: a generation ago, the classicist Eric Havelock earned a prominent position beside Marshall McLuhan and Walter Ong as a pioneer in the study of media and
culture. More recently, Jay Bolter and James O'Donnell have emerged among the most
creative analysts of the changes around us. Richard Lanham's insights derive much of their
strength from his sense of history and from this recognition that debates about electronic
media now raging continue discussions underway since the continuous European tradition of literate culture took shape in the fifth-century BC.

The enthusiasm with which many classicists have embraced the new technology has several causes. First, the book—the physical object with two covers and rectangular pages bound together—has been grossly misrepresented. The codex is a relatively late product and our earliest references to the codex appear in the poems of Martial during the late first century CE, after the Greeks and the Romans had built up more than eight hundred years of an intensely felt textual culture. The great library of Alexandria, when in the first century BC it caught fire for the first time, was therefore stuffed full of scrolls and not books.

Virgil, writing in the first century BC, was one of the most influential intellectual figures and successful poets who ever lived. He produced poems that played to a passionate immersion in and commitment to literary texts. But Virgil lived in a world of scrolls—he probably never saw a book in his entire life. I have yet to see any cogent argument that the arrival of the codex improved the quality of literature or made possible more keenly felt literary sensibilities than those that we can, by dint of much hard work and skill, recover from the work of Virgil or the Hellenistic Greek poets who preceded him. I have no desire to play off Virgil against Dante, or Homer against Shakespeare or to argue that the cultures of the codex or that of print are inferior to that which was in place when the codex first began to appear. But I see no basis at all for an argument that book culture per se allowed human beings to reach higher levels of literary creativity or to participate in a richer intellectual world than the written culture that preceded it.

Second, it is not at all clear that the effects of the codex upon reading were, on the balance, at all good for that intense linear reading which we celebrate as the starting point of literary experience. The comparison between printed book and later twentieth century computer screen has not carried us very far. The real comparison should be between the codex and the scroll.

It would be interesting to perform experiments comparing the experience of readers working through a continuous text, from beginning to end, in a codex and in a continuous scroll. It would not be easy to design a convincing experiment that probed these differences if all of the participants in this experiment had grown up in book cultures: we would have to compare the impressions of those who grew up handling scrolls to those whose parents had, as impressionable children, listened to their own parents read codices to them in bed. I suspect that a published essay called "The Aristotle Elegies," lamenting the fall of that scroll culture which the great Athenian intellectual had helped to define, would have found a sympathetic audience in the second century CE.

The codex was successful not for literary but for utilitarian reasons. First, the book, with its flat pages laid on top of one another, takes up less space than a scroll: codices take up less "shelf-space." Second, because codices readily support writing on both sides, they could store roughly twice as much information per square inch. Despite the wastage that comes from having bottom and top margins and empty space near the binding, codices are essentially a double-density storage medium—a savings especially significant before the development of inexpensive paper. Third, even in manuscript form and before the settled conventions of running headers, standard page numbers, tables of contents, indices and other aids solidified in the age of print, books are far better suited to random access than scrolls. It is hard to imagine that you could ever unroll a lengthy scroll as quickly as you can flip the pages of the codex.

It was the codex that encouraged a culture of rapid, silent reading. Readers of a scroll expected to read slowly. Words were run together and paragraphs were not marked—storage media was expensive but processing time was less of a concern because readers expected to spend more time working their way through the document: silent (and thus rapid) reading was a relatively late development. Readers who sounded out the words before them experienced the text both visually and aurally—thus drawing upon more than one sense at a time and anticipating a learning practice that cognitive scientists encourage. Full-blown book culture—which married the codex to mechanical reproduction—produced a world of vast documents, quickly written and even more quickly consumed. Concentrated, self-consciously literary novelists such as Proust, James and, of course, Joyce, wrote against this tendency, saturating the ultimate codex genre, the novel, with that density of meaning and of reference which we can find already in Virgil (and, indeed, in the haunting prose of Thucydides). The great novelists were thus renewing, in a different medium and genre, that literary intensity which writing allows us to trace thousands of years further back. They were trying to charge the non-linear and rapidly-read codex with the literary texture that emerged with the texture of the linear and slowly-read scroll.

The preeminent literary genre of the book may well be the novel, but the preeminent genre of the book is the utilitarian reference tool—the accountant's ledger, the maintenance manual and, above all, the bulging filing cabinet (itself nothing less than a mass of fluid codices). To sacralize the book as an object in the defense of a literary or cultural ideal is thus a losing cause for two reasons. First, the book itself is part of the problem, for if we accept the book in place of the scroll, then we have reinforced that utilitarian logic that leads to the electronic hypertext as an entirely logical and defensible continuation.

Second, if we, as defenders of books and book culture, do not take into consideration the culture that precedes the book, we open ourselves to severe criticisms on both scientific and traditional grounds. Not only is our argument profoundly flawed but, if our understanding of history and literature is so shallow that we are oblivious to almost a millennium of Greco-Roman literary achievement, then how can we expect anyone else to respect the past? We certainly cannot all spend years studying Greek and Latin, but if we entirely ignore Greco-Roman antiquity, we weaken the cause of all cultural memory and of that culture to which the scroll, the codex and the printed books have all contributed.

Media constrain the intellectual paths that we can and do pursue, but human creativity can sooner or later exploit the potential of any medium flexible enough to permeate a society. Different forms of media are relatively neutral: the printed book gave us not only the novel and the massive reading audience but tabloids that cynically play to the seamiest instincts that North American mass culture can tolerate—and academic publications just as cynically aimed at reviewers and at the tenure/promotion/better jobs etc. that these reviewers will confer. To attribute such phenomena to a relentless technological determinism is a self-defeating strategy, because it can justify the role of querulously superior bystander.

But if media are relatively neutral with respect to one another and susceptible to development in various ways, media themselves are not neutral. Once we transfer our ideas from the wetware between our ears and inscribe them in some artificial medium, whether a Sumerian clay tablet or an expert system for analyzing Greek morphology, storing our ideas over time and transmitting them to people whom we have never physically seen, we have entered a new world. The most cogent issues that we face today were already striking sparks classical Greece—long before computers, printing presses or the codex. On the one hand, classical literary texts exhibit a technological boosterism comparable with which the capital hungry modern entrepreneur should sympathize. The lyric poet Pindar, a professional well paid for his skills and for the celebrity that he could confer, begins one poem by thumbing his nose at the sculptors with whom he competed for contracts to perpetuate the memory of the rich and successful:

> I am not a sculptor, to make statues that stand motionless on the same pedestal. Sweet song, go on every merchant-ship and rowboat that leaves Aegina, and announce that Lampon's powerful son Pytheas won the victory garland for the pancratium at the Nemean games, a boy whose cheeks do not yet show the tender season that is mother to the dark blossom. (Pind. Nem. 5.1–6 [tr. Svarlien])

The famous athlete may erect a statue commemorating his deeds at Delphi and Olympia—these sites were, by the end of antiquity, crammed with statues and functioned very much like modern sports halls of fame—but statutes, however imposing, can only be in one place at one time. When Pindar composed a poem, the text generally consisted of a few hundred words that could be readily copied and that could spread on every ship, great and small, throughout a Greek speaking world that extended from Spain to Russia. Neither Pindar nor his patrons had ever heard of copyright—nor is it likely that they would have found much to commend this modern concept. Poet and patron alike depended for their success on the furious, uncontrolled circulation of the written text. The poet accumulated wealth by receiving generous gifts in exchange for each poem, and the cumulative fame of prior work lead to the next job—in this regard, the poet earned money much more like a modern architect than author. The patron paid the poet because he wanted his name to be known as broadly as possible in space and as deeply as possible in time to come—in the case of Lampon, surely one of the more successful investments in history, since we still possess the poem above, recalling Lampon and his son Pytheas each time that we read it.

The tragic drama *Prometheus Bound* is even more audacious. Zeus has punished Prometheus for giving mortals the gift of fire. At the center of this play stands a speech in which Prometheus recounts the many benefits that he had conferred on mortals:

> But I do not speak of this; for my tale would tell you nothing except what you know. Still, listen to the miseries that beset mankind—how they were witless before and I made them have sense and endowed them with reason. I will not speak to upbraid mankind but to set forth the friendly purpose that inspired my blessing.
>
> First of all, though they had eyes to see, they saw to no avail; they had ears, but they did not understand; but, just as shapes in dreams, throughout their length of days, without purpose they wrought all things in confusion. They had neither knowledge of houses built of bricks and turned to face the sun nor yet of work in wood; but dwelt beneath the ground like swarming ants, in sunless caves. They had no sign either of winter or of flowery spring or of fruitful summer, on which they could depend but managed everything without judgment, until I taught them to discern the risings of the stars and their settings, which are difficult to distinguish.
>
> Yes, and numbers, too, chiefest of sciences, I invented for them, and the combining of letters, creative mother of the Muses' arts, with which to hold all things in memory. (Aesch. PB 445–461)

Ostentatiously turning its back on earlier visions of a glorious heroic age (such as we see in Hesiod and Homer), this fifth-century Prometheus envisions a near Hobbesian early man whose life is nasty, brutish and short: before Prometheus, men had been help-less, utterly at the mercy of their environment. The speech goes on at some length cata-loguing the various technical skills for which Prometheus was responsible, including (in the passage quoted above) architecture, an astronomically based calendar, and (in subse-quent sections) domestication of animals, sea faring, medicine, and metallurgy. At the core of Prometheus' gifts stand numbers, mathematics and writing—the mother of the Muses' arts, which holds all things in memory.

Fifth-century Greeks were acutely sensitive to the impact that an artificial storage sys-tem had exerted upon their culture. Their society remained, for the most part, oral contracts were pronounced before witnesses rather than signed and writing occupied a position closer to computer programming (i.e., a technical skill, fully mastered by a rel-ative few) than modern writing (i.e., a fundamental skill which society expects, at least, all its members to acquire). Greeks did not have to be literature themselves to recognize that writing was something new and different.

Certainly, the power of (then) modern information technology provoked, in classical Athens, anxiety as well as triumphalist visions. Euripides' Phaedra committed suicide but left behind a letter falsely accusing Hippolytus, her stepson, of sexually assaulting her (Eur. Hipp. 885–886):

Theseus, Phaedra's husband, takes the message at face value. Hippolytus, confronted by a written message but, unable to interrogate the writer (Eur. Hipp. 1021ff.), is unable to defend himself. His father, to the dismay of the chorus, puts more credence in the un-interrogated writing of Phaedra than in a solemn oath sworn by Hippolytus (Eur. Hipp. 1036–1037), thus dramatizing the dangers of transferring authority from speech and to contemporary information technology—we might compare the modern image of an in-nocent trapped by misinformation that had "gotten into the computer." Writing both sub-verted and conferred authority: written law was, at least in the letter, fixed and, in theory, could be reviewed by all. Writing thus reduced the leeway of judges and of those who were expert in traditional wisdom. At the same time, writing allowed new laws to take on an instant authority that only usage over time could confer in a traditional society. Someone embroiled in a court case could appeal to the fact that a law was still agraphos, unwritten, to defend himself (e.g., Andoc. 1.85–86), but Athenians, who, like contem-porary Americans, were remarkable for their reliance upon new media, were also deeply skeptical of these technologies. The Thucydidean Perikles, in his idealizing description of Athenian society, boasts that his fellow-citizens pay particular attention to those laws that are unwritten (agraphos: Thuc. 2.37.3). Elsewhere we hear that Perikles was especially scrupulous to respect these unwritten laws which constituted the traditional culture and morality of Greek culture (Lys. 6.10).

Sophocles' Antigone, of course, turns upon the ambiguities of written law and on the overzealous legislation of an (initially at least) progressive leader. Creon begins by following the most enlightened and indeed radical strand of Greek political thought when he asserts that he will subordinate his own personal interests and affections to those of the city-state (Soph. Ant. 163–210), but he ultimately wilts before Antigone and her stubborn defense of "unwritten laws" (Soph. Ant. 450ff.). The play critiques modern ideas (especially those of Protagoras) and the modern technology of writing at once.

Thucydides, the Athenian writer who did much to invent not only history but also the academic monograph, offers perhaps the most sustained and interesting example of that excitement which some Greeks felt for the new technology of his time. Herodotus published what may have been the first "book-length" prose work in the continuous tradition of Western tradition, but Thucydides played D. W. Griffith to Herodotus' Edison, for, just as Griffith is credited with inventing film as a medium in its own right and not an imitation of stage, Thucydides produced a prose work that was conceived as a written document rather than a script for, or transcript of, performance. Thus, after a description of his methodology and of the pains that he took in collecting his data, Thucydides contrasts his work with that of his predecessors:

> The absence of romance in my history will, I fear, detract somewhat from its interest; but if it be judged useful by those inquirers who desire an exact knowledge of the past as an aid to the interpretation of the future, which in the course of human things must resemble if it does not reflect it, I shall be content. In fine, have written my work, not as an essay which is to win the applause of the moment, but as a possession for all time. (Thuc. 1.22.4)

Thucydides did not write for performance—perhaps to underscore this point, he wrote many passages that are so complex and impenetrable in language that ancient speakers of Greek (like Dionysus of Halikarnassos) could scarcely understand them. Thucydides wrote prose that needs to be studied and that no general audience could ever grasp from a single, oral performance. He defied the glibness of style and the laxness of method that he attributed to those who had gone before him, creating a refined prose work designed to withstand generations of close study. And in this he was spectacularly successful. Thucydides' *History of the Peloponnesian War* remains a staple not only in ancient history, but in political philosophy and international relations as well. Robert Strassler's 1996 Landmark edition of *Thucy-*

*dides,* undertaken as a labor of love by an investment banker, became an unexpected hit, striking a chord of interest that no one—least of all Strassler—had anticipated.

But if Thucydides affected an austerely intellectual rigor and refused to appeal to the popular culture of his time, he nevertheless saw in his written work the source for an emotional engagement that would exceed in intensity and outlast cheap sensationalism. The Funeral Oration which Thucydides attributes to Pericles presents an idealized vision of Athens. Perikles does not claim that Athenian temporal power would be permanent—he does not even anticipate a thousand year Reich. He does, however, boast that Athens' reputation would never die. At the climax of his oration, delivered in honor of those who had died fighting Sparta and its allies (and the direct cultural ancestor of the Gettysburg Address, Pericles articulates his vision of Athenian greatness:

> For this offering of their lives made in common by them all they each of them individually received that renown which never grows old, and for a sepulchre, not so much that in which their bones have been deposited, but that noblest of shrines wherein their glory is laid up to be eternally remembered upon every occasion on which deed or story shall fall for its commemoration. For heroes have the whole earth for their tomb; and in lands far from their own, where the column with its epitaph declares it, there is enshrined in every breast a record unwritten with no tablet to preserve it, except that of the heart. (Thuc. 2.43)

The above passage is remarkable for its apparent dismissal of writing. Athenian glory only has real existence insofar as it penetrates individual hearts and as real human beings emotionally embrace the memory of Athens. Written documents themselves are nothing. Human recognition—and especially a recognition that includes heart as well as head—is the only true form of glory.

Nevertheless, there is no contradiction between the austerity of Thucydides' own rejection of sensationalism and the vision laid out by the Thucydidean Pericles. Athens' glory will endure over time and it will fire the minds of those who come after, but largely because Thucydides has composed, in cool written form, his best exposition of what really happened. The written history, subject to scrutiny and criticism for all time, would be the seed from which profound emotion would grow. And, indeed, this is precisely what has happened, for it is through Thucydides that we still must largely view the Athens of empire and democracy.

In Thucydides' view, the austerity of his work was not so much a rejection of passion and emotion as it was a tactical retreat from sensationalism and a foundation for emotions that would be deeper and more firmly rooted. Thucydides, for all the dour realism that his writing affects, pursues an optimistic intellectual goal that is progressive in the truest sense of the word.

But if the methodology that Thucydides espouses in the opening of his history, the vision of Athens that his Pericles unfolds after one year of war, and even Athenian material power point towards a progressive vision of history, events themselves follow a more ambiguous course. Athens, the sea-power and financial center, falls to the supposedly obsolescent Sparta and its allies. A terrible plague claims Pericles among its victims, and venal leaders who cannot maintain Athenian greatness arise. The historian himself makes it clear that he can describe, but not assuage, such problems as plague (2.48.3) and the collapse into barbarium (3.82.2).

Above all, the austere utilitarianism with which the (otherwise unknown) Diodotus prevents Athens from committing genocide at Mitylene degenerates into the brutal reasoning and pitiless slaughter on the island of Melos. Neither writing nor money—two fundamental indices of fifth-century modernism and keys to Athenian culture—could prevent a perceived social collapse as war dragged on for almost thirty years.

Thucydides lived through a period of bitter disillusion that the British elites after the "Great War" or their American counterparts after Vietnam would quickly reckon. Plato spent his life trying to resolve the problems that Thucydides articulates in his history, above all the notion that "might makes right" and the justice is an ideological illusion. His greatest work, the Republic, takes its departure from the crass power politics and brutal realism that we find in Thucydides' Melian dialogue and establishes for justice a value that transcends any utilitarian measures. Born into the highest reaches of Athenian society, Plato grew up as the values which had defined his class weakened and an international, in many ways attractive, society, centuries old, seemed to be dissolving around him. The central problem for Plato was the same as that which ultimately confronted Thucydides: the technology and social "progress" of the fifth century failed to sustain itself. But where Thucydides was a grown man before war tore his world apart, Plato was born into a world of slaughter, plague and anxiety. He never experienced a "Periclean age," in which Athens, however anxious about the future, dominated the Greek world. He grew up among the intellectual wreckage of a "lost generation." Plato, in other words, confronted a world readily comparable to that of the late twentieth century industrialized democracies.

Plato also exhibits a much more nuanced view of contemporary information technology than his older contemporary. Just as Plato, in the opening of *The Republic* recapitulates ideas about power politics that we find in Thucydides, he summarizes in the Phaedrus the same optimism that we can trace in the *Prometheus Bound* and in *Thucydides*.

Plato's Socrates recounts the story of Theuth, an Egyptian Prometheus, who invented numbers and arithmetic and geometry and astronomy, also draughts and dice, and, most important of all, letters (Plat. Phaedr. 274d):

> The story goes that Thamus said many things to Theuth in praise or blame of the various arts, which it would take too long to repeat; but when they came to the letters, "This invention, O king," said Theuth, "will make the Egyptians wiser and will improve their memories; for it is a drug (pharmakon) of memory and wisdom that I have discovered." (Plat. Pheadr. 274e)

This, of course, is essentially the same argument that we encountered in *Prometheus Bound*. Writing constitutes artificial memory and extends the range of human intelligence. It accompanies the other applied arts and that culture on which upon which these applied arts depend. Thucydides would apply this notion far more subtly, demonstrating in his history concretely how a scientific, written account of events could immortalize the events of his time and extend the subsequent memory of humankind. Plato, however, only introduces the conventional boasts of writing so that the Egyptian king Thamus can critique them:

But Thamus replied,

> Most ingenious Theuth, one man has the ability to beget arts, but the ability to judge of their usefulness or harmfulness to their users belongs to another;
>
> and now you, who are the father of letters, have been led by your affection to ascribe to them a power the opposite of that which they really possess. For this invention will produce forgetfulness in the minds of those who learn to use it, because they will not practice their memory. Their trust in writing, produced by external characters which are no part of themselves, will discourage the use of their own memory within them. You have invented a drug (pharmakon) not of memory, but of reminding; and you offer your pupils the appearance of wisdom, not true wisdom, for they will read many things without instruction and will therefore seem to know many things, when they are for the most part ignorant and hard to get along with, since they are not wise, but only appear wise. (Plat. Phaedr. 274e–275a)

Jacques Derrida made this passage of the Phaedrus famous in literary studies: the ambiguities of the Greek word are very similar to those of Greek pharmakon, and Derrida was able to use the issues involved here to help dramatize the ambiguities of language. This paragraph, for all its apparent simplicity, is extremely dense, alluding backwards to a range of themes from earlier Greek literature, while at the same time anticipating the fundamental objection to modern media. On the one hand, writing externalizes knowledge, giving that knowledge an existence outside the human brain and thus allowing that knowledge to outlive frail biological wetware, but knowledge externalized, available on demand for casual access, never wholly absorbed or internalized in any one mind, becomes information—a commodity that anyone can acquire, rather than knowledge, much less wisdom or the studied and cultivated ability to apply knowledge judiciously. Plato is directly attacking that optimism that we can see in Thucydides, but the attack is tactical rather than strategic. Thucydides envisions a world in which his austere written history will excite human wonder and passion. Plato looks to a world of couch potatoes who cannot remember what passed through their minds a day before and of slick consultants who market a veneer of expertise.

Thucydides and Plato differ in their emphases: Thucydides, for all the overt pessimism that runs through much of his history, in his practices implies an optimism over the value, if not the utility, of written history: whether or not we learn from the past to control the future, we can lose ourselves in the reasoned contemplation of Athens and its struggles. Plato focuses instead upon the effect of writing as artificial memory, as knowledge disembodied from the human brain. If Plato focuses upon the negative consequences of writing and thus pushes in a direction different from that of Thucydides, the contrast emerges precisely because both writers share the same values: each measures the value of writing according to the impact that it has upon the reader.

The shared values of Thucydides and Plato animate the best of the critique aimed against information technology, twenty five hundred years ago and today. But, of course, any argument about technology derives its force from some larger context, in this case the general purpose of education. Two attitudes have contended furiously for as long as we can trace arguments about education. According to one position, conventionally associated with Plato, knowledge has value in and of itself. This argument can take an abstract form in which some transcendent Truth—perhaps scientific, perhaps philosophical, perhaps religious—is the source of all value. Conversely, this argument can be relentlessly practical: education is valuable because it produces useful knowledge, i.e., knowledge that allows us to better master our environment, to preserve or restore our health, to satisfy our physical needs and appetites of all kinds etc. These two variations of this attitude are, of course, generally related—they struggle ceaselessly, for example, within the U.S. National Science Foundation, as the proponents of basic and applied science compete for resources. Nevertheless, for the pure mathematician and the engineer, information technology—writing, print, electronic storage—is essential because it allows us to create shared structures of knowledge far greater than any one brain could encompass.

According to the second attitude, education has value not so much because of the knowledge that it produces as because of the impact that it exerts upon human character. This position, like its counterpart, has both an abstract and an applied wing. All systems for the perfection of human character, whether the Christian quest for salvation, the Confucian drive towards self-improvement or the Buddhist yearning for transcendence, order the disparate impulses and conditions of human life in a grand quest for some transcendent project. In its more applied form, this education leads to a republican rhetorical tradition in which neither abstract truth nor even, contrary to general perception, short term successes are the object.

The republican rhetorical tradition has little to do with bamboozling yokels; it assumes, instead, a contest of words and eloquence among equals, all of whom quickly learn the cheap tricks of argumentation and who, as a group, set de facto standards for discourse. The republican rhetorical tradition, from Pericles and Cicero to Lincoln and Churchill, challenges its practitioners to perfect their command of language and their understanding of the values that their fellows share. Such speakers depend for the success both upon the eloquence of what they say and upon the moral authority which they accumulate over time. At their best, they redefine their societies, winning consent for bold ideas and for shared efforts that renew and invigorate their societies. Promulgating drivel or barbarism may succeed in the short term but ultimately undermines the republican system, leading to chaos or an authoritarian society, both of which squelch the rough give-and-take among political peers.

Of course, there are few who purely embody either position, but Plato is remarkable precisely because he manages at once to champion both education as the source for truth and as the engine for moral perfection. (Postmodern society, conversely, comes to close to rejecting both, insofar as it dismisses notions of transcendent truth and undercuts any notion of moral perfection.) The arguments that swirl about the transformation of the book depend largely upon the dichotomy between these two attitudes. Those who most enthusiastically champion new technology often do so because their eyes have fixed upon the expanded edifice of knowledge that we can construct in this brave new digital world. Whether their visions focus more upon the beauty of a vast new shared society of knowledge or upon the material benefits to society (or themselves) that such new knowledge may bring, for them artificial memory and, ultimately, artificial intelligence are attractive precisely because they separate elements of intellection from the warm tissues of the human body.

We humanists, insofar as we are humanists, belong to the second tradition. Ultimately, the ideas that we pursue do not add to our scientific understanding or produce new mechanisms for the manipulation of the physical world. Insofar as we are humanists, we have forsworn such tangible and practical goals. Our ideas have no value if they do not, as ideas, command attention and interest of other living beings. Insofar as we are humanists, we have also forsworn theology and do not, in our professional capacities, further the awesome religious movements that have proven uniquely capable of moving humanity. Insofar as we are humanists, we dedicate ourselves to the life of the mind, whether Aristotle's life of contemplation or Cecil's struggles in the forum of our own time. None of these categories is, in practice, absolute. Those of us who study past cultures must also contribute to our knowledge of the subject, while our colleagues in science and engineering believe that character and intellect must develop together. If we in the humanities do not passionately explore our fields, then we are not true humanists but priests of a static dogma. If scientists and engineers do not develop moral or rhetorical skills, they will become corrupt or ineffective. Nevertheless, the federal government does not invest vast sums of money into scientific research to develop character or to foster civic republicanism, and the production of knowledge in the humanities matters only insofar as it affects, directly or indirectly, the undergraduate curriculum or some audience beyond the specialists.

Digital libraries have captured the imagination of researchers in classics, old and young, conservative and radical, for over a generation: after receiving the endorsement of an international body of scholars, the Thesaurus Linguae Graecae (TLG) at UC Irvine began in 1972 to build a database of all early Greek literature—for us, the TLG allows us to explore our core data in ways that had been physically impossible and, insofar as we value the production of knowledge, we have long admired the TLG and its electronically transmogrified books. Nevertheless, the real value of this new technology lies less in how it enhances our research and the sheltered conversation of specialist with specialist as it allows us to redefine the relationship between researchers and the rest of the world. We need to ask two basic questions, one quantitative, the other qualitative: what effect does the new technology have on the raw number of those intellectually engaged with antiquity (or in any area of the humanities) and on the quality of that engagement. If no one were to study some area in the humanities except specialists, then the game is up for that area and its days as identifiable sub-discipline are probably numbered. On the other hand, it is not clear what value we offer if we worry only about engaging non-specialists and reduce ourselves to entertainment: if we subordinate ourselves wholly to popular tastes and do not challenge our audience to rise above the passivity of network television or even mass produced weekly magazines, then we may add to the quantity of content available but we will become just another category of programming. Our goal must be to demonstrate that culture extends beyond the market-driven popular culture of our time and that even the Discovery Channel and *Time Magazine* constitute can do no more than arouse interest in larger topics that require more extensive thought.

The quantitative argument is easy to address. A reasonably successful academic publication might sell 1,000 copies, most of which will normally sit unused in university libraries or faculty offices. The potential audience on the Internet is at least 10,000,000 machines, four orders of magnitude larger—since the average sales of academic publications is certainly not rising and the number of people with access to the World Wide Web is certainly not shrinking, this ratio is going to increase during the foreseeable future. But even if only an infinitesimal percentage of machines ever visit any given site, the number can readily dwarf that of print: as of fall 1997, the WWW version of the Perseus digital library on ancient Greco-Roman culture attracts upwards of 7,000 visitors per day. Only half of the identifiable Internet addresses come from higher education (*.edu). A survey of the access logs and of the mail that we receive makes it clear that we are not only reaching conventional academics but grade school children and adult learners resuscitating their knowledge of Greek and Latin. We are reaching office parks, rural homes, schools, and even military installations. We have users not only in Europe and the English-speaking world, but in Japan and South America—where students of Greco-Roman culture had had little contact with experts on North America and Europe. Virtually nothing that we, as academics, publish will find its way into the Walden Books chains or the general school and public library system. Everything that we now publish freely on the Web is immediately available in a substantial percentage of classrooms, public libraries and homes. But, of course, simply making available documents designed for a print medium and written by professors for other professors will not get us very far. Redesigning our publications so that they can reach this wider audience is the major challenge that confronts the next generation of humanists.

But as soon as we focus on adapting ourselves to this new audience so that we can promote the quantitative increases in our audience that all of us in the humanities desperately need, we must decide on what our audience will be and what kind of experience we hope to foster. The greatest danger here is transferring habits of thought and usage that are the products of print technology into an electronic environment with different constraints and possibilities.

Technology, even when revolutionary, generally has an immediate impact upon the tactical decisions that we make (e.g., how to manage a ship powered by coal rather than wind) and it may ultimately have strategic implications (e.g., the need to maintain a world wide network of coaling bases) but it need not affect the overall goals involved (e.g., control of the sea). Writing made possible the historical study of literature, qualitatively changing the way in which we could interact with the distant past. Subsequent advances in information technology such as the codex, printing and electronic systems have revolutionized the way in which we study literatures of the past, but the Alexandrian scholars of the third century BC, transported to the early twentieth-century Library of Congress or a digital library project would quickly recognize what their later colleagues were doing.

Nevertheless, if the possibilities of a new technology allow us to redefine how we go about pursuing our larger goals and indeed to rethink which ideal goals we can reasonably pursue, then we must look for the constraints of a prior technology that we have internalized into our present work lest we confuse bugs in the system with features. Classicists, for example, rarely write anything for a wide audience: the university presses that have published our major ideas as books and brokered our careers prod us to write for a general audience but, in classics, this largely means that we translate the Greek and Latin, reduce our footnotes, and explain some of our ideas—all fairly superficial changes. Of course, we have very little reason to change the way that we write: virtually no one outside the academy will ever see any of our publications and our real audience consists of our colleagues in classics or (if we are very ambitious) one or more adjacent academic specialties (e.g., philosophers who have an interest in Plato). But many of us, enmeshed in the system of publication, tenure, promotion and the parochial recognition of our peers, not only overlook the fact that such isolation renders our field untenable in the long run but even perceive our isolation not as a terrible weakness and danger to our field but as a sign of our intellectual rigor and purity. Throughout academia, the communities that we establish become hostile enclaves, their inhabitants eager to drive out anyone not fluent in the local patois.

The study of classical literature—and this holds true for classical literatures in China, India, and the Islamic world—introduces its audience into a complex, interlocking network of documents. First, reading classical literatures—Greco-Roman, Chinese, Islamic—requires mastery of a demanding language no longer in current usage. This linguistic mastery, challenging as it may be, constitutes only the initiation into a textual world that may be small in size—all of Greco-Roman literature can be stored in a single large book-case—but that no human being can fully master. Second, classical literatures that have flourished and elicited study over centuries generally rely upon a core of exceptionally successful works that accomplish two radically distinct, and often opposed, goals at once. On the one hand, they can appeal to those with little knowledge of the field—Homer, Greek Tragedy and Plato, for example, continue to be read in English by audiences with little knowledge of ancient Greek culture; Latin literature may not have quite the same appeal in English translation, but high school students continue to struggle through authors such as Virgil and Cicero.

Students can encounter these works at an early age and enjoy them—I learned early on in my teaching career from student evaluations, for example, that whatever my audience thought of my lecture style, ideas, exams, grading etc., they almost invariably came to enjoy and admire Greek drama. Nevertheless, these works can be read and reread throughout a lifetime: a reader intellectually engaged in the *Iliad* or *The Republic* can take away new insights from each fresh reading from the age of seventeen through advanced age.

Third, classical literatures are cumulative: each time that we devote a major effort to mastering any one author, we enhance our understanding of many other texts as well. This is certainly true about any literature—the more we know about the cultural and literary context, the more ways in which we can view an individual work. The more we know about Homer, the better we can understand not only Virgil but Plato as well, each of whom wrote in the shadow of the *Iliad* and the *Odyssey*. The Homeric Epics stand at the beginning of European literature and have no surviving antecedents, but the more we learn about archaic society, the better we can understand these poems as well. Professional classicists can expect to increase their intellectual range, studying new texts for the first time, rereading well-known authors with wholly new sets of questions, and tangibly deepening the experience of reading any given text. Some texts, such as the Homeric Epics or Greek Drama, are so rich and complex that sensitive readers can study them from childhood to old age and still continue to learn something with each rereading. Even before vast bodies of information and ideas from archaeology, literary theory, anthropology, sociology, art history, cognitive science, linguistics and other disciplines were available to challenge and transform the way that we study these texts, we had more than enough to support the life of the mind from childhood onwards.

Insofar as we only reach students from the ages of roughly eighteen to twenty-one, we are not living up to our larger mission. We need, of course, to teach students to think and to prepare them for their work in later life, but we must never confuse this aspect of our task with the task as a whole—our students (and their parents) already worry far too much about where they will be at twenty-five or thirty and not nearly enough about where they will be at forty, sixty or eighty. Ideally, we are providing our students with a foundation of knowledge upon which they can draw throughout their lives. Our students may well have little time in the years after they graduate for much besides establishing their careers and establishing families, but most will, sooner or later, begin to hunger for something beyond their daily lives. The BA in classics may later develop an interest in twentieth century Latin American literature or Japanese Film, but reading Homer should provide that BA with a sense of how to engage artistic creations in a disciplined fashion. Conversely, we need to be able to support an interest in our fields that arises long after college.

Book culture has served professional academics and intellectuals well—or at least those who have access to major libraries—but it has had much more limited success in helping a wider audience cultivate sustained interests over a long period of time. Public libraries, book clubs, mall bookstore chains and other outlets can only do so much. It is simply impracticable for most of those outside of a university environment to cultivate sustained areas of interest—nowhere outside of academia is that depth of print information available that can satisfy or stimulate a voracious interest in most subjects. A curious twelve-year-old living in an affluent suburb with a model public library can quickly exhaust its traditional printed resources on Human Evolution or Inner Asian History. Her thoughtful fifty-two-year-old compatriot may simply not have the time in her schedule to visit a library with any regularity. The growth of cable programming on history and science reflects the frustrated hunger for ideas and the limitations of the traditional print library in isolation.

Digital technologies such as CD-ROM (which let us disseminate hundreds of inter-linked books) and, of course, the Internet (through which we can reach millions of documents) are still in their infancy, but they are already beginning to redefine both what questions we academics can ask and, more importantly, who can ask what. We can, for example, see signs of a revolutionary change in one core area of classics. However well our students may learn classical languages in their student days, they have traditionally had little prospect of retaining these skills later in life, when their careers and family obligations allow them to broaden their interests and when they are often hungry to read works such as the *Iliad* or *The Republic* again. When our former students wish to return to Plato or Virgil, their linguistic knowledge has receded and they lack the support system to work their way through the language. Now, however, we provide not only raw access to many Greek and Latin texts on the World Wide Web but, more importantly, links between source texts and reading aids of various kinds, including lexica, grammars, commentaries, and morphological analyses of individual words. In some cases, we make faster and more widely available functions that could be done in a library or if the reader had assembled a bookshelf full of reference works.

In other cases, we allow readers to perform functions or ask questions that have never before been possible. While a great deal remains to be done, we have already been able to transform the way in which those beyond the academy can interact with Greek and Latin literature. Already, we have begun to hear from former classics majors who never expected to read Greek or Latin again and who are now able to consider resuscitating their knowledge. At the same time, we can now begin to tell our students that the work which they do at twenty will serve them again at forty or seventy. By changing the relationship between our core texts and the wider public, we change the value that these texts have for our traditional full-time students.

Millions of people may not develop a passionate interest in Greek and Latin language in the immediate future, but numbers are not the point, since the example of classical languages could be replicated throughout the intellectual world. Every discipline in the humanities has functions that books can only imperfectly support. Printed illustrations are very expensive: it is extremely difficult to study art from books because there are never enough pictures or enough details. Nor have the weaknesses of print publication enhanced the value of the original objects—in developing a visual database of Greek art we grew accustomed to curators fearful that digital images, if too good, could lower interest in the originals. All of our experience to date indicates that the opposite is true: the better the published documentation and the fuller the pictures, the greater the interest in the original. This is the positive side of the "papparazzo principle." Likewise, virtual reconstructions of vanished spaces, especially when these reconstructions are linked to digital libraries of information about the culture represented.

Our greatest goal as intellectuals is to create a seamless web of knowledge so that the curious may pursue their interests as far as their will and ability take them, rather than as far as traditional print publication has allowed. The viewer captivated by Branagh's *Hamlet* should be able to compare Branagh's *Hamlet* with that of Olivier and Zefferelli, survey the kinds of questions experts on the play have raised, even compare the First Folio edition with the version of the play as adopted in a given performance. The technical barriers to such a seamless web of knowledge are relatively modest. Simple access to academic publications now safely ensconced in research libraries will have little affect because these publications were written by specialists and for specialists. We must think long and hard about how we write, cultivating ways to make our ideas more readily accessible to an open-minded and interested public. Some ideas may be too complex, but often jargon and academic shorthand needlessly obscure our main points. Most publications may address minutiae and points of little general applicability, but the core issues that we are exploring and a large body of data should be readily accessible. Such a finely designed web of knowledge would indeed help both the general public and researchers. As one colleague observed, describing the function of an astrolabe in terms comprehensible to a twelve year old made the description more useful for non-specialist scholars unfamiliar with astrolabers.

As a humanist, I see little to lose from electronic media. We have, like medieval monks in their monasteries, cultivated and maintained a magnificent culture of learning in our universities, but it is our obligation to seize upon every means at our disposal not only to help our own research but also to reach that wider audience. Artificial dichotomies between paper and electronic media only distract us from the question of who does what. As a classicist, I know full well that print did not create a new kind of textuality that was qualitatively superior to what went before but allowed the experience of textuality to reach more people than scribal culture ever could. We may smile at the "sweatness and light" that Matthew Arnold saw at the core of intellectual life—we are more apt to challenge conventional pieties and focus upon uncomfortable truths. We certainly have a much broader range of interests than those of Arnold's Oxford, but our mission is the same: to reach out and communicate our ideas—and, equally important, our passionate engagement with those ideas to the widest possible audience. Our work has barely begun: while our large goals—to increase knowledge and to communicate what we have learned—may not change, we must, in the years to come, rethink every aspect of our work.

## Bibliography

Birkerts, S. 1994. *The Gutenberg Elegies.* Winchester, MA: Faber and Faber.

Crane, G. 1989. "Creon and the 'Ode to Man' in Sophocles' Antigone." *HSCP* 92: 103–116.

Flory, S. "Who Read Herodotus' Histories." *AJP* 101 (1980): 12–28, contains a nice discussion of the problems that Herodotus had to consider. The audience for such a huge book must have been small, and creating this work in the fifth century was something of a miracle and a selfless turning away from the mass audience. There is a lot of material to work with in this article.

Stoll, C. 1995. *Silicon Snake Oil: Second Thoughts on the Information Highway.* New York: Doubleday.

Thomas, R. 1989. *Oral Tradition and Written Record in Classical Athens.* Cambridge: Cambridge University Press.

# 9 Potholes on the Information Superhighway: Congress as a Publisher in Nineteenth-Century America

Oz Frankel

*You may read the President's message and read nothing about it there,*
*Nothing in the reports from the state department or treasury department . . . or in the daily papers, or the*
*weekly papers,*
*Or in the census returns or assessors' returns or prices current or any accounts of stock.*
—Walt Whitman, "Song for Occupations"

In April 1853, a minor political squabble broke out on the Senate floor over the publication of a report by John Russell Bartlett, the outgoing Commissioner of the Mexican Border Survey. Appointed by the Whig administration three years earlier, Bartlett was a Rhode Island publisher and co-founder of the American Ethnological Society. His tenure was marred by constant friction between this inexperienced explorer and a cast of hostile military subordinates. Recurrent allegations concerning mismanagement and incompetence were made, but the dispute that did the greatest injury to the commissioner's reputation touched directly upon the purpose of the survey. Bartlett was willing to compromise with the Mexican government over the location of the borderline, a stance that, according to his foes in Congress, amounted to betraying U.S. interests. Under these circumstances, he was quickly ousted by the new Democratic administration of President Franklin Pierce.[1]

Nevertheless, it was a Democrat, the Texan Senator Sam Houston, who proposed that despite his removal Bartlett still be authorized to compose a report on the geography, natural history and indigenous tribes on both sides of the Mexican border. Houston offered editorial guidelines for the prospective report—illustrating the extent to which lawmakers intervened in the production of such official documents. The Indian subject matter, he suggested, should follow the example set by Henry Schoolcraft's volumes on the history and current state of the Indian tribes of America—a mammoth project sanctioned by Congress a few years earlier. The natural history segment should take after another celebrated government publication—David Dale Owen's report on the geology of Lake Superior. Houston further suggested limiting the length of the report to one thousand pages bound in two volumes to be paid for from the contingency fund.[2]

The senator did not expect Bartlett's work to be anything other than an expensive document to produce. Nevertheless, the whole country from California to the Atlantic was awaiting the report, he claimed. "I think the character of this information is about as important as any that has come before the Senate."[3] To further his point he told his colleagues that in the distribution of Owen's geological report to remote parts of the union, many copies were stolen from the mailbags before reaching their destinations. Houston's story was met with skeptical chuckles in the chamber. Somehow, the deep concern displayed by this rugged frontiersman toward books and their publication (let alone toward a report penned by a political foe) seemed to be out of character. But Houston insisted. The thefts demonstrated the value of the work, and the great desire of the people for intelligence. Congress should print more books. He told his colleagues that he had practiced great care in sending the reports back home, spending hundreds of dollars to protect them in boxes at least until they reached his state. "I am not afraid of the mails being robbed in Texas," he declared with a certainty that prompted another round of laughter and provoked a fellow southerner to retort that the Carolinas would prefer not to be held answerable "for all the literary thieving or plagiarism that may take place."[4]

Houston's mannerism aside, in the three decades that preceded the Civil War, government, and especially Congress, sponsored a multitude of publishing ventures. Beginning in the late 1810s, Congress committed itself to fund serial publications that commemorated federal history with titles such as the *American State Papers, Annals of Congress,* and *The Works of President John Adams.* In the 1840s, large printing initiatives shifted to the exploration of the West. John C. Frémont's highly stylized narrative on his travels across the Rockies to California dazzled the public mind and heralded a new age of the "Great Reconnaissance" and territorial expansion. Frémont's early reports were enormously popular, issued in 10,000 copies each and republished by private printers to respond to the overwhelming demand. By the 1850s, the routine production of expedition accounts became a luxurious affair. Government issued large tomes bound in leather and embellished with exquisite woodcuts or astonishingly expensive hand-colored steel engravings. The most stupendous were the thirteen volumes on the natural history of the American West issued in the wake of a large cluster of expeditions to determine the route of the future transcontinental railroad.[5] The publication of these reports with their "life-like" depictions of western reptiles and shrubs cost twice as much as all of the actual expeditions combined—well over $200,000. In addition to such special enterprises, Congress issued the perpetually swelling body of petitions, memorials, resolutions and similar staples of legislative and executive ephemera.

This massive production and dissemination of printed matter seems to support the notion that providing information became a vital dimension of state power and the governing process in the nineteenth century. Other government actions also helped sustain networks for diffusing knowledge—for instance, the patronage of Washington publications that articulated the views of the administration, or the low postal rates, akin to a subsidy, which were guaranteed to all newspapers. One of the pillars of this government-sponsored information highway was the ability of congressmen to use the postal services free of charge, their so-called franking privilege.[6]

Writing in the context of the present anxieties (or jubilation) over the demise of print culture in the digital bowels of cyperspace, Geoffrey Nunberg recently pointed to the role of the state in what he otherwise calls the "phenomenology of information." His critique emphasizes two dimensions of "information" that are habitually (and significantly) overlooked: its historicity (as a modern creation) and materiality. Libraries, museums, daily newspapers, or, in our case, state publications—all received their standard configuration only in the nineteenth century. These informational genres impose a particular form of organization and registration on their content and yet concurrently strive for self-effacement. They endow "information" with its reified material properties such as uniformity or quantifiability. At the same time, the semantic features assigned to "information," such as objectivity and autonomy, reflect the power of the institutions that produce or underwrite (as well as the practices that surround) these informational tools, for instance the authority of the state or the daily ritual of purchasing and perusing a newspaper. One feature in the making of modern "information" has been, therefore, the suppression of explicit authorship and its substitution with institutional or phenomenal authorship.[7]

Indeed, the modern state created powerful apparati, purposefully devised to provide mass, uniform, transparent and ostensibly authorless facts, befitting "the age of information;" for instance, the national census. But rather than offer a master narrative on the ascendance of the state through the dispensation of knowledge, in what follows I will demonstrate the inevitable dissonance and cracks in the informative performances of the state in the context of my particular historical episode—mid-nineteenth century production of reports and other documents by the federal government. Two arguments are central to my analysis. Without neglecting Nunberg's important insights, I will argue first that the material facets of state publications—the physical properties that rendered them books and artifacts—often eclipsed any informative purpose, or at least never ceased calling attention to themselves; and second, that the making of government documents actually aggrandized rather than diminished individual authors and authorship.

That official publications had numerous and somewhat opposing assignments beyond the façade of information is relevant to both contentions. For example, the publication of narratives and scientific knowledge on the West was conceived of as a national undertaking that glorified both government action and national know-how. The grandeur of the newly acquired western empire was replicated or simulated by the splendor of those volumes. It was manifested prominently in their aesthetic work that was, besides their literary content, an effect of tangible features such as their binding, font-size, and quality of engravings. These reports were roving monuments that could be sent across the nation, or even across the Atlantic, for inspection and admiration.

By the early 1850s, the federal government was printing each of its published papers in 1,500 copies, but in every congressional session about ten to twenty documents received much greater publicity (unmatched by any parliamentary literature in Britain, for instance).[8] Circulated in between 5,000 and 100,000 copies, these large editions were allocated through congressional representatives and senators to hundreds upon hundreds of libraries, learned associations, and athenaeums as well as to state and local governments. Other copies were dispatched to supporters in their home districts. In addition, Congress funded, either fully or in part, books on historical or scientific topics. Congress usually owned the manuscripts for those books and subscribed for perhaps 1,000 or 2,000 copies. The publisher could sell as many additional volumes as he chose at the price paid by Congress. Only the *Statutes at Large,* published by Little, Brown, was deemed government property. An act of Congress required that office holders bequeath those copies to their successors. Individual states also became invested in publishing initiatives, albeit on a smaller scale. For instance, in the late 1830s, the legislature of New York launched a wide-ranging natural history survey of the state. In 1847, it commissioned a study of the Iroquois nations that were residing on western New York reservations; a report that featured a census of the Iroquois nations supplemented by chapters on aboriginal history, mythology and archeology.[9]

Governmental printing, in general, was largely under the purview of Congress and a notable domain for party patronage (until the establishment of the Government Printing Office in 1861). The federal legislature had similarly broad discretion concerning which executive papers to publish and in what manner. In a few cases, Congress and the administration were at odds over the publication of an executive document. Most famously, soon after the conclusion of the Civil War radical Republican lawmakers insisted on making public Carl Schurz's report on the condition of the former confederate states despite president Andrew Johnson's protests. Johnson had dispatched Schurz on his tour, but became increasingly concerned by the pro-Reconstruction views of his envoy.[10]

During the middle decades of the nineteenth century, government documents had a singular presence as conveyors of factual matter, side by side with other, more ubiquitous vessels of information such as the commercial press, party papers, pamphlets and books. The short passage taken from Walt Whitman's "Song for Occupations" at the beginning of this chapter is one demonstration—there are many others in the historical record— of the availability, as well as the presumed authority of these documentary papers. (For the poet who purported to steer his readers toward personal and political recognitions that transcend print and language, these repositories of measurable facts, of "information," were, of course, hopelessly wanting.) The reading public experienced official papers either first hand or, more typically, through long excerpts in the daily press and reviews in journals. A good example of a much-anticipated periodical report was the bulky *Annual Message* of the president. This communication, presenting documents and reports from executive departments, was dispatched to specific newspapers in central locales ahead of time so that they would be able to examine and publish it on the day of its formal presentation to Congress.[11] The demand for unmediated access to government publications (as well as other reports generated by myriad reform and civic organizations) containing undiluted, "raw" facts corresponded with the spirit of antebellum political participation in which the distance between lawmakers and citizens was expected to collapse. It is also another indication of the unprecedented predominance of printed matter and practices of reading in American public life and politics during this period. The citizen/ reader nexus (as in the idea of the "informed voter") would be all the more celebrated during the Progressive Era at the turn of the twentieth century. However, by then, the press' digestive might as well as its claim to be a medium of "objective" news (rather than a presenter of "authentic" facts) would serve as a buffer between the voter-as-reader, on the one hand, and unaltered primary sources, on the other. A similar mediating function would be assumed by a plethora of newly emerging scientific discourses, experts and institutions.[12]

Official print output was integrated into concrete exchange relationships between congressmen and their constituents. Typically, Representative Abraham Lincoln wrote in May 1848 to a supporter, "I will place your name on my book, and send you such documents as you desire, when I can get them." Lincoln predicted that the publication in question, featuring transcripts of official correspondence on the war with Mexico, would be, when completed, the "best electioneering document" for his party.[13] Senator Charles Sumner, to give another example, furnished numerous congressional papers to the abolitionist Theodore Parker, including documents on Cuba and Haiti and other material concerning the slave trade. This collaboration took place shortly after the publication of *Uncle Tom's Cabin,* when Parker was assisting Harriet Beecher Stowe in compiling documents to vindicate her characterization of slavery in what would become *A Key to Uncle Tom's Cabin.*[14]

In a few cases, individuals were cultivating private collections of such complimentary reports. The Boston reformer Samuel Gridley Howe, a long time friend of Sumner, often asked the senator to supply him with particular volumes and concurrently solicited other Massachusetts congressmen to complete the missing parts of the series. During the same year in which he published the first edition of *Leaves of Grass* (1855), Whitman requested Senator William Henry Seward to grant him "public documents, your speeches, and any government, congressional or other publications of general interest, especially statistics, census facts &c."[15] Responding to such recurrent applications was part of the lawmaker's routine.

The most popular government publication was arguably the annual agricultural report of the Patent Office. It was an illustrated volume featuring a medley of articles and correspondences on field cultivation and animal husbandry, better seeds, improved grafts, and other such useful or simply interesting details. The report for the year 1858, to give one example, is a 552-page octavo affair that opens with a series of woodcuts, the first of which is a large depiction of the Yak of Tibet. Inside, a rather inconspicuous essay contemplates the introduction of the Yak to the Great Plains as a means to improve the condition of the Indian tribes and to expedite their civilization "for the possession of property is a strong bond of society."[16] (The decision to display the Yak at the beginning of the report had less to do, it seems, with the gravity of the proposal than with the impressive illustration of the humped mammal.) The report itself offers articles on farming and education, a piece on the classification of midwestern weasels ("The Quadrupeds of Illinois Injurious and Beneficial to the Farmer"), and reports on new brands of grapes and apples. More than a hundred pages are populated with short descriptions of local agricultural societies and the segment on agricultural statistics is occupied by a continent-long list of queries, exceeding 1,700 items, for ordinary readers who wished to contribute to future reports. Such questionnaires were a customary vehicle of mid-nineteenth century efforts at "interactivity."

In an early discussion about the printing of the Patent Office's report on agriculture, Representative David K. Cartter from Ohio argued that Congress owed the public such an account. His rationale betrayed more than a trace of regional animosity. "West of the mountains, the people got nothing from the Government but intelligence. Of the $30,000,000 which were annually taken from the people, to supply the Treasury, why should they not be permitted to receive back five mills on the dollar, in the way of information?"[17] But another congressman, Albert Gallatin Brown, countered that if the purpose of generating more reports was informing the people, why not print the House Journal in tens of thousands of copies. The real target of issuing the agriculture report could not be concealed. "We all know very well what an effect might be sometimes produced by sending a book to some particular constituent, in a doubtful part of the district, in securing his exertions in favor of the member who had sent it."[18] Despite these and other reservations, the number of printed copies of this report accelerated dramatically. In 1880, the Commissioner of Agriculture complained that while the print run was larger than that of any annual book ever published, it was not yet half-large enough to meet the "reasonable and pressing demand."[19] By the conclusion of the century, 400,000 copies left the printing press every year.

Decisions on printing or procuring particular documents were thus made with great attention to the reading preferences of voters—an assessment that was conspicuously colored by party affiliation and local considerations. When the House considered producing an extra 10,000 copies of a report from the Treasury on statistics of commerce and navigation, Representative John A. McLernand, a Democrat from Illinois, suggested cutting the number by half. He saw the report as a Whig document that promoted the goals of trade and the controversial concept of "internal improvement." As a source of practical information, it best suited the narrow interests of merchants and boards of trade, he further maintained. "It was such a document as the mass of the people would neither have leisure nor taste to trace into its arithmetic details."[20]

In the fall of 1850, the Senate debated the purchase of a compilation known as Hickey's edition of the Constitution. The resolution called for acquiring 10,000 copies of Hickey's primer, which, in addition to the Constitution, featured Washington's inaugural and farewell addresses and some statistical details "illustrative of the genius of the American Government, and the development of its principles."[21] This work had already been ordered in thousands of copies. Responding to questions concerning the legislative utility of the motion, Senator George E. Badger explained that the objective was simply wide distribution. "I know of no books which either House of Congress has at any time circulated which is so valuable, and so generally acceptable, and so much desired by our constituents as this very book."[22] Senator David Rice Atchison contended that the Constitution was more diffused and more easily obtained than any other document. It could be purchased in every bookstore across the land, served as the preface of every state constitution and was featured in numerous digests of laws.

However, the senator's skepticism did not dominate the discussion. One colleague argued that Congress paid much more for inferior documents. "If Congress never goes into extravagance till it does it in circulating the Constitution of the United States among the people, we shall be a very economical Government, indeed."[23] Senator M. Gwin suggested that if Atchison had tired with franking his books, then he was willing to take charge of the extra share. Gwin's county (San Francisco) had not received the books last time they were given away, and they certainly wanted their due allowance. Senator Issac P. Walker reported to have letters from those in favor of the abolition of the franking privilege who, nevertheless, still wished the government to put Hickey's book in the hands of every citizen of the United States. "I believe I can say that in Wisconsin it has had a good effect on the sentiments and political opinions of the people, and has introduced a high feeling of patriotism wherever it has been read."[24] The resolution was accepted 22 to 19.

A public appetite for books (as much as for the facts and figures they contained) fueled the traffic in official documents. Congress was not just imparting knowledge into an ethereal public sphere, but in the business of producing actual books. The material culture of bookmaking and the phenomenology of book-consuming (of which collecting and displaying were constitutive practices as much as perusing and reading) at times overwhelmed the demands of "information." Thus, for instance, the House of Representatives busied itself with the question of whether the President's *Annual Message* for the year 1850 ought to be issued in two parts (separating the Secretary of War's reports from the rest) or in one volume. The Printing Committee guaranteed no additional delays in production, and promised that doubling the number of volumes would allow for the distribution of the *Message* among a much-expanded group of constituents. This prospect, however, inspired more apprehension than enthusiasm. One member charged that dividing the reports would render it difficult to monitor their precise trajectories. Congressmen would have to keep a list and send the second installment to all of those who received the first. Otherwise, he predicted, they would face disgruntled voters. Indeed, Congressman Wenthworth confirmed that in the previous year, when the *Message* was bound in three parts, he got himself into trouble by dispatching different segments to different people.

Subsequently, he was deluged by requests for the two missing sections. The house decided therefore to limit the production to a single volume.[25]

The debate over the President's *Annual Message* took place while a new policy was rendering government publications ever closer to books. Large executive reports (over 250 pages) in the octavo *Congressional Series* would be bound as a matter of policy anchored in renewable legislation. Representative William McWillie exhibited for the inspection of the House a host of alternative bindings. Binding could be done for less, he explained, but the Printing Committee figured that if congressional documents were to be treated better, the work should be done in half-morocco. That December a resolution was proposed to bind in a "superior manner" the forthcoming 3,000 copies of the "Reconnaissances of Routes from San Antonio to El Paso." Why should Congress spend 30 cents a copy, more than double the ordinary expenditure on binding? The Committee explained that the reports featured "a large number of beautifully executed plates" and therefore were "of sufficient excellence and value" to justify the extra cost.[26] Senator Hannibal Hamlin concurred. "It is indeed an ornament, and adorned with some of the finest specimens of engravings that I have ever witnessed."[27] Government documents, therefore, were made to be judged by their covers rather than by their content alone. Endowing reports with an opulent, book-like exterior opened, as we shall see, a new expanse for aesthetic signification.

Frequent attempts at book publishing lured the legislature into becoming an agent in the marketplace, outside the realm of legislation or policy supervision, as a producer and consumer of books. This intervention of a representative body in an actual—not metaphoric—line of production was fraught with tension. By binding its documents, Congress transcended its own boundaries. (Commissioning its various printing tasks, the legislature either set the price or offered the job to the lowest bidder. In the case of binding, it appeared that congressmen were negotiating special deals with merchants and literally bringing the marketplace to the chamber by presenting various commercial products there.) In tedious debates, lawmakers increasingly sounded like booksellers, comparing the value of muslin, leather and other forms of binding, and arguing over the best methods of preserving books that were destined to make long journeys in postal bags. Mockingly, Senator John P. Hale accepted his colleagues' presumption that without proper binding valuable documents would be doomed. Indeed, fine binding was the only rationale for their survival.

> Now, if it is worthwhile to print these documents to send to our friends, it is certainly worthwhile to put upon them this nine-penny binding; for instead of tearing them up, as they would inevitably do if they were not bound, they allow them a place on the shelves of

their libraries, there to remain, sir, like many of our documents here, never to be opened and read again.[28]

Members of Congress also voted for a substantial package of costly books for the benefit of their own libraries. In each session, new representatives and senators would receive a set of the more elaborate productions; presumably, to assist them in their legislative work. In the case of an on-going series (such as the *American State Papers*), lawmakers were entitled to new installments years after they left Washington as long as the fecund project continued to generate more volumes. When in December 1847 the Secretary of the Senate was instructed to furnish each new member with such an offering, one senator remarked that the Senate was ostensibly voting $700 or $800 pay increases for each senator.[29] Members of both chambers found it very difficult to retire this custom. The monetary value of the books rose so much that letters arrived from relatives of deceased congressmen requesting the remaining volumes of specific publishing projects as still their due.[30] To add to the scandal, it turned out that many government publications were acquired from representatives and others by private speculators and sold in bookstores in DC, Boston, and other cities to those who did not have the right political connection to obtain them gratis.

The material dimension of government information was particularly salient in the publication of exploration accounts. Official texts on the West customarily gravitated toward, and were arranged around, palpable objects. Various products of cartography were prominent along with illustrations reproduced by an array of technologies, including woodcuts, lithographs, and metal engravings that were sometimes painstakingly colored by hand. Whether depicting birds or bison, a desert view or an aboriginal rite, these artifacts were the costliest to produce, and the articles of western reportage most prized by explorers and readers alike. Their scientific merit—for they were supposed to represent nature with great fidelity—was supplemented or supplanted by their monetary value and aesthetic desirability. This multifaceted designation of worth corresponded to the opinion expressed by an 1848 congressional committee that Frémont's achievement in explorations culminated in a collection of employable objects from minerals and birds' plumage to drawings of western scenery. The production value of expedition reports was paramount. Such considerations also applied to other, similarly crafted, scientific and bureaucratic reports. Even a staunch advocate of principled science such as Joseph Henry, the first secretary of the Smithsonian Institution, proudly commented on the report that inaugurated the Smithsonian Contribution to Knowledge series—an illustrated archeological survey of the Midwest—"I think it will make one of the most beautiful books ever published in this country."[31]

An army of printers, engravers, mapmakers, and binders in Washington, Baltimore, Philadelphia and New York was recruited to execute the task of making these ornate documents. Great skills of coordination were consequently required. During the 1840s, many publication projects were managed directly by the Secretary of the Senate and the Clerk of the House of Representatives. Entering a gap between publication frenzies and an absence of any governmental branch established for that purpose, congressional staff had to make decisions that bordered on editorial rather than technical preferences. In the case of Gales and Seaton's *American State Papers* and other documentary enterprises, the Clerk and the Secretary were given explicit editorial powers.[32] By the 1850s, the executive departments incrementally assumed some of these functions. The Navy and the Department of the Interior supervised expeditions' reports while the War Department was in charge of printing the large-scale Pacific Railroad surveys.

Not merely a completion of government action in the market of information, or the realization of expeditions in print, the publication of a few famous reports became itself an expedition, i.e., a complicated and somewhat risky project that demanded great resources and manpower. It was an endeavor that could go awry, or simply subvert the conventional equilibrium between action and reportage. At times, it seemed easier (let alone cheaper) to send ships to remote oceans or a group of soldiers to uncharted deserts rather than to publish a book describing those ventures. The famous U.S. Exploring Expedition to the Pacific Northwest (led by Captain John Wilkes) took four years to conclude in 1842. The publication of the subsequent reports—first predicted to require a single year—took another thirty years but was never completed. In 1861, an English botanist wrote to an American colleague regarding this project: "Who on earth is to keep in their heads . . . such a medley of books—double-paged, double-titled, and half finished as your Government vomits periodically into the great ocean of Scientific bibliography."[33]

Other reports did not fare much better. Schoolcraft's Indian volumes and the Pacific Railroad surveys, to mention two perennial projects, yielded printed assortments of miscellaneous articles, badly edited and in stunning disarray. A single official or a few officers sitting in Washington could not master the deluge of letters, reports and other documents generated by these massive undertakings. The state thus could (and did) get lost in its printing expeditions. Political wrangling, bureaucratic inexperience, the incredible number of specimens that were truly impossible to classify within a short time, and the enormity of the printing volume contributed to what seemed to be verging on ineptitude.

Questions were recurrently posed, within Congress and elsewhere, concerning the duty of government to provide information and the type of knowledge that lent itself to such circulation. Government's presence in the publishing marketplace was also addressed. Senator James A. Pearce (Maryland) warned that state patronage of books was so often solicited that, unless curbed, Congress would become "a great publishing establishment, that authors and editors may avoid the risk of trade."[34] A related point was raised by the executor of James Monroe's will who petitioned Congress to purchase the late president's correspondence for its proper publication. Among other arguments, he mentioned Congress's previous commitments to publish documents by early republic presidents. If those undertakings would be executed rightly, the commercial value of Monroe's papers would inevitably decline and the project would become financially unfeasible. Implicit in this reasoning was the notion that Congress was morally responsible for the public consequences of its intervention in the business of publishing. Support was not just necessary for the preservation of national memory, but a matter of fairness as well.[35]

Lawmakers deliberated over whether they should merely respond to the reading desires of their constituents, or whether it was their duty to elicit public attention toward the less easily read and not-so-exquisite products of the printing press that were still essential to the affairs of the state. Government expenditure was also at issue. The entire effort of registering and departing information rendered the federal government vulnerable to another type of criticism that became even more vitriolic in the twentieth century, namely that government is a compulsive printer. To add to the measure of awkwardness exhibited by the state in fulfilling its information duties, the material excess of official publications was compounded by another surplus—the problematic of double authorship—one originated in government as a corporate institution and the other with individual subjects.

Such doubts and concerns were evident in the episode with which I began—the debate over the printing of Bartlett's report. Senators claimed that some publication initiatives were too exorbitant and others contained inaccessible piles of details and were thus practically useless except for wrapping loaves of bread in Washington markets. To those among the senators who maintained that the Senate should not publish a book whose content was unknown (or, in fact, was yet to be written), Senator Sam Houston, the publication's sponsor, replied that that was precisely why the book should be printed—so senators could learn something about the topic. "He may give us a very entertaining lecture upon the manners, customs, and peculiar habits of Mexico."[36] This rhetorical trickery rested on the ambiguity of the Senate's double role as both producer and consumer of information and the further confusion between lawmakers and voters as readers.

Senator James Mason charged that Bartlett chose various routes far from the border for a purpose. "[T]he commissioner—God knows where—[was] exploring the interior of Mexico, perhaps, and collecting material for a book."[37] In a dispute over another printing project (a controversy that, following Jonathan Swift's title, was dubbed the "The Battle of the Books"), Senator Hamlin maintained that every person who wished to publish a book attached himself to some expedition or survey. The enterprising would-be-author was granted an opportunity to report to the department that retained him and thus was guaranteed a book at the expense of the House or the Senate. It was, therefore, not that government commissioned individuals to perform tasks, but that individuals harnessed government to help them fulfill their personal ambitions. Was congressional largess indulging a cadre of writers? Senator Robert Hunter saw in the printing of books at government's expense two types of hazardous desires: the craving of private authors for personal fame, and the consequent demand of the public to have books for free, an appetite that government would never be able to satisfy in full. For other detractors of official publications the greatest offenders were to be found in the bureaucracy itself. A Senate committee protested that heads of executive bureaus had become aspiring "book makers." They kept clerks working all year round, the committee alleged, obtaining material with which to inflate their annual reports.[38]

It did not escape senators that the proposed Bartlett publication circumvented the entire rationale of reporting, for the Department of the Interior, its addressee, was evidently uninterested in such a communication. In fact, before the Senate debate Bartlett had already submitted a written account to his superiors in the Department, thereby fulfilling the bureaucratic imperative and the ritual of submitting a report. However, there was still the question of the grand "Report" which he hoped would combine his personal journal with the scientific findings of the expedition and would be accompanied by the illustrations of the expedition's artist, Henry Pratt. Bartlett's allies promoted the notion that his public service earned him the privilege of conceiving his report under congressional auspices. Likewise, when a congressional select committee recommended in 1848 to publish the third of Frémont's expedition narratives, they argued that the explorer's refusal to exploit his achievements in the service of government rendered it a matter of justice to allow him to complete his expeditions "which only want the finishing hand of their author to erect a monument of honor to himself and of utility to his country."[39]

John Wilkes's greatest achievement after coming ashore in 1842 was probably his success in convincing Congress that the individuals who were part of the Exploring Expedition should be employed in the publication effort. He further established a continuum between his command on the high seas and his supervision of the publication project. Once again, fairness and justice were invoked. Professing views close to Wilkes's, an article in the *American Journal of Science and Art* maintained that the knowledge that had been accumulated by the Exploring Expedition should not be kept by the few, but rather shared with the nation, the people who bore the expense of the journey. In a like manner, it would be right if the work was consigned to those who participated in the voyage. "Each will prepare his own report, reap his own honors, and be held responsible for his own facts."[40]

Government reports, back then as now, were signed documents closely associated with individuals. Frémont who, regardless of his supporters' claim, did capitalize on his trail to California fame, eventually made a political career on the foundation of his authorial voice. In 1856, he became the first presidential nominee of the Republican Party. Moreover, the craving of army officers, lawmakers and others to assert themselves in print also endowed official reports with a surplus of style. That style often conformed to recognizable model-narratives and yet carried individual markers. In numerous expeditions, and similar operations, reports were based on personal diaries. Government officials commonly transmitted anecdote-saturated accounts on incidents, crucial and trivial, whose only organizing principle was the vantage point of their authors moving in space and time.

The literary properties of Frémont's famous narratives have been attributed often to his wife, Jessie. In general, crafting the text of an expedition report was a work of collaboration (much like producing the report as a book) that, in this case, involved Charles Preuss, the expedition's cartographer, and John Torrey, the pioneering botanist who was entrusted with the botanical and zoological collections. The narrative segment was Frémont's responsibility. As prescribed by convention, the report was to be arranged chronologically following the expedition's itinerary, therefore ignoring the vast terrain that stretched outside the immediate vicinity of its slender path.

In the weeks after his return to his home in St. Louis at the conclusion of his travels (October 1842), Frémont faced the seemingly uncomplicated task of preparing such a chronology. Alas, three days of arduous work yielded only a tremendous headache and a nosebleed. At this point, his wife entered the scene of (report) writing. Jessie Benton Frémont (the daughter of Frémont's chief ally in Washington, Senator Thomas Hart Benton) volunteered to sit at the desk recording her husband's words. Initially dictating from his notes, Frémont soon moved into a more conversational tone, reportedly 'forgetting himself' in his oral retelling. According to one of Jessie Frémont's biographers, "freed from all self-consciousness, unhampered by the nagging thought of the mechanics of writing, [Frémont] happily recounted the story of his adventures to the woman he loved. In answers to her eager and adroit questions, he simplified, clarified, and dramatized his experience."[41] This narrative on the making of the narrative is tangential to the story of the expedition itself and complements the cultural work that Frémont's report has performed as a text that linked (or triangulated) nature, American nationalism and a gendered self. Future scholars would disagree about the respective contributions of the husband and wife team. Jessie Frémont was an avid reader in the classics and familiar with other expeditions' accounts as well. Undoubtedly, no less important was Frémont's determination to offer a popular, readable document. His political backers and the press expected that of him.

In one of the best-known passages of his first expedition narrative, Frémont described standing next to a hurriedly hoisted American flag on (what he mistakenly thought to be) the tallest summit in the Rockies, peering over the majestic abyss below. The silence was interrupted only by a single bumblebee, which was duly captured and put into a book otherwise used to dry botanic samples. Without directly alluding to the concept, Frémont's description is a conventional exposition on the theme of the sublime, employing one of the sublime's most common circumstances—the individual overlooking a dangerously magnificent view from a top of a mountain. Peril was signified by the threat to his person posed by climbing enormous rocks as well as by the topography of the Rockies that evoked a mightier force. Arriving at the peak, Frémont encountered nothing other than absolute stillness and silence. The uncanny appearance of the bee in a spot that appeared to be beyond the reach of animated life, prompted ambivalence; a sense of identification with the path-breaking bee that was probably "the first of his species to cross the mountain barrier, a solitary pioneer foretells the advance of civilization." Concurrently, however, the bee provoked a burst of aggression. "I believe that a moment's thought would have made us let him continue his way unharmed, but we carried out the law of this country, where all animated nature seems at war."[42] The bee's demise was inevitable.

Frémont's early reports served as a model for the expeditions of the next two decades. The genre became ever more patriotic in the aftermath of the war with Mexico, generating documents such as the 1848 compilation of reports by Lieutenant Colonel William Emory, Lieutenant James W. Abert and Lieutenant Colonel Philip St. George Cooke, titled "Notes of Military Reconnaissance from Fort Leavenworth in Missouri to San Diego, in California." The range of plotting strategies that controlled these texts is beyond the scope of this discussion, but the creation of a stylistic continuity under the patronage of government is an important feature of the state's contribution to print culture. This fidelity of style was not exhausted by the characteristics that are commonly associated with Frémont's reports, namely a certain chauvinistic emotionalism and a tendency to engage in detailed, graphic descriptions. More intriguing, perhaps, was the way these subsequent documents were able to reproduce uncanny moments of the kind that brought together Frémont and the wandering bee on the top of the Rockies.

Emory's journal began on August 2, 1846, with him standing alone looking in the direction of Bent's Fort. While watching an enormous American flag flying forcefully, he noticed that the flag was waving against the direction of the wind and threatening to break the ash pole on which it was hoisted. "The mystery was soon revealed by a column of dust to the east, advancing with about the velocity of a fast walking horse—it was 'the Army of the West.' I ordered my horses to be hitched up and, as the column passed, took my place with the staff."[43] Lieutenant Abert's narrative commenced with his arrival at Fort Bent's where he suffered from fever and experienced hallucinations:

> At this time my disease had obtained such an influence over my senses, that days and nights were passed in delirium and a mental struggle to ascertain whether the impressions my mind received were true or false. Even my sight was affected, and when I gazed on Bent's fort, the building seemed completely metamorphosed, new towers had been erected, the walls heightened, and, as I then thought, everything put in readiness to resist an attack of the New Mexicans.[44]

The proclivity of physical objects in Bent's Fort to defy the rules of nature further developed Frémont's estrangement motif. The misplaced bee on the mountain is substituted here with buildings and a flag that are strangely animated by a dream-state (or an intoxication) that has both personal and national underpinnings. All three moments, in fact, seemed to displace the peculiarity that originated from the presence of expeditions in the vistas of the West onto the physical world, natural and man-made. Strangest of all may be that these incidents found their way into official military accounts. Importantly, the moment of capturing the bee in the book was also the point in time when the West was "won" and became American.

Authorship in government publications was also manifested in interesting market relations between government employees and the texts they wrote in their official capacities. Officers of the army corps of engineers received hundreds of copies of their reports for personal use. In the case of the Exploring Expedition, the congressional Library Committee decided to permit each author to print from the typeset 100 to 150 copies for three-fifths of the contract price, provided the writers would sell them at low prices.[45]

In a few instances, individuals battled over their respective claims of authorship in official documents. Wilkes's habit of copying material from general histories and lifting passages from crewmembers' journals endeared him neither to reviewers nor to his men. The government claimed all notes taken by participants during the expedition. In fact, officers were obliged to keep daily journals and to record all incidents on board ship or on shore that "tend to illustrate any transaction or occurrence which may take place, or afford any information in regard to the manners, habits, or customs of natives and the position and characters of such places as may be visited."[46] Subsequently, Wilkes had at his disposal the works of his subordinates, which he mined relentlessly. To make matters worse, he issued a personal copyright for future commercial editions of his *Narrative*. Wilkes intoned that this account was not identical to the original report he had submitted to the Navy Department upon his return, but a distinct document written specifically at the request of the Joint Library Committee that supervised the project on Congress's behalf. Presumably a reward for a naval officer conducting extra work, he nevertheless chose to explain the unusual copyright in terms of personal integrity. "My object in so doing was to protect my reputation, being unwilling that a garbled edition should be printed by others."[47] Wilkes's claim over his text (as well as his men's bitterness over the violation of theirs) may be better understood in light of the tremendous growth and professionalization of authorship in antebellum America. It was also derived from the principle of deservedness that guided the concurrent expansion (still in a rudimentary form) of what would be commonly known as "intellectual property" into other domains of knowledge and expertise, for example, the lecture circuit. This concept coexisted strenuously with a lingering conviction in Victorian America that the dissemination of knowledge to the public at large should be a remuneration-free, self-rewarding civic duty.[48]

A decade later, in 1859, a private act of Congress granted the ethnologist Schoolcraft a special 14-year copyright to republish his six volumes on the Indian tribes of America. Congress was responding to an appeal by Mary Howard Schoolcraft acting on behalf of her husband who by then was sick and bed-ridden. In another twist that further exemplified the confusion over governmental and personal stakes in such documents, Seth Eastman, the project's celebrated illustrator, launched a counter campaign, claiming he had been injured by Congress's gesture toward the ailing Schoolcraft. He demanded proper compensation for his artwork. His petition failed to win congressional support. The Schoolcrafts were similarly unsuccessful in their commercial bid. Apparently, there was a limit to the public's interest or to its willingness to pay full price for these volumes.[49] This was not the first time that Schoolcraft contemplated reissuing the congressional project as a private work. The Commissioner of Indian Affairs approved his application for such an initiative as early as June 1853. "The only motive the Gov. had in ordering the publication was to preserve and diffuse the information it contained of a people fast fading away [i.e., the native tribes]," wrote the Commissioner. "A private edition would more completely effectuate this object by more widely diffusing this great national memorial."[50]

John Russell Bartlett was ultimately unable to secure support in Congress for his particular venture. Senator Houston could not possibly be a very persuasive advocate for the project, especially when he conceded during the debate on the Senate floor that despite his impassioned call for printing Bartlett's and other comparable accounts he had never glanced at a government report with the exception perhaps of the agricultural volume. Things did not improve when he further admitted that his unlikely embrace of Bartlett's cause had largely to do with the fact that Andrew Gray, Bartlett's chief surveyor and a prospective contributor to the report, was a fellow Texan. The Senate finally decided not to proceed with the debate, thus practically killing the motion to publish Bartlett's report.

The dispute over this particular report would later digress into a verbal duel between two authors, positioning Bartlett against his successor, (by then) Colonel William Emory. For the rest of the 1850s they verbally assaulted each other, directly or through proxies, over their performances as commissioners and the comparative value of their respective accounts. Whereas Congress issued Emory's report in a lavish form, Bartlett had to satisfy himself with a commercial publisher, finally bringing his work to print in 1854 under the title, *Personal Narrative of Explorations and Incidents in Texas, New Mexico, California, Sonora, and Chihuahua.*[51] The *New York Herald,* among others, continued to call for an official edition of Bartlett's ethnological collection:

> It is matter of surprise to all who visit Washington that no museum or gallery has yet been erected by our government for the purpose of preserving portraits characteristic of the Indian Tribes of the United States, together with their articles of manufacture, their weapons of war, and implements of husbandry. Every nation in Europe possesses such collections, il-

lustrating the history, manners, customs and arts of their primitive inhabitants, which are more highly prized than those collections exhibiting mere advanced state of civilization. Such a collection, illustrative of our Indian tribes, would, at this moment, be regarded as most valuable and interesting in London or Paris. Do they possess less interest for us who possess the soil of these aborigines?[52]

This celebration of the Indian past, another national project, sought as its site a museum in Washington (that would become a reality only in September 1999) or, alternatively, the type of museumification afforded by books such as Bartlett's or Schoolcraft's. The *New York Times* joined the chorus. It would be to the credit of any government to present these facts to the world. "How differs this from sowing freely and reaping sparingly?—appropriating liberally for the prosecution of the work, yet, by refusing appropriations for publishing, reaping no other fruits rather than the Commissioner's *Personal Narrative*."[53] Bartlett himself protested that "[n]o public officer has ever before met with the treatment that I have." All reports of American surveys and explorations, whether domestic or otherwise (including expeditions to the Amazon), were officially published and distributed without charge. The public should judge who was wronged, government or him.[54] Emory countered in the *Washington Union* alleging that his predecessor was still in possession of government property, most importantly, sketches made by the commission's artists that had "both intrinsic and mercantile value."[55]

In a reversal of roles, when the first volume of Emory's report was completed in 1857, the *Herald* attacked it as one of those tomes crafted to glorify their authors.[56] It was labeled "a ponderous volume" brimming with more expensive illustrations than any similar government work—no less than ninety-nine steel, copper and stone engravings, twenty woodcuts. "[N]ever have we seen so many illustrations presenting so few features of interest, sixty-four of them being views of the desert directly on the western portion of the boundary, and consequently offering little variety." The article poked fun at Emory's arrogance in calling a mountain near Rio Grande after himself. A sketch of that mountain was, in fact, embossed on the cover of the report. By depicting Mount Emory on the binding, Emory the officer turned author was able to sign or inscribe his report both inside and outside. The illustration enhanced the function of the document as a monument; although its national significance was obviously threatened by Emory's own bloated sense of self.

Emory's critics claimed that the cost of printing his report was $233,000, not to speak of the expense for the scientific crew, which the writer estimated to be more than $70,000. Another newspaper did not neglect to mention that the engravings for the

Emory report were done in Paris and that foreign artists were preferred over Americans. "Possibly the French may beat us in the toads and lizards, but we do not believe that anything is gained by sending away the engraving of the botanical illustrations."[57] Despite a measure of cynicism that seems to have been a fixture of public reactions to government print products (and the omnipresence of party loyalties), the views expressed in the press during the debate over the fate of Bartlett's report gave ample evidence of a persistent ambivalence over the government's role in disseminating knowledge. They also demonstrated the diversity of modes of criticism—political, scientific, literary, and aesthetic—that official publications were subjected to in the daily and the periodical press.

The tension between the tendency of "information" to be molded into succinct, orderly, easily retrievable (and transportable) bits of knowledge and the actual material characteristics of state documents was amplified by the authorial aspirations of officials, the political and national ambitions of lawmakers and the reading sensibilities of the public. It is also true that despite recurrent attempts at reform and retrenchment, the proverbial attachment of officials and politicians to the printing press died hard, if it can be said to have ever perished. More importantly, however, the state was literally (and literarily) entrapped among first, the requirement for political transparency, which encouraged representatives and bureaucrats to sustain a vast public archive in print, supposedly created to allow the public to peer into the inner workings of government. Second, the contending public demand for usable knowledge. And lastly, government's insistence on representing the nation in ways that exceeded political representation through scientific, literary and aesthetic documentation of the country, its social "condition," history and nature.

The didacticism of the latter assignment was targeted by the *Chicago Tribune* journalist George Townsend in his 1873 book *Washington: Outside and Inside*. He selected as an example the industrious commissioner of the Land Office, Joseph Wilson, who each year presented a voluminous report on the state of the public domain, new surveys, land sold as well as topics that extended far beyond his call of duty, from the history of gold to, as Townsend wrote, "other problems of empire and extension."[58] Wilson also had a propensity to produce exorbitantly expensive maps, one of which was 12 square feet and charted the past, present and prospective routes to the Pacific. Townsend formulated two opposing approaches toward such productions. One was that the Land Commissioner's diligence should be greatly appreciated. "The nation rejoices to see itself in the light of its rivals, and to see the century in the light of the past;" or, "the Federal State ought to waste not expense to understand and properly represent itself, both before its own citizens and the world."[59] The counter argument was that economy should take precedent, and also that "the Republic is not a high school, and a Land Commissioner is not a Professor of History."[60]

Thus, only in its simplest form can the problematic of government as a source of information or knowledge be reduced to questions of veracity and volume—although, then as now, these are the most often articulated charges against the medium of government publications. Curiously, it is sometimes unclear whether government tells us too little or too much. This suspicion endures even from the perspective of the last decade. Two examples spring to mind. First, there was Hillary Rodham Clinton's health-care report. For critics, this gigantic document, thousands of pages long, signified by its sheer size and unreadability the excess of unbridled bureaucracy. More recently, Kenneth Starr's best-selling voyeuristic account combined a glut of detail with a stylistically excessive narrative structure. Yet, the parade of dozens of boxes of evidence on the stairs of the Capitol Building only raised suspicions about concealed information. Sometimes, it seems, government engages in deception by bombarding us with indigestible piles of information, by telling us "everything."

## Notes

1. At stake was the future railroad route to the Pacific, which southern senators hoped would pass through Texas along the 32nd parallel to southern California. On the Mexican Boundary Survey, see William Goetzmann, *Army Exploration in the American West, 1803–1863* (New Haven: Yale University Press, 1959), 152–208; Gray Sweeney, "Drawing Borders: Art and the Cultural Politics of the U.S.–Mexico Boundary Survey," in *Drawing the Borderline: Artist Explorers of the U.S.–Mexico Boundary Survey,* ed. Dawn Hall (Albuquerque: The Albuquerque Museum, 1996), 23–79.

2. *Congressional Globe,* April 5, 1853, 32nd Cong., 3rd Sess., 312. Henry Rowe Schoolcraft, *Inquiries Respecting the History, Present Condition, and Future Prospects of the Indian Tribes of the United States* (6 vols., Philadelphia: Lippincott, Grambo & Co., 1851–1857); David Dale Owen, "Report of a Geological Reconnaissance, of the Chippewa Land District of Wisconsin, and the Northern Part of Iowa," Senate Executive Document 57, 30th Cong., 1st Sess., serial 509. Also, see Owen, *Report of a Geological Survey of Wisconsin, Iowa, and Minnesota* (Philadelphia: Lippincott, Grambo & Co., 1852).

3. *Congressional Globe,* April 5, 1853, 312.

4. Ibid., 313–314.

5. *American State Papers: Documents, Legislative and Executive, of the Congress of the United States,* (38 vols., Washington, DC, 1832–1861); *Annals of Congress: The Debates and Proceedings in the*

*Congress of the United States,* (42 vols., Washington, DC: Gales & Seaton, 1834–1856); *The Works of John Adams: Second President of the United States* (Boston: Little, Brown, 1850–1856); "Exploring Expedition of the Rocky Mountains in 1842, and to Oregon and North California in 1843–1844, by Brevet Captain J. C. Frémont," Senate Document 174, 28th Cong., 2nd Sess., serial 461. *Reports of Explorations and Surveys to Ascertain the Most Practicable and Economical Route for a Railroad from the Mississippi River to the Pacific Ocean* (12 vols. in 13, Washington, DC: A. O. P. Nicholson, Printer, 1855–1860).

6. Culver H. Smith, *The Press, Politics, and Patronage: The American Government's Use of Newspapers, 1789–1875* (Athens, GA: University of Georgia Press, 1977); Donald A. Ritchie, *Press Gallery: Congress and the Washington Correspondents* (Cambridge, MA: Harvard University Press, 1991); Thomas C. Leonard, *The Power of the Press: The Birth of American Political Reporting* (New York: Oxford University Press, 1986); William E. Ames, *A History of the National Intelligencer (Chapel Hill: University of North Carolina Press, 1972).*

7. Geoffrey Nunberg, "Farewell to the Information Age," in *The Future of the Book,* ed. Geoffrey Nunberg (Berkeley: University of California Press, 1996), 120. Also, see Richard Terdiman, *Discourse/Counter-Discourse* (Ithaca, NY: Cornell University Press, 1985). Nunberg's approach is influenced by the writing of Walter Benjamin, especially "The Storyteller" and "The Work of Art in the Age of Mechanical Reproduction," in *Illuminations,* ed. H. Arendt (New York: Schocken, 1969).

8. For example, in 1849 Congress printed extra copies of the following documents: "Coast Survey," 4,500; "Report on Commerce and Navigation," 10,000; "Patent Office Report on Agriculture," 100,000; "Patent Office Report on Machines," 50,000; "King's Report on California," 10,000; "Banks of the United States," 5,000; "Foster and Whitney's Mineral Report," 10,000; "Proceedings Relative to the Death of General Taylor," 30,000.

9. Great Britain. House of Commons. *Report from the Select Committee on Parliamentary Papers,* HC 1852–1853 (720) XXXIV, 178. Michele L. Aldrich, "New York Natural History Survey, 1836–1845," Ph.D. diss., University of Texas, Austin, 1974; "Report of Mr. Schoolcraft, to the Secretary of State, Transmitting the Census Returns in Relation to the Indians," New York, Senate Document 24, 1846. Schoolcraft expanded and republished the report privately as *Notes on the Iroquois; or Contributions to American History, Antiquities, and General Ethnology* (Albany: Erastus H. Pease & Co., 1847).

10. "Report of Carl Schurz on the States of South Carolina, Georgia, Alabama, Mississippi, and Louisiana," in *Message of the President of the United States,* Senate Executive Document 2, 39th Cong., 1st Sess., serial 1237; Hans L. Trefousse, *Carl Schurz: A Biography* (Knoxville: University of Tennessee Press, 1982), 158–160.

11. By the second session of the 40th Congress (1868), the cluster of executive documents known as the "Annual Message of the President," reached almost 11,000 pages and cost

approximately $110,000 to print. The message was issued in three thousand copies while an abridgment was printed in a massive 35,000 copies. Senate Report 247, 40th Cong., 3rd Sess., serial 1362, 3.

12. For a discussion of the role of parliamentary papers in British public life see, Oz Frankel, "Scenes of Commission: Royal Commission of Inquiry and the Culture of Social Investigation in Early Victorian Britain," *The European Legacy,* 4, no. 6 (December, 1999), 20–41.

13. James L. Harrison, *100 GPO Years, 1861–1961* (Washington, DC: Government Printing Office, 1961), 54.

14. Charles Sumner to Theodore Parker, [copy] Jan 6, 1853, *Theodore Parker Papers, Massachusetts Historical Society,* vol. X, 262.5; Sumner to Parker, [copy] March 27, 1853; Ibid., vol. X, 263.5; Parker to Sumner; 18 August, [copy] 18[53?]; ibid., vol. VI, 261; Harriet Beecher Stowe, *A Key to Uncle Tom's Cabin: Presenting the Original Facts and Documents upon which the Story is Founded* (Boston: J. P. Jowett & Co., 1853).

15. December 5, 1855; quoted in Betsy Erkkila, *Whitman the Political Poet* (New York: Oxford University Press, 1989), 129.

16. *Report of the Commission of Patents for the Year 1858: Agriculture* (Washington, DC: James B. Steedman, 1859) or, House Executive Document 105, 35th Cong., 2nd Sess., serial 1012, p. 239.

17. *Congressional Globe,* March 7, 1850, 31st Cong., 1st Sess., p. 475.

18. Ibid.

19. Harrison, *100 GPO Years,* p. 54.

20. *Congressional Globe,* January 17, 1850, 31st Cong., 1st Sess., p. 172.

21. *The Constitution of the United States of America,* ed. William L. Hickey (Philadelphia, 1848); *Congressional Globe,* September 23, 1850, 31st Cong., 1st Sess., 1923.

22. Ibid.

23. Ibid.

24. Ibid.

25. Ibid., December 31, 1850, 31st Cong., 2nd Sess., 139.

26. Ibid., December 18, 1850, p. 77. The document under consideration was Senate Executive Document 64, 31st Cong., 1st Sess., serial 562.

27. *Congressional Globe,* December 19, 1850, 96. Also Ibid., July 26 1850, 31st Cong., 1st Sess., 1464.

28. Ibid., 332.

29. Ibid., December 14, 1847, 30th Cong., 1st Sess., 22. The complimentary set for 1848, for example, was a mixture of legal, historical and "reference" works: *Congressional Globe* (16 vols.), *Revised Statutes* (31 vols.), *Register of Debates* (5 vols.), *Contested Elections* (1 vol.), W. Hickey's *Constitution, Senate Land Laws* (2 vols.); Peter Force's *American Archives* (6 vols.), Gales & Seaton's *American State Papers* (21 vols.), Blair Rives *Diplomatic Correspondence* (7 vols.). Printed Circular from Thomas J. Campbell, Clerk to the House of Representatives, January 15, 1849, Letters to the Clerk of the House of Representatives, *National Archives,* RG 233; HR 30C-B10.

30. For instance, Arabelle Carter to Thomas Campbell, Clerk of the House of Representatives, July 23, 1849, Ibid., RG 233; HR 30C-B1.

31. Joseph Henry to Asa Gray, May 23, 1848, Historic Letters, *Gray Herbarium Archives,* Harvard University.

32. In the case of the U.S. Exploring Expedition, a small publishing apparatus was established under the supervision of the Joint Committee on the Library of Congress. See Anita M. Hibler, "The Publication of the Wilkes Reports, 1842–1877," Ph.D. diss. George Washington University, 1989, 178.

33. Joseph Hooker to Asa Gray, quoted in Barbara Novak, *Nature and Culture: American Landscape and Painting, 1825–1875* (New York: Oxford University Press, 1980), 129.

34. *Congressional Globe,* August 26, 1850, 31st Cong., 1st Sess., 1668.

35. "Petition of Samuel L. Gouverneur," Senate Misc. Document 10, 30th Cong., 2nd Sess., serial 533.

36. *Congressional Globe,* April 5 1853, 32nd Cong., 3rd Sess., 312.

37. Ibid., 313.

38. Senate Report 247, 40th Cong., 3rd Sess., Serial 1362, 6. At issue was congressional support for a manuscript on the commercial potential of southeastern Asia written by a private citizen, Aaron H. Palmer, and titled, "A Comprehensive View of the Principal Independent Maritime Countries of the East."

39. Senate Committee Report 226, 30th Cong., 1st Sess., serial 512, 2.

40. "Brief Account of the Discoveries and Results of the United States Exploring Expedition," (reprint from the *American Journal of Science and Arts,* vol. xliv) (New Haven: B. L. Hamlen, 1843), 4.

41. Catherine Coffin Phillips, *Jessie Benton Frémont: A Woman Who Made History* (San Francisco: John Henry Nash, 1935), 69.

42. *The Expeditions of John Charles Frémont,* ed. Donald Jackson and Mary Lee Spence (3 vols., Urbana: University of Illinois Press, 1970–1980), vol. I, 270. On the motif of the sublime in nineteenth century American art, see Novak, *Nature and Culture,* 18–77.

43. "Notes of Military Reconnaissance from Fort Leavenworth in Missouri to San Diego, in California" [By Lieut. Col. W. H. Emory, with Examination of New Mexico by Lieut. J. W. Abert, and Report of Lieut. Col. St. George Cooke on his March from Santa Fé to San Diego] Executive Document 41, 30th Cong., 1st Sess., serial 517, 15. The House of Representatives ordered that 10,000 extra copies of each of the reports be printed out of which 250 would be given to every reporting officer.

44. Ibid., 419.

45. Senate Document 405, 29th Cong., 1st Sess., serial 477, pp. 10–11. Charles Wilkes, *Narrative of the United States Exploring Expedition, During the Years 1838, 1839, 1840, 1841, 1842* (5 vols., Philadelphia: C. Sherman, 1844).

46. Instructions of James K. Paulding, Secretary of the Navy to Charles Wilkes, quoted in Daniel C. Haskell, *U.S. Exploring Expedition, 1838–1842, and its Publications, 1844–1874,* (New York: New York Public Library, 1940), 34.

47. "Report from the Joint Library Committee," House Report 160, 28th Cong., 2nd Sess., serial 468, 6.

48. See Donald M. Scott, "Knowledge and the Marketplace," *in The Mythmaking Frame of Mind: Social Imagination and American Culture,* ed. James Gilbert et al. (Belmont, CA: Wadsworth Publishing Co., 1993), 91 112.

49. Private Bill no. 9, 35th Cong., 2nd Sess.; Mary Howard Schoolcraft to the House of Representatives Committee of Indian Affairs, January 21, 1859, Committee Papers, RG 233; HR 35A-D8.7, *National Archives.* "Report [to accompany Bill S. 308] on Seth Eastman's Memorial," March 23, 1860, Senate Committee Report 151, 36th Cong., 1st Sess., serial 1039; "The Committee on Claims on Seth Eastman's Memorial," February 7, 1867, Senate Committee Report 160, 39th Cong., 2nd Sess., serial 1279.

50. Commissioner of Indian Affairs George Manypenny to Henry Schoolcraft, June 11, 1853, RU 75 Letters Received, Misc., *National Archives.*

51. John Russell Bartlett, *Personal Narrative of Explorations and Incidents in Texas, New Mexico, California, Sonora, and Chihuahua* (2 vols., New York: D. Appleton & Company, 1854); William H. Emory, *Report on the United States and Mexican Boundary Survey* (2 vols. in 3, Washington, DC: A. O. P. Nicholson, 1857–1859); Emory's report was published in three large quarto volumes. Congress decided to print 10,000 copies of the first volume, the narrative (August 15, 1856). The botanical and zoological volumes were circulated in 3,000 copies only.

52. *New York Herald,* March 12, 18[50?], The John Carter Brown Library, *Bartlett Papers: Mexican Boundary Commission,* Microfilm Edition, Scrapbook, reel 11, 149.

53. *New York Times,* June 16, 1854.

54. *Washington Union,* [April, 1854] "Bartlett Papers: Mexican Boundary Commission," Scrapbook, reel 11, p. 277, clipping 2.

55. Major Emory to General Robert B. Campbell, April 24, 1854, reprinted in the *Washington Union,* April 1854, ibid., 279.

56. Republished in [*Providence Daily*] *Journal,* July 14, 185[8?], ibid., 312.

57. Ibid., 352, clipping 1.

58. George Alfred Townsend, *Washington, Outside and Inside,* (Hartford, CT: James Betts & Co., 1873), 240.

59. Ibid.

60. Ibid., 241. Townsend argued that if government wished to cater to authors and authorship it should sign an international copyright law and leave the people to make their own maps and books.

# 10 Prophetic Peasants and Bourgeois Pamphleteers: The Camisards Represented in Print, 1685–1710[1]

Daniel Thorburn

This essay examines a hot news item in the northern European press at the end of the seventeenth and beginning of the eighteenth centuries. The story deals with the religious revival of a group of peasants from southern France, and throughout this discussion, I will be interested less in the Camisards themselves, as these peasants came to be known, than in the experiences and arguments of the literate consumers of print media. The episode of the Camisards and the public controversy that followed offer an interesting lens through which to view media in transitions, and should inform any contemporary discussion of media change. The debates about the Camisards demonstrate the coexistence of older forms of oral culture and newer forms of printed discourse over two hundred and fifty years after the advent of the printing press. We do, nonetheless, see early political uses of print media at a time when such debates were technically illegal. And, in fact, the relative merits of print and oral culture were themselves the subject of the debates.

Within the bounds of a loose narrative of the history of the Camisards from the first prophets following the Revocation of the Edict of Nantes to their arrival in London and the public controversy which followed, I discuss what I've divided—according to both chronological and generic criteria—into three groups of printed sources on the Camisards. The first group, published in the late seventeenth century, attempts simply to report on the religious revival in the Cévennes and often takes the form of compilations of letters or testimonies. This group of pamphlets demonstrates clearly that despite the fact that the printing press had been used in Europe for roughly two hundred and fifty years, the Camisards' message was seen as powerful and genuine precisely because it was orally transmitted. There was, in the end, a deep skepticism toward the printed word, even among the literate classes.

The second group, dating from 1702 and the official commencement of Louis XIV's War of the Cévennes, represents a literate appropriation of the Camisard cause for strictly political purposes by Protestant opponents of the French king. In this section, we will see that although political discussion and debate was technically illegal in France, and historians of the public sphere have routinely asserted that such debate did not arise in France until the second half of the eighteenth century, the printed representations of the Camisards and the War of the Cévennes exemplify just such a debate. Furthermore, we see not only the printed arguments of lettered elites, but the oral proclamations of illiterate peasants as an integral part of public, printed debate.

The third group is the mass of pamphlets and books that appeared in London after the Camisards' arrival there. This last group demonstrates that elites in Europe were themselves engaged in a debate about comparative media, arguing the relative worth of print and orality. The pamphlets and books discussed in this last section demonstrate the main lines of argument in opposition to the Camisards and to spiritual possession in general and show that in its essence, the debate concerned the legitimate sources of biblical or religious authority. The Camisards were opposed because of the social group from which they came and because their message was spread orally.

### Celebrating the Oral

> And it shall come to pass afterward, that I will pour out My Spirit on all flesh; your sons and your daughters shall prophesy, your old men shall dream dreams, your young men shall see visions.[2]

The Edict of Fontainbleau of October 18, 1685, which revoked the Edict of Nantes and ended roughly one hundred years of limited toleration of the Huguenots, offered the Protestant ministers two choices: either they could convert to Catholicism or they had fifteen days to leave France. Even before the Revocation, of course, Huguenots had been fleeing France to take refuge mainly in Switzerland, Holland, and England, and in the month or so immediately preceding the Edict, royal soldiers forced whole communities to convert. In July, for example, 21,000 of the 22,000 Protestants in Béarn converted in a few days, and similar forced conversions occurred in September and October throughout the south of France.[3] The intendant of Poitiers, Lamoignon de Bâville, was so content with the "abjurations générales" in the Cévennes during the first weeks of October that he wrote, "There is not a single parish which has not been fully cleansed."[4] Of the 128 ministers in Languedoc and the Cévennes in October 1685, fifty-four converted to Catholicism and seventy-four left the country, mainly for

Geneva or other Swiss towns, joining the twenty or so who had fled in the preceding two years.[5]

Louis XIV probably assumed that once the Protestant ministers were removed and their temples destroyed, the Reformed religion would cease to exist in his realm. What he did not predict, however, was the strength of the Huguenots' oral culture, specifically the degree to which their religious mentality had been rooted in the psalm-singing and Bible-reading that characterized Protestant services. Royal efforts to force young Cevenols to receive Catholic schooling achieved little, as parents, according to Bâville, "destroyed each evening all the good that the teachers were able to do" during the day.[6]

By January 1686, lay preachers, or *prédicants*, began preaching clandestinely at secret assemblies usually held at night in secluded, outdoor locations. The metaphor of the "desert" referred to both the physical and spiritual isolation of the Huguenot assemblies,[7] and the Huguenots found comfort not only in their meetings, but also in the belief that the persecution they endured was part of God's scheme for the coming of the millennium. Early in the century, the works of Pierre du Moulin had circulated widely in the south of France and predicted that the end of the trials of the true church would come with the resurrection of the Two Witnesses in 1689.[8] Du Moulin's grandson, the exiled Huguenot minister Pierre Jurieu, whose work was also read in the south of France, used different calculations to arrive at the same date.[9]

In the summer of 1685, after a plague of grasshoppers invaded the Mediterranean coast and the dragoons continued to terrorize the Cévenols, the Huguenots of the Desert first had contact with Jurieu's millennial writings,[10] and in later years they were certainly aware of his *Pastoral Letters* and *Accomplissement des Prophéties*.[11] After fleeing France, Jurieu, who held a position as pastor and Professor of Hebrew and Theology at Rotterdam, celebrated the secret assemblies of the Cévennes in his *Pastoral Letters* as well as in his later publications. An installment of the *Pastoral Letters* was written roughly every two weeks and a collection of the first twenty-four was published in both French and English in 1689. The letters were specifically addressed to the Huguenots remaining in France, although they were also translated into English, Dutch, German, and Hungarian. In the very first of these letters, Jurieu glorifies the secret assemblies of the Cévennes:

> for more than four months time there have been Assemblies almost every day in the Cévennes, and in adjacent parts, for the offering up of Prayers and Supplications to God, sometimes in Woods, and at other times in Caves, and Rocks, and Dens of the Earth. The Dragoons, which almost always surprize them, put them to the Sword according to their

Instructions, they Kill and Hang, and drag them into Prisons: but all signifies nothing, they assemble nevertheless.[12]

Himself a minister, Jurieu saw the necessity of *prédicants*. His fourth letter reveals respect for oral religious expression and skepticism toward written sermons when he urges the Protestants in France to preach among themselves and emulate the secret assemblies of the Cévennes:

> You must assemble amongst your selves as often as you can, read the Scripture together, and good Books of Christian morality, and you must recal what you can remember of former Sermons. You must mutually comfort one another by good Prayers, and good Conversations, and good Discourses, which without being studied are oftentimes of greater edification than Sermons on which the fancy of a Preacher hath toiled and labored many days. To conclude, you must imitate the zeal of your Brethren of Languedoc.[13]

But the people of the Cévennes did not merely recite those biblical passages and sermons they could remember. The first prophets appeared in the Cévennes in 1687–1688. They were usually—but not exclusively—female adolescents and they urged their followers to repent for their sins and expect the Day of Judgment. Isabeau Vincent is the best known of the first generation of prophets. A sixteen-year-old shepherdess, she cried out in her sleep one night in 1688 and began to sing the Ten Commandments. Huguenots gathered in her uncle's house while she preached in her sleep and her body displayed wild agitations and contortions. These gatherings continued for four months before she was arrested and placed in a convent. But she continued her wild ecstasies, thus embarrassing the Catholic officials, and was eventually released. Once free she preached repentance and deliverance in her sleep at outdoor assemblies, and soon others, often children as young as eight or nine, emulated her.

When they could locate the assemblies, the royal dragoons attacked them and arrested the *inspirés,* often killing a few individuals in the dispersion. But this violent oppression only corroborated the millenarian expectations of the trials of the true church.

In 1689 *A Relation of Several Hundreds of Children and Others that Prophesie and Preach in their Sleep* was printed in London and contains translations of letters and extracts from letters originally written in French. I will describe the text in some detail, for it crystallizes those aspects of the Cévenol prophets that so intrigued literate observers. The letters describe various instances of children *inspirés,* anticipating readers' doubts about the divine origin of the inspirations. For example, the first letter, originally written in Geneva, admits that "there is something in this story which at first seems ridiculous" and "it looks like a thing only fit to be laughed at."[14] The second letter also notes, "to determine with what Spirit these Prophets are possessed, whether with the Spirit of God or with the Devil, whether with Art or Disease, I leave to wiser than me to judge."[15] Another is even more unsure: "it is so surprising and amazing, that . . . I could not but doubt a little such extraordinary Matters."[16]

Yet the overall emphasis of this collection of testimonies is to convince the readers of the miraculous occurrences described. First, the letters and testimonies exhibit great sympathy for the young prophets, who face cruel persecution at the hands of royal and Catholic officials:

> It must make a Man sad, when one afterwards sees the Prisons of Grenoble, Cret and of Valence full of those preachers, of all Ages and Sexes, and of those that have heard them Preach, of what Quality or Condition soever they be; When one sees Barns and Farm houses pulled down or burnt, because those Children have preached there, and that Vally full of Souldiers that are there on purpose to ruine the Inhabitants.

Yet despite the persecution, the *inspirés* continued preaching and their numbers increased: "when one sees that two of them are Arrested, there presently appear six others, and that among those that heard them and that were carried to Prison, there are some that before they came thither fall down, fall asleep, and Prophesy."[17]

Of course, other factors support the claims of divine inspiration. That the *inspirés* were uneducated shepherds or peasants is often used in their support. The very fact that their message was expressed orally implied an unadulterated sincerity and the simple eloquence of the preaching impressed observers. The author of one letter claims that he "never heard so good Prayers, nor more lively Exhortations" and another claims that the young shepherdess through whom the Holy Spirit had preached the night before spoke with "as much eloquence and Energy as can be imagined, and in as good Terms."[18] Hillel Schwartz generalizes, "the youth of the *inspirés,* their illiteracy or idiocy, their unsophisticated habits and rural background stood as proof of purity for Huguenots of the Desert."[19]

The oral power of the Camisards message was enhanced by the fact that some of the *inspirés* preached in French, not the dialect of the *pays,*[20] and many of the testimonies in the collection claim that such a miracle represented further proof of divine inspiration, as did the fact that none of the prophets preached "any thing but what is Orthodox."[21]

But the final proof of the legitimacy of the prophets lay in the fact that men of "worth" and "reputation" were themselves convinced. One of the letters in the collection relates the testimony of a "Physician and Philosopher" who examined a prophetess:

> he examined the Eyes, Pulse, the beating of the Heart of the Shepherdess, five different Nights, and daies, That notwithstanding the agitation she is in all the Night, she has her Pulse as quiet as one that is in a deep sleep, and her Body insensible. She has preached, saies he, from the third of February to the twenty eighth of May, the time that he wrote, but does not find her fell the least weary, rising as fresh in the Morning as if she had neither said nor done any thing.[22]

The author of another testimony was a lawyer described as "an able Man in his Profession, and of great Repute, and besides not Credulous and a Philosopher." One letter claimed that a shepherd's exhortations to repent and prophesies of the impending deliverance of the church convinced not only "Country Fellows, but . . . a considerable Gentleman, . . . a Merchant that is an ingenious Man, and . . . two Philosophers."[23]

The mixture of social groups that characterized the international Camisard controversy as a whole is seen clearly in the *Relation*. The editor, who provides a brief introduction, scattered commentary, and summaries of missing portions of the letters, was obviously an educated Englishman, perhaps an exiled Huguenot. The letters themselves were written by educated Huguenots from Geneva, Savoy, or France itself. And most importantly, the letters all highlight extended quotations from the oral preaching of the *inspirés*, who, as I mentioned, were largely illiterate, female shepherdesses, peasants, or wool carders.

In the end, the mixture of doubt and belief found in this collection of letters and reports is summed up: "such doubtful things are reported . . . yet there appears likewise much Sincerity."[24] Jurieu's position is similar. After describing an event when a "Man without Learning" had a divine vision one night, Jurieu writes,

> I know not whether it were the force of his zeal, and imagination which produced this effect, or whether it were actually a Voice from Heaven; however it were, all the reasonings and warnings of his Father, who turned both his Vision and Design into Ridicule, could not hinder him from following his Call, which he esteemed as coming from Heaven: he gathered Assemblies, he spake there with so much success, and with so much order and method, for a person of his quality, that everyone was surprized by it, and all that heard him edified by it.[25]

In short, it was precisely the illiteracy of the prophets and the oral quality of their message that not only garnered local support to the religious revival, but also convinced literate observers of the authenticity of the movement.

Gatherings like those described in the *Relation* and in Jurieu's *Pastoral Letters* continued for more than a decade, as did their persecution by Catholic and royal authorities. In
the first years of the eighteenth century a new group of prophets began trance-preaching.
The second generation of *inspirés* was more militant than the first. Whereas the first generation urged its followers to repent for their sins and expect God's deliverance, the second generation added violent aggression to millenarian expectations. In contrast to the
first generation of prophets who, as I mentioned, were largely female adolescents, this
second generation was almost entirely male and, in their twenties, older than the first.
They often wore white, wool shirts, thereby earning the name Camisards or sometimes
White Camisards.

In 1702 Abraham Mazel had "several revelations which told [him] to prepare to take
up arms with [his] brothers to combat [their] persecutors."[26] That summer, when the
abbé du Chayla and the local dragoons interrupted a Huguenot assembly and took some
prisoners, Mazel and his followers responded. The next night they attacked the abbot's house, freeing the prisoners and killing the abbot. Louis XIV responded by sending 20,000 troops into Languedoc, thus beginning officially the War of the Cévennes.

We can only speculate what might have happened had the Catholic and royal officials
not responded to the *prédicants* with such violent repression. In persecuting the peasants,
weavers, and shepherds of the Cévennes, however, Louis XIV made heroes out of them.

### Politics in Print

A word, nay a Letter, oftentimes changes the whole Sense of a Discourse.[27]

The fact that Louis was forced to send such extensive forces into the Cévennes demonstrates what an embarrassment the Camisards had become for him. He was certainly responding to printed propaganda. Legally, any publication at the time was required to gain
the approval of royal censors, and political discussion was forbidden. Historians of the
public sphere have generally followed Jürgen Habermas's assertion that before the middle
of the eighteenth century, political representation was made "not for but 'before' the
people."[28] The episode of the Camisards, however, attests that not only was there a vigorous public sphere debating the War of the Cévennes, but Louis XIV actively took part
in the debates. Even before the war officially began, M. de Brueys received royal patronage to write a book entitled *Histoire du fanatisme de notre temps* which was little more
than a denunciation of the Cévenol prophets.[29] In 1704 the crown wrote a letter to Pope

Clement XI complaining that the Camisards had been aroused by Protestants in Savoy and elsewhere.[30] And later, in 1712, the Marquis de Torcy arrested and jailed a man assumed to be "the first *nouvelliste* of the war of the Camisards."[31]

There was already a vigorous literature of Protestant opposition to Louis XIV when peasants and shepherds began trance preaching in the Cévennes. How did the Camisards' cause enter this discourse? How could an educated, literate class of Protestants, who themselves were continually attacking the 'irrationality' or 'superstition' of Catholicism, endorse and celebrate the wild agitations, sexual exhibitionism and millenarianism that characterized events in the Cévennes? In short, it didn't. Even Jurieu expressed doubts about the divine inspiration of the Camisard prophets, despite the fact that he espoused a millenarian ideology himself. A few other pamphleteers briefly mention the popular prophesying of the Camisards only to dismiss its importance. Clark Garrett generalizes, "the exiled Huguenot clergy had always looked with disfavor on the prophets, and . . . questioned whether the mood of ecstatic defiance that they encouraged was indeed in the best interest of their faith."[32] Nevertheless, many Protestant writers did favor the Camisard cause, and they phrased their arguments according to contemporary English political theory: a poor group of peasants was defending its traditional liberties against a despotic tyrant.[33]

A telling example is the pamphlet *A Wonderful Account from Orthez, in Bearne, and the Cevennes, of Voices heard in the Air, singing the Praises of God.* Printed in 1706 in London, the pamphlet contains letters and other testimonies dating from 1686 which relate a variety of divine miracles that had been occurring in the south of France. The section of the pamphlet containing the letters themselves resembles closely the form and content of the *Relation* discussed above. Yet despite the sensationalist title and the inclusion of letters describing angelic psalms coming from the sky and the prophetic inspirations of several shepherds and others, the whole first part of the pamphlet, obviously written for its publication in London, is a description of the persecution of the Protestants in France going back to the Wars of Religion of the sixteenth century with particular attention to the Saint Bartholomew's Day massacres.

The main task of those defending the Camisards in print is to demonstrate the lawfulness of the cause. They are concerned with demonstrating that the Camisards cannot be called 'rebels,' a term obviously reserved for unlawful insurrections. The anonymous author of *A Compleat History of the Cevennees* of 1703 writes in the dedication to Queen Anne, "The Imputation of Rebellion to this People is only a false gloss to amuse a giddy Multitude."[34] Pierre Boyer makes this argument by drawing a parallel between the Camisards and the English Revolution of 1688: "let the Cevenois go under what Name soever in other Countries, they ought not with English Men, and Protestants, to pass for Rebels; since they act upon the same Principle, by which the late Revolution was happily accomplish'd."[35]

Even when the Revolution of 1688 is not specifically named, its precedent is still important, for many of the arguments that justified the ousting of James II are used to legitimize the Camisard revolt. To demonstrate that the Camisards are within the law when taking up arms against their king, these authors provide endless details of the cruelties and persecutions Protestants in France have undergone and claim that Louis XIV is no longer the just king of the realm:

> Was there ever a greater piece of Cruelty and Injustice than to persecute these faithful and innocent Subjects; to banish some from the Kingdom, to transport others into desert Islands, to make Galley-slaves of others; and to take away the Lives of others by the most exquisite Torments. Now if provok'd by these Barbarities the poor Remains of the Protestants in France have taken up arms to defend those Rights and Liberties, which God, Nature and their Kings have given them, do they deserve the odious name of Rebels?[36]

These writers make it clear, however, that before taking up arms the Protestants attempted on several occasions to make their discontents known to their king, in hopes of some relief from persecution. Since a copy of a petition of the Protestants to Louis XIV was translated into English and printed in London in 1680, evidence was readily available to support this claim.

The writers defending the Camisards further claim that the Protestants in France were always strongly royalist. Boyer writes that the Protestants never considered themselves rebels or acted upon any "Republican Principle" but "at all times, they have been the firmest Support of their Monarchy, and maintain'd the rightful Succession to the Crown of France."[37] According to Guy Howard Dodge, the exiled Protestants were always royalist, and Pierre Jurieu is exemplary in this regard. Dodge refers to the period after the implementation of the dragoons in 1681 as the period of "desperate royalism" in Huguenot political thought.[38] In the sixteenth pastoral letter, Jurieu argues that of the three types of government (monarchy, aristocracy, democracy), monarchy is the best. Citing Romans 13, he claims that although the power of the sovereign does not originate in divine law, one is obliged by divine law to obey.[39] The anonymous *Manifesto of the Cevennois,* translated from French and reprinted toward the end of *A Compleat History,* declares, "The Kingdom of France never had any Subjects more faithful and submissive to their kings than our Fathers and we have constantly been," but "since they employed the Force of Arms to destroy us . . . we had also an unquestionable Right to oppose with Force. For it is a right of Nature, authorized by the Laws of God and Man."[40]

The literate, English defenders of the Camisards argue that by subjecting the Protestants to such cruel persecution and, above all, by revoking "several Edicts equivalent to our Acts of Parliament," most importantly the Edict of Nantes which the king had sworn to uphold in his coronation oath, "the Prince has not Broke down the Fence of Laws in this particular part of the kingdom only, but in several other Provinces the Nobility are divested of their ancient Authority." After all, "the Prince is to be considered no longer as such, than whilst he continues to model his government to the Law of the Nation." For "if a lawful Prince . . . breaks his Oath and Bounds, and Reigns Arbitrarily, he becomes a Tyrant and a Usurper."[41]

Not only has Louis XIV abused the natural rights and liberties of all his subjects, these authors argue, but the people of the Cévennes have special privileges. They descend from the Waldensians and Albigensians and, thus, their religious practices have a long tradition of the "Gothic Spirit of Liberty" and the "Truth of the Gospel." Under Louis XIV, however, the Protestants of the Cévennes "have been strip'd of their rights and Liberties, without the least Colour of Equity and justice."[42]

Another measure of the cruelty of Louis XIV, according to the author of *A Compleat History,* was his refusal to allow the Protestants to emigrate. It is merely another example of their persecution, helping to legitimate armed rebellion:

> First of all they supplicate their Prince in the most dutiful manner, to grant them a Toleration of their Worship, and when that was denied to them, to suffer them in the next place, to fly to another Country. This being likewise refused, and their restless Persecutors will continuing to load them with new pressures, who can blame them for force? . . . Reduc'd to this miserable condition, they had recourse to the oldest Law of Nature, I mean that of Self-Preservation.[43]

Undoubtedly, these arguments about the constitutional basis of religious toleration in France and legitimate resistance to the king would have meant little to Louis XIV himself—in France at this time they would indeed have been revolutionary—but in England they were more convincing, and were used to urge the English sovereign to send military troops and money to help the Camisards.

Abundant precedents are cited of the English crown aiding the Protestants in France against their tyrannical king; the examples of Elizabeth and Charles I are mentioned by several authors. Above all, it is to defend the Protestant interest that not only England but the other Protestant countries ought to aid the Camisards. Boyer writes that "Christian Charity" and "Reasons of Interest" should encourage "Protestant Princes and States to procure the Restoration of the Reformed Religion in France" and that England in particular has such a responsibility because of the precedents of English intervention during the Wars of Religion. He further asks, "what may not the Cevenois, and all the Protestants of France hope from the most Gracious, the Pious, the Victorious Queen Anne, a Queen who is not only the Defender of the Faith, by Hereditary Title, but the Nursing-Mother of the Church, by a particular Appointment of heaven?"[44] Another writer claims, "Naturally, the Protestant Princes and States . . . ought to protect and maintain the Protestant Subjects of other Princes" and refers to Queen Anne as "as zealous and Strenuous a Defender of the Protestant Interest both at home and abroad, as the great Heroine of the World, and her Glorious Predecessor, Queen Elizabeth was."[45]

Modern historians often argue that by the second half of the seventeenth century—specifically after the Thirty Years' War—wars were no longer waged simply on the basis of religion. Such may, in fact, have been the case, although the rhetorical value of such arguments had clearly lost no vigor. In any case, the argument about the necessity to defend the Protestant interest is not merely an evocation of imagined religious solidarity. It is closely tied to the political interests of the various nations of Europe which felt threatened by Louis XIV and his perceived aim of universal monarchy. Many authors claim that a military campaign should be undertaken in the Cévennes not merely to protect the Protestants there, but as part of an effort to thwart Louis XIV's ambitions towards universal monarchy. The author of *A Compleat History* writes that the Camisards:

> have the most reason to expect Assistance from some of the Protestant Estates. And undoubtedly nothing can contribute more to the suppressing the power of France, than such a Thorn in its side, which will soon affect the Vital and Noble parts, such a little Wound that has rancour in it, may soon fester, and so cause a Gangrene thro' the whole Body Politick.[46]

Boyer writes in less colorful but more emphatic language: "the general Fate of Christendom depends, in a manner, on the particular Destiny of the Camisards . . . whoever shall maturely and impartially consider the present State of Europe, will soon acknowledge the Truth of this Assertion."[47] Thus, the pretensions and tyrannies of Louis XIV demand not only that the French subjects take up arms against him, but that the other powers of Europe do the same.

The timing of the publications of these writings corresponded exactly with the arrival of Anne to the throne of England, and should be seen as part of an effort to ensure that Anne continued William's war against France. Even during the Nine Years' War there was a movement in Parliament in opposition to a strong war effort. The "country" voice urged that England should not be the principal power in the war, but only an auxiliary one, and mercantile interests were also opposed to an increased military effort, since trade with the Mediterranean and west Africa had been damaged severely by the war. In 1702, as Anne took the throne, the French were in "effective possession of the entire Spanish empire," particularly the whole Spanish Netherlands.[48] These pamphleteers who claimed to be defending the Camisards were clearly more concerned about maintaining the war against France out of fear of France's international power.

In short, the Camisard controversy and the War of the Cévennes gave rise to a vigorous public debate regarding French and international politics. This is noteworthy, for it represents a political use of printed matter over half a century before most historians have dated the full development of the public sphere in France. But in using the Camisards for their own political purposes, the literate opponents of the French king changed the terms of debate and transformed the image of the Camisards. Whereas the Camisards saw their struggle as a local one, that is, against the local intendants, priests, and dragoons, their literate defenders from Holland and England place the Camisard cause within the larger context of the Huguenot struggle in France, with considerable emphasis on the Wars of Religion not only in Languedoc, but throughout the realm. Versed in contemporary political theories, they present the Camisard revolt as simply one manifestation—a particularly dramatic one, certainly—of legitimate opposition to Louis XIV's despotic rule and efforts towards universal monarchy. Presenting the Camisard revolt in these terms, they both rationalize and radicalize it. Until well into the War of the Cévennes, the Camisards themselves never attacked the legitimacy of the French king. They believed him to be ignorant of the oppression to which they were exposed and hoped that once he was made aware of the situation, he would put an end to it.[49] Their literate, Protestant defenders, however, claim that Louis had broken the contract to govern by the laws of the kingdom, and was no longer the legitimate sovereign. These accounts, then, although claiming to defend the Camisards, appropriated the Camisard cause for their own ends and, in the process, the distinctive features of the Camisard rebellion—prophetism and millenarianism expressed in oral proclamations—were ignored or repressed altogether.

## Competing Media

> The consideration of obliging the Publick at this time, when the discourse of every Coffee-
> house is about the affairs of the Camisards or Cevennois, I take to be a sufficient excuse for
> Publishing these Papers.[50]

By 1704 it was apparent that royal forces were subduing the rebels despite the Camisards' superior knowledge of the local mountains and valleys and a few minor Camisard victories early on. In that year, Abraham Mazel, who had been a prophet and military chief of the Camisards, fled the country for Geneva. His prophetic inspirations and eschatological fervor were not well received there, and after attempting to reside in other Swiss towns as well as failing in a couple of military efforts to re-enter Languedoc, he arrived in London in 1706. Similarly, Elie Marion, one of the few literate Camisards, left for Switzerland in 1704 and continued to London after a failed military endeavor in Languedoc.[51] These two joined Durand Fage and Jean Cavalier de Sauve[52] who had been in London for a couple of years and had just gained attention by proclaiming prophetic warnings before small audiences.

By the time Marion and Mazel arrived in London, Fage and Cavalier had already established a procedure that would cause a stir among London's literate class. They would gather in a house in front of an audience and two or three scribes. When one of them entered their prophetic agitations, the scribes would take down their statements and then sign an oath swearing that they had done no more than preserve what was uttered by the prophets. Just as the testimonies of physicians, lawyers and merchants gave credibility to the original occurrences in the Cévennes, so "the stature of their followers increased the appeal of Fage, Cavalier and (soon) Marion."[53] The swearing of oaths by the scribes also testifies to the public nature of the prophetic gatherings and the centrality of the oral prophecies.

In 1707 a deluge of publications from London addressed the French prophets. Maximilien Misson, a Huguenot refugee from Normandy,[54] collected many of the transcriptions by scribes as well as extracts from related books, pamphlets, and letters, and published them as *Le theatre sacré des Cevennes*. John Lacy published an English translation entitled *The Cry from the Desart*, which included a controversial preface.[55] Marion published his *Avertissemens prophétiques*, which was immediately translated into English, and Lacy came out with his own version, *The Prophetical Warnings of John Lacy*.

That same year literature in opposition to the prophets began to appear. An English translation of *Fanaticism renouvélé* was finally published (the French original dating from 1704) and contained a preface referring specifically to Marion's *Prophetick Warnings* and *The Cry from the Desart*. George Keith published a pamphlet denouncing the Quakers but felt obliged to provide a preface and postscript denouncing the Camisards as well. The next few years witnessed a continued outpouring of anti-Camisard literature. Schwartz has located over seventy-eight pieces in opposition to the Camisards published in London between 1706 and 1710 and several others published in the next few years. These numbers exclude any publications originating from the continent, even if they were later translated.[56]

The public debate surrounding the Camisards after their arrival in London is interesting in terms of comparative media specifically because the debate itself centers on the relative merits of print and orality. Prophecies and apparitions had since the Middle Ages been the only avenues for the lower classes—especially women—to gain religious authority, and since the sixteenth century those types of religious expression had increasingly come under scrutiny by the Catholic and Protestant churches. But this debate in London expresses explicitly what made literate elites so nervous about the oral religious culture of peasants and the lower classes. The opposition to the French Prophets centered on two points: the base social origins and moral character of the individual prophets and the fact that divine knowledge conveyed orally obviated the need for the Bible and its literate interpreters.

The main text supporting the Camisards in this debate, *Le theatre sacré des Cévennes*, resembles in many ways those pamphlets discussed in section I. The book is an extensive anthology of excerpts relating to the Camisards in Languedoc and London, even containing pieces of books or other testimonies blatantly opposed to the Camisards. Misson admits that the inclusion of an excerpt from *L'histoire du fanatisme de notre temps* did not help his cause, but maintains, "I had neither any shame in including it nor any fear of leaving it out." He also refers to several other books and pamphlets published in opposition to the Camisards, and addressing the objections of some, he refuses to debate those writers who had published anonymously."[57]

The majority of Misson's excerpts were taken from dictations given by illiterate Camisards in London, either issued in prophetic trances or recounted as memories of occurrences in the Cévennes. Most of the excerpts relating to the Camisards in the Cévennes corroborate the descriptions by Jurieu and the other sources discussed in section I. Several testimonies describe outdoor gatherings at night where one or more female prophets were overtaken by divine possession and preached repentance and deliverance before royal dragoons interrupted the meetings and arrested or killed several in attendance.

In the second edition of his *Enthusiastic Imposters, No Divinely Inspired Prophets,* Richard Kingston discusses each of the excerpts from the *Le theatre sacré* in order and denounces every one. The first edition of his work had been published anonymously, and his decision to put his name on the second might have been motivated by Misson's comments. Kingston responds specifically not only to *Le theatre sacré,* but to other publications, including Marion's and Lacy's *Prophetick Warnings.*

Throughout the 220-page book, Kingston makes several distinct arguments against the Camisards, but never does he deny the possibility of divine inspiration altogether. Instead, he denounces the moral character of individual Camisards, who display "wicked Lives and Behaviours."[58] A few examples of Kingston's refutation of individual testimonies will serve adequately as examples of his arguments. An excerpt from a letter by Mathieu Boissier is the third item in *Le theatre sacré.* One day in 1697 Boissier was in Dauphiné when he went to a secret assembly and heard a young, female *prédicant.* Soon "the Spirit seized her and she made a great prayer." The description follows along the same lines as those described in section I. Boissier writes,

> She made a discourse so excellent, so moving and so well followed, with a boldness so sacred and such great zeal, that one was forced to believe that there was something in her which was not human. A poor, young girl of this sort was surely not capable in any manner of speaking in such a way.[59]

Kingston simply denounces Boissier's character, and the fact that so many of the Camisards came from peasant families is now used against them: "he is descended from one of the meanest Families of Loriol in Dauphiné and can scarcely write." Kingston further claims that even Jacques Mazel found the Camisards in London "to be a wretched sort of people."[60]

Kingston concludes that in general "we may clearly discern, that they who took the Depositions, that are inserted in the Sacred Theatre, disguised the Thoughts of the Witness; and by the Address of their Pens, made a Flourish of Miracles, where there was none at all." (Note again the deceptive quality of print.) But most of Kingston's argument resorts to a simple defamation of the moral character of individual Camisards. Durand Fage is called "a poor Devil . . . such a Composition of Knave and Fool" and Jean Cavalier de Sauve "an errant Coward, and a Vagabond" who "kept Company with a Woman of no great Reputation."[61]

Many of the arguments Kingston makes are similar to those of others writing in opposition to the Camisards. Originally published in French in 1704 and translated into

English in 1707, *Fanaticism Reviv'd* contains denunciations by various Catholic and royal officials. The anonymous author of the preface, who also specifically refutes Lacy's preface to *The Cry from the Desart,* believes that if the Camisards are possessed at all "it must be by the Spirit of the Devil," and he also defames their moral character by describing their promiscuous behavior:

> it cannot be deny'd, but that there remain'd very evident Tokens of their Love, Like-mindedness, Sympathy and Goodness to one another in the Sevennes, all the Young Wenches, who frequented their Meetings having been found fruitful in bringing forth Sons and Daughters to the Prophets from their first meeting in Publick, til they were entirely suppress'd.[62]

This book claims that "the source of all this Fanatick Rage, and the Original of the rising of the rebellious Hugonots" is due to one individual, William of Serre, who went to Geneva one day and read Jurieu's *Accomplissement des prophéties.* When he returned to the Cévennes, "he gather'd among the poor People, a parcel of Boys and Girls" and convinced them that God had given him His spirit, which he could in turn give to them and make them prophets. They would have to "prepare themselves for the receiving of that rare Gift by repeated Fasting." By making them fast for several days every week, "he dry'd up their Brain, distracted their Intellects, and easily fill'd them with wild Notions." Soon these new false prophets "drew such Numbers after them, that the Country [was] over-run with Fanaticks." All the Camisards' prophetic activities as well as their rebellious "Cruelties and Murders" are due, according to these arguments, to the devious "Design" of one "crafty Knave."[63]

Just as much of the discourse of the defenders of the Camisard insurrection discussed in section II centered on the barbarous cruelties of the dragoons, so is *Fanaticism Reviv'd* filled with accounts of various "Bloody Murders, Barbarious Desolations by Burning, Horrid Sacriledges, and other Villanies committed" by the Camisards. And just as the fact that the illiterate Camisard prophets spoke in French rather than their Languedocien dialect provided credibility to their trances, the fact that they could not speak other languages is used against them: "They tell us that in their Extatick Fits they spoke good French, who knew nothing of that Language before, it is very strange, if that were true, they should not have the same Privilege in another Tongue."[64]

Thus, we see that most of the arguments denouncing the Camisards do not deny the possibility of divine possession or millenarianism, but claim that the Camisards are impostors or enthusiasts, that they are deluded or even satanically possessed.[65] The opposition to the Camisards from those who themselves espoused millenarian expectations expresses well what I see to be the central conflict between the Camisards and their literate opponents: the Camisard debate in London was essentially a debate over the legitimate sources of religious authority. Edmund Chishull was an Anglican minister who himself displayed a "millenarian bent"[66] but opposed the Camisards because of the revolutionary implications of their brand of millenarianism[67] and because, very simply, they challenged his own authority. In his 1708 pamphlet entitled *The Great Danger and Mistake of all New Uninspired Prophecies,* Chishull assures his readers that the coming of the millennium would not be preceded by chaos and confusion, and that, most of all, the clergy must maintain their role as spiritual leaders.[68] Kingston was also bothered that the Camisards "advanced with Design to destroy reveal'd Religion and all good Government in the reform'd Churches of Jesus Christ"[69] and George Keith states the argument best, writing that "this notion of theirs," that illiterate peasants and women might receive the word of God,

> renders not only the Protestant Ministry useless, but the Whole Scripture it self and the Words and Writings of those extraordinary Inspired Prophets, to be of equal Authority with the Holy Scriptures, yet although they do not affirm this positively, yet it is the proper and genuine consequence of their Notion.[70]

We see clearly, then, that the essence of the opposition to the Camisards was a defense of the institutions of the church, the Bible, and the clergy as the legitimate source of religious authority.[71] Educated ministers, not illiterate peasants, are to serve as religious leaders, and the written Bible, not oral proclamations, are the source of religious knowledge.

## Conclusions

This story might be interpreted to indicate the success of print media over older forms of oral culture. Indeed, though the Camisards' early success was due to the authenticity associated with their oral messages, in the end, their movement was suppressed and the literate ministers maintained their control over religious authority and asserted the importance of the written word as the source of divine knowledge. In addition, the episode of the Camisards offers evidence that print media was carving itself out a new niche as a vehicle for public political debate.

However, although the Camisards had become the latest in a long line of targets in the increasing "rationalization" and institutionalization of religious practice, and a stress on the written word was part of that process, the popularity of the Camisards, even two hundred fifty years after the spread of the printing press throughout Europe, reveals a deep mistrust of the printed word. Very simply put, the religious revelation of the illiterate peasants was seen as legitimate precisely because it was oral, because it was not diluted by the written word. Only in this way can we understand the long transcriptions of Camisard prophecies and the importance of the scribes in London.

All these documents also shed light on the historical development of the public sphere and demonstrate the coexistence of old and new media. Several of the documents I've examined are themselves collections of testimonies and extracts from letters or other pamphlets or books. This is particularly the case with *Le theatre sacré des Cevennes, A Relation of Several Hundreds of Children,* and *A Wonderful Account.* In each of these pieces, in fact, the editor's voice is limited to the preface and a thin strand running through the collection, summarizing missing sections of text or providing brief biographical profiles of the individual authors. But in other literature as well, documents in whole or partial form are provided for readers' scrutiny. The printed sources that contain collections of letters and testimonies and make an effort to document occurrences in the Cévennes (or in London) and present them to the reader correspond closely to what Habermas describes as a precursor to the unofficial press. To Habermas, "news itself became a commodity" and "printed journals often developed out of the same bureaus of correspondence that already handled hand-written newsletters."[72]

However, the case of the printed representations of the Camisards makes it clear how we must amend Habermas's original formulation.[73] In my first suggestions, I can follow Keith Baker. Habermas argues that the public sphere only emerged with the "polarization of state and society" in the mid-eighteenth century, and under the absolute monarchs before that time, public representation was made "before" the people. He clearly underestimates the role of opposition to the crown and the extent to which the crown was forced into printed debates. Baker maintains, "the concept [of public opinion] took on meaning in France in the context of a political crisis of absolutism." He continues, "by accepting the logic of a politics of contestation . . . the royal government unwittingly conspired with its opposition to foster the transfer of ultimate authority from the public person of the sovereign to the sovereign person of the public."[74] Baker claims this transformation was apparent by the end of Louis XV's reign, although evidence here shows that even under Louis XIV, the monarchy was not only extremely sensitive to printed opposition, but even hired writers and engaged in public debates.[75]

Baker also remarks that "the public" should not be reduced simply to "sociological terms,"[76] questioning Habermas's assumption that the public sphere was a distinctly bourgeois formation. Throughout the printed documents I have examined, the testimonies of illiterate peasants and shepherds were transcribed and consumed by a literate class and, in fact, this sort of testimony represents a fair proportion of the printed discourse on the Camisards. Peter Stallybrass and Allon White argue that the public sphere was always a "mixture . . . in which aristocratic values and leadership were combined in a complex and uneven manner with the conservative desires of the squirearchy and the aspirations of the bourgeoisie in the City and the professions, and could never be a homogeneous one."[77] I would carry this argument even further, stressing the participation in the public sphere of popular—even rural and illiterate!—social groups.[78] In other words, forms of oral culture found an outlet in print media and, in the case of the Camisards at least, print may even have helped to glorify the oral. Even if many of those cited in *Le theatre sacré* and other documents were not intentionally contributing to a public debate in print, certainly Mazel dictated his memoirs of the War of the Cévennes to Charles Portalès in 1708 with the expressed desire to counter some of the opposition that had been aggressively voiced against him and his followers. In addition, there were two literate Camisards, Elie Marion and Jean Cavalier, the latter of whom was "obliged to draw up this brief recitation of adventures and misfortunes" in order to refute the "evil of these writers . . . distorting, in the most unjust manner, our activities, by the invention of the most vile lies in order to blacken us in the eyes of the public."[79]

The story of the Camisards and the printed discourse surrounding them must also be placed within the larger story of the Reformation and the Enlightenment, in which elite social groups increasingly separated themselves from popular culture and attempted to rationalize religion.[80] Clearly, at the turn of the eighteenth century, literate classes were, with some exceptions, skeptical of prophetism, but were not yet able to dismiss it entirely. The seriousness with which even those opposing the Camisards approached the subject suggests that popular prophetism expressed orally was still powerful enough to represent a threat to educated classes. And the fact that even those who espoused a type of millenarianism, such as Edmund Chishull, still opposed the Camisard prophets, demonstrates that what was opposed was unofficial religious authority, especially religious authority with millenarian and revolutionary potential, in the hands of lower classes.

## Notes

1. This chapter was first conceived in a graduate seminar at Berkeley directed by Carla Hesse. Her initial guidance was indispensable. At the conference at MIT, Robert Darnton and David Thorburn both offered helpful advice.

2. Joel 2:28.

3. Bost (1912), 32, 34–35.

4. Cited in ibid., 36.

5. Richardot in the introduction to Misson, ed. (1978), 24.

6. Cited by Richardot in ibid., 31.

7. See Deyon (1971).

8. For du Moulin's numerical calculations, see Schwartz (1980), 15.

9. In *The Accomplishment of Spiritual Prophecies* (1687) Jurieu links the coming of the millennium to late seventeenth-century international politics.

10. Schwartz (1980), 16.

11. Although beyond the scope of this essay, the influence of outside, printed sources on the Camisards deserves attention in its own right, especially in regard to the transition from peaceful, adolescent, female prophets to militant, adult, male prophets.

12. Jurieu (1689), 12.

13. Ibid., 75–76.

14. *A Relation of Several Hundreds of Children and Others that Prophesie and Preach in their Sleep* (1689), 2–4. Henceforth I will refer to this text simply as *Relation*.

15. Ibid., 7

16. Ibid., 30–31.

17. Ibid., 3–4.

18. Ibid., 7, 13.

19. Schwartz (1980), 31. In section III we will see opponents of the Camisards center on these same characteristics, that is, the Camisards' peasant background and illiteracy, as proof of the fallacy of their religious expression.

20. That the *inspirés* spoke *en langue* certainly astonished contemporary observers. Since the Huguenot services had always involved Bible-reading and psalm-singing, all in French, it is not surprising that the Cévenols would speak their local dialect in everyday life and yet possess a French religious vocabulary. Later, in section III, we will see English opponents of the Camisards ask why the prophets were limited to French and could not speak English when in England.

21. *Relation*, 7. Garrett (1985) argues that the orthodoxy exhibited in the preaching of the *inspirés* serves as proof of the vitality of local oral culture.

22. *Relation,* 13.

23. Ibid., 15, 19.

24. Ibid., 17.

25. Jurieu (1689), 77.

26. Mazel and Marion (1931), 5.

27. *Relation,* 35.

28. Habermas (1989), 8.

29. I have been unable to locate a copy of this book, although Misson includes an excerpt in his *Theatre sacré des Cévennes* (1707).

30. Klaits (1976), 198.

31. Ibid., 55. Klaits's whole book demonstrates clearly how sensitive Louis XIV was to printed propaganda of all sorts. For another specific example of the 'absolute' monarch entering a printed debate during this period, see Baker (1990, 207–09) who briefly discusses the French crown competing with the Huguenots over the representation of the English Revolution of 1688.

32. Garrett (1987), 33.

33. Both Rothkrug (1965) and Dodge (1947) claim that the opposition to Louis XIV was going through a process of "secularization" over the course of Louis XIV's reign. While I do not oppose such a view—indeed much of my research might corroborate that argument—I think Dodge ignores the genuinely religious aspects when he argues that Jurieu's *Accomplissement des prophéties* "had a tendency, probably intentional, to cloak with the apocalyptic guise the diplomatic manoeuvres of the Protestant states at the time" (37).

34. The pages of the dedication are not numbered.

35. Boyer, *The Lawfulness glory and advantage of Giving Immediate and Effectual Relief to the Protestants of the Cévennes* (1703), 6.

36. Boyer, *The Cevennois Reliev'd, Or else, Europe Enslaved* (1703), 7.

37. Ibid., 5.

38. Dodge (1947), 7.

39. See the summary of Jurieu's political philosophy in Dodge (1947), 45–48.

40. *Compleat History,* 196, 203.

41. Ibid., 186, introduction, 157.

42. Ibid., 36, 196, 189.

43. Ibid., 193.

44. Boyer, *Cevennois Reliev'd,* 9, 37.

45. *Compleat History,* introduction.

46. Ibid., 35.

47. Boyer, *Cevennois Reliev'd,* 38.

48. Jones (1979), 281–283, 288–290.

49. In the memoirs of Marion and Mazel as well as that of Jean Cavalier, all of which cover only the period after the official beginning of the War of the Cévennes, it is understood that Louis XIV had sent troops into Languedoc, but the enemies still remain the local dragoons, Bâville and the Maréchals de Montrevel and de Villars.

50. *Compleat History,* introduction.

51. Marion was a law student at Toulouse when the insurrection began in 1702. These events are recounted in most of the secondary literature and Marion's own version is found in chapters XI-XV of *Mémoires inédites* (1707).

52. Jean Cavalier de Sauve should not to be confused with his well-known cousin, the Colonel Jean Cavalier de Ribautes, a Camisard military leader of considerable reputation who published his *Mémoires sur la guerre des Camisards* in 1726.

53. Schwartz (1980), 73. The third chapter of this volume provides an excellent summary of the initial establishment of and controversy surrounding the French prophets.

54. According to Charles Bost, Misson, the son of a pastor, fled to England when the local church was closed by the French king in 1682. He was initially skeptical and for six weeks refused to visit the *inspirés* in London. See Mazel and Marion (1931), appendix IV.

55. Several anti-Camisard writers specifically mention Lacy's introduction to this work and argue at length against it. Unable to locate the English version, I am, unfortunately, working with the French original.

56. Schwartz (1978), 85–90.

57. Misson (1978), 48, 52.

58. Kingston (1707), 56.

59. Misson (1978), 62–63.

60. Kingston (1709), 37–38, 42.

61. Ibid., pp. 43, 59–60.

62. *Fanaticism Reviv'd* (1707), preface.

63. Ibid., 2–4, 23–24.

64. Ibid., title page, preface.

65. Schwartz (1978) argues that these explanations for the Camisards all reflect the same assumptions about the relationship of soul to body.

66. Ibid., 66.

67. Schwartz (1980) argues that for the Camisards "life itself was in jeopardy," especially after the intense persecution by the dragoons from 1698 to 1700, and "Camisard millenarian prophesy was consequently that of cataclysm" (283). On revolutionary attachments to millenarianism among the poor of the Middle Ages, see Cohn (1970).

68. Chishull (1708), 16–17.

69. Kingston (1709), 169.

70. Keith (1707), 82

71. It should not be surprising that of the twenty-six opponents of the Camisards for whom Schwartz (1978) has found biographical information, nineteen held ecclesiastical positions (82–83). However, I would not argue that opposition to the Camisards depended on personal interest in the ecclesiastical power structure. As mentionend above, most exiled Huguenots, not only the ministers, also opposed the Camisards' prophesying.

72. Habermas (1989), 21.

73. For a general overview of Habermas's description of the public sphere, see Calhoun (1992), 1–48.

74. Baker (1990), 171–172.

75. See p. 9 above. Much of the discussion in Klaits (1976) demonstrates the extent to which the monarchy under Louis XIV was intensely sensitive to printed opposition of all sorts and often countered that literature with propaganda of its own.

76. Baker (1990), 172.

77. Stallybrass and White (1986), 83.

78. Historians of pre-Revolutionary Paris have also found that songs, rumors, and other oral messages made their way into printed media. See, for example, Darnton (1996) and Farge (1994). However, these works only address Paris and the later eighteenth century. The Camisards, however, were rural peasants, and their messages made their way into international print media by the end of the seventeenth century.

79. Cavalier (1973), 23.

80. On prophetism in Italy and its persecution by the Catholic Church, see Niccoli (1990). On the Spanish Inquisition's efforts to distinguish true revelation from "enthusiasm," see Keitt (1998). For a general statement of the "withdrawal" of European elites from a whole range of popular practices in the mid-seventeenth century, see Burke (1978), especially chapters 8 and 9.

## Primary Sources

*An Account of a Dream at Harwich in a Letter to a Member of Parliament about the Camisards.* London: B. Bragg, 1708.

Boyer, Pierre. *The Lawfulness, Glory, and Advantage of Giving Immediate and Effectual Relief to the Protestants in the Cevennes.* London: J. Nutt, 1703.

———. *The Cevennois reliev'd, or else, Europe enslaved.* London: J. Nutt, 1703.

Bulkelley, Sir Richard. *An Answer to Several Treatises Lately Published on the Subject of the Prophets.* London: for B. Bragg, 1708.

Calamy, Edmund. *A Caveat Against the New Prophets.* London, 1708.

Cavalier, Jean. *Memoirs sur la guerre des Camisards.* Paris: Payout, 1973 [1726].

Chisholm, E. *The Great Danger and Mistake of all New Uninspired Prophesies Relating to the End of the World.* London: S. Manship, 1708.

Claude, Jean. *Les plaintes des Protestants, cruellement opprimez dans le royaume de France.* Cologne: Pierre Marteau, 1686.

*Clavis Prophetica, or, A Key to the Prophesies of Mons, Marion and the other Camisards.* London: F. Morphew, 1707.

*A Compleat History of the Cevennes.* London: Nich. Cox, 1703.

*Fanaticism Reviv'd: or, the Enthusiams of the Camisars.* London, 1707.

Joutard, Philippe, ed., *Les Camisards.* Paris: Gaillimard/Julliard, 1976.

———, ed. *Journaux Camisards, 1700–1715.* Paris: Union générale d'éditions, 1976.

Jurieu, Pierre. *The Pastoral Letters of the Incomparable Pierre Jurieu Directed to the Protestants of France Groaning under the Babylonish Tyranny.* London: T. Fabian, 1689.

———. *The Accomplishment of Scriptural Prophesies of the Approaching Deliverance of the Church.* London, 1687.

Keith, George. *The Magick of Quakerism, or the Chief Mysteries of Quakerism Laid Open. To which are added a Preface and Postscript relating to the Camisards.* London, 1707.

Kingston, Richard. *Enthusiastic Imposters, No Divinely Inspir'd Prophets.* London, 1709.

Lacy, John. *The Prophetical Warnings of John Lacy.* London, 1707.

Marion, Elie. *Avertissemens prophétiques.* London, 1707.

Mazel, Abraham and Elie Marion. *Mémoires inédites,* ed. Charles Bost. Paris: Librairie Fischbacher, 1931 [1708].

Misson, Maximilien, ed. *Le theater sacré des Cevennes.* Brignon: Presses du Languedoc, 1978 [1707].

*The Present French King Demonstrated an Enemy to the Catholick as Well as Protestant Religion.* London: Tim Goodwin, 1691.

*A Relation of Several Hundreds of Children and Others that Prophesie and Preach in their Sleep.* London, 1689.

*Les voeux d'un patriote* (Amsterdam, 1788). [Originally published as *Les Soupirs de la France esclave qui aspire après la liberté* (1689)].

*A Wonderful account from Othez, in Bearne, and the Cevennes, of voices heard in the air.* London, 1706.

### Secondary Sources on the Camisards

Alameras, C. *La révolte des Camisards* (1960).

Ascoli, Georges. "L'Affaire des prophètes français à Londres," *Revue du XVIIIe siècle* 3 (1916).

Bosc, Henri. *La guerre des Cévennes,* 4 vols. Presses du Languedoc/Curandera, 1985.

Bost, Charles. *Les prédicants protestants des Cévennes et du Bas-Languedoc, 1684–1700,* 2 vols. Paris: Honoré-Champion, 1912.

———. "Les 'Prophètes des Cévennes au XVIIIe siècle," *Revue d'histoire et de philosophie religieuse* 5 (1925).

Colas, Dominique. *Civil Society and Fanaticism: Conjoined Histories,* trans. Amy Jacobs. Stanford: Stanford University Press, 1997. chapter 6 and passim.

Court, Antoine. *Histoire des troubles des Cévennes.* Marseille: Lafitte Reprints, 1975 [1760].

Deyon, Solange. "La résistance protestante et la symbolique du desert," *Revue d'histoire moderne et contemporaine* 18 (1971).

Douen, Orentin. *Les premiers pasteurs du Desart, (1685–1700).* Paris: Grassart, 1879.

Ducasse, A. *La guerre des Camisards.* Paris: Hachette, 1978.

Garrett, Clarke. *Spirit Possession and Popular Religion from the Camisards to the Shakers*. Baltimore: Johns Hopkins Press, 1987.

————. "Spirit Possession, Oral Tradition, and the Camisard Revolt," *Popular Traditions and Learned Culture in France*, ed. Marc Bertrand. Saratoga: Anma Libri, 1985.

Joutard, Philippe, and Daniel Ligou. "Les deserts, 1685–1800" in *Histoire des protestants en France*. Toulouse: Privat, 1977.

Mazoyer, Louis. "Les origins du prophétisme cévenol (1700–1702)," *Revue historique* 162, 1947.

*La Revocation de l'Edit de Nantes dans les Cévennes et le bas-Languedoc,* Actes du Colloque de Nîmes, 1985. Nîmes: Editions Lacour, 1986.

Schwartz, Hillel. *The French Prophets: The History of a Millenarian Group in Eighteenth-Century England*. Berkeley: University of California Press, 1980.

————. *Knaves, Fools, Madmen, and that Subtitle Effluvium: A Study of the Opposition to the French Prophets in England, 1706–1710*. Gainesville: University of Florida Press, 1978.

## *Other Secondary Sources*

Baker, Keith Michael. "Public Opinion as political invention" and "Inventing the French Revolution" in *Inventing the French Revolution*. New York: Cambridge University Press, 1990.

Bossy, John. *Christianity in the West, 1400–1700*. New York: Oxford University Press, 1985.

————. "Godparenthood: The Fortunes of a Social Institution in Early Modern Christianity," in *Religion and Society in Early Modern Europe, 1500–1800,* ed. Kaspar von Greyerz. London: Allen and Unwin, 1984.

————. "Blood and Baptism: Kinship, Community and Christianity in Western Europe from the Fourteenth to the Seventeenth Centuries," in *Sanctity and Secularity: The Church and the World: Studies in Church History,* ed. Derek Baker. New York: Oxford University Press, 1973.

Burke, Peter. "How to be a Counter-Reformation Saint," in *Religion and Society in Early Modern Europe, 1500–1800,* ed. Kaspar von Greyerz. London: Allen and Unwin, 1984.

————. *Popular Culture in Early Modern Europe*. New York: Harper and Row, 1978.

Calhoun, Craig, ed. *Habermas and the Public Sphere*. Cambridge, MA: MIT Press, 1992.

Christian, William. *Apparitions in Late Medieval and Renaissance Spain*. Princeton: Princeton University Press, 1981.

————. *Local Religion in Sixteenth-Century Spain*. Princeton: Princeton University Press, 1981.

Cohn, Norman. *The Pursuit of the Millennium*. New York: Oxford University Press, 1970.

Darnton, Robert. *The Forbidden Best-Sellers of Pre-Revolutionary France.* New York: W. W. Norton, 1996.

Dodge, Guy Howard. *The Political Theory of the Huguenots of the Dispersion with Special Reference to the Thought and Influence of Pierre Jurieu.* New York: Columbia University Press, 1947.

Eisenstein, Elizabeth L. *The Printing Press as an Agent of Change: Communications and Cultural Transformations in Early-Modern Europe,* 2 vols. New York: Cambridge University Press, 1979.

Farge, Arlette. *Subversive Words: Public Opinion in Eighteenth-Century France,* trans. Rosemary Morris. University Park: Pennsylvania State University Press, 1995.

Furet, François and Jacques Ozouf. *Reading and Writing: Literacy in France from Calvin to Jules Ferry.* New York: Cambridge University Press, 1982.

Habermas, Jürgen. *The Structural Transformation of the Public Sphere: An Inquiry into a Category of Bourgeois Society,* trans. Thomas Burger. Cambridge, MA: MIT Press, 1989.

Jones, J. R. *Country and Court: England 1658–1714.* Cambridge, MA: Harvard University Press, 1979.

Kagen, Richard L. *Lucretia's Dreams: Politics and Prophecy in Sixteenth-Century Spain.* Berkeley: University of California Press, 1990.

Keitt, Andrew Wannamaker. "'Inventing the Sacred': Religious Enthusiasm and Imposture in Mid-Seventeenth-Century Madrid." Ph.D. diss., University of California, Berkeley, 1998.

Klaits, Joseph. *Printed Propaganda under Louis XIV: Absolute Monarchy and Public Opinion.* Princeton: Princeton University Press, 1976.

Kreiser, B. Robert. *Miracles, Convulsions, and Ecclesiastical Politics in Early Eighteenth-Century Paris.* Princeton: Princeton University Press, 1978.

Malssen, P. J. W. *Louis XIV d'après les pamphlets répandus en Holland.* Amsterdam, 1936.

Niccoli, Ottavia. *Prophecy and People in Renaissance Italy,* trans. Lydia G. Cochrane. Princeton: Princeton University Press, 1990.

Orcibal, Jean. *Louis XIV et les protestants.* Paris, 1951.

Outram, Dorinda. *The Enlightenment.* New York: Cambridge University Press, 1995.

Popkin, Richard H., ed. *Millenarianism and Messianism in English Literature and Thought, 1650–1800.* Leiden: E. J. Brill, 1988.

Rothkrug, Lionel. *Opposition to Louis XIV: The Political and Social Origins of the French Enlightenment.* Princeton: Princeton University Press, 1965.

Stallybrass, Peter, and Allon White. *The Politics and Poetics of Transgression.* Ithaca: Cornell University Press, 1986.

# 11 Redefining the Home Screen: Technological Convergence as Trauma and Business Plan

William Boddy

Every electronic media product launch or network debut carries with it an implicit fantasy scenario of its domestic consumption, a polemical ontology of its medium, and an ideological rationale for its social function. The scattered public record of these self-representations, in the ephemeral forms of TV commercials, corporate press releases, and trade-press reporting, can offer insights into the larger contexts and implicit assumptions within which media firms operate. The current period of confusion and conflict among the would-be architects of our putative post-television age offers a productive site to investigate the ways in which wider social, technological, and political changes may deform or put into crisis such calculated representations of media apparatus and artifact. The shifting boundaries between analogue and digital, cinema and television, and broadcasting and the Internet, throw into question traditional critical oppositions between domestic and public media reception, active and passive scenarios of consumption, and authored and non-authored texts. As powerful firms within and outside the television industry improvise strategies of competition and alliance around the introduction of digital products and services, new self-serving fantasies of the medium's nature and use will undoubtedly be offered to consumers and policy-makers. We have much to learn in attending to such frankly commercial discourses, despite their ephemeral nature and dubious reliability as forecasters, for such instrumental fantasies of consumption can speak eloquently of the larger cultural ambivalence regarding new communications technologies. This paper represents a modest effort toward this larger goal through an examination of the introduction of a new consumer product in the U.S., the digital "personal video recorder" or PVR in the late 1990s.

One way to assess the significance of technological innovations such as the PVR is to chart their impact upon traditional assumptions about television and its audience, assumptions themselves informed by specific historical forces within and outside of the television industry. The current turmoil around the transition to digital standards throws into stark relief how far the industry has moved from the instrumental fantasies of reception, ontology, and national identity associated with the era of network television in the United States from the 1940s into the 1980s. The first four decades of postwar American television, dominated by the formidable economic and cultural power of three network firms, is noteworthy beyond the phenomenal economic prosperity and relative structural stability that the TV industry enjoyed. As commercial television was consolidated within American economic and cultural life, a remarkably consistent and enduring set of ideas about the general nature and function of the television medium was also elaborated. Responding in complex ways to the self-promoting discourses of industry groups, including network defenses of their economic power, a web of "common sensical," if largely implicit, propositions about the medium permeated public and trade discussions of the TV medium. These assumptions found a place within both popular and elite criticism of television, were invoked by both defenders and antagonists of the industry, and guided policy-makers and legislators concerned with the medium, sustaining an common image of television as quotidian and domestic, advertising-dominated, audio-driven, visually impoverished, female-centered, and passively consumed. In American media scholarship, it was not until the somewhat belated impact of cultural studies approaches to audience research that such constructions underwent systematic revision. Unlike the cultural positioning of cinema in the United States since the 1940s, increasingly associated with the possibilities for artistic status, personal expression, cosmopolitanism, and high cultural prestige, American television was generally construed in terms of its domesticity, liveness, and its role as an indispensable agent of national identity. The significance of the current period of technological innovation within moving-image culture is suggested by the ongoing erosion of the consensus regarding many of these traditional propositions about the nature and uses of commercial television.

Leaders of the three dominant U.S. networks at the height of their enormous postwar prosperity and power had their own reasons for ratifying these imagined essentialized features of the medium. Countless network statements in the mid-1950s linked commercial television's role as nation-builder with the medium's purportedly all-powerful relationship with its domestic audience. In 1954, the year that CBS became the world's largest single advertising medium, CBS network president Frank Stanton told a gathering of journalists: "The most remarkable thing is what the *Public* does. Putting aside all other considerations, the public glues its eyes and ears to newspapers, loudspeakers and television tubes; seeing everything, hearing everything and—heaven help us all—

believing everything." Stanton outlined the importance of the commercial media in constituting American national identity for such a credulous population: "*We give America its daily consciousness of being a Nation. If it weren't for us, private individuals all, and private businesses all, America would not know where it stood or what it felt.*" Stanton concluded by defending television's role as nation-builder: "I am far from saying we are a perfect mirror, or even always a well-polished one, . . . but if this mirror were shattered, the National Countenance would disappear."[1]

The U.S. television networks had specific motives in the mid-1950s for claiming the role of national looking glass and consciousness-maker. Two network firms, CBS and NBC, which controlled only 11 percent of television industry assets, took in an estimated 43 percent of total industry profits in 1955.[2] The previous year, CBS alone captured 28 percent of the profits of the entire television industry, boosted by an annual return of 1,800 percent from the operation of its New York City station.[3] Given their vulnerability to public and regulatory charges of monopoly power, the networks defended their monopoly on live provision of nationwide programming with high-minded appeals to national identity and necessity. For example, CBS's Frank Stanton told a Congressional committee in 1956 that "to curtail or destroy the networks' unique quality of instantaneous national interconnection would be a colossal backward step. It would make the United States much more like Europe than America. In fact, it would be a step in the direction of the *Balkanization,* the fragmentation, of the United States."[4]

If network leaders in the 1950s claimed that U.S. national identity depended upon their unfettered market power, they also argued for their own legitimation via a quasi-electoral mechanism of viewer choice; as Stanton told the Congressional committee, "a network draws its validity in precisely the same fashion as an elected official of government—from election by and of the people."[5] Thus the image of television as a quasi-statist oligopoly serving a domesticated and credulous audience was reinforced by network leaders defending their monopoly powers from the threats of regulation and competition.

In a similar manner, leaders of the two major networks defended their commercial practices before a series of congressional committees in the mid-1950s by associating their operations with ontological and aesthetic claims for the privileged status of live television, what CBS's Frank Stanton called "the very lifeblood and magic of television."[6] During the 1950s, the networks posited this strategic ontology of liveness against competition from potential pay-television services built upon the feature film libraries of the Hollywood studios. In CBS's Annual Report for 1955, Stanton argued that such networks would "highjack the American public into paying for the privilege of looking at its own television sets."[7] In a 1955 CBS pamphlet, Stanton described pay television as "a booby trap, a scheme to render the television owner blind, and then rent him a seeing eye dog at so much per mile—to restore to him, only very partially, what he had previously enjoyed as a natural right."[8] CBS's mid-1950s evocation of pay television as a violation of both television's ontological destiny of liveness and of the "natural rights" of television viewers resonated with the pervasive rhetoric of anti–Americanism in the political discourse of the time and implicitly aligned advertising-supported television with the legitimating operations of the state. Television's association in both elite and public opinion with viewer credulity, liveness, consumer sovereignty, and national identity was sustained by industry leaders and critics alike over the three or four decades of network domination of the U.S. television industry after WWII.

If many of the truisms about American commercial television can be traced back to the era of network ascendancy of the mid-1950s, such associations endured long after network power began to fade in the mid–1970s. The traditional opposition in reception sites between the domestic television receiver and the public cinema screen, with its persistent gender implications, has recently been challenged both by the growing popularity of domestic home-theatre installations and by the prospect of the electronic distribution and projection of feature films in public cinemas. While decried by some critics as the lamentable "domestication" of the theatrical film experience, the 1990s home-theatre boom has provided new masculinist pleasures of technological fetishism and feature-film collecting and connoisseurship and has arguably changed the modes of attention and sociality around which at least some television is consumed in the home. More significantly, prospective changes associated with digital delivery and recording media in the home promise to further de-stabilize traditional notions of the nature of television, its audience, and its links to national identity, as we shall see in the case of the PVR.

It is symptomatic of the current unsettled state of the U.S. television industry generally that the mid-1999 commercial launch of the seemingly-prosaic personal video recorder, a VCR-like appliance which records programs on a computer hard drive and downloads program schedules overnight via an internal modem, has already provoked apocalyptic warnings of the death of commercial television from some TV executives. While a number of major studios and television networks have responded to the personal video recorder by making direct investments in the two start-up manufacturers of the new devices, Replay Networks Inc. and TiVo Inc., other major media firms have threatened to sue the same manufacturers for copyright infringement. Four large media companies—Walt Disney, CBS, the News Corporation, and Discovery Communications—have, in fact, both made direct investments *and* threatened to sue the PVR manufacturers.[9]

One of the novel features of the PVR is its ability to record and replay material at the same time, allowing viewers to record an on-air program as they watch it, walk out of the room for an interval, and resume viewing the recording at the point at which they left, jumping past commercials on playback as desired. Replay's vice-president of marketing reported that tests of the device among consumers indicated that "after they've had the unit a while they stop watching live TV."[10] This new form of time-shifting is merely one sign of the ways in which digital technology, at least in the eyes of many current industry leaders and pundits, is eroding the experience of simultaneity and liveness that has traditionally been seen both as part of television's essential nature and central to its relation to the nation. MIT's Nicholas Negroponte predicted in 1995 that "digital life will include very little real-time broadcast. . . . With the possible exception of sports and elections, technology suggests that TV and radio of the future will be delivered asynchronously."[11] In the same year, Microsoft CEO Bill Gates nostalgically described the communal aspects of the traditional live national television broadcast as instrument of national unity: "When we Americans share national experiences, it is usually because we're witnessing events all at the same time on television—whether it is the Challenger blowing up after liftoff, the Super Bowl, an inauguration, coverage of the Gulf War, or the O. J. Simpson car chase. We are 'together' at those moments." However, Gates argued, "it is human nature to find ways to create synchronous communications into asynchronous forms."[12] Notwithstanding such dubious appeals to human nature or technological will in forecasting the decline of the live nationwide broadcast, other observers have expressed skepticism about the significance of the entire project of television as agent of national identity, a central tenet of the network broadcasting era. As the *New York Times* briskly advised in a January 1999 editorial: "to the lament that we are losing a sense of national community as television grapples with its recombinant future, there is only one thing to say: Get a life."[13] Just as the three powerful networks had economic interests in proposing the nationwide live broadcast as television's unique aesthetic and nation-building mission in the 1950s, specific sectors of the media industry have their own commercial motives in announcing the end of simultaneity in the late 1990s.

If the prospect of digital delivery and storage of television programming has put into crisis the long-standing privileging of the live nationwide broadcast as guarantor of national cohesion, the digital personal video recorder has also re-ignited debates going back to the 1950s over advertising- versus subscription-supported television. The ease with which viewers might skip commercials recorded via the new device has led some industry observers to offer doomsday scenarios for commercial television, as declining advertising revenues force networks to bail out of bidding wars with pay television firms for the most desirable programming. One Young & Rubicam advertising executive told the *New York Times:* "I think conventional television, while not quite dead, is going to do a slow death here," and the chairman of Viacom's MTV Networks told the paper: "I hate to think about Replay and TiVo. We kind of like the world the way it is now."[14] At the same time, the television networks in the 1990s seem uncertain about how to frame the perceived threat to commercially supported television in the ideological terms of their 1950s opposition to pay-television proposals. For Garth Ancier, head of NBC Entertainment, the prospect of the migration of the most popular television programs from advertiser-supported to pay television brought about by the ad-busting personal video recorder "is either anti-American or totally American, depending on how you look at it."[15]

The prospect of large numbers of TV viewers using their PVRs to evade television commercials has also led to predictions that advertisers and broadcasters will respond by creating advertising formats impossible for viewers to escape, including intensive product placement within programs, on-screen banner advertisements, and program-length commercials.[16] A spokesperson for Replay Networks told journalists in August 1999: "We know there will be people who want to skip commercials. The goal for us is to find other ways for companies to deliver their messages."[17] Robert Tercek, senior vice president of digital media for the Columbia-TriStar Television Group at Sony Pictures, described the programming logic of Sony's partnership with WebTV and TiVo by invoking mail-order catalogs as program models: "There's no reason why TV programs in this new media have to be 30 minutes or an hour long. In fact, there are a lot of reasons why you want to make them shorter. It costs you a lot to keep an audience there. . . . J. Crew could be a show—it already is a show, look at the catalog. Or Abercrombie & Fitch. Catalogs already attempt to create a narrative drama to give their products more mystique."[18] Through such programming innovations, commercial broadcasters and advertisers hope to adapt to even the most alarmist scenarios regarding the effects of the PVR upon television advertisers.

One feature of the personal video recorder of enormous appeal to networks and advertisers is its ability to continuously track users' viewing preferences, offering sponsors and broadcasters the long-sought ability to deliver tailored commercials to individually-targeted consumers. General Motors, for example, has experimented with TiVo to allow the replacement of a GM broadcast advertisement with another commercial previously downloaded on the household's PVR, one tailored to the consumer's specific viewing habits and demographic profile.[19] As one industry official told *Electronic Engineering Times*: "We are beginning to see some system operators setting aside a portion of the HDD [hard disk drive] real estate for revenue-producing applications." As the trade journal explained, manufacturers made this choice "rather than leaving the entire storage space under the consumer's control."[20] In the TiVo device, viewers are asked to make simple "thumbs up" or "thumbs down' responses to programs titles on the weekly program guide; the device aggregates and uplinks these preferences for use by advertisers. Despite the rudimentary nature of such viewer data, Jim Barton, TiVo's chief technical officer, argued that "there's actually not that many different types of people. . . . They tend to (fall into) socioeconomic buckets."[21] Despite perceptions of current industry upheaval at the hands of new digital technologies, such crude instrumental constructions of the television audience resonate with decades of postwar U.S. marketing and mass communication research.

The opposing reception scenarios conjured up by the PVR, technologically empowered TV viewers rebelliously zapping commercials versus passive and unwitting consumers being sold to advertisers in ever more perfectly commodified form, suggest the extent to which contemporary digital technologies have evoked wildly differing fantasies of domestic television viewing. In this regard, the personal video recorder represents a case study in the long-predicted merging of television set and computer monitor, a convergence that activates distinct connotations of media use. As John Markoff of the *New York Times* wrote of the PVR, "the idea is to permit people to use television the way Web surfers now use the Internet," including the construction of customized viewer 'channels' of favorite programs.[22] *Business Week* saw in the launch of the two competing personal video recorders a "race to convert television from a one-way affair into an Internet-age interactive medium," and this persistent opposition between interactive Web user and passive TV viewer pervades discussions of digital television.[23]

In addition to its effects on television advertising, another source of industry interest in the PVR concerns its potential as an Internet access provider and tool for what *Business Week* called "couch commerce."[24] As one journalist explained: "If you like the shirt being worn by Bill Cosby on his sitcom, . . . all you'll have to do to purchase it is press a button on your remote and be linked to the site of a major retailer or manufacturer, which already have all your measurements and credit card information."[25] In August 1999, America Online (AOL), the largest Internet service provider in the U.S. with 20 million subscribers, announced it had acquired a minority stake in TiVo; Bob Pittman, president of AOL, said at the time that "AOL has always focused on making the online experience a key part of our members' lives. As consumers want to extend that interactive experience to devices beyond the PC, we see TiVo as a great way to help us deliver our hallmark, ease-of-use and convenience, to the television."[26] At the same time, rivals to AOL see Internet-enabled PVRs as a way to challenge AOL's Internet-access dominance by expanding Internet provision beyond the computer desktop. Such a shift involves the speculative re-definition of the traditional television screen, its location, and the nature of social interaction around it. An executive at the AT&T-owned Excite@Home told the trade journal *Telephony:* "We expect that a high percentage of consumers will want both TV and PC Internet. . . . The PC experience in the den is typically very task-oriented, whereas the television experience is more driven by convenience."[27] One industry official noted that the central question about the success of the PVR remained "how couch potatoes might respond to potentially interactive features."[28] As the *New York Times* put it: "some question whether ReplayTV and TiVo, in predicting revolution, are misreading how viewers watch television: as either passive lumps not sure what they want until they notice that it is on, or as reflexive hunters for new, unanticipated viewing alternatives."[29] This already-familiar rhetoric of empowerment, freedom, and interactivity has marked much of the press coverage of the PVR, frequently explicitly contrasting the active, in-command viewer of new interactive TV with that fabled and disreputable figure of the previous era of network broadcasting, the barely-sentient, lump-like couch potato. However, at least some journalistic observers have expressed skepticism about the likelihood of the PVR overturning that long-established figuration of the television audience. The PVR, according to one journalist, "allows the couch potato to settle even deeper into the cushions," and an enthusiastic *Newsweek* PVR reviewer promised that "you may never get up off that couch again."[30]

While it remains to be seen whether U.S. consumers will demonstrate much of an appetite for the time-shifting and interactive capabilities of the personal video recorder, it is clear that digital delivery and storage systems have already shaken some of the long-standing conventional notions of television's purported essence, reception, and social function. Moreover, the current marketing battles over the definition of the television medium and audience have more than merely commercial consequences; such scenarios of media reception become powerful, if largely unexamined, tools with which the public and policy-makers alike make sense of a changing media environment. The real historical agency wielded by such representations suggests that media historians and activists have much to learn from a consideration of such ephemeral and self-serving material.

## Notes

1. Frank Stanton, Talk to Sigma Delta Chi convention, Columbus OH, November 13, 1954, 14–15. Collection of CBS Reference Library, New York. Emphasis in original.

2. U.S., Congress, House, Committee on Interstate and Foreign Commerce. Network Broadcasting, House Report no. 1297, 85th Cong., 2nd sess. (Washington, DC: Government Printing Office, 1958), 194.

3. U.S. Congress, Senate, Committee on Interstate and Foreign Commerce. "The Network Monopoly," report by Senator John W. Bricker (Washington, DC: Government Printing Office, 1956), 3, 5, 15.

4. Frank Stanton, "Statement of Frank Stanton, President, Columbia Broadcasting System, Inc. before the Senate Committee on Interstate and Foreign Commerce, June 12, 1956," 6. Collection of CBS Reference Library, New York. Emphasis in original.

5. Ibid., 36. Emphasis in original.

6. Frank Stanton, Speech to Second General Conference of CBS Television Affiliates, Chicago, April 13, 1956, 10. Collection of CBS Reference Library, New York.

7. Frank Stanton, "Free vs. Pay-Television," pamphlet (New York: Columbia Broadcasting System, May 19, 1955), n.p.

8. Ibid.

9. Bill Carter, "Aiming a Little Persuasion at Makers of TV Recorders," *New York Times*, August 16, 1999, C5. The diverse corporate investors in Replay and TiVo also include Sony, Philips, DirecTV, America Online, and NBC; individual investors include Paul Allen (co-founder of Microsoft and America's third wealthiest individual), and Netscape founder Marc Andreesen. Emphasizing the ambiguous status of the new storage device within the television industry was Replay's September 1999 selection of Kim LeMasters, a former chief programmer for CBS, as the company's chairman and chief executive officer. See Bill Carter, "Replay Network to Appoint Ex-CBS Programmer as Chief," *New York Times*, September 16, 1999, C8.

10. Replay executive Steve Shannon, quoted in "Here at Last: A Brainy VCR," *Toronto Star*, August 29, 1999, n.p.

11. Nicholas Negroponte, *Being Digital* (New York: Knopf, 1995), 168–69.

12. Bill Gates, *The Road Ahead* (New York: Penguin, 1995), 66. Microsoft, through its WebTV subsidiary, is developing its own version of the personal video recorder.

13. "Whither Television?" *New York Times*, January 4, 1999, A18.

14. Bill Carter, "Will This Machine Change Television?" *New York Times*, July 5, 1999, C1.

15. Ibid.

16. "Taking the Ads Out of Television," *The Economist,* May 8, 1999, n.p.

17. "'Networks Buy into New Personalized TV Technology," *Calgary Herald,* August 19, 1999, F5.

18. Robin Berger, "The Name of Tercek's Game is Interactive," *Electronic Media* (September 13, 1999), 22.

19. "Companies Consider Ways to Target TV Advertising," *Marketing News* (March 15, 1999), 11.

20. Junko Yoshida, "Digital VCRs Packing HDDs Seen as First Front in War to Establish non-PC Home Networks," *Electronic Engineering Times,* August 2, 1999, n.p.

21. Jon Healey, "New Technology Customizes Television Program Selection to Viewer's Tastes," *San Jose Mercury News,* August 18, 1999, n.p.

22. John Markoff, "Two Makers Plan Introductions of Digital VCR," *New York Times,* March 29, 1999, C13.

23. Janet Rae-Dupree and Richard Siklos, "Here's the Next 'Big Thing,'" *Business Week* (August 9, 1999), 38.

24. Ibid.

25. "Here at Last: A Brainy VCR," n.p.

26. "TiVo and America Online Announce Alliance for AOL TV," *Business Wire,* August 17, 1999, n.p.

27. Kelly Carroll and Brian Quinton, "Gaining Ground on a Giant," *Telephony,* August 23, 1999, n.p.

28. Jim Porter, president of Disk/Trend Inc., quoted in "Digital VCRs Packing HDDs," n.p.

29. "Will this Machine Change Television?," C1.

30. Ernest Holsendolph, "Play it Again; or, Maybe, for the First Time," *Atlanta Journal and Constitution,* August 22, 1999, 1p; N' Gai Croal, "(Re) Play that Funky Television Show," *Newsweek* (May 3, 1999), 67.

# II  *Emerging Forms and Practices*

# 12 Homer to Home Page: Designing Digital Books

William J. Mitchell

## Back to the Future?

"Tell me, O Muse, of the man of many devices, who wandered full many ways."
Are we about to hear of a cybernaut surfing the Net? Actually, as the dwindling band of the classically educated will recognize, this is a popular translation of the opening line of *The Odyssey.*

But it's also an excellent starting point for thinking about the character and uses of text in an online world since, in the days of Homer, words had no material embodiment; they floated freely in the air, and faded away as the itinerant poet ceased to speak. In the thousands of years since, humankind has figured out innumerable ways to bind words permanently to matter—to carve them into clay and stone, to print them on paper, to form them out of unlikely things like neon tubes, and furtively to spray them onto walls. Now, in some ways, we're back where we started. If I want to consult the text of *The Odyssey,* I no longer bother to seek out the tattered volume that's somewhere on my shelves; I just go to Google, type in some keywords and click a couple of times, and the bits that I want come flowing down the line to my laptop computer. The ancient text has finally been freed from its long enslavement to materiality; it inscribes itself briefly on my screen, then disappears when I click to dismiss it.

Don't get me wrong. I still love the feel of that old clothbound volume in my hands. I cherish the memories it evokes. I do feel a little guilty about leaving it to gather dust.

But the attractions of the newcomer are just too seductive to ignore. Without having to carry a weighty package of paper around with me, I can get to the digital version at anytime, from anywhere in the world. It doesn't cost me anything. It's never unavailable because it's been borrowed by someone else. I need not fear losing it by accidentally leaving it somewhere. Since it doesn't have a limited number of physical copies, it cannot go out of print. I can instantly copy quotations (without worrying about transcription errors), and paste them into texts—like this very one—that I am constructing myself.

I can click on hot-linked words to discover where they show up in other ancient Greek texts. And (if I were scholar enough to find these capabilities useful) I could go back to the original Greek at any point and click on words to find dictionary entries, run morphological analyses, and even analyze frequencies of occurrence in different contexts. Finally, I can even make a hard copy whenever I need that for some reason. The digital text has new pleasures. Does this make the printed text obsolete? Will printers, binders, bookshops, and libraries soon be things of the past? I don't think so. But the online digital text does take over some of the traditional functions of ink on paper, and it does enable some strikingly new ways of producing, transforming, and using literary material. Its emergence requires writers to reconsider their craft, it forces designers to rethink the task of making language visible, and it leaves publishers anxiously scrambling to find new business models.

### *The Case of* City of Bits

In 1995 I had a chance to explore these questions in a practical context when, with the MIT Press, I published my book *City of Bits.* Since it dealt with the digital revolution and the new relationships that were being created between the material and virtual worlds, we decided that it should be self-exemplifying—that it should appear simultaneously as a hardback and in a full-text World Wide Web version. As far as I know, it was the first book to be published simultaneously in print and on the Web. (At the very least, it could not have had many predecessors.)

We made the marketing people happy by providing a link to an online order form from the opening screen of the Web site; enter your name and address, include your credit card number (in a secure transaction), click to transmit your order, and a copy gets sent to you immediately. Conversely, we published the URL (the address in cyberspace) of the Web version on the dustjacket of the print version. So a reader of either one could always conveniently obtain the other.

We provided free access to the Web version. (As the Web develops, convenient mechanisms for charging for access to online material are being put in place, and these will obviously be crucial to the development of an online publishing industry. But these were not highly developed when we put *City of Bits* online, and attempting to charge just didn't seem worth the trouble at that point). There was some risk in this, of course; why would anyone buy a copy when the online version was right there at no cost? Perhaps we would lose sales. But we guessed that the additional sales generated by the Web site would out-weigh such losses, and there is some good evidence that we were right; in the first two printings, about 2% of the total sales were directly through the online order form, and it is likely that the Web site also stimulated bookstore and mail-order sales. Why should this be so? The answer is that the hardback and online versions added value to the text in different and complementary fashions. (The dimensions of that complementarity will be explored in the discussion that follows.) So readers of the Web version are not necessarily potential customers for the hardback. And lots of people decided that they wanted both, to use in different ways.

### Hardback, Paperback, and No-back

Of course, publishing a book in different versions is not a new idea; it has long been a common strategy to put out both hardbacks and paperbacks. The hardback is more expensive and more robust, and it is aimed at libraries and at buyers who want to keep it permanently on their bookshelves, while the paperback is cheaper is not designed to have such a long life. Depending on the content and the marketing strategy for a particular book, it may appear in hardback only, in paperback only, in paperback with a small number of hardbacks for sale to libraries, or in hardback followed by a less expensive paperback at a later point.

With the Web, the online no-back emerges as a third option at the inexpensive and ephemeral end of the spectrum. It can be used, even by very small publishers, to achieve instant world-wide distribution; certainly we found, with *City of Bits,* that it was quite widely read and even reviewed in some countries long before copies of the hardback were available there. But, since publishers generally have not begun to guarantee the permanent existence of Web sites, you still need a hardback copy if you want to be sure of continued access in the future.

You may also want a well designed, well produced print version for ease of extended reading, portability, and just the sheer pleasure of it. By comparison with even the very best laptop computer, a well-made book is light, tough (you can drop a book without damaging it, but not a laptop), comfortable in the hand, and usable anywhere. It has an extremely high-contrast, high-resolution display, and the access mechanism (turning pages) is a lot nicer than using a mouse and cursor to scroll text down a screen. Indeed, I have often thought that, if Gutenberg had invented the personal computer and printed books had not appeared until the 1980s, we would now be hailing paper and print as a major technological advance!

As forward-looking computer technologists will be quick to point out, things won't stay this way. Computers will become lighter, less fragile, and more portable. The quality of displays will improve. Sophisticated home and office printers will allow production of high quality, personalized print copies on demand. We may even see the emergence of programmable "smart paper" allowing development of devices that combine the virtues of the portable computer and the book. But, for the moment at least, the hardback, the paperback, and the electronic no-back have significantly different properties and roles.

### Getting the Reader's Attention

The first task of a book, especially a trade book that's supposed to attract an audience, is to get itself picked up and read. So the hardback *City of Bits* has a vivid, colorful dustjacket to catch the reader's attention; it's carefully designed to stand out on a bookstore display or a library shelf. When you take it in your hand, you find a brief description and author biography on the flyleaf. Then you can flip through it to see what's inside.

The Web version clearly had to attract attention in very different ways, and making sure that it did so was a key to success. Several strategies were used.

First, a hot link was made from the entry in the MIT Press's online catalogue to the *City of Bits* site. Just as bookstore browsers can pick up a copy of the hardback, Web-surfing catalogue browsers can immediately get their hands on the online version. And the first thing that the online version presents is a welcome page with links to a synopsis, the author's home page, and the table of contents. Thus, to provide one path into the online *City of Bits,* the metaphor of an "electronic bookstore" was fairly closely followed.

Hot links from other Web sites provide a second way in. *City of Bits* was quickly listed in many online, classified Internet and Web guides, "Cool Sites" collections, online newsletters and magazines, home pages of organizations and individuals who wanted to draw attention to it, and online reading lists for classes of various kinds. Some of these links were sought and negotiated by members of the *City of Bits* WWW team, but many appeared spontaneously. Most were one-way, from the other site to *City of Bits,* but some were reciprocal: a fixed "you point to me and I'll point to you" arrangement. The ultimate effect was to create a very large, electronic "catchment" to collect potential readers and efficiently funnel them to the site.

The third strategy for bringing in readers is to attract the attention of Web search engines. Typically, these engines explore the Web periodically to create large indexes and directories, then, in response to users' queries, employ these indexes and directories to provide very rapid access to the relevant Web sites. They perform their explorations in a variety of ways—by looking for specified keywords in the titles or headers of Web documents, by scanning through the documents themselves, or even by searching other indexes and directories. They are usually pretty dumb, since they just look for keyword matches. So, to make sure that your site is not missed by the search engines—which have now become very important tools for finding one's way around the Web—you must make sure that the appropriate descriptors are included in titles and headers, and in the text of the opening pages. Incidentally, you can reliably attract a lot of attention by scattering words like "sex" and "nude" through your text, but it may not be the sort of attention, that you want!

A fourth possible strategy, which we have not used, is closely analogous to pinpoint direct-mail marketing. When Web-surfers access your server, it is technically possible to collect a lot of information about them—who they are, where they are from, what links they followed to get to your site, what browser they were using, what they looked at, and so on. If you are prepared to ignore the obvious privacy issues, you can use this information to target electronic advertising. So, for example, Web-surfers who looked at MIT Press online catalogue entries for other books on related topics might get e-mail promoting *City of Bits*.

### Reading Tools and their Effects

In traditional fashion, the hardback version of *City of Bits* is a narrative divided into chapters on different sub-topics and it has a table of contents and an index to guide the reader through the material. This allows for multiple styles of reading; you can follow a continuous thread straight through from beginning to end, you can jump immediately to particular chapters that interest you, you can use the index to find passages on particular topics, and you can even cruise the index (or the endnotes) to look for entries that may pique your interest. You can skim quickly or you can read more slowly and attentively. You may make notes as you go, or you may not. You may read in strict sequence, or you may jump back and forth.

The physical book is not only a repository of the textual information, but also a reading tool that allows you to pursue these strategies efficiently, and gives you context and feedback as you do so. Its size and shape tells you roughly how much information it contains, and you always know how far through it you are from the relative thicknesses of the stacks of pages under your left and right thumbs. The springiness of the paper allows you to scan quickly by riffling through pages with the book half open, but the mechanical properties of the binding assure that you can also leave it open, flat on a desktop, for more extended and careful study.

Typography signals the hierarchy of information by visually distinguishing headings, sub-headings, and body text. A table of contents right at the front, an Index at the very back, and numbered pages, provide effective search and navigation capabilities. End-notes, with numbered references from the text, allow backup information to be provided without disrupting the flow of the narrative.

The online version provides very different reading tools. Most dramatically, there is no index; it is replaced by an internal search engine that locates instances of user-entered keywords in the text. From the author's viewpoint, this eliminates the intellectual drudg-ery of creating an index. From the reader's viewpoint, it provides greater freedom; you can search for anything, and you don't have to rely on the author's judgment about what was worth including in the index. (I'm told, for example, that many readers immediately type in their own names to see if they're mentioned anywhere!)

The hierarchy of information is also handled differently in the online version, since the screen can only display a limited amount of text at one time, since current bandwidth constraints make it undesirable to download large text files to your browser all at once, and since scrolling through a long segment of text doesn't work nearly as effectively as flipping the pages of a book. The complete text is organized into a hierarchy of small seg-ments, with internal hot-links providing the interconnections among them. At the top of the tree is the table of contents page providing entry points to each of the chapters. Within each chapter, there is the introductory section of text followed by hot links to the subsections that it contains. Finally, there is the relatively short text of each subsection. To allow for sequential reading of the narrative, without having to go up and down the hierarchy, there are "previous" and "next" hot links at the end of each subsection.

Endnotes, of course, are handled by hot links; click on the endnote mark and you imme-diately get the corresponding note. (Cross-references within the text could be handled in a similar way, but there aren't any.) To maintain consistency with the print version, and conti-nuity with tradition, the notes are numbered—but of course, they no longer really have to be, since there's never any ambiguity about which note relates to which point in the text.

Overall, the reading tools provided with the online version have a very interesting effect; they privilege the hierarchical structuring of the book's content and the operation of searching while they make sequentially following the narrative more cumbersome and difficult. (It's no accident, then, that CD-ROM and online books that have these sorts of reading tools have tended to emphasize modular, classified and indexed chunks of content as in encyclopedias and dictionaries, to provide dense cross-referencing within the material, and to construct multi-threaded and branching narratives—in other words, to focus on anything other than long, continuous narrative sequences.) The hardback, on the other hand, privileges skimming, random jumps back and forth, and the continuity of the main narrative thread. So it's probably optimal to read the hardback first, to gain an overview, then to go to the online version for more detailed study and for ongoing reference.

### Fixed Format and Personalized

Good graphic designers exert very considered and precise control over the look and feel of a printed book. Certainly this was the case with *City of Bits*. The designer, Yasuyo Iguchi, chose to set it in Bembo and Meta. She arranged elements on the various different sorts of pages, and deployed white space with care.

She gave consideration to its size, shape, proportions, weight, and rigidity. She chose the paper, the cloth for the cover, and the matte varnish of the jacket so as to create a particular relationship of feels and textures. All of this matters. It all adds up to something that has the characteristic look of a MIT Press book, and that signals something about the product's style, content, and level of sophistication.

But the client-server architecture of the Web does not allow a designer such precise control of the online version; it may be downloaded to many different types of display devices, by many different types of browsers, with many different settings of their various options, to produce screen displays that vary enormously. This can be seen as a disadvantage (and typically is by graphic designers, who don't like the loss of control), and the producers of Web servers and browsers can try to eliminate as many sources of unwanted variation as possible. Or it can be seen as an advantage—opening up the possibility of adapting content intelligently to different contexts and to the needs of different readers; perhaps every reader of *City of Bits* could have a uniquely personalized version.

The issue of producer-control versus user-personalization is a philosophical rather than a technical one; it is technically feasible to implement systems that support either one or both, and to design online productions that either go for a consistent look or encourage personalization. In the online version of *City of Bits,* we tried to exert as much control as possible to assure a reasonably high level of graphic quality, to remain consistent with the print version, and just to keep things simple for ourselves. But, as personalization tools become increasingly sophisticated, it will become more interesting to try to take advantage of them.

## External Hot-Links

Perhaps the most obvious and striking difference between the hardback and the online version is that the text of the online version contains hundreds of hot-links to other Web sites with relevant information on the topics that are discussed. When I discuss online shopping malls, for example, you can just click to go and visit one. And, when I refer to Aristotle's *Politics,* you can immediately access the relevant passage, online, in either English or Greek. Thus the City of Bits site becomes a conveniently organized entry point for exploring an enormous quantity of related information.

Some of these external hot links are to sites that I or my research assistant discovered and consulted when *City of Bits* was being written, but the vast majority have resulted from systematically going through the text, picking out key words, and sending search engines out on the Web to find what was there.

Whenever a search engine discovers a relevant site, we link it in. (You can think of this as a new form of bricolage.) This process has to be repeated at regular intervals, since the Web is growing explosively, and relevant new sites are continually appearing. So the structure of intertextual linkages in which City of Bits embeds itself is a very dynamic thing, and it looked very different, after the site had been up for a few months, than it did when it first went online.

The converse process is to combat link-rot by identifying and removing hot-links to sites that have died, shifted to new locations, or become irrelevant. (If this is not done, a site quickly loses its charm like an untended garden.) To facilitate this, we employ a software tool that automatically runs through the text, checks all the hot-links, and reports all those that don't seem to be working.

Superficially, adding these links may just seem to be a more convenient way to provide endnote citations to related publications. But, on closer inspection, there are some important differences. One is the dynamism that I have noted; print endnotes can only be updated, all at once, when there is a reprint or a new edition, but hot-links can be updated incrementally and at any time. Furthermore, you cannot add too many endnotes to a printed book without making it bulky and unwieldy, but there is no practical limit to the number that you can embed in an online text.

But the most important difference is the shift in scholarly responsibility, and correspondingly in the reader's use of the text, that the substitution of hot-links for endnote citations entails. Recall that endnote citations are normally to printed documents that have been formally published and do not change. A responsible scholar is expected to check the relevance, quality, and usefulness of a cited document, and to give publication date and page numbers; scholars who cite irrelevant or poor-quality publications are not highly regarded. But the author of an online publication cannot attempt to take the same responsibility, since the contents of an externally linked site may change unpredictably, at any time; I might, for example, discover a site containing the text of Aristotle's *Politics,* check it out and assure myself that everything was in order, and then make the link from City of Bits only to discover, some time later, that the operator of that site had subsequently substituted several hundred pornographic GIF files for the philosopher's words. So, external hot-links are very useful, but they have their dangers. Caveat surfer!

As the Web and similar structures mature, there will undoubtedly be an increasing number of sites providing stable, "guaranteed" content, and scholars will have less of a problem. There are, for example, already some refereed online technical journals. But the medium does not automatically enforce document stability in the way print does, so special institutional arrangements will be needed in contexts where such stability is necessary.

### Marginalia and Readers' Comments

Sometimes readers like to scribble their comments in the margins of printed books, and sometimes subsequent readers see these comments and may even add their own responses, but this usually isn't encouraged (particularly with library books) and it isn't a very effective form of discourse. By contrast, online versions of books can easily provide for readers to add their comments, and for these comments to be widely available.

In the online City of Bits, readers can enter an electronic "agora" directly from the site's front door, or from the foot of any page of text. There, they can read the (comments) that other readers have posted. They can also use a simple form to add their own comments. And they can even insert hot-links to other sites that they consider relevant. This agora is organized as a collection of newsgroups, and provides all the usual features of newsgroup support software.

Over time, then, the online version of City of Bits has become encrusted with commentary. It has succeeded in provoking, capturing, and making visible a discourse in a way that is impossible with print. And, in the process, the seed provided by the original text has grown into a considerably larger and richer textual structure.

This evolution is fascinating and exciting to see, but it creates some theoretical conundrums and practical difficulties. The continually growing, transforming structure is actually the work of many hands, yet it has my name on it. In the beginning, it was mostly mine, but it becomes less and less so as time goes on and the online comments accumulate. At what point does it become inappropriate to say that it is "my" text? When does it become more reasonable to call it a collective work?

Who bears moral and legal responsibility for it? Should I treat the agora as a zone in which complete freedom of speech is permitted, or should I, as the author, take responsibility for actively moderating and shaping the discussion? Should I delete blatantly irrelevant and self-serving comments? What if advertisements are posted? What if a reader were to post comments that I found personally offensive and insulting? (Am I obliged to provide that person with a platform?) What if a posting were found to contain slanderous or obscene material, or a neo-Nazi diatribe? These are not the sorts of questions that arise about scribbled marginal comments in printed books, but they have been hotly debated in relation to online newsgroups and bulletin boards. A book becomes a thing of a different kind when it systematically internalizes and reports back the discussion that it has provoked, rather than standing distinct, closed, and aloof from it.

These seem difficult questions, and general answers will probably have to be worked out through experience and debate. In the case of City of Bits, the team that maintains the site has taken a rigorous "hands off" attitude; we occasionally go through and clean out the completely irrelevant postings that sometimes appear, but we leave everything else there. Generally, comments so far have been serious and responsible, so we have not been forced to confront any really troublesome dilemmas. Perhaps we have just been lucky, though.

## Reviews, Mentions, and Translations

Any successful book soon generates a growing body of thematically related, secondary, and derivative texts reviews, commentaries, news articles, mentions in other works, and translations. The City of Bits site keeps a running record of this sort of material (to the extent that the team can keep up with it) and, where possible and appropriate, provides links to it.

As it turned out, the City of Bits site generated a lot of interest, and quickly received many reviews in both the specialist and mainstream media. Perhaps naively, we had hoped that we might add the full texts of all reviews to the site as they appeared. That would have made accessible another, extremely interesting, layer of commentary and elaboration. But the world is not quite ready for that; after a few attempts to secure permissions to reproduce complete reviews online, and generally getting rebuffed or asked to pay exorbitant fees, we retreated to the position of posting short extracts much as they have traditionally been reproduced in jacket copy and advertisements. In the future, though, it may not be so difficult to achieve our original ambition; when the majority of reviews appear in online editions of newspapers and magazines, and the like, it will only be necessary to link to them.

As translation rights have been sold, details on the forthcoming foreign-language editions have been posted in a Translations section of the site. When the translations are completed, we will explore further possibilities. (This will require making new and unusual types of agreements with the overseas publishers, and it is not yet clear how these will work out.) For example, we might simply add online texts of the foreign-language versions to the City of Bits site. We might go further, and provide structures of cross-linkages among the English and foreign-language versions so that multilingual readers might conveniently move back and forth—a particularly useful capability where words and phrases do not have very exact equivalents in other languages, or where there might be ambiguity or debate about the best way to translate things. Or we might encourage the foreign publishers to develop their own Web sites for the translations, then build links to and fro. In the more distant future, it is easy to imagine online books existing as multilingual, geographically distributed sites in which you are asked, on entry, what language you want to use—as American Express cash machines.

## Online Appropriation

In effect, the various external linkages from the City of Bits site appropriate a vast array of existing textual fragments and combine them to form a new work—something that, because of the selection and organization that goes into it, is significantly greater than the sum of its parts. The original *City of Bits* text, as published on paper, is just one of these constituent fragments—though, to be sure, a privileged one. (This shifts to a radically new context the old idea, recognized in intellectual property law, that a collection can be a creative work.)

This strategy of textual appropriation and collage does not run into the sorts of intellectual property difficulties that would arise in creating a large, cross-referenced print collection, since the constituent fragments are merely pointed to rather than repro-duced. The author of an appropriated text does not lose anything in this way. On the con-trary, authors usually post texts online because they want them to be noticed and read, so it is an advantage to attract linkages that might channel readers from other texts and sites.

In sum, an important new literary role has now emerged: the link-editor who locates fragments of text online and combines them into original literary structures by superim-posing patterns of linkages. On a large scale, the operators of Internet guides like Yahoo! play the link-editor role by selecting and classifying online material and providing con-venient point-and-click access from a topic list. Pedagogues play the game when they link words in books and articles to online reference works, such as dictionaries, encyclope-dias, and so on. Critical scholars play it when they create structures of comparisons and contrasts among texts. The City of Bits team certainly played it when they constructed the online version. And, by now, the online City of Bits has been appropriated into a great many online constructions created by others.

When I have discussed this form of appropriation with other authors, some of them have been greatly disconcerted by the idea. They do not like the possibility that their work might be used in ways they cannot control and for purposes that they never intended. (They forget, of course, that authors have never really had very much control over the uses and misuses of their published texts. But embedding in online link structures does make this possibility dramatically explicit.) Others, including myself, are excited by being able to see with new clarity the evolving roles that their texts play in ongoing discourses.

## Stabilities and Instabilities

As we have now seen, the online City of Bits has both stable and unstable elements. The core text, which corresponds to that of the print version, does not change. But the struc-ture of links that it carries is continually adjusted and extended, the contents of the externally linked sites evolve, and the accreted structure of comments, reviews, and translations grows. If I decide to do new print editions, I expect to add the text of those to the online version, and to preserve the earlier edition texts as well. Thus any change in the core text will be carried out in well-defined, modular increments.

A more radical possibility would be to make continual small changes to the core text to reflect new developments and to respond immediately to comments and criticisms. (There is no technical difficulty in doing so.) That way, the text would be kept constantly up to date; there would be no need to keep using an increasingly obsolete and unsatisfactory text while waiting for the right moment to put out a complete new edition. But this would destroy the logical integrity of references within the overall structure. What if, for example, a reader's comment refers to a specific paragraph in the core text and that paragraph is subsequently deleted or significantly altered?

Perhaps the most satisfactory approach would be to preserve successive versions as incremental changes are made. Some fairly straightforward software could then automatically relate comments and other linked material to the appropriate versions. So far, though, we have not had the energy or the disk space for that.

Whatever the balance between stable and unstable elements, though, you never read the same text twice. (Heraclitus would have loved it!) Even the internally stable elements are continually being recontextualized, and so shift in their meaning, as the huge structure that embeds them transforms itself. Furthermore—an alarming thought for historians—it is quite impossible to preserve more than a very partial record of the past states of that transforming structure; it has no distinct boundaries, it is distributed over many different machines in widely scattered locations, and it is far too large and complex to back up on tape. The printed book appeared to give scholars stable, repeatable text modules to work with. Perhaps that was always a myth. With online books, certainly, that myth is increasingly difficult to sustain.

### The End

Hardback and paperback books eventually go out of print. Archival libraries selectively perform the function of preserving books after that point. But what about online books? Since it does take some effort and resources to keep them around, and even more to keep them growing and changing, they are likely to have quite limited lives. How long do they stay available online? What is the electronic equivalent of going out of print? Who is responsible for long-term archiving?

Answers to these questions are likely to vary with the type of book, and may change over time as online publication grows in importance, but I can give a provisional answer for City of Bits online. I regard it as a kind of extended live performance in a vast virtual theater. Eventually, that performance will end. The site that remains will not instantly disappear, but will slowly fade away like an abandoned stage set—as link-rot sets in and as additions and updates are no longer made. As time goes by, there will be fewer and fewer visitors.

In the end, the City of Bits will be an electronic ruin. Like Troy, it will cease to function and to live—becoming, instead, part of the archaeology of cyberspace.

# 13 *Reflections on Interactivity*

Luis O. Arata

Interactivity tends to evoke thoughts of digital media. In literature, digital interactivity is commonly associated with hypertext and more recently with cybertext. Hypertext gives the reader choices to branch out among chunks of text linked by multiple pathways. George Landow traces the origins of this term to Theodor Nelson, who used it in the 1960s to refer to non-sequential writing on a computer.[1] Espen Aarseth looks beyond hypertexts to cybertexts which he defines as involving calculations in their production.[2] Such explorations of other possible ways to generate literature open the question of the very nature of literature as a collection of fixed texts. Literature is moving from its origins in oral traditions to a future that we can hardly envision from current experiments in the new media. As for the arts, they are becoming harder to contain. Fixed objects are increasingly perceived as only fossilized traces of much broader ensembles, organic, in process. The objective nature of museums is turning fuzzy.[3] More generally, Sherry Turkle observes that we are starting to move toward a culture of simulation.[4] This is possible, she points out, because people are increasingly comfortable with substituting representations of reality for the real. How simulation is able to deal flexibly and creatively with the always problematic notion of reality, is perhaps one of the most important epistemological advances of our times.

Yet such developments overflowing traditional boundaries actually recall creative features which have been neglected and now resurface in new guises. The sense of interactivity that dominates the digital media stretches as far back as we care to look into the roots of human creation. The most deliberately interactive books span the ages, from the *I Ching* to Julio Cortázar's *Hopscotch*. In many ways these books are beyond what computer driven texts achieve these days.[5] In an entirely different cultural world, interactivity surfaces right from the start of the *Popol Vuh,* the ancient Maya book of creation, when a narratorial voice speaks of the text as a seeing instrument which can help the viewer understand clearly all there is. The notion of interactivity appears in

Aristotle's notion of tragic catharsis and the pleasures of imitation described in the *Poetics*. I recounted in *The Festive Play of Fernando Arrabal* how theatre developed in ancient Greece as a festive medium using mainly episodic forms. This was a highly interactive mode of creation. It served as vehicle to interconnect performance, audience, and a pre-existing festive background. But this began to change as theatre detached itself from its active web of links. Aristotle rejected the episodic form in favor of the more sophisticated plot-structures which had started to emerge.[6] The constraints of plots have in fact reduced the interactivity of theatre and literature. Such well-made frames tend to tame the imagination and narrow the field of expectations. However, they can enhance a game-like virtuosity through a mastery of specific rules, so that both authors and audiences can rely on artificial yet objectified expectations as marks of excellence.[7] Antonin Artaud used the medium of theatre in an intransitive mode, as incantation, to make what he envisioned as its double reveal itself. Political and philosophical literary texts use the medium in a more transitive way to communicate messages that could effect change. In the arts, André Malraux conceived museums without walls. He wished to see art works move beyond the boundaries of museum walls, and have art history establish dialogues across space and time. Malraux noted how Picasso was interested in the process of creation rather than in the final products. He quoted Picasso saying: "it's always painting that wins in the end."[8] Picasso was satisfied by the certainty that, like cave painters, he had captured something with his creations. What it was, he could not tell. The object captured is not important. Framing only brings the work to an end. The process of interaction is essential for artists. It is now beginning to count for the museum as well.

The exploration of interactivity brings us back to the roots of literary and dramatic creation. It takes us beyond more classic issues such as Eco's question of whether texts are to be used or interpreted.[9] Interpretation becomes one of the many uses of texts, rather than being an alternative. Richard Rorty has already noted that a work of literature is neither a mirror of nature nor a fixed object, thus recalling many other uses of literature including its potential for simulation and modeling which are essentially interactive features. The issues that return when exploring interactivity, not surprisingly, are concerned with the play set in motion through the medium. As it turns out, these are pragmatic issues.

What is an interactive work? Without shutting the door on an open concept, we can say that interactivity points to active interrelations between players and mediums. The interactions can be of many types. The forms of interactivity tend to be as diverse as the artists who make them possible. What the rise of new digital media has done is to widen the focus of interest beyond the object created, to the participation in a process of playing out a multitude of interactions. Interactivity in its most general form is a mode of creation, a way of being, a perspective. The basic characteristics of such a perspective can be grouped tentatively into four areas. An interactive approach favors the use of multiple points of view that can coexist even if they appear mutually exclusive; it celebrates the creative value of play; it is a catalyst for emergence; and it tends to be ultimately pragmatic.

Like a statue on a pedestal or a frozen oracle, the object of creation has been defined classically as something to contemplate. From an interactive perspective, this leaves most of the creation out of the picture. A first quality of an interactive perspective is that it opens multiple points of view through the blurring of boundaries of realities and objects once conveniently fixed. This shifts the emphasis away from the object and tilts it more toward the subject who perceives. Viewers interact with objects in a way that celebrates subjectivity and diversity. Multiple views of a common phenomenon can coexist even if they are mutually exclusive. Objects themselves can remain fuzzy and metamorphic.

The genial French mathematician Henri Poincaré provided a striking illustration of both classical and interactive views in the sciences. Poincaré used to say that when truth is reached, what remains to be done is to sit back and contemplate it. Truth, when perceived in detached, static terms, becomes a precious object that can only be admired from a distance. The world turns into a museum. Look but don't touch.

Poincaré, however, had other more complex and contradictory views. The man who would sit back to contemplate also thought it was impossible to find truth in things in themselves. Truth hovered only in relations among things. He saw in the emergence of non-Euclidean geometries a clear indication of the ephemeral and arbitrary nature of theories: what mattered was not an ontology but convenience of use. He thought that failed theories left a valuable trace even as they vanished, and that trace had the scent of truth.[10]

The second characteristic of an interactive perspective is that it favors open approaches that stimulate play. Unfortunately, the creative function of play at the adult level tends to be underestimated. In cultural studies, Johan Huizinga's *Homo ludens* sparked an interest in play. It was published in 1938 when Herman Hesse was already at work in his novel *The Glass Bead Game*. Both writers situated play as a free activity deliberately outside of ordinary life. Huizinga saw play as an activity originating in the mind, distinct from all other forms of thought as a "second, poetic world alongside the world of nature." In this realm of illusion, the mind is able to break down what Huizinga presupposed was "the absolute determinism of the cosmos."[11] In a similar fashion, Hesse separated Castalia, the domain of the abstract, intellectual & artistic glass bead game, from the domain of sensuous, down-to-earth worldly life. But such view left out the interactive side of play. The ending of *The Glass Bead Game* highlights such conflict. It is precisely the dilemma that Magister Ludi Joseph Knecht faces toward the end of his career. He has reached the limits of the game and begins to find it an empty exercise, all too perfect and formulaic. The world, thought imperfect and chaotic from a Castalian point of view, begins to appear vaster and richer, full of change, history, struggles, and new beginnings. Knecht fears that the isolation of the Castalian game-culture might be its own doom because it has lost the capacity for further growth and change. Castalia has reduced interactivity to a minimum. The only variations allowed are brilliant new moves within the strict rules of the world-like Glass Bead Game. But these moves escape the ongoing changes that take place in the outside world. Knecht foresees that unless Castalia interacts with the world, it will come to an end. Such is the end of all systems that try to remain closed, and exhaust their possibilities.

Huizinga's separation of play from "ordinary life" cuts along somewhat similar lines as Hesse's but is more problematic. Whereas Hesse saw that life was the realm of change, Huizinga considered life fixed in its basic order. Chemist and Nobel laureate Ilya Prigogine bridged this gap and introduced the question of play directly into what Huizinga had imagined was an absolutely deterministic cosmos. Prigogine's work in the area of complex systems explores a world that might function with both laws and play at the same time. In *The End of Certainty,* Prigogine pointed out that scientific laws formulated in traditional ways, describe an "idealized, stable world that is quite different from the unstable, evolving world in which we live."[12] He envisioned science hovering between "the two alienating images of a deterministic world and an arbitrary world of pure chance."[13]

Perhaps Jean Piaget offered the most functional definition of play. He presented play as a type of adaptive action understood in contrast to imitation. Adaptation to situations involves a combination of imitation and play. These two activities are the extremes in the spectrum of adaptive behavior ranging from accommodation to assimilation, respectively. When imitating, we accommodate ourselves to the outside model. But in play we undo the world, so to speak, and assimilate it to our preferences. Adaptation is reached through a balancing of these processes.[14] A way to look at the spread of adaptive attitudes ranging from imitation to play is to gauge them in terms of interactivity: imitation minimizes interactivity, but interactivity increases the more play there is.

Marshall McLuhan used a temperature metaphor to distinguish between what we consider are interactive features. He distinguished between hot and cold media. He wrote that hot media leave little to be filled or completed by the audience. Hot media are low in participation, and cool media are high in participation or completion by the audience.[15] In this sense, the new interactive media is mostly cool.

Sherry Turkle prefers the metaphor of solidity to that of temperature. Cool media for her is soft.[16] It allows for flexible, nonhierarchical interactivity. It embodies the notion of a decentered self. It facilitates bricolage and simulation. Along similar lines, Ian Hacking proposes that hard sciences tend to be indifferent because participation is excluded. Natural laws are supposed to be what they are independently of the observers. But social sciences, far softer, are interactive because there is change introduced by the very process of structuring the sciences.[17] In other words, observations affect what is observed.

Many have already started to question the validity of the metaphorical division of the sciences into a range from hard to soft, noting that there is interaction and lack of objectivity even in physics, in the area of quantum mechanics, for example. The possibility of interactive emergence extends then to all areas of human research and creation. Much depends on how a medium is used rather than on the properties of the medium or on the discipline. As works like the *I Ching* or *Hopscotch* show, hot medium can be used in cool ways. Or, to put it differently, a hard science like physics has plenty of soft spots.

A third and perhaps the most unique feature of an interactive view is that it allows us to consider emergent phenomena without downgrading them by reductions. An emergent phenomenon cannot be predicted. Nor can it be entirely explained away a posteriori. Emergent phenomena are above all those that cannot be predicted by the behavior of their constituent parts. They happen as if on their own. Here we see the crucial role of interactivity. Only through the play or jiggling of interactivity is the stage set for emergent surprises. Marvin Minsky ranks intelligence as one of such surprises. In *The Society of Mind* he investigated how a mind could possibly emerge from an ensemble of mindless little parts. In writing the book, Minsky tried to simulate the process of emergence of possible solutions to the question of how a mind comes into being, by writing collections of short pieces and letting the parts conjure themselves into solutions.[18] Emergent phenomena can be seen as successful yet unpredictable mutations. John Holland has even suggested that life itself may well be an emergent phenomena.[19]

Concerning the digital media, Jim Gasperini has noted the emergence of an interactive aesthetic in the structural ambiguity which permeates decentered computer environments and the internet.[20] He thinks this sense of interactivity is still in its infancy, especially in the area of interactive games. But the development of more user-friendly interfaces and the way the Internet has broken down barriers so that every page is literally next to every other one in the world, are interactive breakthroughs which begin to show the extraordinary richness of the digital media. Eric Drexler suggested that a breakthrough in the order of the Gutenberg revolution has taken place with the advent of digital hypertext. The introduction of movable print made producing texts much easier. Now hypertext and its spread to the Internet, make searching for information incredibly fast and effective.[21]

The investigation of emergent phenomena is truly a new frontier of both the sciences and the arts. The two domains of human creation seem to join hands in this realm of exploration. Science has traditionally dealt with repetitive phenomena, whereas the arts have favored special events charming by their inspiring uniqueness. In the realm of emergence we begin to look into events which are neither regular nor unique. They are surprises that can be managed to happen but never coerced into predictable repetitions. What I suggest is that an interactive perspective helps us map more effectively this new frontier opening between chaos and total order.

The fourth broad characteristic of an interactive perspective is that it favors pragmatic views. Richard Rorty captured the spirit of pragmatism stating that it is the "refusal to believe in the existence of Truth, in the sense of something not made by human hands, something which has authority over human beings."[22] Pragmatism is a self-organizing, bootstrap-like approach.

Rorty pointed out that "the end of human activity is not to rest, but rather richer and better human activity."[23] He envisions solidarity as an expression of this human interactivity directed toward the goal of enhancing our lot in the world in an all-inclusive rather than exclusive way. The method of working in solidarity hinges on what Rorty calls a "new fuzziness" in which "objectivity" gives way to "unforced agreement."[24] The expression of this creative solidarity is democracy: "a conception which has no room for obedience to a nonhuman authority, and in which nothing save freely achieved consensus among human beings has any authority at all."[25] Following John Dewey, what Rorty stresses is the notion of interactive participation, of being an agent rather than a spectator.

From a pragmatic point of view, objectivity is an illusion. What Rorty proposes instead is to acquire habits of action to deal with the world. Pragmatic interactions should not force preconceptions on others. Agreements for action should come from reaching positions of solidarity and working toward common purposes freely chosen. In this sense, pragmatism favors a local flexibility. In the absence of absolutes, what works, works— within a context that by necessity must be local.

Rorty suggests that the reward for pragmatists is Dewey's sense of democracy with its utopian possibilities and sense of hope. He believes that we can mitigate our finitude by self-creation rather than by invoking untenable and ultimately confining truths. This creative imagination begins with self-imagining: an inward interaction which gives rise to processes and models to interact with the world. The pragmatic high value of feedback, a deep concern with reflexivity, is perhaps the most critical navigating tool of a mature interactive perspective.

Finally, interactivity itself can be brought under focus. What does interactivity have to offer in its approach that we did not already have? I have suggested that it is best suited to deal with multiple perspectives, it invites emergence, offers a broader sense of play, and has a pragmatic outlook. In other words, an interactive view celebrates a constructive flexibility well suited for navigating in open, changing, or unknown environments. But such outlook also exposes us to the risks of the new, to sudden conflicts, disintegration, fragmentation, and other unpleasant surprises. When science is more open to the whims of the imagination it may be more vulnerable to ridicule. Literature may lose the greatness of canonical values. The message in the new media may turn out to be hollow, mindless. Creativity could be compromised. Minsky already warned that total interactivity leads to chaos. He argued in the appendix to *The Society of Mind* that insulators are needed just as much as interactive links.

Borders have shifted from autocratic theories to democracies of models. Politics are evolving from dogmatisms to networks of pragmatic solidarities. A drift in cultural plates is changing the artistic landscape. And as new architectures metamorphose the imagination, science also seems to overflow its banks and touch uncharted domains. The Internet is emerging as a model of constructive freedom to link with few insulations or barriers. Upon reflection, I suggest that these reconfigurations are best explored from an interactive perspective that moves us from teleology to play.

But an interactive perspective does not exclude other approaches. Its tendency toward decentering and autonomy does not negate hierarchical structures. This perspective is one more tool at our disposal, another creative instrument to enhance our flexibility. And in order to learn how to manage the initial anarchism of total interactivity, we must put to good use all the tools we have at hand. The development of new links is not enough. We must also develop new ways to manage those links. The development of flexible management tools is a critical and challenging part of our interactivity.

Finally, couldn't we say that all creative works are always produced by interactions? Yes, to varying degrees, unless, of course, we think they originate from one-way divine inspiration, from the whispers of muses.

*Notes*

1. George P. Landow, *Hypertext 2.0: The Convergence of Contemporary Critical Theory and Technology* (Baltimore: Johns Hopkins University Press, 1997), 3.

2. Espen Aarseth, *Cybertext: Perspectives on Ergodic Literature* (Baltimore: Johns Hopkins University Press, 1997), 75.

3. Robert Markley warns in *Virtual Realities and Their Discontents* (Baltimore: Johns Hopkins University Press, 1996) that the new media is not displacing the old ones. The book stresses that we must remain skeptical of the notion that a new form can place itself above what has come before. I agree. Virtual reality is a new modeling medium sprouting among the many others we already have. Any claim to transcend other forms of expression goes against the grain of an interactive perspective. Such claim would also be unproductive. The fascinating issue is not hierarchical, but how the new media interacts with previous ones and stimulates transitions.

4. Sherry Turkle, *Life on the Screen: Identity in the Age of the Internet* (New York: Simon & Schuster, 1995), 20.

5. Cortázar favored active readers rather than armchair ones, as he put it. *Hopscotch* celebrates his notion of interaction by inviting the reader to follow at least two paths through the text. Works that focus on plot are the least interactive in this sense. The interactive nature of Maya textuality is rather different in that readings are based on spiritual links with the text. Readings vary depending on the quality of such links. Texts are not fixed. The *I Ching* also contains this type of interactive quality of reading, although here it is enhanced with the throwing of sticks or coins to arrive at one of sixty-four hexagrams. Espen Aarseth noted the hypertextual nature of the *I Ching* and argued that it is the first expert system based on the principles of binary computing (Landow 1994, 64–65).

6. Luis O. Arata, *The Festive Play of Fernando Arrabal* (Lexington: University Press of Kentucky, 1982), 1. The episodic form reappeared during the revival of theatre in the Middle Ages, and has continued to crop up since then in many playful guises.

7. Such was the case with classical French tragedy made to follow neo-Aristotelian rules of time, place, and action. Shakespeare, fortunately, had enjoyed a much freer hand.

8. André Malraux, *Picasso's Mask* (New York: Da Capo Press, 1994), 98.

9. Umberto Eco, *Interpretation and Overinterpretation* (Cambridge: Cambridge University Press, 1992), 93.

10. Henri Poincaré, *Science and Hypothesis* (New York: Dover, 1952), xxvi, 50, and 143.

11. Johan Huizinga, *Homo ludens* (Boston: Beacon Press, 1955), 3–4.

12. Ilya Prigogine, *The End of Certainty* (New York: The Free Press, 1997), 26.

13. Ibid., 189.

14. Jean Piaget, *Six Psychological Studies* (New York: Random House, 1968), 8.

15. Marshall McLuhan, *Understanding Media* (Cambridge, MA: MIT Press, 1994), 23.

16. This mirrors a solidity scale common in the sciences. Physics is considered the hardest discipline.

17. Ian Hacking, *The Social Construction of What?* (Cambridge, MA: Harvard University Press, 1999).

18. Marvin Minsky, *The Society of Mind* (New York: Simon & Schuster, 1986).

19. John H. Holland, *Emergence: From Chaos to Order* (Reading, MA: Addison Wesley, 1998).

20. Jim Gasperini, "Structural Ambiguity: An Emerging Interactive Aesthectic." In Robert Jacobson, ed. *Information Design* (Cambridge, MA: MIT Press, 1999), 301–316.

21. Eric Drexler, *Engines of Creation* (New York: Anchor Books, 1986). Of course, Drexler wrote this book before the Internet took off as a hypermedium, but his observations carry over quite well.

22. Richard Rorty, *Achieving Our Country* (Cambridge, MA: Harvard University Press, 1998), 27.

23. Richard Rorty, *Objectivity, Realism, and Truth* (Cambridge: Cambridge University Press, 1991), 39.

24. Ibid., 38.

25. *Achieving Our Country,* 18.

# 14 *Forms of Future*

Michael Joyce

---

This chapter is shrouded in images of and allusions to Berlin, not merely because it serves, I think, as a locale for legitimate wariness about magical transformations. The transformation of the book that I know best involves interactive fiction. Indeed, in Berlin I was asked to talk about the state of interactive fiction. To say interactive fiction is what I know best, of course, does not necessarily mean that I am he who knows best about it, nor does it mean to suggest that interactive fiction is as yet anything but a marginal activity taking place at the sheltered edge of a plain scoured by winds of transformation.

The margin, whether the edge of the campfire or the hedge which shielded forbidden Irish bards, has been more or less the storytellers' place from the first. My friend, Charles Henry, a great librarian and a technological visionary, often recounts his vision of the earliest story-telling technology. The cave paintings, he reminds us, could only be seen in patches of light from the rudimentary torchlamps—no more than fire upon a flat stone—held by our European ancestors of millennia ago. Those, too, were stories disclosed by little and surely interactively.

So I will discuss what I can see, the edges of things illuminated by a brief fire in my hand. I will console myself with an understanding that prophecy is cheap in this age of suppressed memory. The market analyst and the technological guru tell the future by economic quarters but count on having their prognostications forgotten by the time the stock market closes that day. For most technologists the measure of the future is a sound bite, an animated gif, or a mouse click. I have written elsewhere that in our technologies, our cultures, our entertainments and, increasingly, the way we constitute our communities and families we live in an anticipatory state of constant nextness.

In this constant blizzard of the next, we must nonetheless find our way through both our own private histories and the cumulative history of our cultures. Not a history in the old dangerously transcendent sense, but a history of our making and our remembering alike:

a history nearer to that which in "The Special View of History" the poet Charles Olson defines as "the function of any one of us . . . not a force but . . . the how of human life."

The hyperfiction novelist Shelley Jackson writes, "History is only a haphazard hop-scotch through other present moments. How I got from one to the other is unclear. Though I could list my past moments, they would remain discrete (and recombinant in potential if not in fact), hence without shape, without end, without story. Or with as many stories as I care to put together."

I am aware as I begin that digital technology attracts many of you because it promises the excitement of speed, the quickness of the present moment, the dizziness (or the Disneyesque) of next. I hope I do not disappoint you with my slowness. Artists tell the future in millennia, a glacial measure which even (or especially) at the beginning of a new one is already haunted by the past, both the past gone and the past yet to be. The future of fiction is its past, though that future, too, is a fiction.

The emergence of a truly electronic narrative art form awaits the pooling of a communal genius, a gathering of cultural impulses, of vernacular technologies, and most importantly of common yearnings which can find neither a better representation nor a more satisfactory confirmation than what electronic media offer.

It seems self-evident that multimedia of the sort we see now on the Web or CD-ROM is not likely to find a general audience. There is astonishing creativity everywhere (and I will point to some specific locales in a survey of interactive fictions at the end of this talk) but there has not as yet emerged any form which promises either widely popular or deeply artistic impact.

Nor is it likely that a haphazardly swirling chaff of java tools and plug-ins will suddenly reach a point of spontaneous combustion and bring forth a new light. The current state of multimedia does not repeat the case of the motorcar where widespread parallel technological developments led to a sufficient shift in sensibilities to make the mass distributed assembly line seem a technological event threshold. The form of multimedia itself has no obvious audience, nor any obvious longing which it seeks to fulfill.

To be sure there will be electronic television, perhaps even the much vaunted, ubiquitous push technology that is breathlessly championed by pseudo-religious cargo cults, techno-onanist publications, and infotainment empires. Yet push technology is merely radio for the eyes in which infobits flutter across the field of vision like papers falling from a virtual tickertape parade.

There will likewise be an electronic marketplace (perhaps there already is) for it is only an extension of the shopping mall with its shelves full of branded trademarks, surrounded by the architectural goulash of the gated suburb, and the holy shrines of the ATM card. The electronic marketplace will in this way parallel the course of the videotape rental industry in which an island of catalogues floats upon a sea of porn.

There are three general views about the failure of a true electronic form to yet emerge. Before I discuss them I wish to note that I have been quite intentionally using the term multimedia for the electronic television and electronic marketplace in order to distinguish such multimedia not merely from hypermedia but also from an electronic form yet to emerge but which has occasionally shown itself in almost magical, if incremental, transformations in our consciousness and indeed our sense of the real.

For now, though I will return to it later as a figure of more fundamental morphogenetic change, perhaps the image of Christo and Jeanne-Claude's *Wrapped Reichstag* can stand as a figure for these veiled changes, the pre-emergent and imminent forms of future whose edges push against the shrouded cloak of time like a baby's elbows push against a mother's belly.

One view of why a true electronic form has yet to emerge holds that we are in an age similar to that of the silent film and that a rich and powerful art form will emerge synergistically as the result of multiple, individual explorations upon the part of cultural producers coupled with simultaneously rising audience sophistication and expectations.

Yet the form of multimedia does not lead naturally from the marriage of eye and memory which film promised. Contemporary life leaves little time for those domestic and public mysteries of life lived in common which feed drama. Nor does multimedia provide the shadow box for the psychoanalytic model of detached personality as does television. Multimedia neither extends the page into some inevitable dream of technicolor longing to which its surface previously aspired, nor does it endow the unruly moving image with the staid conventionality of the page.

The second view about the failure of a true electronic form to yet emerge holds that authorship will turn from the creation of distinctly marked, individual stories to the creation of potentiated storyworlds, maintained and extended communally or by software agents which poll communal tastes. In such worlds individual audience members assume identities, spawn transitory narratives, and populate communities according to the logic of the storyworld, the accidental encounters of their inhabitants, and the story generation algorithyms of software agents alike. The dream of the software agent and the storyworld is the dream of Sheherezade's mother, a longed for happily-ever-after which is both outside the womb and yet no longer in the world. That dream doomed Berlin once before, before this rebuilding, the dream of a history outside history, a history at history's end. I think we all must be wary that dreams without ends do not summon the Reich of Virtual Reality, do not awaken the Avatar führer.

The third view is perhaps an extension of the second. It holds that language slides inevitably toward image. From Jaron Lanier's 1960s hippy, utopian view of unmediated, grokking communication through Virtual Reality to the network executives (of either the broadcast or inter networks) who see the web as packaging for a particular kind of targeted entertainment, not unlike the wrapper on a frozen egg roll, a Victoria's Secret brassiere, or the picture-in-picture headshots of interchangeable experts who appear over the shoulder of interchangeable infotainment news show hosts.

Total belief in the unmediated image is the behavior of cults. The Heaven's Gate cult knew what it saw beyond Hale Bop. Total belief in the unmediated image is denial of the mortality of the body. Yet outside the occult we live in a patchwork of self and place, image and word, body and mind. "Suppose we thought of representation," the philosopher and literary critic W. J. T. Mitchell suggests in his book *Picture Theory,* "not as a homogeneous field or grid of relationships governed by a single principle, but as a multidimensional and heterogeneous terrain, a collage or patchwork quilt assembled over time out of fragments."

We will come to see (we have come to see) that electronic texts expose the patchwork ("expose" perhaps in the way of a photograph) and recall the body. "Suppose further," Mitchell says, " that this quilt was torn, folded, wrinkled, covered with accidental stains, traces of the bodies it has enfolded. This model might help us understand a number of things about representation." The image Mitchell summons here is clear, the stained quilt is the Shroud of Turin, the bride's gift from her grandmother, the wedding night sheet, the baby's blanket. The image is clear but it does not proclaim its self-sufficiency.

The new electronic literature will distinguish itself by its clarity. It will seem right. I say literature because any literacy, even a visual or transitory one, expresses itself in a literature. Nor do I mean the kind of clarity that media purveyors speak about in terms of better authoring tools or more intuitive interfaces. I mean a new human clarity.

In the recent and important special issue of *Visible Language* regarding New Media Poetry and guest edited by Eduardo Kac, the French electronic poet and theorist Phillipe Bootz quotes Jean-Pierre Balpe's assertion that because computer authors "do not question at all the notion of literature [but] on the contrary claim they belong to it and feed on it. The fact that they bring us to reconsider its nature and consequently its evolution seems unquestionable."

The strengths of interactive fiction as a literary form increasingly seem to reside, quite curiously for me, in its realism or how truly it lets us render the shifting consciousness and shimmering coherences and transitory closures of the day-to-day beauty of the world around us. Hyperfiction seems equal to the complexity and sweetness of living in a world populated by other, equally uncertain, human beings—their dreams, and their memories.

Hyperfiction isn't a matter of branches but rather of the different textures of experience into which language (and image) leads us. Hyperfiction is like sitting in a restaurant in the murmur of stories, some fully known, some only half-heard, among people with whom you share only the briefest span of life and the certainty of death.

To be sure interactive fictions are an intermediate step to something else, but what that something might be is a question fit for philosophy. All our steps are intermediate. This one seems to be veering toward television, God help us, perhaps even television imprinted on your eyeballs. I put my trust in words. Media seers may talk about how we won't need stories since we will have new, virtual worlds, but soon those new worlds, too, will have their own stories and we will long for new words to put them into.

Do not mistake me. I am not saying that hyperfiction enjoys an obvious audience which multimedia lacks. I am however saying that language—with its instrinsically multiple forms, with its age-old engagement of eye and ear and mind, with its ancient summoning of gesture, movement, rhythm and repetition, with the consolation and refreshment it offers memory—offers us the clearest instance and the most obvious form for what will emerge as a truly electronic narrative art form.

The new electronic literature will seem self-evident, as if we have always seen it and, paradoxically, as if we have never seen it before. Berlin at this moment seems the ideal figure of what moments ago I called the astonishing creativity of an emerging electronic literature, a Berlin in which the cranes crosshatch a sky whose color, rather than being William Gibson's color of television, is not yet known, a sky whose expanse promises a new clarity (*eine neue Klarheit*).

Despite the earnest impulses of government bureaucracies and the imperial appetites of transnational conglomerate capital all of the busyness of the Berlin skyline—while not purposeless—is nonetheless to no purpose. This is good. We need to move beyond purpose, to what the monk and poet Thomas Merton calls the "freedom which responsibilities and transient cares make us forget." We need to be free of technology to be free in technology. Like the overarching apparatus of our technologies, the scaffolding which criss-crosses Berlin is bandaged air. Beneath it lies the promise of new clarity, indeed even the unthinkable possibility of a *Kristall Tag,* an inversion of history, in which our world reforms itself as a globe of glass in which the fractures of the darkest nights are never again forgotten but rather where these healed-over fractures form a prism for a new light to shine through in all its differences. Through such a new prism the wounds of a world torn apart would both flow like tears and crystalize like roses at intervals in the way that the hearts of martyrs do under glass reliquaries in a cathedral. The new electronic literature will seem old, as old as any human story, in its newness as old as birth.

The new Berlin heals over itself and in the process becomes itself differentiated by its own perception of gathering forms. The way in which a thing is both still itself and yet no longer itself is what Sanford Kwinter identifies as the singularity of catastophe theory in which "a point suddenly fails to map onto itself" (58) and a new thing is born. This is, of course, the genius of Christo and Jeanne-Claude's *Wrapped Reichstag* in which the thing seen is not the thing wrapped and yet evokes and insists upon it, and meanwhile the thing unwrapped is no longer the thing that was wrapped and yet promises to be what it was then.

This healing-over traces a circle like that of the Zen paradox, the circle whose center is nowhere and whose circumference is everywhere. In writing some years ago about the emergence of a city of text I cited Wim Wenders's angelic vision of the great Berlin film, *Wings of Desire,* in which angels walk among the stacks of a library, listening to the musical language which forms the thoughts of individual readers. Into this scene, shuffling slowly up the stairs, comes an old man, who the credits identify as Homer. "Tell me, muse, of the story-teller who was thrust to the end of the world, childlike ancient. . . . With time," he thinks, "my listeners became my readers. They no longer sit in a circle, instead they sit apart and no one knows anything about the other. . . . " The new electronic literature will restore the circle as it always was and, paradoxically, as it never was before.

I suggested earlier that we live in constant nextness. Thomas Merton speaks of the nextness of "Computer Karma in American Civilization" in which:

> What can be done has to be done. The burden of possibilities has to be fulfilled, possibilities which demand so imperatively to be fulfilled that everything else is sacrificed to their fulfillment. (25)

The new electronic literature will bear the burden of possibilities in the way the earth bears the air.

Steven Johnson, the editor of the defunct Webzine FEED, recalls the passage in Walter Benjamin's essay "The Work of Art in the Age of Mechanical Reproduction," where "Benjamin talks rhapsodically about the cultural effects of slow-motion film" as an instance of how difficult it is "to predict the broader sociological effects of new technologies."

"I've always liked this passage," Johnson says, "because it seems so foreign to us now, reading Benjamin fifty years later. If you imagine all the extraordinary changes wrought by the rise of moving pictures, slow-motion seems more like a side-effect, a footnote or a curiosity-piece."

Confronted by Johnson's observation, I wondered instead whether Benjamin was right and we have missed the point of the technology. Perhaps we are all watching too fast. In his book of interviews Wim Wenders quotes Cézanne, "Things are disappearing. If you want to see anything you have to hurry." Yet in another place Wenders says, "Films are congruent time sequences, not congruent ideas. . . . In every scene my biggest problem is how to end it and go on to the next one. Ideally I would show the time in between as well. But sometimes you have to leave it out, it simply takes too long. . . ."

The current generations of Berliners are, of course, citizens of the time in between and as such bear the responsibility which so many of us do in the constant state of changing change which constitutes networked culture. Many of you here are likewise from the generation of the time in between, and you too bear the burden of its telling, a process which, despite our technologies, requires constant generation and generations alike. One day Potzdamer Platz will be, however, temporarily complete. One day the world will lack a memory of what happened here; it is a storyteller's task to remember in the midst of dizzying change. The new electronic literature will show the time in between, which is nothing less than the space which links us through our differences.

And so, as I turn, finally, to the brief survey of interactive fiction which I promised earlier, I hope you will forgive me if I turn a critical eye toward the paradoxical lack of any obvious sense of what links us in these fictions. It is this lack of the "betweenus," to use the word which Helene Cixous coined, more than any technical lack, which momentarily stops us short of a mass electronic medium or a lasting artform. Nor do I exempt myself from this criticism. Although my hyperfictions are sincere attempts to negotiate whatever clarity I could find in linkage and multiplicity of voices, I have as yet found nothing truly self-evident to show you. No new clarity, no new city-of-text beneath the cranes and scaffolds, no promised land, not even a wire frame Frankenstein awaiting the flesh of textual space.

I also hope as I begin this survey that you will recall the modest intention with which I began, that is to say what edges I think I can glimpse of forms of future.

Let me say something briefly about my current work, the Web fiction, *Twelve Blue*. I have often been critical of the way the Web impoverishes hypertext. The Web is a pretty difficult space in which to create an expressive surface for text. It seems to me that the Web is all edges and without much depth and for a writer that is trouble. You want to induce depth, to have the surface give way to reverie and a sense of a shared shaping of the experience of reading and writing. Instead everything turns to branches.

With this fiction, I decided to stop whining and learn to love the Web as best I could, to honor what it gives us at present and to try to make art within the restrictions of the medium. *Twelve Blue* explores the way our lives—like the Web itself or a year, a day, a memory, or a river—form patterns of interlocking, multiple, and recurrent surfaces. I've tried to use frames and simple sinking hyperlinks to achieve a feeling of depth and successive interaction unlike most Web fictions. The idea is to put the links within the text and outside the interface and thus have the fiction echo with possibilities and transform the day-to-day, page to page, rhythm of the Web into a new music of swirling waters and shades of blue. So while there is only one text link in any screen (and that one disappears when it is followed), the whole of the text is not only surrounded by the visual threads of its various linked narratives but threaded through with shared visions, events, and situations for which the reader's sensibility supplies the links.

The drawing came first, the threads creating a kind of score in the sense of John Cage, a continuity of the various parallel narratives. When the threads veer nearer to each other—or in at least one instance cross—so do their narratives. The twelve lines became months but also characters or pairings of them as well (that is, sometimes a character has her own line and another line she shares with someone paired to her, although not necessarily within the narratives threads). The twelve threads do not start with January at the top but rather November, the year of my year. I then made eight different cuts across the y-axis, though in my mind they were more fabric strips or something like William Burroughs's compositional cuts.

Within these eight longitudinal strips the various stories take place and intermingle. Obviously, however, since narrative goes forward horizontally and time here is represented vertically, there is something of a displacement in which events along a single thread in fact violate the larger time of the characters sensibilities. Thus the drowning deaf boy of the story floats across various threads through different seasons until his body surfaces at the end. Beyond this, I gave myself some other simple constraints. For instance, the already mentioned one of only one text link per frame and another of having every screen contain the word blue.

Meanwhile I have barely begun another webfiction which takes place on an island in-habited by several historical characters (St. Francis, William Wordsworth and his sister Dorothy, and the engraver and book illustrator Bernard Picart). It is a novel about the re-lationhips between word and image and the slippages as each lapse into each other. Parts of it are in a local pidgen of the island, whose name we never quite get, although the locals call it Banyan (or Yamland in some parts). In the words of the fiction pidgen also enters through occasional typos, which themselves enter the pidgen, since typos are thought to be sacred in this place, i.e., divine inspiration, the devolution of the word, logo into imago, or so I think at present.

A moment ago I invoked Frankenstein and so let me begin my survey of interactive fic-tion with Shelley Jackson's extraordinary disk-based hypertext novel, *Patchwork Girl, or a Modern Monster,* a work attributed to Mary/Shelley and Herself. This hyperfiction seems to oscillate in its voices among these three attributed authors and at least once engages in a dialogue with Derrida. It is a fiction of continuous dissection, in which both Mary Shel-ley's monster and Frank Baum's girl of Oz are successively cut and repatched in the way of Xeno's paradox. This is a getting nowhere which gets somewhere. "I align myself as I read with the flow of blood," says Shelley Jackson's triple narrator:

> that as it cycles keeps moist and living what without it stiffens into a fibrous cell. What hap-pens to the cells I don't visit? I think maybe they harden over time without the blood visi-tation, enclosures of wrought letters fused together with rust, iron cages like ancient elevators with no functioning parts. Whereas the read words are lubricated and mobile, rub familiarly against one another in the buttery medium of my regard, rearrange themselves in my peripheral vision to suggest alternatives. If I should linger in a spot, the blood pools; an appealing heaviness comes over my limbs and oxygen-rich malleability my thoughts. The letters come alive like tiny antelopes and run in packs and patterns; the furniture softens and molds itself to me.
>
> (I do not know what metaphor to stick to; I am a mixed metaphor myself, consistency is one thing you cannot really expect of me.)
>
> What I leave alone is skeletal and dry.

Dissection and Frankensteinian cyborgization also informs the very provocative collaborative Web work of Noah Wardrip-Fruin and others, titled *Gray Matters,* itself a brilliant unbinding of book and body and the link each represents between creation and reception.

On the Web I am currently very much taken by the work of Tim McLaughlin whose language constantly meditates in the presence of image and mediates the nature of image. McLaughlin's work with the architects, Thomas Bessai, Maria Denegri, and Bruce Haden for the Canadian biennale pavilion, *Light Assemblage* is an extraordinary exploration of how word makes place and place enables language. His *25 Ways to Close a Photograph* perhaps most nearly approaches the self-evident quality that I have demanded of electronic literature, exploiting rather than working within the constraints of the Web.

Although not strictly a fiction, I am very fond of *Memory Arena* and *Who's Who in Central & East Europe 1933* done by Arnold Dreyblatt in collaboration with the Kulturinformatik, Dept. of the University of Lüneburg which Heiko Idensen first introduced me to. As Jeffrey Wallen notes in his introduction, this work takes "the ordinary and the bureaucratic . . . to a further extreme through their own logic of fragmentation, listing, juxtaposition, and leveling" giving us "a haunting glimpse of an absence."

I know that this conference has previously been graced by Mark Amerika, whose overly earnest but nonetheless likeable *Grammatron* is weighed down by a quasi-theoretical agenda, a perplexing nostalgia for cyberpunk, and the already discussed impossibility of multimedia.

A similarly likeable brilliance, but without the nervousness of multimedia, suffuses the work of both Marjorie Luesebrink and Adrianne Wortzel with a serenity of surface if not yet a fully new clarity. Luesebrink's *Lacemaker* Webfiction (written as M. D. Coverley at <http://gnv.fdt.net/~christys/elys_1.html>) inside the also very compelling Madame de Lafayette site of Christy Sheffield Sanford is a variation upon Cinderella. Wortzel's *Ah, Need* turns the inevitable probing of surface which multimedia elicits to something more of an experience of liguistic surface.

Finally I am especially fond of *Flygirls,* the Web fiction of the Webwench, Jane Loader of *Atomic Cafe* fame. Its dusty rose to khaki trim retro look, its elegiac quality, and most of all its rich expanse and compelling writing are smart in the double sense of intelligence and style. This site seems an actual aerodrome but with the narrative spine of the race stretching over the rose-lit space, the links like lavender vertebrae.

My own feeling, however, is that the most provocative works are taking place outside the Web in what might be called natural electronic spaces, the vernacular technologies of game engines, MOOs and most especially the kinetic texts of electronic poetry where language finally finds its natural element in motion—not in a window but as a window, not as a single surface but as the aural, visual, and proprioceptive experience of successive surfaces. I do not think I am wrong to include hypertext fiction among these natural electronic environments, despite the current feeling in media and publishing and among certain critics that their time came and passed. This is hardly the literature of the present and will likely not be the literature of the future, and yet I am convinced that the literature of the present cannot continue without it and the literature of the future will not only encompass it but in some sense depends upon it.

An extraordinarily exciting international collaboration involves the Dublin-based but Derry-born writer, Terence MacNamee, the electronic artist and programmer, Eoin O'Sullivan in Derry, an American hyperfiction writer, Noah Pivnick and his colleague and co-producer, Rachel Buswell (info at <http://www.ulst.ac.uk/hyperfiction/Welcome.html>). This group is in the midst of creating a fiction in the form of the Derry city walls, utilizing the Quake game engine as a locale for what they call networked co-readings. This story, which the authors describe as hypertext in architectural space, includes progressively disclosed texts, ambient sounds, and multiply inhabited story spaces which subvert the mythic war engine of Quake toward a literally dynamic consideration of the possibility of reconciliation. The fictional space invites the reader to explore walls and the link they represent between insider and outsider, reader and writer. Their fiction thus takes its place rather than takes place within a naturalized electronic space, not unlike how Judy Malloy in the early stages of *Brown House Kitchen* would set up space inside a room at *LambdaMOO* and begin to tell her stories, ignoring the protests, until the story made its own space.

Of my experiences of virtual reality thus far, I remember only one with a visceral excitement and longing: the experience of moving in and out of planetary spaces of text within a 2-D rendering of 3-D typographic space which I experienced in the work of the late Muriel Cooper together with David Small and Suguru Ishizaki at MIT's Visible Language Workshop. "Imagine swooping into a typographic landscape: hovering above a headline, zooming toward a paragraph in the distance, spinning around and seeing it from behind, then diving deep into a map," Wendy Richmond described it perfectly in *WIRED*, "A virtual reality that has type and cartography and numbers, rather than objects—it's like no landscape you've ever traveled before, yet you feel completely at home."

Making space through and in and of language distinguishes the kinetic poets featured in Visible Language whose work seems to me very much in the spirit of Muriel Cooper and her group. This includes Eduardo Kac's holopoems, John Cayley's cybertexts, E. M de Melo e Castro's videopoemography, Philippe Bootz's work on a functional model of *texte-a-voir,* and most importantly Jim Rosenberg's extraordinary body of theory and poetry leading toward an "externalization of syntax analogous to the externalization of the nervous system manifested in computer networks."

This is a call for a language outside itself, a language that goes out into the world. In his chapter "Walking in the City" in *The Practice of Everyday Life,* Michel de Certeau spies this externalization in the figure of the wanderer who looks beyond "the absence of what has passed by" to "the act itself of passing by" (97). The act of passing by is Olson history as the "how of human life." It takes place and makes place alike in the city of text.

There is a city of text and it, too, mutates and thrives beneath an umbrella of construction cranes and a crenellated skin of scaffolding, beneath SGML, XTML, VRML, and HTML, inside the plug-in, the data stream, the web crawler, the game engine, the Photoshop filter, and so on. As with Berlin, what matters most is not what life goes on beneath but what life emerges and in what light we come to see each other in the act of passing by.

## Works Cited

Balpe, Jean-Pierre. L'Imaginaire Informatique de la Litterature, paper presented at a 1993 conference.

De Certeau, Michel. *The Practice of Everyday Life,* trans. Steven Randall. Berkeley: University of California Press, 1983.

Jackson, Shelley. *Patchwork Girl, or a Modern Monster,* on computer disk. Watertown, MA: Eastgate Systems, 1995.

Kwinter, Sanford. "Landscapes of Change: Boccioni's Stati d'Animo as a General Theory of Models." *Assemblage* 19 (1992): 55–65.

Merton, Thomas. *Woods, Shores, Desert.* Santa Fe: Museum of New Mexico Press, 1982.

Mitchell, W. J. T. *Picture Theory: Essays on Verbal and Visual Representation.* Chicago: University of Chicago Press, 1994.

Olson, Charles. *The Special View of History,* ed. with an introduction by Ann Charters. Berkeley: Oyez, 1970.

Richmond, Wendy. "Muriel Cooper's Legacy." *WIRED 2.10,* 1994.

Rosenberg, J. "The Interactive Diagram Sentence: Hypertext as a Medium of Thought." *Visible Languages 30,* no. 2 (1996): 102–118.

# 15 *Stitch Bitch: The Patchwork Girl*

Shelley Jackson

---

It has come to my attention that a young woman claiming to be the author of my being has been making appearances under the name of Shelley Jackson. It seems you have even invited her to speak tonight, under the misapprehension that she exists, that she is something besides a parasite, a sort of engorged and loathsome tick hanging off my side. May I say that I find this an extraordinary impertinence, and that if she would like to come forward, we shall soon see who is the author of whom.

Well? Well?

Very well.

I expect there are some of you who still think I am Shelley Jackson, author of a hypertext about an imaginary monster, the patchwork girl Mary Shelley made after her firstborn ran amok. No, I am the monster herself, and it is Shelley Jackson who is imaginary, or so it would appear, since she always vanishes when I turn up. You can call me Shelley Shelley if you like, daughter of Mary Shelley, author of the following, entitled "Stitch Bitch" or, Shelley Jackson, that impostor, I'm going to get her.

I have pilfered her notes, you see, and I don't mind reading them, but I have shuffled the pages. I expect what comes of it will be more to my liking, might even sound like something I would say. Whoever Shelley Jackson may be, if she wants me to mouth her words, she can expect them to come out a little changed. I'm not who she says I am.

## Body Not Whole

We're not who we say we are.

The body is not one, though it seems so from up here, from this privileged viewpoint up top. When we look down that assemblage of lobes and stalks seems to be one thing, even if it looks nothing like our ID photo, but it routinely survives dissolution, from hair loss to loss of limb. The body is a patchwork, though the stitches might not show. It's run by committee, a loose aggregate of entities we can't really call human, but that have what look like lives of a sort; though they lack the brains to nominate themselves part of the animal kingdom, yet they are certainly not what we think of as objects, nor are they simple appendages, directly responsible to the conscious brain. Watch white blood cells surround an invader, watch a cell divide. What we see is not thinking exactly, but it is "intelligent," or at least ordered, responsive, purposeful. We can feel a sort of camaraderie with those rudimentary machinic minds, but not identity. Nor, if we could watch a spark dart across a synaptic gap in a brain, would we cry out "Mom!" or "Uncle Toby!" for thinking is conducted by entities we don't know, wouldn't recognize on the street. Call them yours if you want, but puff and blow all you like, you cannot make them stop their work one second to salute you.

The body is not even experienced as whole. We never see it all, we can't feel our liver working or messages shuttling through our spine. We patch a phantom body together out of a cacophony of sense impressions, bright and partial views. We borrow notions from our friends and the blaring organs of commerce, and graft them on to a supple, undifferentiated mist of smart particles. It's like a column of dust motes standing in a ray of light, patted and tatted into a familiar shape. Our work is never very successful, there are always scraps floating loose, bits we can't control or don't want to perceive that intrude like outsiders on the effigy we've constructed in our place. The original body is dissociated, porous and unbiased, a generous catchall. The mind, on the other hand, or rather discursive thought, what Zen calls monkey-mind and Bataille calls project, has an almost catatonic obsession with stasis, centrality, and unity. Project would like the body to be its commemorative statue or its golem, sober testament to the mind's values and an uncomplaining servant. But the statue doesn't exist except in the mind, a hard kernel like a tumor, set up in the portal to the body, blocking the light. The project of writing, the project of life, even, is to dissolve that tumor. To dismantle the project is the project. That is, to interrupt, unhinge, disable the processes by which the mind, glorying in its own firm grip on what it wishes to include in reality, gradually shuts out more and more of it, and substitutes an effigy for that complicated machine for inclusion and effusion that is the self.

### Write Mutt

My favorite writing is impure, improper, and disorienting.

Ecstatic or fantastically systematic, hybrid in form or of uncertain genre, incomplete or overwrought, too little or too much, it staggers off the straight and narrow line. Like

Sterne's famous drawing of the flight path of Tristram Shandy, it digresses. It runs backwards and sideways or in all directions at once. Some of the best writing in print works this way, despite the prevailing winds from start to finish, which favor the linear plot and the sober pilot. Hypertext, on the other hand, is nonlinear almost by default. I think we have no real idea yet what will come of this difference, though it is well to keep in mind that the surrealists had their greatest influence on perfume ads and paperback book-covers. Every new form will inspire mediocre works as well as great ones, and while even mediocrity can be interesting when the form is new, it doesn't remain so. Difficult going, novelty and strangeness sharpen the eye, the ear, the mind, but hypertext will acquire its own conventions and become easier and more commonplace. Probably we will only bother to describe and marvel at it for a little while; then it will just be another thing people do, and it will cloak itself in a new kind of ordinariness that will only drop away in weird moments of alienation or historical awareness, like when you realize that someone had to invent the book, and suddenly that iconic shape looks wry and marvellous again.

I hope the flexibility of electronic media means they evolve many different conventions, a sort of articulation of the possibilities, rather than a narrowing. (Let books take inspiration from them and evolve as well.) Let styles and forms proliferate along with points of view. Borrow and lend, write mutt, and don't be intimidated by that goose-stepping Mickey Mouse and his armed henchmen ordering you to keep mum: if it's in your head it's yours to express. Write about what interests you, no matter how sniffy the world gets, even if it's kid Lolita getting her kicks off Humbert or pissing on a crucifix. Write in whatever WAY interests you, even if nobody wants to publish something that "experimental," that "bad," that old-fashioned, new-fangled or unfathomable. (This is why I like the Internet. Every crank with a web page can put forward whatever crackpotpourri she pleases.) Read everything, William Burroughs AND Charles Dickens, Patricia Highsmith AND Gertrude Stein. The boundaries between genres and disciplines keep people dumb and inflexible and make them careerists of the imagination. You can't let other people decide what is important to think or write about. Other people are wrong. This is a good rule of thumb. (But also keep in mind that you are someone else's "other people.")

What I want to read: disrespectful texts, because humor and the shuffling around of stuff loosens the categories; useless texts, that refuse to be adopted by practical purposes of any description. Beautiful strange constructions of language. Lies, collaborations, collage. Borderline texts that don't know if they're fact or fiction, serious or tongue-in-cheek. Texts that want to take over the world, piratical texts, bristling with signposts pointing "outa here". Hybrid works, recombinant works, fairy tales and folk songs, rants and dreams; preposterous, infectious. Luscious, dizzy, baroque works. Austere, impersonal, crystalline works. These may not be novels. They may not be hypertexts. If it were possible, I would like to replace the word "hypertext" in the following with a word of my own coining, partly because "hypertext" is a horribly spiky word that makes me picture a coked-up rooster on a go-cart, but also because what I have to say applies to any gorgeously non-linear piece of writing, not just ones you can read on your computer screen.

## Everything at Once

You're not where you think you are.

In non-linear writing, and in hypertext most obviously, everything is there at once and equally weighted. It is a body whose brain is dispersed throughout the cells, fraught with potential, fragile with indecision, or rather strong in foregoing decisions, the way a vine will bend but a tree can fall down. It is always at its end and always at its beginning, the birth and the death are simultaneous and reflect each other harmoniously; it is like living in the cemetery and the hospital at once; it is easy to see the white rectangles of hospital beds and the white rectangles of gravestones and the white rectangles of pages as being essentially synonymous. Every page-moment is both expectant and memorializing.

Hypertext doesn't know where it's going. "Those things which occur to me, occur to me not from the root up but rather only from somewhere about their middle. Let someone then attempt to seize them, let someone attempt to seize a blade of grass and hold fast to it when it begins to grow only from the middle," said Kafka. It's got no throughline. Like the body, it has no point to make, only clusters of intensities, and one cluster is as central as another, which is to say, not at all. What sometimes substitutes for a center is just a switch-point, a place from which everything diverges, a Cheshire aftercat. A hypertext never seems quite finished, it isn't clear just where it ends, it's fuzzy at the edges. You can't figure out what matters and what doesn't, what's matter and what's void, what's the bone and what's the flesh; it's all decoration or it's all substance. Normally when you read you can orient yourself by a few important facts and let the details fall where they may. The noun trumps the adjective, person trumps place, idea trumps example. In hypertext, you can't find out what's important so you have to pay attention to everything, which is exhausting like being in a foreign country; you are not native.

Hypertext is schizophrenic: you can't tell what's the original and what's the reference. Hierarchies break down into chains of likenesses, the thing is not more present than what the thing reminds you of; in this way you can slip out of one text into a footnoted text and find yourself reading another text entirely, a text to which your original text is a footnote. This is unnerving, even to me. The self may have no clear boundaries, but do we want to lose track of it altogether? I don't want to lose the self, only to strip it of its claim to naturalness, its compulsion to protect its boundaries, its obsession with wholeness and its fear of infection. I would like to invent a new kind of self that doesn't fetishize so much, grounding itself in the dearly-loved signs and stuff of personhood, but has poise and a sense of humor, changes directions easily, sheds parts and assimilates new ones. Desire rather than identity is its compositional principle. Instead of this morbid obsession with the fixed, fixable, everyone composing their tombstone over and over. Is it that we want to live up to the dignity of our dead bodies? Do keep in mind the dead disperse, and even books, which live longer, come apart into different signatures.

### No-Place

I'm not where you say I am.

Hypertext blurs the distinction between subject and object, matter and the absence of matter. We no longer know where it does its thinking, or what it is driving at. (It's no one and no-place, but it's not nothing.) Instead, there is a communicating fabric spread out over a space without absolute extent, a place without placement (a place without placemats, I almost wrote, which is good too). In the no-place of hypertext, there's finally room to move around, like an orifice I can fit my whole body into, instead of just my finger or my p-p-p-pen. I adore the good old-fashioned book, but I don't fit into it very well. As a writer or a reader, there's always some of me hanging untidily outside, looking like a mess, an excrescence, something the editor should have lopped off and for which I feel a bit apologetic. To make something orderly and consecutive out of the divergent fragments that come naturally feels like forcing myself through a Klein bottle.

I can't help seeing an analogy between the editorial advice I have often received to weed out the inessentials and lop off the divergent story lines, and the life advice I've received just as often to focus, choose, specialize. You don't show up for tennis in a tutu and a catcher's mask, it's silly. But in this place without coordinates I cautiously began to imagine that I could invent a new game, make a novel, if we still want to call it that, shaped a little more like my own thoughts. It is as though somebody chewed a hole in a solid and irrefutable wall, and revealed an expanse of no-space as extensive as the space we live in, or as though the interstices between things could be pried apart without disturbing the things themselves, to make room for what hasn't been voted into the club of stuff.

## Gaps, Leaps

You won't get where you think you're going.

A conventional novel is a safe ride. It is designed to catch you up, propel you down its track, and pop you out at the other end with possibly a few new catchphrases in your pocket and a pleasant though vague sense of the scenery rushing by. The mechanism of the chute is so effective, in fact, that it undoes the most worthy experiments; sentences that ought to stop you in your tracks are like spider webs across the chute. You rip through, they're gone.

Non-linear writing likes give and take, snares and grottos, nets and knots. It lacks thrust. It will always lack thrust; thrust is what linear narrative is good at. As far as I'm concerned, we can trust thrust to it. It means we'll need other reasons to keep readers reading—assuming that's what we want—than a compulsion to find out what happens next. There's no question that hypertext will lose or never acquire those readers for whom a fated slalom toward the finish line is the defining literary experience; hypertext's not built for that. Probably it is because linear text's so well-built for it that it has become the dominant narrative style in the novel. But there are other reasons to read. I can be caught in that slalom myself, but I emerge feeling damp, winded and slightly disgusted. It is a not entirely pleasant compulsion disguised as entertainment, like being forced to dance by a magic fiddle. It becomes harder and harder to imagine going anywhere but just where you're going, and words increasingly mean just what they say. (Common sense reality does the same thing: there is little opportunity for poetic ambiguity in the dealings of everyday life.) Plot chaperones understanding, cuts off errant interpretations. Reading a well-plotted novel I start by knowing less than I know about my own life, and being open to far more interpretations, which makes me feel inquisitive and alive. I finish by knowing more than I want to know, stuck on one meaning like a bug on a pin.

In a text like this, gaps are problematic. The mind becomes self-conscious, falters, forgets its way, might choose another way, might opt out of this text into another, might "lose the thread of the argument," might be unconvinced. Transitional phrases smooth over gaps, even huge logical gaps, suppress contradiction, whisk you past options. I noticed in school that I could argue anything. I might find myself delivering conclusions I disagreed with because I had built such an irresistible machine for persuasion. The trick was to allow the reader only one way to read it, and to make the going smooth. To seal the machine, keep out grit. Such a machine can only do two things: convince or break down. Thought is made of leaps, but rhetoric conducts you across the gaps by a cute cobbled path, full of grey phrases like "therefore," "extrapolating from," "as we have seen," giving you something to look at so you don't look at the nothing on the side of the path. Hypertext leaves you naked with yourself in every leap; it shows you the gamble thought is, and it invites criticism, refusal even. A plot is designed to keep you reading the next thing until the end, but hypertext invites choice. Writing hypertext, you've got to accept the possibility your reader will just stop reading. Why not? The choice to go do something else might be the best outcome of a text. Who wants a numb reader/reader-by-numbers anyway? Go write your own text. Go paint a mural. You must change your life. I want piratical readers, plagiarists and opportunists, who take what they want from my ideas and knot it into their own arguments. Or even their own novels. From which, possibly, I'll steal it back.

## Banished Body

It's not what we wish it were.

The real body, which we have denied representation, is completely inimical to our wishful thinking about the self. We would like to be unitary, controlled from on top, visible, self-contained. We represent ourselves that way, and define our failures to be so, if we cannot ignore them, as disease, hysteria, anomaly. However:

> The banished body is unhierarchical. It registers local intensities, not arguments. It is a field of sensations arranged in space. It has no center, but a roving focus. (It "reads" itself.)
>
> It is vague about size and location, unclear on measurements of all kinds, bad at telling time (though good at keeping it).
>
> It is capacious, doesn't object to paradox, includes opposites—doesn't know what opposites are. It is simultaneous.
>
> It is unstable. It changes from moment to moment, in its experience both of itself and of the world.
>
> It is easily influenced; it is largely for being influenced, since its largest organs are sensing devices. It is permeable; it is entered by the world, via the senses, and can only roughly define its boundaries.
>
> It reports to us in stories, intensities, hallucinatory jolts of uninterpreted perceptions: smells, sights, pleasure, pain.

It is neither clearly an object nor simply a thought, meaning or spirit; it is a hybrid of thing and thought, the monkey in the middle. Its public image, its face is a collage of stories, borrowed images, superstitions, fantasies. We have no idea what it "really" looks like.

Because we have banished the body, but cannot get rid of it entirely, we can use it to hold what we don't want to keep but can't destroy. The real body, madcap patchwork acrobat, gets what the mind doesn't want, the bad news, the dirty stories. In hysteria, the body starts to tell those stories back to us—our kidneys become our accusers, our spine whines, our knees gossip about overheard words, our fingers invent a sign language of blame and pain. Of course, the more garbage we pack into that magical body the more we fear it, and the more chance there is that it will turn on us, begin to speak, accuse us. But that body bag is also a treasure-trove, like any junkyard. It knows stories we've never told.

### Boundary Play

We don't think what we think we think.

It's straightforward enough to oppose the self to the not-self and reason to madness. It's even possible to make the leap from here to there, though coming back presents some problems. But the borders between are frayed and permeable. It's possible to wander that uneven terrain, to practice slipping, skidding in the interzone. It's possible, and maybe preferable for the self to think of itself as a sort of practice rather than a thing, a proposition with variable terms, a mesh of relationships. It's possible for a text to think of itself that way. ANY text. But hypertext in particular is a kind of amphibious vehicle, good for negotiating unsteady ground, poised on its multiple limbs where the book clogs up and stops; it keeps in motion. Conventional texts, on the other hand are in search of a place of rest; when they have found it, they stop.

Similarly, the mind, reading, wants to make sense, and once it has done so it considers its work done, so if you want to keep the mind from stopping there, you must always provide slightly more indicators than the mind can make use of. There must be an excess, a remainder. Or an undecidable oscillation between possibilities. I am interested in writing that verges on nonsense, where nonsense is not the absence of sense, but the superfluity of it. I would like to sneak as close to that limit as possible without reaching it. This is the old kind of interactive writing: writing so dense or so slippery that the mind must do a dance to keep a grip on it. I am interested in writing this way for two reasons. One, because language must be teased into displaying its entire madcap lavish beauty. If you let it be serviceable then it will only serve you, never master you, and you will only write what you already know, which is not much. Two, because the careful guarding of sense in language is not just analogous to but entirely complicit in the careful guarding of sense in life, and that possibly well-intentioned activity systematically squelches curiosity, change, variety, & finally, all delight in life. It promotes common sense at the expense of all the others.

### Reality Fiction

It's not what it says it is.

Reality thinks it "includes" fiction, that fictional works are embedded in reality. It's the boast of a bully. But just because reality's bigger doesn't make it boss. Every work of art is an alternate "world" with other rules, which threatens the alibi of naturalness our ordinary reality usually flaunts. Every fictional world competes with the real one to some extent, but hypertext gives us the chance to sneak up on reality from inside fiction. It may be framed as a novel, yet link to and include texts meant to be completely non-fictional. Thus the pedigreed facts of the world can be swayed, framed, made persuaders of fiction, without losing their seats in the parliament of the real, as facts tend to do when they're stuck in a novel. Hypertext fiction thus begins to turn around and look back on reality as a text embedded in a fictional universe.

Ironically, that might make us like reality better: it's reality's hegemony that strips it of charm. Reality is based on country cottage principles: what's homey must be true. It is a tolerable place to live. What's dreadful is the homey on a grand scale, Raggedy Ann and Andy turned Adam and Eve, cross stitch scenes of the Grand Canyon, the sun cast as the flame snapping behind the grate, the ocean our little kettle. Those goofy grins turn frightening on a cosmic scale; the simplicity that makes it easy to pick up a coffee cup is not suitable for managing a country, or even a conscience. The closure of the normal is suffocating at the very least. By writing we test the seams, pick out the stitches, trying to stretch the gaps between things to slip out through them into some uncharted space, or to let something spring up in the real that we don't already know, something unfamiliar, not part of the family, a changeling.

### The Feminine

She's not what he says she is.

The banished body is not female, necessarily, but it is feminine. That is, it's amorphous, indirect, impure, diffuse, multiple, evasive. So is what we learned to call bad writing. Good writing is direct, effective, clean as a bleached bone. Bad writing is all flesh, and dirty flesh at that: clogged with a build-up of clutter and crud, knick-knacks and fripperies encrusted on every surface, a kind of gluey scum gathering in the chinks. Hypertext is everything that for centuries has been damned by its association with the feminine (which has also, by the way, been damned by its association with it, in a bizarre mutual proof without any fixed term). It's dispersed, languorous, flaunting its charms all over the courtyard. Like flaccid beauties in a harem, you might say, if you wanted to inspire a rigorous distaste for it. Hypertext then, is what literature has edited out: the feminine. (That is not to say that only women can produce it. By feminine, I mean only what convention has given that label. Women have no more natural gift for the feminine than men do.)

### *Constellation*

I'm not what you think I am.

I am a loose aggregate, a sort of old fashioned cabinet of curiosities, interesting in pieces but much better as a composite. It's the lines of traffic between the pieces that are worth attention, but this has been, until now, a shapeless sort of beauty, a beauty without a body, and therefore with few lovers. But hypertext provides a body, a vaporous sort of insufficiently tactile body but a body, for our experience of the beauty of relationships. It is like an astronomy of constellations rather than stars. It is old-fashioned, in that sense. It is a sort of return, to a leisurely old form, the sprawling, quizzical portmanteau book like the *Anatomy of Melancholy* ("a rhapsody of rags gathered together from several dung-hills, excrements of authors, toys and fopperies confusedly tumbled out," as Burton himself described it) to the sort of broad cross-fertilization of disciplines that once was commonplace, only hypertext does not provide so much courtly guidance across the intellectual terrain, but catapults you from spot to spot. (The wind whistles in your ears. It aerates the brain. You begin to feel like a circus performer, describing impeccable parabolas in the air, vacating every gesture before it can be fixed, wherever anyone thinks you are is where you've just been, sloughing off afterimages. You feel pared down, athletic, perfectly efficient.) The athletic leap across divides has its own aesthetic, and so does the pattern those leaps form in the air or, to be more exact, in the mind. People spend their lives forging such patterns for themselves, but only the cranks and the encyclopaedic generalists with vague job descriptions, the Bill Moyerses, have the nerve to invite others to try out their own hobby-horse ride through the World of Ideas. More often these are private pathways, possible to make out sometimes in a novelist's oeuvre (rare butterflies turn up in Nabokov's fiction enough to make you guess that he was a lepidopterist, if you didn't know already) as a system of back alleys heading off from the work at hand, but not for public transit. Until recently, that is, since the Internet seems to be making possible a gorgeous excess of personal syntactical or neural maps, like travel brochures for the brain. What results isn't necessarily worth the trip, but some of it will be: art forms take shape around our ability to perceive beauty, but our ability to perceive beauty also takes shape around what forms become possible.

## *We Like to Make Statues*

We are not who we wish we were.

We like to make statues of ourselves. The Greeks marched ever-more-perfect bodies out of antiquity, slim vertical columns, like a line of capital Is, a stutter of self-assertion. But works of words are self-portraits too, substitute bodies we put together, then look to for encouragement. Boundaries of texts are like boundaries of bodies, and both stand in for the confusing and invisible boundary of the self. The wholeness of an artwork helps firm us up; in its presence we believe a little more in the unity we uneasily suspect we lack. As a result we have an almost visceral reaction to disorderly texts. Good writing is clear and orderly; bad writing inspires the same kind of distaste that bad grooming does, while experimental novels are not just hard to read, they're anti-social. Proper novels are duplicate bodies to the idealized ones we have in our heads, the infamous "thin person struggling to get out." They're good citizens, polite dinner guests.

Books, of course, like other bodies, fall apart. Literally, and also in the invisible body of the text, because language is libidinous, and the most strait-laced sentence hides a little hanky-panky under the dust ruffle. But monkey brain doesn't want to think about that, project can't hear, and so the novel, over the course of time, has become, despite the most flagrant tendencies toward polymorphous perversity and transgender play, a very stalwart announcement of nothing much. A sturdy who cares. One writes, one produces literature, and as Bataille says, "one day one dies an idiot." A project without any particular purpose that I can see, besides the announcement that project exists, that there is purpose and order, a sort of recitation of what we already know. The novel has become the golem, the monster that acts like everyone else, only better, because the narrative line is wrapped like a leash around its thick neck. I would like to introduce a different kind of novel, a creature who's entirely content to be the turn of a kaleidoscope, an exquisite corpse, a quilt on which copulas copulate, the chance encounter of an umbrella and a sewing machine on an operating table. A patchwork girl.

The hypertext is the banished body. Its compositional principle is desire. It gives a loudspeaker to the knee, a hearing trumpet to the elbow. It has the stopped stories to tell, it mentions unmentionables, speaks unspeakables; it unspeaks. I don't mean to say it has different, better opinions than novels can muster up, that it's plugged with better content. Hypertext won't make a bland sentence wild or make a dead duck run quacking for the finish line. Fill a disjunctive structure with pablum and you will only cement the world's parts more solidly together, clog the works with glue. It's not opinions I'm interested in, but relationships, juxtapositions, apparitions and interpolations. Hypertext is the body languorously extending itself to its own limits, hemmed in only by its own lack of extent. And like the body, it no longer has just one story to tell.

## Collage

We don't say what we mean to say.

The sentence is not one, but a cluster of contrary tendencies. It is a thread of DNA—a staff of staphylococcus—a germ of contagion and possibility. It may be looped into a snare or a garotte. It is also, and as readily, a chastening rod, a crutch, an ID bracelet. It is available for use. But nobody can domesticate the sentence completely. Some questionable material always clings to its members. Diligent readers can glean filth from a squeaky-clean one. Sentences always say more than they mean, so writers always write more than they know, even the laziest of them. Utility pretends to peg words firmly to things, but it is easy to work them loose. "Sometimes the words are unfaithful to the things," says Bachelard. Indeed they are, and as writers, we are the agents of misrule, infidelity, broken marriages. We set up rendezvous between words never before seen in company, we provide deliciously private places for them to couple. Like the body, language is a desiring machine. The possibility of pollution is its only life. Having invented an infinitely recombinant language, we can't prevent it from forming improper alliances, any more than we can seal all our orifices without dying.

In collage, writing is stripped of the pretense of originality, and appears as a practise of mediation, of selection and contextualization, a practise, almost, of reading. In which one can be surprised by what one has to say, in the forced intercourse between texts or the recombinant potential in one text, by the other words that mutter anagrammatically inside the proper names. Writers court the sideways glances of sentences mostly bent on other things. They solicit bad behavior, collusion, conspiracies. In fact, we are all collage artists. You might make up a new word in your lifetime—I nominate "outdulge": to lavish fond attention on the world, to generously broadcast care—but your real work will be in the way you arrange all the stuff you borrow, the buttons and coins, springs and screws of language, the frames and machinery of culture. We might think of Lawrence Sterne who, when accused of plagiarism, answered the charge with an argument that was itself a plagiarism.

### Constraints & the Book

It's not all you think it is.

I have no desire to demolish linear thought, but to make it one option among many. Likewise, I'd like to point out that the book is not the Natural Form it has become disguised as by its publicists. It is an odd machine for installing text in the reader's mind and it too was once an object of wonder. Turning the page, for example, has become an invisible action, because it has no meaning in most texts, the little pause it provides is as unreflective as breathing, but if we expected something different, or sought to interpret the gap, we might find ourselves as perplexed by that miniature black-out as by any intrusive authorial device we get exercised about in experimental literature or hypertext. Similarly, the linear form of the novel is not a natural evolutionary end, but a formal device, an oulipian constraint, albeit one with lots of elbow room. Like all constraints, it generates its own kinds of beauty, from graceful accession to linearity to the most prickly resistance. My favorite texts loiter, dawdle, tease, pass notes, they resist the linear, they pervert it. It's the strain between the literal and the implied form that's so seductive, a swoon in strait laces that's possibly sexier than a free-for-all sprawl. Constraints do engender beauty, Oulipo and evolution prove that, but maybe we've shown well enough how gracefully we can heel-toe in a straight line. We can invent new constraints, multiple ones. I think we will: just because I advocate dispersal doesn't mean I'm as impressed by a pile of sawdust as I am by a tree, a ship, a book. But let us have books that squirm and change under our gaze, or tilt like a fun-house floor and spill us into other books, whose tangents and asides follow strict rules of transformation, like a crystal forming in a solution, or which consist entirely of links, like spider-webs with no corpses hanging in them. Language is the Great Unruly, and alphabetical order is a contradiction in terms.

*Against History*

It was not how they said it was.

   I see no reason why a nonlinear work can't serve up an experience of satisfying closure not drastically different from that of reading a long and complicated novel, though it will do it differently. But I'm not sure closure is what we should be working toward, any more than a life well lived is one that hurtles without interruption toward a resounding death. A life that hurls itself ahead of itself seeking a satisfaction that must always remove itself into the future will be nothing but over in the end, and the same with those greased-lightning luge-novels. Don Delillo said in a reading in San Francisco that the writer sets her pleasure (his pleasure, is what he actually said), her eros, against the great, megalithic death that is history's most enduring work. I take that death to be not just the literal ex-tinction of life after life, but the extinguishing of the narrative pulse of all those lives un-der the granite gravity of history recorded. History is a cold, congealed thing, but if it is not too far past, there are strands of DNA, molecules of story imbedded in it, which can be rejoined and reanimated by a sufficiently irreverent Frankensteinbeck. Not the same as life, fiction has a funeral flavor to it, no question, a stony monumentality life luckily lacks; it has the thudding iambic footsteps of the Undead, but this is all to the good, be-cause everyone listens to a monster. Writers can't make facts react backwards, redo what's done, but what we have left of what's done is stories, and writers tell those better than most people. The incredible thing is that desire suffices against history, against death, against the hup-two lock-step of binary logic and the clockwork of common sense. What we imagine is all that animates us, not just texts, but also people. A beaker of imaginal se-cretions makes us all desire's monsters, which is what we ought to be.

"Let's Be Going": A Parent Reads GeekCereal

Peter Donaldson

October 24, the first day of the "Transformations of the Book" Conference at MIT was the last day—or possibly the last day—of GeekCereal. It was a kind of collective Web diary my son coordinated for about a year and a half as part of his duties as Gardener in Chief of Cyborganic Gardens, a web-based on and offline community, whose various web activities were supplemented by real life dinners every Thursday (TNDs) at Cyborganic's South of Market headquarters. My wife Alice told me that it might be the end, and that I should try to read his final post, but I didn't get to it until Sunday. As the bright yellow "cereal box" splash screen came up (more flakes! more nuts!), and Caleb's cartoon likeness and one-line teaser appeared, two days after they should have been supplanted by Rebecca and Jeremy's posts, it was clear Alice had been right—"Sayonara Cyborganic" was the headline (see fig. 16.1).

Caleb was born in 1968, the annus mirabilis of the new age, when I had been suspended from graduate school and from my not very lucrative stipend as a preceptor in English at Columbia, while my Lawyers' Guild counsel traded memos with my thesis adviser (who was also the head of the faculty senate discipline committee) over the niceties of whether it was possible to be guilty of trespassing in one's own office in Hamilton Hall. As the years passed and fervor gave way to prudence (we had more than our chains to lose), Alice and I retained, as is not unusual in academic Cambridge, a connection with those times, though ever more faintly. All of our children went through the alternative programs in the Cambridge schools, descendants of the parent-run nursery schools and playgroups we had joined as early members.

So we had a sense of pride, as if Caleb were carrying on the family business of hapless non-Marxist revolt, when he was drawn into the orbit of the nascent Web culture, running chat lines, reading proof for Wired and HotWired, managing a devoted staff of friends and disciples at CNET Online, apparently in the belief that, somehow, technology and community could converge. Having worked at MIT since Caleb's first birthday, I

Figure 16.1    "Sayonara Cyborganic," GeekCereal Web Site (<http://sharon.net/gc/>).

was less sanguine—but in the past few years I too had been influenced by unexpected optimism, and was drawn to explore electronic tools for teaching literature. Unlike Caleb,
who had mastered enough Pascal or whatever it was to have all the records of Cambridge
Rindge and Latin School at his disposal from his Freshman year on, I had no aptitude for
computers (the Datateknik cover story on my project noted, in Swedish, that even the
laserdiscs refused to obey my nervous commands, and attributed the project, reverently
but incorrectly, to the genius of Nicholas Negroponte), but I had wonderful collaborators, and a strong will, and persisted. Like Caleb, I thought we were using technology to

make things better. I began, in tentative ways, even to imagine we were using it to change the world. Our mutual interests and hopes became a strong bond. When I could, I even got some free consulting and moral support from Caleb and his group, who had become highly paid web designers, flown in, at times, to rescue complex projects from their incompetent initiators. I couldn't afford the full treatment, but appreciated the good advice they gave in passing.

In 1995, their communitarian instincts led to the forming of a web community that would also be a company; that would be realistic and professional as well as alternative-cultural, kind, and smart. That was Cyborganic, and its birth was heralded by a wonderfully goofy and fairly accurate story in *Rolling Stone,* with a double page upside-down picture of the house on Ramona Street, with cable strung from every landing, and a geek at every window ("That's Trish! That's Sonic!—is that Caleb up there?—why didn't he stay on the second floor where we could see him better?"). Though all the geeks came off well, Caleb seemed to be the hero of the piece, at least to us, with a header proclaiming, "if Caleb has any fears of jumping, he isn't showing it." Our stacks of copies of the issue, with Lenny Kravitz on the cover of each one, have hardly faded. (Visitors pick them up to read the latest rock and roll high fashion news and then put them back in the pile quietly when they realize they're a few years out of date.)

The Cereal itself (http://sharon.net/gc/) was a joy to look at, to read, and to navigate. The seven "geeks" were each responsible for a main post on their day, and "side orders," comments from the others, were optional but frequent; a flawless interactive calendar kept track of all entries, allowing you to follow one character through the weeks, or to follow a thread or a story. GeekCereal launched when Caleb and his friends had an entire six months of writing in the archive—this was an unfolding story of their lives in and around multimedia gulch that had a history at its inception.

The Cereal provided us, as parents, with glimpses of Caleb's life we hadn't had before and a fuller picture of things we already did know—his leadership, his love of cooking for large groups of friends, his hard work and kindness were much in evidence; his "side orders" were often compassionate and understanding, and even when the tone was angry, he seemed to point the way to productive modes of expressing anger in this oddly private, oddly public medium that others could imitate—and they did. His acknowledgment of our role in his life, and his affirmation of his bond with his brother and sister were moving beyond words, and perhaps could not have been communicated to us in such depth through any other medium, reading what he had written primarily to share with friends and with unknown visitors to the site.

One post discussed his giving up smoking (we never knew he smoked), his love of reggae and hip hop came into better focus, and, as East coast mostly folks we learned about the Western rite: fetish parties, bondage a go-go (Caleb disapproved, but seemed to know a lot about it); Reggae on the River; Burning Man ("good God, don't go!" we wished, while his posts teased readers with claims that he would sit this year's event out, only to provide them with a last minute on-site post from the desert). We gathered, from GeekCereal and the pictures posted on Bianca's Smut Shack (how did we wind up there?) that Burning Man was some kind of desert youth festival in which people burnt very large effigies and dressed bizarrely or went naked amid the pyrotechnics. Steev's post was an exuberant celebration of human anatomical diversity, newly seen and appreciated.

Unlike Woodstock, the geeks, before and after the event, were openly anxious about their role, their dress or undress, the propriety of their demeanor: "I don't know if I'm ready for Burning Man" was the theme. Alice and I, years before, never started for Woodstock, as the baby needed feeding and the news of hundred mile traffic jams was discouraging, but we didn't know anyone who would admit to anxiety about how they might look or appear there.

Through the Web, we were also able to follow Caleb's secret but gradually revealed mission to India, where he participated, as an early "scout" (see Numbers 14:24, the passage we had in mind when we named him, and see also his account of that naming in his FAQ) in the wiring of the Dalai Lama's compound at Macleod Ganj. The India post was the only one with a photograph—a beautiful view of the Himalayas, where one of the Western visitors got lost after dark; the local lamas said prayers, were unruffled and comforting, and the young man returned safely.

We came to rely on the Friday serving, and noticed that the comic book image of Caleb, that accompanied every post (strange at first, too quirky to be our son) came to seem more and more like him. At times it seemed to BE Caleb, more present than the pictures on the mantel.

We were moved by his stories of his love for his partner Tricia, a wonderfully gifted, quiet, and reflective person. She had been a classmate and friend at Yale, but Caleb had not dared to try to date her during their college years. When she migrated to the Bay Area, like Caleb she worked in "new age" publishing—first at Wired as an associate art director, then at Yoga Journal. At Cyborganic she was the designer (with Sonic, Queen of the Universe) of GeekCereal, and then went on to work for Third Age. She had moved from the East to be with Caleb, and there is a media-in-transition lesson somewhere in the story of their reunion.

Tricia visited friends in Berkeley for a few days several years ago, and renewed her acquaintance with Caleb by chance. Then she left. The story goes—it has several versions, oral, written and webbed—that Caleb then wrote her a twenty page handwritten letter and sent it by surface mail (no email for this communication). There was no response for weeks, and then she showed up in her tiny red car (not the canonical Alfa Romeo roadster, but close enough so that I think of her driving over the Bay Bridge to Berkeley like Dustin Hoffman in *The Graduate*). She had quit her job, loaded up her belongings, and driven out. They've been together since. Most romantic stories I've heard lately have involved the Internet as matchmaker; perhaps the use of the mail and the internal combustion machine will seem as archaically romantic in a year or two as Daphnis and Chloe does now.

When Caleb was at Yale, he and a friend were selected to deliver the Class Speech at graduation, which at Yale is a stand-up comedy retrospective you have to audition for. We were entranced, but found the next day, when the event was covered in the Yale campus paper, that we had missed nearly every double entendre ("play" to us suggested either the Boston Celtics or theories of the "ludic" in the Middle Ages). The paper even took note of the massed parents in their clueless delight, missing every vulgarity. Well—it was better than Marian Wright Edelman's speech on the same occasion, which seemed to me inappropriately self congratulatory, contrasting her own social commitments with the supposed irresponsibilty of the privileged young. I'm still impatient, though guiltily so, when the Children's Defense Fund calls for a donation.

The Web version of Caleb's life and that of his friends offered many similar interpretive challenges—we often missed the point of elegantly lewd posts, Alice missing a bit more than I, usually.

In March of last year, while I was at a conference in Atlanta, Alice called to say that Caleb had called and would call me with an important message; I guessed what it was about, as Caleb had been hinting at spending a considerable portion of his boom or bust savings on a diamond (a diamond!—no hippy crafted silver and flawed opal for the webhead generation). I was exhausted after a long day, trying to sort out Hal Varian's unsettling futuristic vision of academic assessment using web citations and making notes on Peter Lyman's humane and wise account of his trip to China and the preciousness of the freedom of speech on the internet. I left the television on loudly so I wouldn't fall asleep and miss the call—when it came, images of a village that had fallen prey to a deadly outbreak of ebola flickered on the screen; I had a bad connection. Caleb's message was brief—he'd proposed to Tricia, she'd accepted and I could read about it at length in his post tomorrow. He too was tired, and couldn't really talk, but he wanted me to hear this news by phone.

So the phone had become the way to show respect for parents—but the canonical version was the Web page, and it was indeed rewarding to read; reflective, funny, loving, wastefully extavagant and wonderful; it was a treasure for us, and we copied text and snapped screenshots (command, shift, 3) to save it. We understood the double and the triple entendres. It was better than a phone call.

Now GeekCereal was ending—a prey to the vicissitudes that might befall any idealistic community structured as a corporation. The touch of gold rush fever had been there, we might now guess, from the beginning (we have seen it in academia too, but there's no El Dorado in educational multimedia either, at least not for those who sought it most ardently); the geeks who wrote for the Cereal had actually been contractors and employees (though some had wanted to be partners)—and they had not been paid. There was no revenue with which to pay them, and the venture capital and its supplements had dried up; relationships suffered; one geek was already in small claims court with a case against the founder. Caleb sounded the knell, and he did it with elegance and care.

Although posts had been infrequent in the last few weeks, and the "side order" responses had almost disappeared, all four of the remaining Geeks responded. Rocky was perplexed, and almost disbelieving—"so this means you are backing out of the project? that's all it seems it could be, i guess . . . unless one person can decide it's over for everyone." Steev was rueful but accepting and grateful for having participated. He was the geek who seemed to us to have changed most over the months, from a nervous beginner, a technical guy whose only convergence with these high style webheads seemed to be his purple hair (at least the obligatory "Steev" caricature has purple hair) to an effective and interesting writer. His posts combined wide-eyed and naive appreciation for the wonders of the web world (especially at Burning Man) with an engaging down to earth and direct style.

The mysterious Jeremy (does he still wear a long skirt, and why? where will he go after Apple?) was brief—he can be found at satori.net. Each of the geeks now referred us to their home pages, and some promised to keep writing and told us where we could find what they wrote. I read Allison's side order last—and followed the link to her home page at floozy.com. It brought tears to my eyes, as the screen displayed the conclusion of the Phaedrus. As the day cools and the dialogue ends (though these precious moments preserved on papyrus rolls and transcribed in the medium of print now reach us in cyberspace), friends depart. Socrates offers a prayer, to Pan and all the gods:

Grant that I may become beautiful within, and that whatever outward things I have may be in harmony with the spirit inside me. May I understand that it is only the wise who are rich, and may I have only as much money as a temperate person needs.—Is there anything else we can ask for Phaedrus? For me that prayer is enough.

Phaedrus asks him to offer the prayer on his behalf as well, "since friends have all things in common." Socrates replies, concluding the dialogue, with words that appear on Allison's page in large blue character, underlined.

## <u>Let's be going.</u>

And that was how the serial ended, an ending worthy of Plato's great precursors, Calvin and Hobbes (I mean the final Sunday panel, that shows an expanse of white, of newly fallen snow; and either the child or the tiger remarks, as the strip ends forever, "Let's go exploring!"). In my reading, on that day, it didn't even occur to me that these words were also a link. As Alice and I re-traversed the end of Cyborganic the next day, I noticed that Allison's post let us know that she hadn't changed her page in months. In fact, as we now discovered, "let's be going" led to a series of marvellous quotations, from Huang Po, Sufi mystics, American transcendentalists, Montaigne—and, of course, to much else. "Let's be going" is Allison's signature link.

And so at the end of the cereal we began to learn more, belatedly, about Allison, and her particular sensibility, to revisit old and revered texts we had in common and to follow her lead into new paths. We couldn't know where following these connections might lead. Given the personal and legal tangles these folks had got themselves into, even how long these posts might remain on the Internet as Cyborganic went under, we didn't know—but the transformation of what had been an important part of our lives had been marked. The cereal ended for us with deeper understanding of the medium, and its special way of articulating endings and beginnings, with gratitude for a form of connection that could not have existed in any other form, and with the sense that we understood, a little better, the restlessness of grown children at the end of family visits.

Let's be going.

*Note:* This chapter first appeared as hypertext on MIT's Media in Transition Web site with links to GeekCereal and other sites. See <http://web.mit.edu/m-i-t/articles/index_donaldson.html>.

# 17 Private Uses of Cyberspace: Women, Desire, and Fan Culture

Sharon Cumberland

---

*The writing of an erotic story is a public articulation of desire . . . what begins as a private act, a woman, a computer, becomes a community of women and computers. To place a story on the internet mirrors and amplifies the act of writing it in the first place.*

—helen

The subject of this essay is fiction writing on the Internet, specifically, the erotica written by women in the context of fan culture. Fan fiction is a genre of non-commercial writing that features an original plot using characters and settings from commercially produced film and television. Such fiction has been a social and literary phenomenon since fans started writing their own *Star Trek* episodes in the 1960s, though some would argue that fan fiction can be traced back to early literary parodies and sequels such as Lydgate's *Siege of Thebes* (a continuation of *The Canterbury Tales*) or the many "metanovels" that have been written as sequels to such works as Austen's *Pride and Prejudice,* Conan-Doyle's *Sherlock Holmes,* or Stowe's *Uncle Tom's Cabin.*[1] While a great deal of critical attention has been given recently to fan cultures and fan arts in all media, my particular focus is on the proliferation of fan fiction on the Internet and the communities that have encouraged fans to become writers as well as readers.[2] In this essay I examine the way in which women are using the paradox of cyberspace—personal privacy in a public forum—to explore feelings and ideas that were considered risky or inappropriate for women in the past. I will suggest that the protection and freedom of cyberspace is enabling these writers to defy many of the social taboos that have inhibited self-exploration and self-expression before the emergence of the Internet.

## *Problems of Internet Research*

> But how do I prove to other fen [plural of "fan"] that I'm real, if I only interact with fandom virtually? How does anyone?"
> —Kass

Any discussion based upon Internet phenomena must begin with a disclaimer (confession might be a better word) concerning the limitations of "cyberfacts" and, by extension, the limitations of any claim a scholar makes based upon them.[3] The virtues of cyberspace are access and anonymity, which I call the "paradox of cyberspace" because of the incongruity of hidden identities seeking and finding exposure to the public. Cybercitizens can express thoughts and ideas in a public forum while concealing identifying markers that in the past might have caused their voices to be dismissed or diminished: race, gender, age, appearance, and economic status, to name the most obvious general categories. These virtues are two-sided coins, however, each with a corresponding "vice" or problem for scholars.

Untold millions have access to cyberspace, and the number of people going online increases every day. Google.com, the dominant search engine on the World Wide Web, documents 1.4 billion unique pages, of which 71.2% were less than one year old in December, 2000. Furthermore, cyberspace is equally weighted. While certain "homesteads" are very large, such as GeoCities (5.5 million pages) and America Online (1.7 million pages), one homepage or threaded discussion is as valid as any other. There is no capital city in cyberspace, and no Great Chain of Cyber-being. Without a central point from which a hierarchy can be constructed, even a modest commitment of resources will enable the humble to stake a claim in cyberspace beside the mighty. The corresponding "vice," however, is that quantification of Internet phenomena is nearly impossible because the number of participants is so vast. For instance, the volume of fan fiction on the Internet makes it impossible for me to verify some basic facts for this essay, such as how many fan communities there are on the Internet, how many fan fiction writers are posting stories on the Internet, and how many of these writers are women, (not to mention how many are heterosexual, lesbians, married, single, mothers, etc). As with any large media group, one can use sampling methods to estimate general numbers, and then use ethnographic methods to create a sense of individual characteristics. But like Neilson ratings for television and telephone polling for elections, the results are highly stylized constructions for which no verification exists.

The other virtue of cyberspace is anonymity, which permits self-expression without retaliation, both for the historically oppressed and for those with unpopular or unconventional ideas, as well as for those who wish to experiment with their identities. The corresponding "vice" is that you don't know who you're talking to and cannot verify claims of identity short of meeting informants face to face. For instance, I have interviewed many writers of fan fiction for this essay, and I believe that they are women because they say they are. But though I have no reason to doubt them, I also have no way to authenticate their identities unless I attend fan fiction conferences to meet them in person. Until new conventions or new technologies emerge to address this issue, a certain amount of unscholarly faith in the good will of cybercitizens is required for studying the Internet. As Kass observes, "[U]ntil we meet in RL [real life]—or if we never meet in RL—we have to take each others' identities on faith".[4] This essay makes a reasonable (i.e. highly personal) investment in the good will of the writers I quote.

## Women in Disguise

> Anonymity isn't important, but there's just too much crap in the world around the issues of homosexuality for me to waste my time trying to explain to people why I write what I write if I don't have to. It's primarily a pragmatic approach for me.
> —elynross

In her article entitled "Drag Net: From Glen to Glenda and Back Again . . . Is it Possible?," Sherry Turkle examines the benefits of concealing one's biological gender while participating in multi-user discussion groups (MUDs). Since male and female gender identity must be constructed in real life anyway, she argues, reconstructing identity in a MUD by changing gender enables both men and women to escape the expectations of their biological sex and to gain insight into the opposite sex. While the authors of internet fan fiction do not, as a general rule, conceal their genders, the majority of them—especially those writing erotica—conceal their real life identities with pseudonyms, as does "elynross," a prolific writer of the erotic genre called "slash."

Pseudonyms, avatars, and "handles" allow writers to avoid the real world "crap" that many of the women who write fan erotica would face if their work was published under their legal names, or in the print media. The ability to conceal identity on the Internet grants the woman author a level of liberation, like those in Turkle's MUD culture, that goes beyond first amendment rights. For while authors who publish in print media are free to write uncensored erotica, social mores inhibit most women writers from doing so. By writing on the internet under pseudonyms, women can go directly to their readers without risking their reputations with editors, publishers, or—as Henry Jenkins describes in *Textual Poachers*—anti-erotica fans. In pre-internet times the only way to buy fan erotica was to attend conferences and buy fan zines sold by the authors themselves. This made the authors vulnerable to being "outed" (publicly humiliated) by those who wished to discourage the use of their celebrity heroes in sexually explicit stories.

This ability to go directly to the reader on the Internet is the second part of the cyberspace equation. In the past, the desire or need for privacy would have either limited the author's access to an audience or would have placed the author at risk of discovery. In cyberspace, however, the audience for anonymous fan erotica is very large, since people can access and read it in the privacy of their homes. (Google.com reports that the number one search term on the World Wide Web is "sex"). Though it is impossible to know precisely how large the readership for adult fan fiction may be, a conservative approach would be to assume that the readership is at least as large as the "writership" because, as we shall see below, fan fiction writers are part of an actively supportive community that encourages writing as much as reading.

Bearing in mind the impossibility of actually quantifying the phenomenon, I turned to Yahoo's WebRing program on the Internet to determine the scope of the fan erotica "writership" and their productions. WebRing allows any interested person with a home page about a special topic to become a "ringmaster" by inviting others on the internet who have relevant sites to join in their ring. As the WebRing advertisements claim, there are "84 affinity groups (in the ringworld directory), 66,000 rings on any conceivable topic, and 1.5 million member sites." The press release goes on to say that "The WebRing system can support an unlimited number of separate and distinct Rings across the Internet." This allows the visitor to move through the indirection of cyberspace in what feels like a circular pattern, either by jumping from site to site in a designated order or skipping along the ring randomly. Though Web rings are not comprehensive (there is no guarantee that all *Star Trek* home pages are on *Star Trek* Web rings, for instance) using web rings to select samples of fan populations offers some sense of the extent of the fan community devoted to erotic fan fiction on the Internet.

Though I could only explore a fraction of the choices offered on the Adult Fan Fiction web ring because of the extremely large size of the field, at the time of this writing there were 145 separate rings listed in the ringworld sub-directory. A more comprehensive category, "alternative fan fiction," includes lesbian and gay fan fiction and all permutations of S&M and bondage. In this division there were 601 webrings, with over fifteen thousand individual sites. By selecting one percent of these sites and averaging the number of stories on each—more than a dozen stories per homepage—a rough estimate suggests that there are over 180 thousand fan-authored erotic stories on the "alternative fan fiction" list.[5] If there is even one non-writing reader for every writer in the alternative fan fiction webring, then the readership for this genre alone is thirty thousand.

Although there is no way to prove the widely held impression that the majority of these writers are women, some fan writers themselves identify their communities as predominantly female, as does delle, a writer in the *La Femme Nikita* universe who says that their authors "are, to the best of my knowledge, 99.9% female." Different fandoms will have different gender proportions, of course, but if fan writers reflect the general population of cybercitizens, then at least half of fan fiction writers are female—a very conservative estimate given early claims that as many as ninety percent of fan writers were women. While few researchers accept that claim across all fan communities today—if for no other reason than that more and more male writers are contributing to fandoms on the Web (assuming, of course, that they are not gender experimenters)—fan culture, especially fan erotic culture, still has a the earmarks of a woman's community: interest in topics such as the status of women in society, women's ability to express desire, the blurring of stereotyped gender lines (powerful women; nurturing men), as well as enthusiastic discussion and support groups for new writers. Regardless of numbers, however, there is no doubt that women benefit from the ability to explore their erotic fantasies on the Internet, and to share them with enthusiastic and supportive "sister" writers.

## Fanfic Communities

> Is this noble? Is this arrogance? To hope that my writing can give someone the desire to push
> on? Ease them out of their pains for a while? Make them giggle?
> —James Walkswithwind

Ethnographic studies conducted over the past ten years have documented fan communities and their creative productions, as well as the migration of these communities to the Internet.[6] A remarkable aspect of the development of online fandoms and fan fiction ("fanfic") communities is the culture of inclusion that embraces anyone (including men) who joins in, both as readers and writers. I have written elsewhere about the powerful sense of sisterhood that develops among women who work together to build websites for their collaborative writing focused on iconic celebrity figures.[7] Much larger communities have formed around fandoms devoted to television and film, such as *Xena: Warrior Princess, The X-Files, Buffy the*

*Vampire Slayer, The Sentinel, The Professionals, Highlander, Hercules, Babylon 5,* and all iterations of *Star Wars* and *Star Trek,* to name only a few of the hundreds listed on general fan Web sites. As James Walkswithwind suggests in the quotation above, motivations for fanfic writing are non-commercial, and focus on imaginative identification not only with the appropriated protagonists from popular culture, but with the community of fanfic readers. Within general fandoms, the writers of fanfic—their sites, symposia, support sites, and rec sites (recommendations of favorite stories or expert writers)—make an elite subculture.

Though the term "elite" seems to contradict the concept of inclusiveness and equality found on the Internet, talent among fanfic authors is cultivated, appreciated, and awarded status in the community since these writers have the ability to extend the sagas of favorite characters and to invest them with the sexuality and interior lives that are only implied in the commercial productions. In an article that compares fanfic writing to the Northwest Indian gift-giving tradition of the potlatch, fan author Rachel Sabotini describes the basis for "creation of status within the fan community" as the giving of gifts: "The gifts—art, songvids, and fan fiction—all require some level of artistry to master and are thus highly prized". Fanfic communities have many methods of encouraging writers to hone their skills for their own sakes and for the sake of the community.

An excellent example is *Lunacy's Fan Fiction Reviews,* a rich online support system for the communities devoted to *Xena Warrior Princess* and *Star Trek: Voyager.* On her large and detailed site, Lunacy offers resources for both readers and writers, easing the way for readers to gain the expertise required to attempt fan writing. For the neophyte there is a glossary of several hundred terms used in fanfic culture, including definitions for various genres (slash, het, alt, gen, Mary Sue . . . ), common abbreviations (TPTB: The Powers That be; UST: Unresolved Sexual Tension . . . ), terms specific to particular fandoms (*X-Phile,* n. Also *'phile:* an X-Files fan; *PGP,* adj. Acronym for Post Gauda Prime: stories set after the *Blake's* 7 series finale, which took place on Gauda Prime . . . ), and terms specific to the writing of fanfic (*beta,* v. to edit a fanfic story; *canon,* n.: refers to facts established by the original fiction . . . ). On a separate page of Lunacy's site are definitions of sub genres in the *Xena* and *Voyager* universes, such as "Uber-Xena," "Warlord/Slave," and "Hurt/Comfort," with detailed descriptions of their histories, nuances, and variations. Lunacy includes links to essays that describe the art of fanfic writing, recruiting and working with a "beta reader" (volunteer story editor), and official Web sites, as well as to the original series and plot summary sites (for learning the "canon" and tracking studio activity).

One of the most impressive offerings for *Xena* and *Voyager* fanfic writers is Lunacy's Experts Directory, which contains twenty-four topic headings under which volunteers can list their areas of expertise for fanfic writers to consult. From "Animals" to "Weapons," there are over a hundred experts willing to advise on languages, ancient coins, black-smithing, medicine and herbs, karate, musical instruments, and myriad other areas that will make the futuristic universe of *Star Trek* or the ancient universe of *Xena* seem more authentic. Finally, Lunacy offers hundreds of reviews of *Xena* and *Voyager* fanfic, organized by genre, author, and special topics. On her "Highest Recommendation" page she leads the reader to the most polished exemplars of each genre, giving both the apprentice writer and the fan reader the means of enjoying and studying the best in the field. Sites like Lunacy's offer a profound service to the fan community that enables the fanfic culture to exist by educating and encouraging the newest readers, the most experienced writers, and fans at all stages on the continuum between. Their efforts enable authors like Walkswithwind to write as an act of both community and personal creativity; to "give someone the desire to push on," or, to quote an earlier passage in his essay, to let them "read something erotic that makes them smile, laugh, cry, turn to someone and say 'let's get naked.'"

### E-Genres: emotional, erotic, electronic

> *I don't read or write fanfic to get more of the show. I read fanfic to get what was missing in the show.*
> —Lorelei Jones

"Getting naked" is the central act of the e-genres of fanfic, in which "e" stands not only for "electronic" but for "erotic" and "emotional." It is that which is "missing" in almost all of the commercial film and television stories that inspire fanfic writers. Lorelei Jones continues:

> I read for a favorite character who didn't get enough screen time. I read for overt declarations of love or physical intimacy. I read for realistic consequences to actions, a sense of continuity, deeper exploration of a theme barely touched on in the show. I read for the things I wish had been in the show but weren't.

Reading and writing erotica on the Internet is not simply a matter of exploring the forbidden, but of exploring the fully human. Popular culture productions in America tend to valorize violence and a type of clever, shallow relationship in which the protagonists "meet cute" and short-circuit their intimacy with snappy dialogue. Yet the commercial characters in film or a television series who must perform these abbreviated versions of their potential humanity—Spock and Kirk, Xena and Gabrielle, Han Solo and Princess Leia, for example—all have the capacity for love, physical intimacy, and emotional depth, since without this potential they would not attract even the 18–25 year old male who is target of most popular culture productions. Given the demographic that runs

Hollywood, however, intimacy and complexity must be implied rather than allowed to interfere with the physical action that sells tickets and advertising.

Thus, a great deal of fan fiction is the product of longing by women for stories that bear some semblance to the realities of the human struggle for understanding, affection, and communication—all the things that studios believe would be slow and boring if developed on the screen. And sex, while not boring, needs to be slow—or approached slowly in the context of character-driven relationships—in order to have the emotional content that women find satisfying. Clearly the Internet's unique combination of personal privacy and access to a sympathetic public has enabled a huge subculture of adult fan fiction to thrive, in which the abbreviated characters of popular culture can be "fleshed out" by fan writers. "Getting naked" is both an emotional and an erotic act, in which the soul of a character as well as the body is exposed.

Though there are many permutations of e-genres emerging on the Internet, the three major forms are "het" or heterosexual fiction, "alt." or lesbian fiction, and "slash" or homoerotic fiction. Women who write for adult audiences are experimenting with and challenging the conventional gender definitions imposed upon them in real life by imagining themselves into characters experiencing a full range of erotic engagement. In cyberspace, where a woman can avoid criticism of (or even identification with) her own writing, fanfic writers are able to explore areas of curiosity and concern that could not be explored in print media. In real world print environments, women writers would have to pass through editorial hierarchies or expose themselves to the expectations of gender appropriateness. When asked if they would have written erotica if they had not found fanfic on the Internet and sympathetic readers, most of the fanfic writers I interviewed answered in the same vein as Killashandra: "I *do* think I would have written regardless, but whether I would have written pure erotica? I doubt it. Not without the community of other women out there reading it and responding to it".

### Het: Female ≠ Fanatic

> *Knowing that I am not alone in my appreciation of Antonio Banderas as an actor gives my "obsession" with him approval and validates it.*
> —Deena Glass

Because heterosexual erotica is the most conventional and (apparently) least transgressive of the e-genres, it is the most likely to conjure up the classic stereotype of female fans as desperate women who are "fanatics" for an iconic celebrity male. The image of a female whose love endangers a male hero is a basic trope (Adam/Eve; Odysseus/Calypso; Launcelot/Guenivere, etc.) that constructs the female as a renegade who is untrustworthy unless controlled by a powerful male. Yet the modern image of an anonymous female fan swooning over a celebrity male is the invention of the romantic age. Women fainting at Chopin concerts and Byron chased through the streets of London, foreshadow hysterical Elvis and Beatles fans—always-young females, always screaming and crying, overwhelmed by unrequited and unrequitable lust. This image of the anonymous female fan represents a threat to male authority. She functions outside the domestic sphere (and cannot be kept at home); she expresses open desire for a man who is not her mate (implying by her behavior that she would give him sexual favors if only he would accept them); and she is hysterical in public (out of patriarchal control). The female fan is, in effect, the woman who makes the private public, who makes sexuality, which was confined to the domestic sphere, a matter of public display. She humiliates the men who are charged with controlling her.

That, at least, is the patriarchal subtext handed down through ages of male-authored literature (with some notable exceptions, including Chaucer's *Wife of Bath's Tale)*. Yet the erotic genre called "het" (predominantly woman-authored fanfic which engages male and female protagonists in erotic relationships) seems to come from a parallel universe in which men have as much capacity for emotional attachment and meaningful communication as do women. The image of women as rogue characters, whose unbridled lust for men endangers hearth and home (as in *Fatal Attraction),* is replaced with passionate yet rational relations between the sexes. As a fan of the Spanish actor Antonio Banderas, I have followed the het fiction written in Web communities devoted to him since 1994. Fan writers use his many film characters as protagonists for sequels and expansions of such films as *The 13th Warrior* and, at the time of this writing, the erotic thriller *Original Sin*. Yet in every case I have found the het erotica written about the Banderas iconic hero to be as much focused on complexity and communication as on sex. Other fandoms devoted to het treatments of characters like the *X-Files'* Fox Mulder make no apology for their open lust for their erotic hero, with sites devoted to the actor who portrays Mulder bearing such titles as the David Duchovny Estrogen Brigade, and DROOL (David's Revelry of Obsessed Lusters). Without the patriarchal presence that converts het lust into home-wrecking, desire into danger, or fans into fanatics, women writing and reading het erotica on the Internet are free to share and enjoy their common fantasy of sexy, communicative, non-oppressive males. And, as Deena Glass observes, the company of other women in the Banderas fanfic community legitimizes and validates her "obsession."

## Alt.: The f/f Alternative

> As is the case with m/m slash, the majority of writers seem to be female but the difference, at least with XWP [Xena Warrior Princess] fanfic, is that many of the female writers are lesbian or bisexual—though certainly not all. We have many fantastic het AND male writers.
> —Maribel Piloto

Erotic fanfic that pairs female protagonists, such as *Xena Warrior Princess*'s Xena with the bard Gabrielle, or *Star Trek: Voyager*'s Captain Janeway with Borg shipmate Seven of Nine, is referred to as "alternative fiction" or "alt.," sometimes expressed as f/f, meaning female to female. The presence of a slash, in the fanfic world, has always indicated homoerotic sex scenes—a venerable convention dating from the Kirk/Spock *Star Trek* erotica of the 1970s zine culture. (Even though "slash" is a general term for homoerotic fiction, it is sometimes used, however, as a general indication of sex in fanfic, with m=male and f= female: m/m, f/f, m/m/f, f/f/m, m/f . . . ).

Fanfic writers in the alt. community present the sexual passion between female protagonists as natural and inevitable, rather than as transgressive relative to a heterosexual worldview. While both Xena and Captain Janeway could be interpreted within their settings as "masculine" women who hold positions of power and authority traditionally occupied by men, gender struggles are not a thematic strain in either canon. Janeway does not have bitter and disobedient men around her who disrespect her authority, nor does Xena struggle to assert herself in a male-dominated world. Furthermore, their partners in the alt. iterations—Seven of Nine and Gabrielle—are not playing particularly "female" roles relative to their partners. Seven of Nine is a Borg-enhanced human whose detachment is reminiscent of the Vulcan Mr. Spock and the android Data in previous *Star Trek* series, while Gabrielle is as athletic and energetic as her warrior counterpart. Male characters in each series occupy the full spectrum of masculinity, from drag queens, to mild dependency on women, to equal partners with women, and chest-thumping he-men. Female characters follow the same full range of gender types, giving the genders equal sway by acknowledging that there are many ways to be both male and female. Because of the basic sympathy of the original series characters to lesbian (or feminist) issues, the re-conceptualized alt. universe is highly plausible.

For example, fan writer G. L. Dartt has accomplished the notable feat of adding two complete seasons to *Star Trek: Voyager* by writing 50 stories in her own alt. universe. Called the "Just Between" series, or the "JB universe," the episodes conform to the canonical behavior of characters and, in general terms, to the events in the television series. The difference, however, is in the richness of Janeway's interior life, as she struggles over the inappropriateness of falling in love with a female subordinate (whereas the Janeway of the TV series remains aloof from emotional attachments). The first two episodes, "Just Between Us," and "Just Between Them," are classic "First Time" stories in which the reader shares in the emotional tension of both protagonists as they come to terms with their love for each other, go through the first awkward stages of private and public encounters, and find the balance between their personal and professional lives. The love story between Janeway and Seven of Nine is told in the context of other characters familiar to *Voyager* fans, and against a full program of events and plot developments, so that the *Voyager* setting is not a mere backdrop for a love story or a PWP (Plot What Plot?) sex story. Dartt not only constructs a tense story line concerning an alien culture that may (or may not) be as hospitable as it seems, but also manages to address contemporary issues of concern to the lesbian community without allowing ideological intrusiveness.

For instance, in "Just Between Them," Janeway and Seven of Nine are dancing at a formal event hosted by aliens whose world they are visiting. As they dance, they discuss the difficulty of not being able to touch each other in public whenever they feel moved to do so. Janeway asks Seven, "Does it really bother you that you can't touch me unless we're alone?" Her partner answers that it does, but that she understands how it would make others feel if they have private moments in their professional settings: " . . . were I to touch you in the way that I like to touch you, it would make others uncomfortable as well . . . and that is not good for the functionality of the ship." The conversation addresses several layers of problems that the protagonists face: the distinction between a captain and her subordinate, the distinction between public and private behavior, the need to maintain the good will of the crew, and the ability to read each other's signals. But outside the universe of *Voyager,* which takes place three hundred years into the future in a time when, presumably, no prejudice exists against homosexual expression, the episode carries a contemporary subtext concerning the plight of homosexual couples. In early twenty-first century America, neither gay nor lesbian couples have the freedom of displaying affection in public to the same degree that heterosexuals enjoy. The discussion between Janeway and Seven transposes the essential dilemma facing contemporary lesbians into the present and offers the reader some advice and comfort on a difficult aspect of life.

Convincingly written alt. fiction performs another service to its readership by modeling for the heterosexual community lesbian relationships that are successful and natural as well as passionate. Without being two-dimensional moralists (they are, after all, writing erotica) the authors of the alt. fanfic I have read, which I selected from Lunacy's Highest Recommended page, demonstrate that lesbian relationships are as normal—even ordinary—in their arguments, disappointments, and passions as heterosexual relationships. And as Maribel Piloto notes, not all readers and writers in the alt. community are lesbian and bisexual. Het fans of alt. provide the world with one more group of people who do not demonize alternative lifestyles.

## Slash: Queen (King?) of E-genres

> Slash fiction, devoted to same gender couplings, produces consumers of nearly exclusively one gender. This is a sexual community, an explicit community, in which desire is looked upon as normal and a fixation with sex is rewarded, with readership, with feedback. This, for many women, is a community that is significantly lacking in life off the Internet.
> —helen

Of all the erotic genres of fan fiction on the Internet, "slash" is the most evolved, analyzed and, if sheer volume is an indication, the most popular. There are hundreds of slash pages devoted to fandoms of all kinds, as well as chat rooms, discussion groups and symposia devoted to analyzing the genre. There is an annual conference for writers and readers of slash, in addition to slash discussion groups in the major fan conferences world wide.[8] And while the history and evolution of slash is well documented and will not be repeated here, it presents the most complex analytical issues of all the erotic genres, since, as helen points out, "in a slash story, there is no place for a woman—thus, the writer is nowhere and everywhere. She must be both the aggressor and the recipient of romantic overtures." This point—the whereabouts of a woman author in the m/m world of slash— is the subject of much discussion in the slash community.[9]

The debate follows two major themes through fan discussions. The first theme is preoccupied with whether or not a protagonist is gay if he is portrayed as having sex with another male protagonist, and whether this constitutes a departure from canon. This discussion, set in motion by Joanna Russ in 1985, implies that the author is straight identified, since she is worried that a favorite character may be diminished by being labeled gay.[10] In a culture that persists in seeing gayness as "effeminate," as Shomeret observes in "Is Methos a Woman?," the heterosexual female reader or writer will have difficulty imaging sex with a favorite character if he is feminized, since she herself wants to be his opposite. Put another way, how can she have sex with him if he's playing the female role?

The second, related, discussion theme is whether or not the female author is projecting herself into the story as a man or a woman, which is to ask, obliquely, whether or not the author is experiencing androgyny, a transgendered (phallic) experience, or an out-of-body experience when writing or reading slash. The Internet has changed the terms of this discussion a great deal, since women slash fans are no longer confined to the objectivity of the printed word, but can enter into the spirit of interactivity, subjectivity, and experimentation that the Internet has encouraged. Sherry Turkle has written extensively on the subject of online identities, as observed earlier, and there is no reason to suppose that experimentation with gender is less prevalent in slash culture than it is in the MUD culture she identifies, though its implementation is somewhat different. In the privacy of the home, writing under a pseudonym and with the encouragement of a community that will never "out" you to your friends and family, gender experimentation has lost its undercurrent of seediness and danger. Slash writers and readers are no longer constructed as "perverts" or "pornographers" as Russ used the terms in 1985.

Two examples of slash fiction from the *Highlander* fandom will demonstrate the range of possibilities for slash writers and readers for projecting or experimenting with their sexual projections onto protagonists. D/M stories involve Duncan MacLeod, an immortal born in Scotland 400 years ago, and Methos, the oldest living immortal, born five thousand years ago. In the *Highlander* universe, potential immortals only achieve immortality if they suffer untimely death (after which they inexplicably wake up again). They can be killed innumerable times and return to life, as long as they are not decapitated. Since Methos suffered his "first death" in his early thirties, he remains that age forever, in spite of his five thousand years. Duncan, killed in his mid-thirties, is likewise vital and—need it be said?—handsome and sexy for eternity. Methos is slender, birdlike, winsome, and one for whom discretion is the better part of valor. Duncan is brawny, powerful, aggressive, one for whom valor involves every martial art known to man. For the slash writer, this is a match made in heaven.

The physical stature of each protagonist suggests that the answer to Shomert's question is yes, Methos is a woman, and Duncan is the man, or, to use language from the gay porn world, Methos is the bottom, Duncan the top. "Interlunation" by Bone follows this general pattern of small = feminine, large = masculine, but constructs Methos as a "pushy bottom," one who makes passive aggressive demands on his top so that it is clear to the reader who is in charge of the emotional encounter. Unlike gay porn, however, Bone delays sexual interaction between the protagonists until the character's situation and relationship has been fully developed. So much of the development has happened in the commercial aspect of the fan universe (which is why readers are required to "do their homework" by mastering the series canon before reading) that sex is delayed only enough for anticipation. Although Bone calls her story "less than a real plot, but more than a PWP," the sex scenes that comprise most of the action occur simultaneously with both men's thoughts, memories, and emotions as they discover that sex is a form of forgiveness and renewal. Thus the reader or writer who is "everywhere and nowhere" may move from top to bottom with her favorite character, but is always rewarded with the rich interior lives that distinguish slash from porn.

The second *Highlander* story draws its pleasures from inverting the D/M relationship and making Methos a slaveholder and Duncan the slave. *The Seduction of the Desert Prince* is an illustrated novel of twenty-three chapters by a writer's collective called The Krell. Set in an alternative universe, (meaning, in slash culture, a setting other than that provided by the creators of the television series) it takes place in a non-specific past and is set in the romantic, imaginary desert first presented in *The Sheik*. Though there are extended sex scenes, they are few in number and embedded in a plausible and suspenseful plot. Duncan and Methos are canonical in that they conform to the essence of their personalities and obey the laws of the *Highlander* universe. But the reader and writers have the pleasure of seeing the brawny Duncan chained like Samson at Methos's feet, forced to serve his sexual pleasures with initial reluctance, growing enthusiasm, and then—as their emotional needs take precedence—as an equal and a free man.

In e-mail exchanges with the authors of this novel, one member of The Krell told me that she wrote what she wanted to read since erotica in bookstores is focused on sex and not relationships: "I write erotic stories because I like to explore the themes of emotional intimacy, and I write fan fiction because it lets me do that with characters that already interest me." This is a perfect summation of slash fiction—erotica that occurs only in the context of emotional relationships, involving familiar and favorite characters. Whether the reader or writer sees herself as experimenting with male identity and sexuality, as a disembodied power to whom powerful males are subject, as a woman masked in a male body, or as some other variation of gender mixing, the most satisfying slash seems to integrate the best of both worlds—emotional complexity with the simple pleasure of great sex.

### Conclusion: Original Borrowings, Communal Pleasures

> *We're in the business of stealing ideas. That's what we* **do.** *We take cultural offerings and we manipulate them, involve ourselves in them, shape them to our taste. Besides which, Shakespeare wasn't exactly Original Story Guy, either.*
> —Justine

Women are using the paradox of cyberspace—personal privacy in a public forum—to explore feelings and ideas that were considered risky or inappropriate for women in the past. The protection and freedom of cyberspace is enabling these writers to defy many of the social taboos that have inhibited self-exploration and self-expression before the emergence of the Internet. At the same time, the inclusiveness of fanfic communities has encouraged more and more women (and some men) to participate actively by writing their own stories. Fan writers have found the resources—such as Lunacy's Experts Directory—to support their inventions, beta readers to critique them, audiences to read them, and symposia to debate their meaning and worth. Our notions of the relationship between sexuality and privacy are challenged by the fact that many—perhaps the majority—of these women would not have written erotica in the absence of a community of appreciative female readers. The Internet fanfic world provides these authors with safe, anonymous and, paradoxically, public places to meet with like-minded women in order to experiment with ideas of sexuality and gender identity.

The sum of this activity is community—a place where the cultural offerings of a detached and commercialized world are manipulated and "shaped to our taste." Women are using erotica not only to explore their inner lives, but also to expand their outer connections with the world. Fanfic Web sites have, in effect, become women's clubs, where erotica can be safely explored without damage to the reputation, the career, or the domestic life.

## Notes

1. See !Super Cat, *A (Very) Brief History of Fanfic* [Online] (Rebecca Lucy Busker, 1999 [cited August 10 2001]); available from <http://www.trickster.org/symposium/symp5.htm>.

2. For an introduction to fan culture and fan media, see Henry Jenkins, *Textual Poachers: Television Fans and Participatory Culture, Studies in Culture and Communication* (London: Routledge, 1992); Camille Bacon-Smith, *Enterprising Women: Television Fandom and the Creation of Popular Myth,* ed. Dan Rose and Paul Stoller, *Series in Contemporary Ethnography* (Philadelphia: University of Pennsylvania Press, 1992); Cheryl Harris and Alison Alexander, eds., *Theorizing Fandom: Fans, Subculture and Identity, Hampton Press Communication Series: Communication Alternatives* (Cresskill, NJ: Hampton Press, 1998); and Henry Jenkins, "Quentin Tarantino's *Star Wars?:* Digital Cinema, Media Convergence, and Participatory Culture," in this volume.

3. The instability of Internet sources is a well-documented problem that I will not address here. For a discussion of online documentation issues, see Janice R. and Todd W. Taylor Walker, *The Columbia Guide to Online Style* (New York: Columbia University Press, 1998) and Joseph

Gibaldi, *MLA Style Manual and Guide to Scholarly Publishing,* 2nd ed. (New York: Modern Language Association of America, 1998).

4. Some would argue that search engines, such as Google and Yahoo, constitute hierarchical powers because they control the terms that allow cybercitizens to find one another. As media companies converge (the dystopian argument goes) barriers to entry will constrict competition in cyberspace. This argument is focused on the commercialization of cyberspace and may not have the same implications for non-commercial enterprise such as fan fiction. Programs such as WebRing provide non-commercial web communities with ways of finding one another apart from search engines. See Robert McChesney, "So Much for the Magic of Technology and the Free Market: The World Wide Web and the Corporate Media System," in *The World Wide Web and Contemporary Cultural Theory,* ed. Andrew and Thomas Swiss Herman (New York: Routledge, 2000).

5. See Rebecca Lucy Busker, *Cereta's Fanfic Symposium* [Online] (1999–2001 [cited June 5 2001]); available from http://www.trickster.org/symposium/. Many fan fiction writers are the most insightful critics of their own work and cultures. I am grateful to Cynthia Jenkins for introducing me to this symposium and many other rich sources of fan criticism and analysis.

6. For another approach to estimating the scope of fan fiction on the Internet see Mary Ellen Curtin, *The Fan Fiction Universe: Some Statistical Comparisons* [Online] (1999–2000 [cited]; available from <http://www.eclipse.net/~mecurtin/au>. Curtin's conservative estimate of general fan fiction stories on the Internet, based upon counting archived stories in the largest fandoms, is over half a million (in 2000).

7. See the citations listed in note 1 as well as Nancy K. Baym, *Tune In, Log On: Soaps, Fandom, and Online Community* (Thousand Oaks, CA: Sage, 2000); Julian Dibbell, *My Tiny Life: Crime and Passion in a Virtual World* (New York: Henry Holt, 1998); Harris and Alexander, eds., *Theorizing Fandom.* Marc A. and Peter Kollock Smith, ed., *Communities in Cyberspace* (New York and London: Routledge, 1999); and Sherry Turkle, *Life on the Screen: Identity in the Age of the Internet* (New York: Touchstone, 1997).

8. Two fan conferences devoted entirely to slash are ZebraCon, which had its sixteenth biannual meeting in October 2002, and Escapade, which had its thirteenth annual meeting in February 2003. Both conferences protect slash writers and media artists from moral and legal objections by limiting attendance to their own membership.

9. While the chapter on slash in *Textual Poachers* covers both history and ideological issues, a more recent article gives an update on the status of the genre. See Shoshanna Green, Cynthia Jenkins, and Henry Jenkins, "Normal Interest in Men Bonking: Selections from The *Terra Nostra Underground* and *Strange Bedfellows,*" in *Theorizing Fandom: Fans, Subculture and Identity,* ed. Cheryl Harris and Alison Alexander, Hampton Press Communication Series (Cresskill, NJ: Hampton Press, 1998). For fan discussions see especially helen, *nt* [Online] (2001 [cited

August 13, 2001]); available from <http://www.waxjism.net/helen/domnatrix.htm> and Busker, *FanFic Symposium* [cited].

10. See "Pornography By Women For Women, With Love" in Joanna Russ, *Magic Mommas, Trembling Sisters, Puritans and Perverts: Feminist Essays* (Trumansberg, NY: Crossing, 1985).

## Bibliography

Austin, Shelley. *Web Ring Press Release* [Online]. Yahoo.com, 1999 [cited October 8, 1999]. Available from <http://nav.webring.org/cgi-bin/navcgi?ring=adultfic;list>.

Bacon-Smith, Camille. *Enterprising Women: Television Fandom and the Creation of Popular Myth.* Philadelphia: University of Pennsylvania Press, 1992.

Baym, Nancy K. *Tune in, Log On: Soaps, Fandom, and Online Community.* Thousand Oaks, CA: Sage, 2000.

Bone. *Interlunation* [Online]. 2000 [cited June 18, 2001]. Available from <http://business/mho.net/houseofslash/bslash.htm>.

Boutin, Paul. "1.6 Billion Served: The Web According to Google." *Wired* (December 2000): 118–119.

Busker, Rebecca Lucy. *Cereta's Fanfic Symposium* [Online]. 1999–2001 [cited June 5, 2001]. Available from <http://www.trickster.org/symposium/>.

Cat, !Super. *A (Very) Brief History of Fanfic* [Online]. Rebecca Lucy Busker, 1999 [cited August 10, 2001]. Available from <http://www.trickster.org/symposium/symp5.htm>.

Clerc, Susan. "Estrogen Brigades and 'Big Tits' Threads: Media Fandom Online and Off." In *Wired Women: Gender and New Realities in Cyberspace,* ed. Lynn Cherny and Elizabeth Reba Weise. Seattle: Seal Press, 1996.

Cumberland, Sharon. "The Five Wives of Ibn Fadlan: Women's Collaborative Fiction on Antonio Banderas Websites." In *Reload: Rethinking Women + Cyberculture,* ed. Austin Booth and Mary Flanagan. Cambridge, MA: MIT Press, 2001.

Curtin, Mary Ellen. *The Fan Fiction Universe: Some Statistical Comparisons* [Online], 1999–2000, available from <http://www.eclipse.net/~mecurtin/au>.

Dartt, G. L. *Just Between Them* [Online]. 2001 [cited August 13, 2001]. Available from <http://www.northco.net/~janeway/JBSeries/Seson1/jb02them.htm>.

delle. *The Overuse of H/C, or, Why Do We Torture Our Characters (and, Perhaps, Our Readers?)* [Online]. Rebecca Lucy Busker, 2000 [cited June 5, 2001]. Available from <http://www.trickster.org/symposium/symp50.htm>.

Dibbell, Julian. *My Tiny Life: Crime and Passion in a Virtual World*. New York: Henry Holt, 1998.

Gibaldi, Joseph. *M. L. A. Style Manual and Guide to Scholarly Publishing*. 2nd ed, New York: Modern Language Association of America, 1998.

Glass, Deena. Electronic mail, 1999.

Green, Shoshanna, Cynthia Jenkins, and Henry Jenkins. "Normal Interest in Men Bonking: Selections from the *Terra Nostra Underground* and *Strange Bedfellows*." In *Theorizing Fandom: Fans, Subculture and Identity,* edited by Cheryl Harris and Alison Alexander, 9–38. Cresskill, NJ: Hampton Press, 1998.

Harris, Cheryl, and Alison Alexander, eds. *Theorizing Fandom: Fans, Subculture and Identity,* Cresskill, NJ: Hampton Press, 1998.

helen. *nt* [Online]. 2001 [cited August 13, 2001]. Available from <http://www.waxjism.net/helen/dominatrix.htm>.

Jenkins, Henry. "*Quentin Tarantino's Star Wars?:* Digital Cinema, Media Convergence, and Participatory Culture." in this volume. See also <http://web.mit.edu/21fms/www/faculty/ henry3/starwars.html>.

————. *Textual Poachers: Television Fans and Participatory Culture*. New York and London: Routledge, 1992.

Jones, Lorelei. *Reasons for Fanfic and Impact on Characterizaton* [Online]. Rebecca Lucy Busker, 2000 [cited June 5, 2001 2001]. Available from <http://www.trickster.org/symposium/symp67.htm>.

Justine. *And Now Back to Our Show: A Rant by Justine* [Internet]. Rebecca Lucy Busker, 1999 [cited October 4, 1999]. Available from <http://trickster.org/radiofree/justine/Rant1.html>.

Kass. *Becoming Real or, the Invisible Fan* [Online]. Rebecca Lucy Busker, 2000 [cited June 5, 2001 2001]. Available from <http://www.trickster.org/symposium/symp65.htm>.

Killashandra. Electronic mail, October 4, 1999.

McChesney, Robert. "So Much for the Magic of Technology and the Free Market: The World Wide Web and the Corporate Media System." In *The World Wide Web and Contemporary Cultural Theory,* ed. Andrew Herman and Thomas Swiss, 5–36. New York: Routledge, 2000.

Piloto, Maribel. Electronic mail, September 6, 2000.

————. *Lunacy's Fan Fiction Reviews* [Online]. 2001 [cited August 13 2001]. Available from <http://www.geocities.com/Area51/Shire/6930>.

Russ, Joanna. *Magic Mommas, Trembling Sisters, Puritans and Perverts: Feminist Essays*. Trumansberg, NY: Crossing, 1985.

Sabotini, Rachel. *The Fannish Potlatch: Creation of Status within the Fan Community* [Online]. Rebecca Lucy Busker, 1999 [cited June 5, 2001]. Available from <http://www.trickster.org/symposium/symp41.htm>.

Shomeret. *Is Methos a Woman?* [Online]. Rebecca Lucy Busker, 1999 [cited June 5, 2001]. Available from <http://www.trickster.org/symposium/symp19.htm>.

Smith, Marc A., and Peter Kollock, ed. *Communities in Cyberspace*. New York and London: Routledge, 1999.

Turkle, Sherry. *Life on the Screen: Identity in the Age of the Internet*. New York: Touchstone, 1997.

Walker, Janice R., and Todd W. Taylor. *The Columbia Guide to Online Style*. New York: Columbia University Press, 1998.

Walkswithwind, James. *Musings* [Online]. Rebecca Lucy Busker, 2000 [cited June 5, 2001]. Available from <http://www.trickster.org/symposium/symp46.htm>.

# 18 Quentin Tarantino's Star Wars? Digital Cinema, Media Convergence, and Participatory Culture

Henry Jenkins

*For me the great hope is now that 8mm video recorders are coming out, people who normally wouldn't make movies are going to be making them. And that one day a little fat girl in Ohio is going to be the new Mozart and make a beautiful film with her father's camcorder. For once the so-called professionalism about movies will be destroyed and it will really become an art form.*
—Francis Ford Coppola

*We're going to empower a writer, somewhere in the world, who doesn't have filmmaking resources at his or her disposal. This is the future of cinema—Star Wars is the catalyst.*
—Jason Wishnow, maker of the digital film *Tatooine or Bust*

Maybe you received a digital postcard from someone you know during the height of the Monica Lewinsky scandals. Like so much that circulates on the Net, it came without any clear-cut attribution of authorship. The same image now appears on a variety of Web sites without much indication of its origins. Given such an image's decentralized circulation, we have no way of knowing whether it was seen by more or fewer people than saw the Elian Gonzales spoof of the "Whazzup" commercials or the image of Bill Gates as a Borg from *Star Trek: The Next Generation.* Yet, few of us could be ignorant of the source material it parodies—the Brothers Hildebrant's famous poster for the original release of *Star Wars.* In this contemporary and somewhat off-color version, Bill Clinton thrusts his power cigar skyward as a scantly clad Monica clings to his leg, her black thong barely visible through her translucent white robe. The sinister face of Ken Starr looms ominously in the background; Hillary shields Chelsea's eyes from this frightful spectacle.

This grassroots appropriation of *Star Wars* became part of the huge media phenomenon that surrounded first the release of the digitally enhanced original *Star Wars* trilogy in 1997 and the subsequent release of *The Phantom Menace* in 1999. Spoofs and parodies of

*Star Wars* were omnipresent the summer of 1999. The trailer for *Austin Powers II: The Spy Who Shagged Me* toyed with trigger-happy audiences eagerly anticipating their first glimpse of *The Phantom Menace* preview reel. It opened with ominous music, heavy breathing, and a space ship interior, as a narrator explained, "Years ago, a battle was fought and an empire was destroyed. Now the saga will continue." The chair revolves around to reveal not the anticipated Darth Vader (or his later-day counterpart, Darth Maul), but Doctor Evil, who shrugs and says, "You were expecting someone else?" Bowing before the media phenomenon, *Austin Powers* was released with the slogan, "If you see only one movie this summer, see . . . *Star Wars*. If you see two movies, see Austin Powers." Doonesbury did a series of cartoons depicting the "refuge camps" awaiting entry into the *Star Wars* films. Weird Al Yankovich, who had previously been successful with a music video, "Yoda," offered his own prequel with "The Saga Begins." *Mad TV* ran two spoofs—one that imagined Randy Newman composing feel-good music for the film, while another featured George Lucas as an obnoxious, overweight male fan who seeks inspiration by dressing in an Ewok costume and who hopes to introduce Jar Jar's aunt "Jar-Jar-Mina" in his next release. David Letterman proposed casting smooth-voiced singer Barry White as Darth Vader. Accepting Harvard's Hasty Pudding Award, Samuel L. Jackson offered his own imitation of how Yoda might have delivered his lines from *Pulp Fiction*. Almost all of us can add many more entries to the list of mass-market spoofs, parodies, and appropriations of the *Star Wars* saga—some aimed at the film's director, some at its fans, and others at the content of the series itself, with Jar Jar Binks bashing becoming the order of the day.

I begin with these various commercial spoofs of *Star Wars* as a reminder that such creative reworkings of science fiction film and television are no longer, and perhaps never were, restricted to fan culture, but have become increasingly central to how contemporary popular culture operates. Too often, fan appropriation and transformation of media content gets marginalized or exoticised, treated as something that people do when they have too much time on their hands. The assumption is that anyone who would invest so much creative and emotional energy into the products of mass culture must surely have something wrong with them. In this essay, I will take a very different perspective—viewing media fans as active participants within the current media revolution and their cultural products as an important aspect of the digital cinema movement. If many advocates of digital cinema have sought to democratize the means of cultural production, to foster grassroots creativity by opening up the tools of media production and distribution to a broader segment of the general public, then the rapid proliferation of fan-produced *Star*

*Wars* films may represent a significant early success story for that movement. Force Flicks, one of several databases for fan film production, lists almost 300 amateur-produced *Star Wars* films currently in circulation on the Web and identifies an even larger number of such works as "in production." There is a tremendous diversity of theme, approach, and quality represented in this sample of the current state of amateur digital filmmaking. Some of the films have developed enormous cult followings. Amazon.com, the online bookseller, reports that sales of *George Lucas in Love* was outselling *The Phantom Menace* among their video customers, while *Troops* (which offers a *Cops*-style behind-the-scenes look at the routine experience of stormtroopers serving their hitch on Tatooine) was featured in a two-page spread in *Entertainment Weekly,* and its director, Kevin Rubio, was reported to have attracted offers of production contracts from major studios.

In this essay, I will explore how and why *Star Wars* became, according to Jason Wishnow, a "catalyst" for amateur digital filmmaking and what this case study suggests about the future directions popular culture may take. *Star Wars* fan films represent the intersection of two significant cultural trends—the corporate movement toward media convergence and the unleashing of significant new tools that enable the grassroots archiving, annotation, appropriation, and recirculation of media content. These fan films build on long-standing practices of the fan community, but they also reflect the influence of this changed technological environment that has dramatically lowered the costs of film production and distribution. I will argue that this new production and distribution context profoundly alters our understanding of what amateur cinema is and how it intersects with the commercial film industry. In the end, I want to propose the fan film aesthetic as a significant middle ground between the commercial focus of the new "dot-coms" and the avant-garde aesthetics of the "low-res" film movement, an approach that facilitates grassroots cultural production by building on our investment in mainstream culture.

## Media in Transition: Two Models

### Media Convergence

Media critics, such as Robert McChesney, have noted that the current trend within the entertainment industry has been toward the increased concentration of media ownership into the hands of a smaller number of transmedia and transnational conglomerates.[1] Horizontal integration, that is, the consolidation of holdings across multiple industries, has displaced the old vertical integration of the Hollywood studios. Certain companies, such as Viacom and Time Warner, maintain interests in film, cable, and network television;

video, newspapers, and magazines; book publishing and digital media. What emerged are new strategies of content development and distribution designed to increase the "synergy" between the different divisions of the same company. Studios seek content that can move fluidly across media channels. Following the "high concept" logic that has dominated the American cinema since the 1970s, production companies favored films with pre-sold content based on material from other media ("books"); simple, easily summarized narrative "hooks"; and distinctive "looks," broadly defined characters, striking icons, and highly quotable lines.[2]

Initially, this "books, hooks, and looks" approach required the ability to construct ancillary markets for a successful film or television program. Increasingly, however, it has become difficult to determine which markets are ancillary and which are core to the success of a media narrative. The process may start with any media channel, but a successful product will flow across media until it becomes pervasive within the culture at large—comics into computer games, television shows into films, and so forth. Marsha Kinder has proposed the term "entertainment supersystem" to refer to the series of intertextual references and promotions spawned by any successful product.[3] The industry increasingly refers to *Star Trek* or *Star Wars* as "franchises," using a term that makes clear the commercial stakes in these transactions. This new "franchise" system actively encourages viewers to pursue their interests in media content across various transmission channels, to be alert to the potential for new experiences offered by these various tie-ins.

As a consequence of these new patterns of media ownership and production, there is increasing pressure toward *convergence,* the technological integration of the various content delivery systems. Technological convergence is attractive to media industries because it opens multiple entry points into the consumption process and, at the same time, enables consumers to more quickly locate new manifestations of a popular narrative. One may be able to move from watching a television drama to ordering the soundtrack, purchasing videos, or buying products that have been effectively "placed" within the narrative universe.

Such an approach requires the constant development of media content that can provoke strong audience engagement and investment. For this synergy-based strategy to be successful, media audiences must not simply buy an isolated product or experience, but rather, must buy into a prolonged relationship with a particular narrative universe, which is rich enough and complex enough to sustain their interest over time and thus motivate a succession of consumer choices. This approach encourages studios to be more attentive to audience interests, and they are using the Web to directly solicit feedback as well as to monitor unsolicited fan responses to their products.

The strength of this new style of popular culture is that it enables multiple points of entry into the consumption process; the vulnerability is that if audiences fail to engage with the particular content on offer, then that choice has a ripple effect across all of the divisions of the media conglomerate. For every *Batman* that demonstrates the enormous potential of this franchising process, there is a *Dick Tracy* that nearly takes the producing company down with it. In such a world, intellectual property that has proven popular with mass audiences has enormous economic value, and companies seek to tightly regulate its flow in order to maximize profits and minimize the risk of diluting their trademark and copyright holdings. *Star Wars* is, in many ways, the prime example of media convergence at work. Lucas's decision to defer salary for the first *Star Wars* film in favor of maintaining a share of ancillary profits has been widely cited as a turning point in the emergence of this new strategy of media production and distribution. Lucas made a ton of money, and Twentieth Century Fox learned a valuable lesson. Kenner's *Star Wars* action figures are thought to have been key in re-establishing the value of media tie-in products in the toy industry, and John Williams's score helped to revitalize the market for soundtrack albums. The rich narrative universe of the *Star Wars* saga provided countless images, icons, and artifacts that could be reproduced in a wide variety of forms and sold to diverse groups of consumers. The serialized structures of the films helped to sustain audience interest across a broad span of time and to provide an opportunity to revitalize it as each new sequel or prequel is released. Despite an almost two-decade gap between the release dates for *Return of the Jedi* and *The Phantom Menace*, Lucasfilm continued to generate profits from its *Star Wars* franchise through the production of original novels and comic books, the distribution of video and audio tapes, the continued marketing of *Star Wars* toys and merchandise, and the maintenance of an elaborate publicity apparatus, including a monthly glossy newsletter for *Star Wars* fans. The careful licensing of the *Star Wars* iconography enabled Lucasfilm to form strategic alliances with a multitude of corporate partners, including fast food franchises and soft drink bottlers, which sought to both exploit and enlarge public interest in their forthcoming release. As a consequence, by spring 1999, it was impossible to go anywhere without finding yourself face to face with the distinctive personas of Darth Maul, Queen Amidala, or Jar Jar Binks.

This climate of heightened expectations also fostered the production of the various commercial *Star Wars* parodies mentioned earlier, as other media producers sought to "poke fun" at the hype surrounding *Star Wars* phenomenon while tapping into audience awareness of the film's impending release. Letterman's spoofs of *Star Wars* were as much a part of the publicity campaign for the movie as were the appearance of Natalie Portman and the other film stars on his program. The good-natured trailer of *Austin Powers* played with the audience's anticipation of *Star Wars* and became a vehicle for creating media buzz about both works.

### Participatory Culture

Patterns of media consumption have been profoundly altered by a succession of new media technologies that enable average citizens to participate in the archiving, annotation, appropriation, transformation, and recirculation of media content. Participatory culture refers to the new style of consumerism that emerges in this environment. If media convergence is to become a viable corporate strategy, it will be because consumers have learned new ways to interact with media content. Not surprisingly, participatory culture is running ahead of the technological developments necessary to sustain industrial visions of media convergence and thus making demands on popular culture that the studios are not yet, and perhaps never will be, able to satisfy. The first and foremost demand consumers make is the right to participate in the creation and distribution of media narratives. Media consumers want to become media producers, while media producers want to maintain their traditional dominance over media content.

A history of participatory culture might well start with the photocopier, which quickly became "the people's printing press," paving the way for a broad range of subcultural communities to publish and circulate their perspectives on contemporary society. The Video Cassette Recorder (VCR) enabled consumers to bring the broadcast signal more fully under their control, to build large libraries of personally meaningful media content, and increasingly, to give them tools that facilitated amateur media production. By the early 1990s, media fans were using the VCR to re-edit footage of their favorite television programs to provide raw materials for the production of music videos. The availability of low-cost camcorders and, more recently, digital cameras has empowered more people to enter directly into the filmmaking process; the power of the camcorder as a means of documentary production was aptly illustrated by the Rodney King video, which placed the issue of police brutality in Los Angeles onto the national agenda. Portable technologies, such as the Walkman and cell phone, enabled us to carry our media with us from place to place, to create our own "soundtracks" for our real world experiences, and to see ourselves more and more connected within a networked communications environment. Computer and video games encouraged us to see ourselves as active participants in the world of fiction, to "fight like a Jedi" or to "outshoot Clint Eastwood." Digital photography and audio-sampling technologies made it easy to manipulate and rework the sights and sounds of our contemporary media environment, paving the way for new forms of cultural expression, such as Photoshop collages and music sampling. These technologies do not simply alter the ways that media are produced or consumed; they also help to break down barriers of entry into the media marketplace. The Net opened up new space for public discussions of media content, and the Web became an important showcase for grassroots cultural production. On one of my favorite Web sites, known as the Refrigerator, parents can scan in their children's artwork and place them on global display. In many ways, the Web has become the digital refrigerator for the "Do-It-Yourself" ("DIY") movement. Prior to the Web, amateurs might write stories, compose music, or make movies, but they had no venue to exhibit their works beyond their immediate circles of family and friends. For example, among those "digital movies" indexed by the various *Star Wars* fan Web sites were Super-8 productions dating back to the original release of *A New Hope* (such as *Star Wars Remake*) but only now reaching a broader audience because of their on-line circulation. The Web made it possible for alternative media productions of all kinds to gain greater visibility.

This ability to exhibit grassroots cultural productions has in turn fostered a new excitement about self-expression and creativity. For some, these grassroots cultural productions are understood as offering a radical alternative to dominant media content, providing space for various minority groups to tell their own stories or to question hegemonic representations of their culture. Groups such as the Goths or the Riot Grrls have been quick to explore these political uses of the Web, as have a variety of racial and ethnic groups. Culture jammers seek to use the power of digital media to call into question the consumerist logic of mass media. Others employ the Web as a means of getting greater visibility, of attracting public notice as a prelude for entering directly into the commercial media world. The Web has become an important showcase for productions of film school students, for example. Still others understand their cultural productions in the context of building social ties within a "virtual community" defined around shared interests. The pervasiveness of popular culture content has made it a particularly rich basis for forming social ties within the geographically dispersed population of the Internet. People who may never meet face to face, and thus have few real-world connections with each other, can tap into the shared framework of popular culture to facilitate communication. Fans were early adopters of all of these media technologies and as a consequence, their aesthetics and cultural politics have been highly influential in shaping public understanding of the relationship between dominant and grassroots media. Such groups seek not to shut down the corporate apparatus of the mass media but rather to build on their enjoyment of particular media products, to claim affiliation with specific films or television programs, and to use them as inspiration for their own cultural production, social interaction, and intellectual exchange.

As more and more amateur works have entered into circulation via the Web, the result has been a turn back toward a more folk-culture understanding of creativity. Historically, our culture evolved through a collective process of collaboration and elaboration. Folktales, legends, myths, and ballads were built up over time as people added elements that made them more meaningful to their own contexts. The Industrial Revolution resulted in the privatization of culture and the emergence of a concept of intellectual property that assumes that cultural value originates from the original contributions of individual authors. In practice, of course, any act of cultural creation builds on what has come before, borrowing genre conventions and cultural archetypes, if nothing else. The ability of corporations to control their "intellectual property" has had a devastating effect on the production and circulation of cultural materials, meaning that the general population has come to see themselves primarily as consumers of—rather than participants within—their culture. The mass production of culture has largely displaced the old folk culture, but we have lost the possibility for cultural myths to accrue new meanings and associations over time, resulting in single authorized versions (or at best, corporately controlled efforts to rewrite and update the myths of our popular heroes). Our emotional and social investments in culture have not shifted, but new structures of ownership diminish our ability to participate in the creation and interpretation of that culture.

Fans respond to this situation of an increasingly privatized culture by applying the traditional practices of a folk culture to mass culture, treating film or television as if it offered them raw materials for telling their own stories and resources for forging their own communities. Just as the American folk songs of the nineteenth century were often related to issues of work, the American folk culture of the twentieth century speaks to issues of leisure and consumption. Fan culture, thus, represents a participatory culture through which fans explore and question the ideologies of mass culture, speaking from a position sometimes inside and sometimes outside the cultural logic of commercial entertainment. The key difference between fan culture and traditional folk culture doesn't have to do with fan actions but with corporate reactions. Robin Hood, Pecos Bill, John Henry, Coyote, and Br'er Rabbit belonged to the folk. Kirk and Spock, Scully and Mulder, Han and Chewbacca, or Xena and Gabrielle belong to corporations.

Fan fiction repairs some of the damage caused by the privatization of culture, allowing these potentially rich cultural archetypes to speak to and for a much broader range of social and political visions. Fan fiction helps to broaden the potential interest in a series by pulling its content toward fantasies that are unlikely to gain widespread distribution, tailoring it to cultural niches under-represented within and under-served by the aired material. In theory, such efforts could increase the commercial value of media products by opening them to new audiences, though producers rarely understand them in those terms.

Consider, for example, this statement made by a fan:

> What I love about fandom is the freedom we have allowed ourselves to create and recreate our characters over and over again. Fanfic rarely sits still. It's like a living, evolving thing, taking on its own life, one story building on another, each writer's reality bouncing off another's and maybe even melding together to form a whole new creation. . . . I find that fandom can be extremely creative because we have the ability to keep changing our characters and giving them a new life over and over. We can kill and resurrect them as often as we like. We can change their personalities and how they react to situations. We can take a character and make him charming and sweet or cold-blooded and cruel. We can give them an infinite, always-changing life rather than the single life of their original creation.[4]

Fans reject the idea of a definitive version produced, authorized, and regulated by some media conglomerate. Instead, fans envision a world where all of us can participate in the creation and circulation of central cultural myths. What is most striking about the quote above is that the right to participate actively in the culture is assumed to be "the freedom we have allowed ourselves," not a privilege granted by a benevolent company. Fans also reject the studio's assumption that intellectual property is a "limited good," to be tightly controlled lest it dilute its value. Instead, they embrace an understanding of intellectual property as "shareware," something that accrues value as it moves across different contexts, gets retold in various ways, attracts multiple audiences, and opens itself up to a proliferation of alternative meanings. Giving up absolute control over intellectual property, they argue, increases its cultural value (if not its economic worth) by encouraging new, creative input and thus enabling us to see familiar characters and plots from fresh perspectives. Media conglomerates often respond to these new forms of participatory culture by seeking to shut them down or reigning in their free play with cultural material. If the media industries understand the new cultural and technological environment as demanding greater audience participation within what one media analyst calls the "experience economy,"[5] they seek to tightly structure the terms by which we may interact with their intellectual property, preferring the pre-programmed activities offered by computer games or commercial Web sites to the free-form participation represented by fan culture. The conflict between these two paradigms—the corporate-based concept of media convergence and the grassroots-based concept of participatory culture—will determine the long-term cultural consequences of our current moment of media in transition.

If *Star Wars* was an important ur-text for the new corporate strategy of media convergence, *Star Wars* has also been the focal point of an enormous quantity of grassroots media production, becoming the very embodiment of the new participatory culture. Fans began to write original fiction based on the *Star Wars* characters within a few months of the first film's release, building on an infrastructure for the production and distribution of fanzines that had first grown up around *Star Trek*. Fan writers sustained the production of original *Star Wars* stories throughout the "dark years," when Lucas had seemingly turned his back on his own mythology, and the release of *The Phantom Menace* provoked an enormous wave of new fan stories on the Web.

Grassroots appropriation and transformation of *Star Wars* has not, however, been restricted to media fandom per se but has spread across many other sectors of the new DIY culture. Will Brooker, for example, notes the persistence of *Star Wars* references in punk and techno music, British underground comics, novels like Douglas Coupland's *Microserfs,* films like Kevin Smith's *Clerks,* and various punk, thrasher, and slacker 'zines. Brooker argues that the rebellion depicted in the *Star Wars* films provides a useful model for thinking about the coalition-based cultural politics that define this whole DIY movement. The Empire, Brooker argues, is a "colonizing force" that seeks to impose top-down regimentation and demand conformity to its dictates. The Rebellion is a ragtag coalition of different races and cultures, a temporary alliance based on constant flux and movement from base to base, and dependent on often decentralized and democratic forms of decision making.[6]

Encouraged by Lucas's romantic myth about grassroots resistance to controlling institutions, these fans have actively resisted efforts by Lucasfilm to tighten its control over intellectual property. Through the years, Lucasfilm has been one of the most aggressive corporate groups in trying to halt fan cultural production. As early as 1981, Lucasfilm had issued legal notices and warnings to fans who published 'zines containing sexually explicit stories, while implicitly giving permission to publish non-erotic stories about the characters. Many fans felt that Lucasfilm was claiming the right to ideologically police their shared "fantasies." Much of the writing of fan erotica was pushed underground by this policy, though it continued to circulate informally. In fall 1997, the Usenet discussion group devoted to *Star Wars* responded to increased traffic sparked by the re-release of the "digitally enhanced" versions of the original films, creating a separate newsgroup where fans could post and critique original fiction set in the *Star Wars* universe. In a rare action, the Usenet hierarchy vetoed the plan, not even allowing it to be presented for a formal vote, claiming that it promoted "illegal activities," i.e., that net discussions of fan fiction encouraged the violation of Lucasfilm's copyright. Many believe that they made this decision based on a series of "cease and desist" letters, issued by Lucasfilm attorneys, aimed at shutting down *Star Wars* fan Web sites or blocking the circulation of fanzines. Controversy erupted again when, in a shift of position that some felt was more encouraging to fans, Lucasfilm offered *Star Wars* fans free Web space and unique content for their sites, but only under the condition that whatever they created would become the studio's intellectual property. Fan activists were sharply critical of these arrangements, both on political grounds (insisting that it set a precedent that went directly against their own argument that fan fiction constituted a legitimate exercise of their "fair use" rights) and on economic grounds (concerned that such arrangements would make it impossible for them to profit in the future from their creative efforts, noting that some *Star Trek* fan writers had been able to turn their fan fiction into the basis for professional novels).

Yet if studio legal departments still encourage the rigorous enforcement of intellectual property law as a means of regulating the flow of media materials, their creative departments often display a rather different understanding of the intersection between media convergence and participatory culture. The culture industry has its own reasons for encouraging active, rather than passive, modes of consumption. They seek consumers who move between different media channels and make meaningful links between different manifestations of the same story. Contemporary popular culture has absorbed many aspects of "fan culture" that would have seemed marginal a decade ago. Media producers are consciously building into their texts opportunities for fan elaboration and collaboration—codes to be deciphered, enigmas to be resolved, loose ends to be woven together, teasers and spoilers for upcoming developments—and they leak information to the media, which sparks controversy and speculation. Media producers also actively monitor and, in some cases, directly participate in the fan discussions on the Web as a way of measuring grassroots response to their productions. The products that are emerging within this new media culture, then, are more complex in their reliance on back story and foreshadowing, more dependent on the audience's familiarity with character history, more open to serialization, genre-mixing, cross-overs between different fictional universes, and more playful in their reliance on in-joke references or spoofing of other media content. As such, these media producers rely on audience access to an archive of episodes on videotape (and on their servers) and the informational infrastructure provided by various fan-generated Web sites and databases. The most adept producers in this new media environment are, in fact, using the Web to reinforce or expand on the information contained in the commercial material.

The old either-or oppositions (co-optation vs. resistance) have long dominated debates between political economy and cultural studies. Approaches derived from the study of political economy may, perhaps, provide the best vocabulary for discussing media convergence, while cultural studies language has historically framed our understanding of participatory culture. Neither theoretical tradition, however, can truly speak to what happens at the intersection between the two. The result may be conflict (as in ongoing legal battles for access to or regulation over intellectual property rights), critique (as in the political activism of culture jammers who use participatory culture to break down the dominance of the media industries), challenge (as occurs with the blurring of the lines between professional and amateur products that may now compete for viewer interest if not revenues), collaboration (as in various plans for the incorporation of viewer-generated materials), or recruitment (as when commercial producers use the amateur media as a training ground or testing ground for emerging ideas and talent). In some cases, amateur media draws direct and explicit inspiration from mainstream media content, while in others, commercial culture seeks to absorb or mimic the appropriative aesthetic of participatory culture to reach hip, media-savvy consumers. These complex interrelationships provide the context for public awareness and response to amateur digital cinema production around *Star Wars*. I will explore more fully the ways that *Star Wars* fan filmmakers have negotiated a place for themselves somewhere between these two competing trends, trying to co-exist with the mainstream media, while opening up an arena for grassroots creativity.

### DUDE, WE'RE GONNA BE JEDI!

Maru *pays homage to* Star Wars *and is intended to demonstrate to everyone who spent their entire childhood dreaming of wielding a light saber that inspired personal visions can now be realized using tools that are readily available to all of us.* Maru *was made using a camcorder and a PC with a budget of about $500. . . . Technology and the new media facilitate the articulation and exchange of ideas in ways never before imagined, and we hope that others will harness the power of these tools as we have in order to share their dreams with the world.*
—amateur filmmakers Adam Dorr, Erik Benson, Hien Nguyen, and Jon Jones

*George Lucas in Love,* perhaps the best known of the *Star Wars* parodies, depicts the future media mastermind as a singularly clueless USC film student who can't quite come up with a good idea for his production assignment, despite the fact that he inhabits a realm rich with narrative possibilities. His stoner roommate emerges from behind the hood of his dressing gown and lectures Lucas on "this giant cosmic force, an energy field created by all living things." His sinister next-door-neighbor, an archrival, dresses all in black and breathes with an asthmatic wheeze as he proclaims, "My script is complete. Soon I will rule the entertainment universe." As Lucas races to class, he encounters a brash young friend who brags about his souped-up sports car and his furry-faced sidekick who growls when he hits his head on the hood while trying to do some basic repairs. His professor, a smallish man, babbles cryptic advice, but all of this adds up to little until Lucas meets and falls madly for a beautiful young woman with buns on both sides of her head. Alas, the romance leads to naught as he eventually discovers that she is his long-lost sister.

*George Lucas in Love* is, of course, a spoof of *Shakespeare in Love* as well as a tribute from one generation of USC film students to another. As co-director Joseph Levy, a twenty-four-year-old graduate from Lucas's alma mater, explained, "Lucas is definitely the god of USC. . . . We shot our screening-room scene in the George Lucas Instructional Building—which we're sitting in right now. Lucas is incredibly supportive of student filmmakers and developing their careers and providing facilities for them to be caught up to technology."[7] Yet what makes this film so endearing is the way that it pulls Lucas down to the same level of countless other amateur filmmakers and in so doing, helps to blur the line between the fantastical realm of space opera ("A long, long time ago in a galaxy far, far away") and the familiar realm of everyday life (the world of stoner roommates, snotty neighbors, and incomprehensible professors). Its protagonist is hapless in love, clueless at filmmaking, yet somehow he manages to pull it all together and produce one of the top-grossing motion pictures of all time. *George Lucas in Love* offers us a portrait of the artist as a young geek.

One might contrast this rather down-to-earth representation of Lucas—the auteur as amateur—with the way fan filmmaker Evan Mather's Web site constructs the amateur as an emergent auteur. Along one column of the site can be found a filmography, listing all of Mather's productions going back to high school, as well as a listing of the various newspapers, magazines, Web sites, television and radio stations which have covered his work—*La Republica, Le Monde,* the *New York Times, Wired, Entertainment Weekly,* CNN, NPR, and so forth. Another sidebar provides up to the moment information about his works in progress. Elsewhere, you can see news of the various film festival screenings of his films and whatever awards they have won. A tongue-in-cheek manifesto outlines his views on digital filmmaking: " . . . no dialogue . . . no narration . . . soundtrack must be monaural . . . length of credits may not exceed ⅟₂₀ the length of the film . . . nonverbal human or animal utterances are permitted . . . nonsense sounds whilst permitted are discouraged . . . all credits and captions must be in both English and French whilst the type size of the French title may be no greater in height than ⅓ the height of the English . . . . " More than nineteen digital films are featured with photographs, descriptions, and links that enable you to download them in multiple formats. Another link allows you to call up a PDF file reproducing a glossy full-color, professionally designed brochure documenting the making of his most recent work, *Les Pantless Menace,* which includes close-ups of various props and settings, reproductions of stills, score sheets, and storyboards, and detailed explanations of how he was able to do the special effects, soundtrack, and editing for the film. We learn, for example, that some of the dialogue was taken directly from Commtech chips that were embedded within Hasbro *Star Wars* toys. A biography provides some background: "Evan Mather spent much of his childhood running around south Louisiana with an eight-millimeter silent camera staging hitchhikings and assorted buggery. . . . As a landscape architect, Mr. Mather spends his days designing a variety of urban and park environments in the Seattle area. By night, Mr. Mather explores the realm of digital cinema and is the renown creator of short films which fuse traditional hand drawn and stop motion animation techniques with the flexibility and realism of computer generated special effects."

The self-promotional aspects of Mather's site are far from unique. The Force.Net Fan Theater, for example, offers amateur directors a chance to offer their own commentary on the production and thematic ambitions of their movies. The creators of *When Senators Attack IV,* for example, give "comprehensive scene-by-scene commentary" on their film: "Over the next 90 pages or so, you'll receive an insight into what we were thinking when we made a particular shot, what methods we used, explanations to some of the more puzzling scenes, and anything else that comes to mind." Such materials often constitute a conscious parodying of the tendency of recent DVD releases to include alternative scenes, cut footage, storyboards, and director's commentary. Many of the Web sites provide information about fan films under production or may even include preliminary footage, storyboards, and trailers for films that may never be completed. Almost all of the amateur filmmakers have developed their own posters and advertising images for their productions, taking advantage of new Pagemaker and Photoshop software packages that make it easy to manipulate and rearrange images using the home computer. In many cases, the fan filmmakers often produce elaborate trailers, complete with advertising catchphrases.

Some of these materials serve useful functions within amateur film culture. The making-of articles that are found on so many of the fan Web sites enable a sharing of technical advice; trading such information helps to improve the overall quality of work within the community. The trailers also respond to the specific challenges of the Web as a distribution channel: it can take hours to download relatively long digital movies and as a consequence, the shorter, lower resolution trailers (often distributed in a streaming video format) allow would-be viewers a chance to glimpse the work and determine if it is worth the effort. Yet, these mechanisms of self-promotion move beyond what would be required to support a functional network for amateur film distribution, suggesting that the fans, too, have come to understand that the art of "high concept" filmmaking (and the franchise system it supports) depends as much on the art of advertising and marketing as on the art of storytelling.

Many of the fans, after all, got their first glimpse of footage from *The Phantom Menace* by downloading the much-publicized trailer. In many cases, fan parodies of the trailer started to appear in the months during which fans were eagerly awaiting a chance to see the film itself. In some early examples, fans simply re-dubbed the original trailer with alternative soundtracks; in other cases, they remade the trailer shot-by-shot. For example, downloading the trailer inspired Ayaz Asif to produce a parody employing characters taken from *South Park*. When an acquaintance, Ted Bracewell, sent him a wallpaper he had drawn depicting *South Park* characters in *Star Wars* garb, the two decided to collaborate, resulting in a quickly made trailer for *Park Wars: The Little Menace,* then for a more elaborately-made "special edition," and then for a series of other shorts based on the *Star Wars* version of the *South Park* characters. The production received such media interest, including an interview with Asif during a Sci-Fi Channel documentary, that the young filmmakers were ultimately invited to air it on Comedy Central, the same network that produced Trey Parker and Matt Stone's series.

Trailervision.com pushes fan cinema's fascination with the trailer format to its logical extreme, releasing a trailer each Monday for a non-existent film. In some cases, these trailers spoof commercial films which hit the theaters that same week, including *The Jar Jar Binks Project, I Know What You'll Want to Do Next Summer, The Wimp Club, Scam 3,* and *American Booty.* These spoof trailers are, in some senses, the perfect genre for the current state of digital cinema—short, pithy, reflecting the amateur filmmaker's self-conscious relationship to commercial media, and recognizable by a mass audience who can be assumed to be familiar with the material that inspired them. These spoof trailers enable amateur and aspiring filmmakers to surf the publicity generated by a current release and thus to get media coverage (as was the case with a surprising number of the *Star Wars* spoofs) or to draw audiences already worked up about the commercial product.

All of this publicity surrounding the *Star Wars* parodies serves as a reminder of what is one of the most distinctive qualities of these amateur films—the fact that they are so public. Mather, for example, reports, "Since I started keeping track in February 1998, this site has been visited by over a half-million people from all seven continents, including such faraway places as Antarctica, Iran, San Marino . . . and Canada." The idea that amateur filmmakers could develop such a global following runs counter to the historical marginalization of grassroots media production.

In her book *Reel Families: A Social History of Amateur Film,* Patricia R. Zimmerman offers a compelling history of amateur filmmaking in the United States, examining the intersection between nonprofessional film production and the Hollywood entertainment system. As Zimmerman notes, a variety of critics and theorists, including Harry Potempkin in the 1920s, Maya Deren in the 1950s, Jonas Mekas and George Kuchar in the 1960s, and Hans Magnus Enzensberger in the 1970s, had identified a radical potential in broadening popular access to the cinematic apparatus, fostering a new public consciousness about how media images are constructed and opening a space for alternative experimentation and personal expression outside of the industrial context of the studio system. Amateur film production emerged alongside the first moving pictures. Tom Gunning has argued that the Lumière Brothers' shorts were best understood within a context of amateur photography in France,[8] while Zimmerman points to the ways that amateur theater movements in the United States, as well as a prevailing entrepreneurial spirit, provided a base of support of amateur filmmaking efforts in the 1910s. However, the amateur film has remained, first and foremost, the "home movie," in several senses of the term: first, amateur films were exhibited primarily in private (and most often, domestic) spaces lacking any viable channel of distribution to a larger public; second, amateur films were most often documentaries of domestic and family life rather than attempts to make fictional or avant-garde films; and third, amateur films were perceived to be technically flawed and of marginal interest beyond the immediate family. Jokes and cartoons about the painfulness of being subjected to someone else's home movies are pervasive in our culture and represent a devaluing of the potential for an amateur cinema movement. Zimmerman cites a range of different critical appraisals that stressed the artlessness and spontaneity of amateur film in contrast with the technical polish and aesthetic sophistication of commercial films. She concludes, "[Amateur film] was gradually squeezed into the nuclear family. Technical standards, aesthetic norms, socialization pressures and political goals derailed its cultural construction into a privatized, almost silly, hobby."[9] Writing in the early 1990s, Zimmerman saw little reason to believe that the camcorder and the VCR would significantly alter this situation, suggesting that the medium's technical limitations made it hard for amateurs to edit their films and that the only public means of exhibition were controlled by commercial media-makers (as in programs such as *America's Funniest Home Videos*).

Digital filmmaking alters many of the conditions which Zimmerman felt had led to the marginalization of previous amateur filmmaking efforts—the Web provides an exhibition outlet that moves amateur filmmaking from private into public space; digital editing is far simpler than editing Super-8 or video and thus opens up a space for amateur artists to more directly reshape their material; the home PC has even enabled the amateur filmmaker to directly mimic the special effects associated with Hollywood blockbusters like *Star Wars*. As a consequence, digital cinema constitutes a new chapter in the complex history of interactions between amateur filmmakers and the commercial media. These films remain amateur, in the sense that they are made on low budgets, produced and distributed in noncommercial contexts, and generated by nonprofessional filmmakers (albeit often by people who want entry into the professional sphere), yet, many of the other classic markers of amateur film production have disappeared. No longer home movies, these films are public movies—public in that from the start, they are intended for audiences beyond the filmmaker's immediate circle of friends and acquaintances; public in their content, which involves the reworking of personal concerns into the shared cultural framework provided by popular mythologies; and public in their aesthetic focus on existing in dialogue with the commercial cinema (rather than existing outside of the Hollywood system altogether).

Digital filmmakers tackled the challenge of making *Star Wars* movies for many different reasons. *Kid Wars* director, Dana Smith, is a fourteen-year old who had recently acquired a camcorder and decided to stage scenes from *Star Wars* involving his younger brother and his friends, who armed themselves for battle with squirt guns and Nerf weapons. *The Jedi Who Loved Me* was shot by the members of a wedding party and intended as a tribute to the bride and groom, who were *Star Wars* fans. Some films—such as *Macbeth*—were school projects. Two high school students—Bievenido Concepcion and Don Fitz-Roy—shot the film, which creatively blurs the lines between Lucas and Shakespeare, for their high school advanced-placement English class. They staged light saber battles down the school hallway, though the principal was concerned about potential damage to lockers; the Millennium Falcon lifted off from the gym, though they had to composite it over the cheerleaders who were rehearsing the day they shot that particular sequence. Still other films emerged as collective projects for various *Star Wars* fan clubs. *Boba Fett: Bounty Trail,* for example, was filmed for a competition hosted by a Melbourne, Australia, Lucasfilm convention. Each cast member made their own costumes, building on previous experience with science fiction masquerades and costume contests. The film's stiffest competition came from *Dark Redemption,* a production of the Sydney fan community, which featured a light-saber-waving female protagonist, Mara Jade. Their personal motives for making such films are of secondary interest, however, once they are distributed on the Web. If such films are attracting worldwide interest, it is not because we all care whether or not Bievenido Concepcion and Don Fitz-Roy made a good grade on their Shakespeare assignment; we are unlikely to know any of the members of the wedding party that made *The Jedi Who Loved Me.* Rather, what motivates viewers to watch such films is our shared investments in the *Star Wars* universe. These amateur filmmakers have re framed their personal experiences or interests within the context of a popular culture mythology that is known around the world.

In a very tangible sense, digital filmmaking has blurred the line between amateur and professional, with films made for miniscule budgets duplicating special effects which had cost a small fortune to generate only a decade earlier. Amateur filmmakers can make pod racers skim along the surface of the ocean or landspeeders scatter dust as they zoom across the desert. They can make laser beams shoot out of ships and explode things before our eyes. Several fans tried to duplicate Jar Jar's character animation and inserted him into their own movies with varying degrees of success. (One filmmaker spoofed the defects of his own work, having Jar Jar explain that he took on a different accent for his part in Lucas's movie and suggesting that he had recently undergone a nose job.) The light saber battle, however, has become the gold standard of amateur filmmaking, with almost every filmmaker compelled to demonstrate his or her ability to achieve this particular effect. Many of the *Star Wars* shorts, in fact, consist of little more than light saber battles staged in suburban rec-rooms and basements, in empty lots, in the hallways of local schools, inside shopping malls, or more exotically against the backdrop of medieval ruins (shot during vacations).

As amateur filmmakers are quick to note, Lucas and Steven Spielberg both made Super-8 fiction films as teenagers and saw this experience as a major influence on their subsequent work. Although these films have not been made available to the general public, some of them have been discussed in detail in various biographies and magazine profiles. These "movie brat" filmmakers have been quick to embrace the potentials of digital filmmaking, not simply as a means of lowering production costs for their own films, but also as a training ground for new talent. Lucas, for example, told *Wired* magazine, "Some of the special effects that we redid for *Star Wars* were done on a Macintosh, on a laptop, in a couple of hours. . . . I could have very easily shot the *Young Indy* TV series on Hi-8. . . . So you can get a Hi-8 camera for a few thousand bucks, more for the software and the computer for less than $10,000 you have a movie studio. There's nothing to stop you from doing something provocative and significant in that medium." Elsewhere, he has paid tribute to several of the fan filmmakers, including Kevin Rubio (the director of *Troops*) and Joe Nussbaum (the director of *George Lucas in Love*).

Lucas's rhetoric about the potentials of digital filmmaking seems to have captured the imaginations of amateur filmmakers, and they are struggling to confront the master on his own ground, to use digital cinema to create a far more vivid version of their childhood fantasies. As Clay Kronke, the Texas A&M University undergraduate who made *The New World*, explained, "This film has been a labor of love. A venture into a new medium. . . . I've always loved light sabers and the mythos of the Jedi and after getting my hands on some software that would allow me to actually become what I had once only admired at a distance, a vague idea soon started becoming a reality. . . . Dude, we're gonna be Jedi." Kronke openly celebrates the fact that he made the film on a $26.79 budget with most of the props and costumes part of their pre-existing collections of *Star Wars* paraphernalia, that the biggest problem they faced on the set was that their plastic light sabers kept breaking after they clashed them together too often, and that those sound effects he wasn't able to borrow from a Phantom Menace PC game were "follied around my apartment, including the sound of a coat hanger against a metal flashlight, my microwave door, and myself falling on the floor several times."

The amateur's pride in recreating professional quality special effects always seems to compete with a recognition of the enormous gap between their own productions and the big-budget Hollywood film they are mimicking. Scholars and critics writing about third-world filmmaking have described those films as an "imperfect cinema," noting the ways that filmmakers have had to deal with low budgets and limited access to high-tech production facilities, making it impossible to compete with Hollywood on its own terms. Instead, these filmmakers have made a virtue out of their limitations, often spoofing or parodying Hollywood genre conventions and stylistic norms through films that are intentionally crude or ragged in style. The abruptness in editing, the roughness of camera movement, the grittiness of film stock, and the unevenness of lighting have become markers of authenticity, a kind of direct challenge to the polished look of a big budget screen production. These amateur filmmakers have also recognized and made their peace with the fact that digital cinema is, in some senses, an "imperfect cinema," with the small and grainy images a poor substitute for the larger-than-life qualities of Lucas's original films when projected on a big screen with Dolby Surroundsound. The trailer for the *Battle of the Bedroom* promises "lots of dodgy special effects," while the team that made *When Senators Attack* chose to call themselves Ultracheese Ltd. In some cases, the films are truly slapdash, relishing their sloppy special effects, embarrassing delivery, and thrift shop costumes. *The Throne Room,* for example, brags that it was shot and edited in only thirty minutes, and it shows. Two hammy adolescents cut-up in home movie footage clearly shot their living room and inserted into the *Throne Room* sequence from *A New Hope* to suggest their flirtation with Princess Leia. In others, the productions are quite polished, but the filmmakers still take pleasure in showing the seams. Setting its story in "a long, long time ago in a galaxy far cheaper than this one," Ceri Llewellyn's technically accomplished *Star Wras* reproduces the assault on the Death Star, using origami-folded paper TIE fighters and a basketball painted white as a stand-in for the Death Star. As the Death Star bursts into flames, we hear a loud boink as the elastic string holding it in space snaps and it falls out of the frame.

If the third-world filmmakers saw "imperfect cinema" as the basis for an implicit, and often very explicit, critique of the ideologies and market forces behind the Hollywood blockbuster and saw their parodies of American genre films as helping to "destroy the very toys of mystification," no such radical goal governs the production of these amateur films. They have, indeed, turned toward parody as the most effective genre for negotiating between these competing desires to reproduce, not to destroy, the special effects at the heart of the contemporary blockbuster and to acknowledge their own amateur status. Yet, their parody is almost always affectionate and rarely attempts to make an explicit political statement.

A notable exception may be *Tie-Tanic,* which directly references the huge corporate apparatus behind *Star Wars*'s success and calls into question the franchising of contemporary popular culture. The filmmaker, John Bunt, re-dubbed a sequence from the original *Star Wars* film depicting a conference between Darth Vader, Grand Moff Tarkin, and other imperial forces so that it now represented a Lucasfilm marketing meeting as corporate executives plot to rob consumers of their entertainment dollars. During a period of "nostalgic consumption" the *Star Wars* trilogy has regained its bid to be the highest grossing box-office success of all time but remains potentially vulnerable to challenge while the producers are nervously awaiting the completion of the prequels. The slow deployment of trailers can hold the audience's attention for only so long in an environment of competing blockbusters. While the studio executives are convinced that "talking pigs will hold the mouse-lovers in line," the real point of vulnerability is teenage girls: "If the rebels arouse sympathy and pathos in adolescent girls, it is possible—however unlikely—that they might find a market and exploit it." Darth Vader warns them that "the ability to control the medium for twenty years is insignificant next to the power of a good chick flick," only to be dismissed, "don't try to frighten us with your demographic ways, Lord Vader." Yet, Grand Moff Tarkin heeds his advice and dispatches him to deal with all challenges to this market segment. In a spectacular finale, which mixes and matches footage, sometimes within the same composite image, from *Star Wars* and *Titanic,* Vader's stormtroopers and TIE fighters open fire on the luxury liner. In several remarkable shots, we see R2D2, C-3PO, and a flaming Ewok among the terrified passengers flying from the sinking ship and watch a TIE fighter swoop down and blow up one of the escaping lifeboats. Rarely has the cut-throat competition between media conglomerates been depicted with such vivid and witty images! Yet, such an overt—and still pretty tame—critique of market forces is the exception rather than the rule.

More often, these amateur filmmakers see themselves as actively promoting media texts that they admire. For example, *Shadows of the Empire* is an unauthorized fan-made adaptation of Steve Perry's commercial *Star Wars* novel. Perry's original novel explored events that occurred between the end of *Empire Strikes Back* and the opening moments of *Return of the Jedi. Shadows of the Empire* has proven especially popular with *Star Wars* fans because it pays significant attention to the bounty hunter, Boba Fett, a character relatively marginal to the original films but central to the fan culture. Frustrated that this novel had never been adopted to the screen, fan filmmakers Jeff Hendrich and Bob Branch created their own serialization of the story: "We pooled every *Star Wars* action-figure and toy that we could beg, borrow or steal to make up the cast of the film. The occasional special guest toy stands in for the characters we just couldn't find and as extras in the crowd scenes." Though the adaptation was unauthorized, it nevertheless follows the logic of the franchise system itself.

*The Qui-Gon Show* aptly suggests the blurring between professional and fan efforts which occurs in this context. The script emerged as part of AtomFilms.com's "Makin' Wookie" competition, a commercially sponsored contest that attracted more than 300 amateur and semi-professional entries, including such promising titles as *Mos Angeles, The Real World—Tatooine, Springer Wars, Star Wars: Close Encounters,* and *Wookie Nights.* Atom-Films then provided a budget for several of the more acclaimed fan filmmakers, including

Jason Wishnow and Evan Mather, to produce a short based on Robert Fyvolent's contest-winning script. As with *The Qui-Gon Show,* many of the films have been distributed through the new commercial sites devoted to digital cinema and in several notable cases, have been released on commercial video.

Even in the absence of such direct commercial connections, the mass marketing of *Star Wars* inadvertently provided many of the resources needed to support these productions. The amateur filmmakers often make use of commercially available costumes and props, sample music from the soundtrack album and sounds of *Star Wars* videos or computer games, and draw advice on special effects techniques from television documentaries and mass-market magazines. For example, the makers of *Duel* described the sources for their soundtrack: "We sampled most of the light saber sounds from the *Empire Strikes Back* Special Edition laserdisc, and a few from *A New Hope. Jedi* was mostly useless to us, as the light saber battles in the film are always accompanied by music. The kicking sounds are really punch sounds from *Raiders of the Lost Ark,* and there's one sound—hideous running across the sand—that we got from *Lawrence of Arabia.* Music, of course, comes from the *Phantom Menace* soundtrack." By contrast, some filmmakers made use of images from the films themselves, but added soundtracks from other sources. *Stooge Wars,* for example, juxtaposes footage of Darth Vader and the stormtroopers with sounds and dialogue sampled from *I'll Never Heil Again,* a Three Stooges short that featured Moe as Hitler.

More broadly, the availability of these various ancillary products has encouraged these filmmakers, since childhood, to construct their own fantasies within the *Star Wars* universe. As one fan critic explained, "Odds are if you were a kid in the seventies, you probably fought in schoolyards over who would play Han, lost a Wookie action figure in your backyard and dreamed of firing that last shot on the Death Star. And probably your daydreams and conversations weren't about William Wallace, Robin Hood, or Odysseus, but, instead, light saber battles, frozen men, and forgotten fathers. In other words, we talked about our legend." Lucasfilm and Kenner may have initially understood the *Star Wars* action figures as commodities, but their cultural effects go much deeper. The action figures provided this generation with some of their earliest avatars, encouraging them to assume the role of a Jedi knight or an intergalactic bounty hunter, enabling them to physically manipulate the characters and props in order to construct their own stories. Fans, for example, note that the Boba Fett action figure, far more than the character's small role in the trilogy, helped to make this character a favorite among digital filmmakers. The fans, as children, had fleshed out Boba Fett's intentionally murky character, giving him (or her) a personality, motives, goals, and conflicts, which helped to inspire the plots of a number of the amateur movies.

Not surprisingly, a significant number of filmmakers in their late teens and early twenties have turned toward those action figures as resources for their first production efforts. For example, *Toy Wars* producers Aaron Halon and Jason VandenBerghe have launched an ambitious plan to produce a shot-by-shot remake of *Star Wars*. Others, such as Damon Wellner and Sebastian O'Brien, two self-proclaimed "action figure nerds" from Cambridge, Mass., formed Probot Productions with the goal of "making toys as alive as they seemed in childhood." Probot has made several action figure movies, including the forty-minute long *Star Wars* epic, *Prequel: Revenge of the Snaggletooth* (which they bill as "homage to the franchise that redefined Movie Merchandi$ing") and *Aliens 5* ("In space, no one can hear you playing with toys"). The Probot Web site offers this explanation of their production process: "The first thing you need to know about Probot Productions is that we're broke. We spend all our $$$ on toys. This leaves a very small budget for special effects, so we literally have to work with what we can find in the garbage. You may be surprised at what you can create with a video camera and some simple household items. . . . If you have seen *Aliens 5,* you may remember Ripley and Bishop running down the computer-generated hallways of the space ship. . . . This effect was done simply by placing the camera directly in front of a TV, having one person holding the action figures up in front of the screen and another person playing the Alien vs. Predator video game. . . . We used a lot of pyrotechnics in the film, and had a fire extinguisher on the set at all times. . . . We used pump-action hairspray (not aerosol!!) and a lighter to create our flame-thrower effect. . . . For sets we used a breadbox, a ventilation tube from a dryer, cardboard boxes, a discarded piece from a vending machine, and milk crates. Large Styrofoam pieces from stereo component boxes work very well to create spaceship-like environments!" Despite such primitive working conditions, Probot has been able to mimic the original film's light saber battles, space weaponry, and holographic images.

No digital filmmaker has pushed the aesthetics of the action figure as far as Evan Mather. Mather's films, such as *Godzilla versus Disco Lando, Kung-fu Kenobi's Big Adventure,* and *Quentin Tarantino's Star Wars,* represent a no-holds-barred romp through contemporary popular culture. The rock-'em sock-'em action of *Kung-Fu Kenobi's Big Adventure* takes place against the backdrop of settings sampled from the film, drawn by hand, or built from Lego blocks, with the eclectic and evocative soundtrack borrowed from Neil Diamond, *Mission Impossible, Pee-Wee's Big Adventure,* and *Charlie Brown's Christmas Special.* Dialogue in Mather's movies is often sampled from the original films or elsewhere in popular culture. *Disco Lando* puts the moves on everyone from Admiral Ackbar to Jabba's blue-skinned dancing girl and all of his pick-up-lines come from the soundtrack of *The*

*Empire Strikes Back.* Mace Windu "gets medieval" on the Jedi Council, delivering Samuel L. Jackson's lines from *Pulp Fiction,* before shooting up the place. The camera focuses on the bald head of a dying Darth Vader as he gasps "rosebud." Rebels and stormtroopers battle it out on the snowy landscape of Hoth while cheery yuletide music plays in the background.

Literary critic Lois Rostow Kuznets has discussed the recurrent motif of toys coming to life across several centuries of children's literature, noting that such stories provide a variety of functions for their readers and authors: "Toy characters embody the secrets of the night: they inhabit a secret, sexual, sensual world, one that exists in closed toy shops, under Christmas trees, and behind the doors of dollhouses—and those of our parents' bedrooms. This is an uncanny (in Freudian terms) world of adult mysteries and domestic intrigue. It can be marginal, liminal, potentially carnival world."[10] Mather and the other action figure filmmakers explore the secrets of the night, blurring the boundaries between different fictional universes, playfully transgressing the family values of the original *Star Wars* films, to encourage our carnivalesque play with their molded plastic protagonists. The humor is often scatological. Yoda eats too many Banta Beans and farts repeatedly in Obi-Wan's face. A naked Barbie spews green vomit into a commode. His characters belch, fart, and barf with total abandon, as they punch, kick, and pummel each other with little or no provocation. *Disco Lando* climaxes with a bloody fistfight between Godzilla and the Virgin Mary. Mather also loves to insinuate tabloid-style secret lives for the various characters. Obi-Wan wakes up in bed snuggling with Lobot. Luke Skywalker enjoys dressing in Princess Leia's skimpy slavegirl costume. As for Leia, Mather shows her smooching with her brother, Luke, and then pulls back to show a whole lineup of panting aliens waiting their turn for the Princess.

Apart from their anarchic humor and rapid-fire pace, Mather's films stand out because of their visual sophistication. In some cases, Mather deftly mixes the visual styles of contemporary filmmakers and borrows heavily from Tarantino in particular. Moreover, Mather's own frenetic style has become increasingly distinguished across the body of his works, constantly experimenting with different forms of animation, flashing or masked images, and dynamic camera movements. Mather has made a virtue of his materials, using the plastic qualities of the action figures to justify a movement into a brightly colored and surreal mise-en-scène.

Yet, if the action figure filmmakers have developed an aesthetic based on their appropriation of materials from the mainstream media, then the mainstream media has been quick to imitate that aesthetic. Nickelodeon's *Action League Now,* for example, has a regular cast of characters consisting of mismatched dolls and mutilated action figures. In some cases, their faces have been melted or mangled through inappropriate play. One protagonist has no clothes. They come in various size scales, suggesting the collision of different narrative universes that characterizes children's action figure play. Recurring gags involve the smashing of brittle characters or dogs gnawing on and mutilating the protagonists, situations all too common in domestic play. MTV's *Celebrity Deathmatch* creates its action figures using claymation, staging World Wrestling Federation-style bouts between various celebrities, some likely (Monica Lewinsky against Hillary Clinton), some simply bizarre (the rock star formerly known as Prince against Prince Charles). Screenwriter/director Steve Oedekerk (*Ace Ventura 2, The Nutty Professor, Patch Adams*) produced *Thumb Wars* using thumbs, dressed in elaborate costumes, as his primary performers and then digitally adding on facial features and expressions. UPN aired the decisively low-tech and low-humor result the week the *Star Wars* prequel opened in the theaters. It is in the context of such unlikely cult television productions that it becomes plausible to see the creation of a high-quality fan film for Web distribution as a "try-out" for gaining access into the media industries.

We are witnessing the emergence of an elaborate feedback loop between the emerging "DIY" aesthetics of participatory culture and the mainstream industry. The Web represents a site of experimentation and innovation, where amateurs test the waters, developing new practices, themes, and generating materials that may well attract cult followings on their own terms. The most commercially viable of those practices are then absorbed into the mainstream media, either directly through the hiring of new talent or the development of television, video, or big screen works based on those materials, or indirectly, through a second-order imitation of the same aesthetic and thematic qualities. In return, the mainstream media materials may provide inspiration for subsequent amateur efforts, which, in turn, push popular culture in new directions. In such a world, fan works can no longer be understood as simply derivative of mainstream materials but must be understood as themselves open to appropriation and reworking by the media industries.

This process is aptly illustrated by considering the work of popular artists like Kevin Smith, Quentin Tarantino, Mike Judge, Matt Groening, and Kevin Williamson, whose films and television series reflect this mainstreaming of fan aesthetics and politics. Their works often deal explicitly with the process of forming one's own mythology using images borrowed from the mass media. One of the protagonists of *Pulp Fiction,* for example, decides at the end that he wants to "wander the earth" like Kane in television's *Kung Fu. Reservoir Dogs* opens with a five-minute discussion of the erotic connotations of Madonna's

"Like A Virgin," defining the characters first and foremost through their relationships to popular culture. Characters in *Chasing Amy* engage in animated debates about the sexuality of the various teens in the Archie comics, while *Dazed and Confused* opens with the scene of high school students trying to recall as many different episodes of *Gilligan's Island* as they can, before one of the women offers a devastating critique of how the series builds on the iconography of male pornography. Kevin Smith's films make recurring in-joke references to *Star Wars,* including a debate about the ethical obligations of the independent contractors who worked on the Death Star (*Clerks*), a comic episode in which Silent Bob becomes convinced that he can actually perform Jedi mind tricks (*Mall Rats*), and a long rant about the "blackness" of Darth Vader (*Chasing Amy*); Smith devotes an entire issue of his *Clerks* comic book to various characters' attempts to corner the market on collectible *Star Wars* action figures.

The protagonist of Williamson's television series, *Dawson's Creek,* decorates his room with posters for Steven Spielberg films, routinely discusses and critiques classic and contemporary films with the other characters on the series, and draws inspiration from them for the creation of his own videos. Tarantino's whole aesthetic seems to have emerged from his formative experiences working at a video store. In such an environment, older and newer films are more or less equally accessible; some movie is always playing on the monitor and providing a background for everyday interactions. These video store experiences encourage a somewhat scrambled but aesthetically productive relationship to film history. Tarantino, Smith, Williamson, and their contemporaries make films that attract the interests of other video store habitues, much as earlier generations of filmmakers—the French New Wave or the American Movie Brats—made movies for other cineastes. Much as the cineaste filmmakers set scenes in movie theatres or made whole movies centering around their protagonist's obsessions with the filmgoing experience, these newer filmmakers frequently cast video store clerks as protagonists (*Clerks, Scream*), celebrating their expertise about genre conventions or their insightful speculations about popular films. This video store aesthetic mixes and matches elements from different genres, different artistic movements, and different periods with absolute abandon. Tarantino's tendency toward quotation runs riot in the famous Jack Flash restaurant sequence in *Pulp Fiction,* where all of the service personnel are impersonating iconic figures of the 1950s and the menu uses different comedy teams to designate different shake flavors. As the John Travolta character explains, "It's like a wax museum with a pulse," a phrase that might describe Tarantino's whole approach to filmmaking. Even his casting decisions, such as the use of *Medium Cool*'s Robert Forster and blaxploitation star Pam Grier in *Jackie Brown,* constitute quotations and appropriations from earlier film classics.

Not surprisingly, the works of these "video store filmmakers" have been deeply influential on the emerging generation of amateur digital filmmakers—almost as influential in fact as *Star Wars* itself. Jeff Allen, a 27-year-old "HTML monkey" for an Atlanta-based Internet company, for example, made *Trooperclerks,* a spoof of the trailer for *Clerks,* which deals with the drab routine confronted by the stormtroopers who work in convenience stores and video rental outlets on board the Death Star. The short spoof, which was immediately embraced and promoted by Kevin Smith's View Askew, was later followed by a half-hour animated film based on the same premise, made in response to the news that *Clerks* was being adapted as an animated network series. Allen's focus on *Clerks* came only after he considered and rejected the thought of doing a *Star Wars* parody based on Tarantino's *Reservoir Dogs.* Similarly, Allen Smith heads a team that is producing a feature-length animated film, *Pulp Phantom,* which offers a scene by scene spoof of *Pulp Fiction,* recast with characters from *Star Wars.* As of late 2002, the team has produced more than ten episodes for the Web, taking the story up to the point where paid assassin Darth Maul races the overdosing Princess Amidala to the home of drug dealer Hans Solo, frantic lest he get into trouble with her jealous gangland husband, Darth Vader. In a particularly inspired bit of casting, Jar Jar Binks plays the geeky college student who, in an installment still in the works, Maul accidentally blows away in the back of Boba Fett's vehicle. "Fan boy" filmmakers like Smith and Tarantino are thus inspiring the efforts of the next generation of amateur filmmakers, who are, in turn, developing cult followings that may ultimately gain them access to the commercial mainstream. The *Pulp Phantom* Web site, for example, includes a mechanism where loyal fans can receive e-mail each time a new installment of the series gets posted.

This cyclical process has only accelerated since the box office success of *The Blair Witch Project,* which presented itself as an amateur digital film (albeit one that got commercial distribution and challenged *Phantom Menace* at the box office in the summer of 1999) and had built public interest through its sophisticated use of the Web. *The Blair Witch Project,* in turn, has inspired countless Web-based amateur parodies (including *The Jar Jar Binks Project* and *The Wicked Witch Project*) and has sparked increased public and industry interest in the search for up-and-coming amateurs who can break into the mainstream, while the bigger budget sequel to *The Blair Witch Project* takes as its central image the explosion of amateur filmmakers who have come to Burkittsville, Maryland, in hopes of making their own documentaries on the mysterious deaths.

## Conclusion

> *I personally find the opportunity to explore this new form of entertainment and creative expression both stimulating and liberating. While much of what we have learned throughout our careers will apply, I am also certain that new and unusual aesthetic values will quickly evolve—shaped by the medium itself, the public and the creative collaborations which this company will encourage.*
> —Ron Howard

> *Just as MTV introduced a new entertainment forum for music videos, we think this new enterprise will offer a new form of entertainment for the rapidly growing population of Internet users. Pop.com has the capability not only to offer a variety of entertainment options, but to tap into an as-yet-undiscovered talent pool that is as global as the Internet itself.*
> —Jeffrey Katzenberg

What is the future of digital cinema? One position sees digital cinema as an extension of avant-garde filmmaking practices, opening a new space for formal experimentation and alternative cultural politics and offering experimental artists access to a broader public than can be attracted to screenings of their works at film festivals, museums, or university classes. Another position, represented by the founders of Pop.com, sees the digital cinema as a potential new site for commercial developments, an extension of the logic of media convergence, a kind of MTV for the twenty-first century. In this vision, established filmmakers, such as Steven Spielberg or Tim Burton, can produce shorter and riskier works, emerging talents can develop their production skills, and works may move fluidly back and forth between the Web, television, film, and computer games. Interestingly, both groups want to tap into the hipness of "DIY" culture, promoting their particular vision of the future of digital cinema in terms of democratic participation and amateur self-expression, pinning their hopes, as Coppola suggests, on the prospect that a "little fat girl" from the midwest will become the Mozart of digital filmmaking. Both visions have inherent limitations: the "low-res" movement's appeals to avant-garde aesthetics, its language of manifestos, and its focus on film festival screenings may well prove as elitist as the earlier film movements it seeks to supplant, while the new commercial version of the digital cinema may re-inscribe the same cultural gatekeepers who have narrowed the potential diversity of network television or Hollywood cinema.

The *Star Wars* fan films discussed here represent a potentially important third space between the two. Shaped by the intersection between contemporary trends toward media convergence and participatory culture, these fan films are hybrid by nature—neither fully commercial nor fully alternative, existing as part of a grassroots dialogue with mass culture. We are witnessing the transformation of amateur film culture from a focus on home movies toward a focus on public movies, from local audiences to a global audience, from mastering the technology to mastering the mechanisms for publicity and promotion, and from self-documentation to an aesthetic based on appropriation, parody, and the dialogic. Coppola's "little fat girl" has found a way to talk back to the dominant media culture, to express herself within a shared language constructed through the powerful images and narratives that constitute contemporary popular culture. She will find ways to tap into the mythology of *Star Wars* and use it as a resource for the production of her own stories, stories that are broadly accessible to a popular audience and, in turn, inspire others to create their own works, as Lucas created *Star Wars* through the clever appropriation and transformation of various popular culture influences (ranging from Laurel and Hardy to *Battleship Yomamoto* and *The Hidden Fortress*).

This third space will survive, however, only if we maintain a vigorous and effective defense of the principle of "fair use," recognize the rights of consumers to participate fully, actively, and creatively within their own culture, and hold in check the desires of the culture industries to tighten their control over their own intellectual property in response to the economic opportunities posed by an era of media convergence. At the moment, we are on a collision course between a new economic and legal culture that encourages monopoly power over cultural mythologies and new technologies that empower consumers to archive, annotate, appropriate, and re-circulate media images. The recent legal disputes around Napster represent only the beginning of what is likely to be a decade long war over intellectual property, a war that will determine not simply the future direction of digital cinema but the nature of creative expression in the twenty-first century.

## Notes

1. Robert McChesney, *Rich Media, Poor Democracy* (Chicago: University of Illinois Press, 1999).

2. Justin Wyatt, *High Concept* (Austin: University of Texas Press, 1995).

3. Marsha Kinder, *Playing with Power in Movies, Television, and Video Games* (Berkeley: University of California Press, 1993).

4. Shoshanna Green, Cynthia Jenkins, and Henry Jenkins, "The Normal Female Interest in Men Bonking," in Cheryl Harris and Alison Alexander (eds.), *Theorizing Fandom* (New York: Hampton, 1998).

5. James H. Gilmore and B. Joseph Pine, *The Experience Economy* (Boston: Harvard Business School, 1999).

6. Will Brooker, "New Hope: The Postmodern Project of *Star Wars,*" in Peter Brooker and Will Brooker (eds.), *Postmodern After-Images* (London: Arnold, 1997). See also Will Brooker, *Using the Force* (London: Continuum, 2002).

7. Paul Clinton, "Filmmakers score with 'Lucas in Love,'" CNN, June 24, 1999, <http://www.cnn.com/SHOWBIZ/Movies/9906/24/movies.lucas.love/>.

8. Tom Gunning, "The Lumière Kinematograph and Amateur Photography Culture: Seizing the Instant," Lecture Presented at MIT Communications Forum, February 25, 1998.

9. Patricia Zimmerman, *Reel Families* (Bloomington: Indiana University Press, 1995), p. 157.

10. Lois Rostow Kuznets, *When Toys Come Alive* (New Haven: Yale University Press, 1994), p. 2.

## *Digital Filmography*

*Alien 5* (Damon Wellner and Sebastian O'Brien), <http://home.earthlink.net/~bsplendor/index.htm>.

*American Booty* (Albert Nerenberg), http://www.trailervision.com/trailerPages/booty_choose.html>.

*Battle of the Bedroom* (Scott Middlebrook), <http://www.geocities.com/Hollywood/Video/6351/botb/botb1.html>.

*Boba Fett: Bounty Trail* (Justin Dix), <http://theforce.net/theater/shortfilms/bountytrail/index.shtml>.

*Dark Redemption* (Warren Duxbury, Peter Mether), <http://theforce.net/theater/shortfilms/darkredemption/index.shtml>.

*Duel* (Mark Thomas and Dave Macomber), <http://theforce.net/theater/shortfilms/duel/index.shtml>.

*George Lucas in Love* (Joe Nussbaum and Joseph Levy), <http://www1.mediatrip.com/per/House_Picks/George_Lucas_In_Love1media.html>.

*Godzilla versus Disco Lando* (Evan Mather), <http://www.evanmather.com>.

*I Know What You Want Next Summer* (Albert Nerenberg), <http://www.trailervision.com/trailerPages/want.htm>.

*The Jar Jar Binks Project* (Albert Nerenberg), <http://www.trailervision.com/trailerPages/jarjar_1.htm>.

*The Jedi Who Loves Me* (Henry Burrows and Adam Ahmad), <http://saturn.spaceports.com/~jedi/>.

*Kid Wars* (Dana Smith), <http://members.xoom.com/ip_president>.

*Kung-Fu Kenobi's Big Adventure* (Evan Mather), <http://www.evanmather.com>.

*Les Pantless Menace* (Evan Mather), <http://www.evanmather.com>.

*MacBeth* (Students of Glen Ridge High School), <http://www.glenridge.org/macbeth/mainpage.htm>.

*Maru* (Adam Dorr, Erik Benson, Hien Nguyen, Jon Jones), <http://theforce.net/theater/shortfilms/maru/index.shtml>.

*The New World* (Clay Kronke), <http://theforce.net/theater/shortfilms/newworld/index.shtml>.

*Park Wars: The Little Menace* (Ted Bracewell, Ayaz A. Asif), <http://www.parkwars.com>.

*Prequel: Revenge of Tall Snaggletooth* (Damon Wellner), <http://home.earthlink.net/~bsplendor/about.htm>.

*Pulp Phantom* (Allen Smith, Dustin Resch, Brian Snook), <http://www.pulpphantom.com>.

*Quenton Tarantino's Star Wars* (Evan Mather), <http:/www.evanmather.com>.

*The Qui-Gon Show* (Robert Fyvolent, Evan Mather, John Stavopoulos, Jason Wishnow), <http://www.evanmather.com>.

*Scam 3* (Albert Nerenberg), <http://www.trailervision.com/trailerPages/scam3.html>.

*Shadows of the Empire* (Jeff Hendricks, Bob Branch), no longer on the Web.

*Star Wars Remake* (Jim Longsma, John Longsma, and Gary Baker), <http://home.earthlink.net/~jimjongsma/StarWarsRemake/Page001.html>.

*Star Wras* (Ceri Llewellyn), <http://www.theforce.net/theater/animation/starwras/index.shtml>.

*Stooge Wars* (Matt Spease), <http://members.xoom.com/Matt_Spease/stoogewars.html>.

*Tatooine or Bust* (Jason Wishnow), <http://www.wishnow.com/production/index.html>.

*Throne Room* (Steve Latham, Ben Latham), <http://homepages.go.com/~lathamfilm/movies.html>.

*Thumb Wars* (Steve Oedekirk), <http://www.thumbtv.com/thumbwars/index.html>.

*Tie-Tantic* (Tri Studio Productions), <http://www.tie_tanic.com>.

*Toy Wars* (Jason VandenBerghe, Aaron Halon), <http://www.toywars.org>.

*Trooper Clerks* (Jeff Allen), <http://www.studiocreations.com/trooperclerks>.

*Trooper Clerks: The Animated One-Shot* (Jeff Allen), <http://www.studiocreations.com/trooperclerks>.

*Troops* (Kevin Rubio), <http://www.theforce.net/troops>.

*When Senators Attack IV* (Ryan Mannion, Daniel Hawley), <http://theforce.net/theater/animation/wsa4/index.shtml>.

*The Wicked Witch Project* (Joe Barlow), <http://www.wickedwitchproject.com>.

*Wimp Club* (Albert Nerenberg), <http://trailervision.com/trailerPages/wimpclub.htm>.

# III  *Visual Culture*

# *19* *Immersion in the Virtual Ornament: Contemporary "Movie Ride" Films*

Constance Balides

---

*The mass ornament is the aesthetic reflex of the rationality to which the prevailing economic system aspires.*
—Siegfried Kracauer, "The Mass Ornament" (1927)

*Think about it, what did you really see? It's all special effects . . . like in the movies.*
—Christine to Nicholas Van Orton, *The Game* (Fincher, 1997)

Computerized special effects are becoming the norm in contemporary Hollywood cinema. These effects are most notable when most spectacular, for example, the running Gallimimus dinosaurs in *Jurassic Park* (Spielberg, 1993), the menacing shadows over Washington D.C. in *Independence Day* (Emmerich, 1996), the fluid morphing in *The Matrix* (Wachowski Brothers, 1999), and the reconstruction of ancient architecture in *Gladiator* (Scott, 2000). Computer graphic images (CGIs) are also used in films for more mundane purposes such as eliminating wires supporting stunt actors, and erasing scratches, shadows, telegraph poles, and sound booms. According to James Cameron, director of *Titanic,* "We're on the threshold of a moment in cinematic history that is unparalleled."[1]

The use of digital technologies is also transforming the identity of cinema. The photographic nature of the cinematic real and the indexical nature of the photographic sign, issues central to contemporary film theory and elaborated in work by André Bazin and by Christian Metz, are less appropriate theoretical points of reference for cinema in a digital age.[2] While the photograph as an indexical sign is linked to its referent in a causal or existential way in the manner of a fingerprint, the computerized image relying on the conventional language of numbers is a symbolic sign, which has an arbitrary relationship to its referent.[3] For a number of media theorists, hybridity is a constitutive feature of computer generated film images, which are photographically realistic even though they are not photographs. The resulting conceptual dilemma, as Lev

Manovich notes, is that digital film images have "perfect photographic credibility, although . . . [they were] never actually filmed." Stephen Prince also points to a paradox in such images due to the fact that they are "referentially unreal" but "perceptually realistic."[4]

Immersion in the spectacle of digital technological effects is a mode of spectatorship associated with these developments. For Peter Lunenfeld, immersion has the status of an operating paradigm in virtual reality, and his suggestive characterization of this investment as "immersion in (synthetic) experience" points to its paradoxical status.[5] CGIs in films are perhaps the most direct cinematic inheritors of Lunenfeld's sense of virtual reality as effecting a real but clearly fabricated experience, and "movie ride" films, a term used in trade periodicals for films that invite spectators to experience the visceral effects of theme park rides, best approximate his sense of investment characterized by immersion. In this paper, I analyze immersion in technological film spectacles associated with "movie ride" effects in films and speculate on the implications of immersion as a cultural logic in contemporary media forms and leisure practices.[6]

In order to delineate the space of spectatorship in the present in a historical manner, I pose two key questions. First, how do immersive strategies enter into public discourse and especially, how has the spectator/consumer of such strategies entered into public debate? My assumption is that the meaning of media forms is not a function of an inherent logic determined by technological characteristics; rather, media forms enter the cultural scene through discourses that make them meaningful in particular ways. Second, what are some broad implications of immersion as a general mode of consumption in relation to changes in the realm of production, especially changes in workers' subjectivity in the contemporary period of post-Fordism? The term, post-Fordism, characterizes shifts in production methods such as flexible specialization (or flexible patterns of production) and economies of scope involving small batch production of a wide variety of products. My general approach, taking an oblique cue from Siegfried Kracauer's analysis of a different period, Taylorism/Fordism, and a different cultural artifact, a synchronized dance troupe performing in Germany in the 1920s, is that the cultural significance of immersive strategies lies in their articulation on an aesthetic level of logics associated with the sphere of production.[7]

## Movie Rides

A specific "sense of immersion" resulting from the "tight linkage between visual, kinesthetic and auditory modalities" in virtual reality discussed by Brenda Laurel extends beyond virtual reality as well as computer graphic images to include a wide range of cultural technologies such as computer games, motion simulator theme park rides, and "movie ride" films.[8] To be sure, there are important differences between immersive experiences, which include varying degrees of sensory intensity and varying levels of imbrication of real spaces with virtual spaces. Contemporary film spectating, for example, involves neither the actual effects of motion on a physical body associated with theme park rides nor the physical interactivity of the user's body in virtual reality;[9] and while the use of head-mounted displays in virtual reality attempts to elide the distinction between real space and virtual space, film viewing retains a sense of the real place of spectating from a seat in a cinema theater or from a sofa in a domestic setting. Mainstream contemporary films, moreover, do not involve an interactive and literal intervention in the development of the story line, which is the case in various projects associated with the Movies of the Future research project at the Media Laboratory at MIT.[10] The increasing popularity of the new trend of reinvigorated 3-D films may change cinematic immersion by effecting a more intense perceptual transformation of the physical position of the spectator.[11] The *immersion effect* in mainstream film now, however, generally works through an imaginary emplacement of the spectator in the world of the film achieved through textual strategies such as the placement of the camera in the literal position of a character (a point of view shot) or one associated with a purported character's view as well as special effects zoom shots created with the use of an optical printer and/or involving computer graphic images suggesting movement inward into the image.

While there are specific ways to characterize immersion as it is associated with different media, the general presence of immersion in these examples supports an argument made by Henry Jenkins that new technologies require models of cultural consumption that take account of a convergence of media forms as distinct from previous models that foreground the specificity of particular mediums.[12] Jenkins, like Manovich, sees this convergence or hybridity as a shift away from a modernist aesthetic concerned with the specificity of a particular medium, an approach that has been important in establishing film as an object in contemporary semiotic and psychoanalytic film theories. The hybrid nature of digital film images, the borrowing of technologies across different media, and an increasing intertextuality between films and computers support the notion of convergence as a dominant media strategy.

The "movie ride" film is the most literal film example of immersive strategies and is also the most explicit example of a convergence between films and theme park rides, a connection that works both ways. Theme park rides borrow film themes, images, and characters but also draw on special effects technologies developed for films and employ personnel working on those effects.[13] The "movie ride" film, for its part, restages the experience of theme park rides through "imperatives of pure sensation" that leave "audiences stagger[ing] back into daylight like passengers unsteadily exiting Coney Island's famous Cyclone."[14] While a version of this kind of film can be traced back to early cinema when cameras were mounted on the fronts of railroad engines, *Star Wars* (Lucas, 1977) is often cited as the originating moment of the "movie ride" film, especially the penultimate scene in which Luke Skywalker navigates his aircraft through a narrow trench in the Empire's battle station of Death Star before blowing it up.[15] This is a scene to which *Independence Day* pays homage and which is endlessly mimicked in children's television programs and advertisements. *Jurassic Park* was noted for its use of CGIs when it was released in 1993 and, along with its sequels, contains a number of "movie ride" scenes, many of which employ CGI effects. A key scene in *Jurassic Park* is a stampede of Gallimimus dinosaurs engulfing Alan Grant, Lex and Tim as they make their way back to the Visitor's Center through the unregulated dinosaur theme park, a scene that was innovative at the time because it tackled the then difficult problem of realistically reproducing blurred motion in the combining of human movement of the characters with computerized movement of the dinosaurs. In the scene, characters along with the spectator via the camera appear to be "inside" this computerized effect. In a later scene, Lex almost falls through a gap in a ceiling tile in the Visitor's Center while Velociraptor dinosaurs are waiting below, and Grant pulls her up and away from danger. In both examples, camera positions enhance the kinesthetic effects of dinosaurs hurtling past or menacing from below.

In *Hackers* (Softley, 1995), a "movie ride" for the spectator is associated with the representation of a hacker's intense relationship to his computer. Joey, a student in a Manhattan high school, tries to demonstrate his proficiency by "hacking a Gibson" at a major corporation in order to gain entry into the Elites, a motley group of student computer experts. Joey's success is represented through a series of accelerated optical and digital zoom shots that propel the spectator into Joey's computer (named Lucy), along a Manhattan city street, past surveillance cameras in the lobby of an office building, down a hallway, past a security control panel at the Ellinson Mineral Corporation, and into the company's mainframe. This movie ride for the spectator is preceded by a shot of Joey looking at his computer screen while a phantasmagoria of algorithms is superimposed on his face, a shot that suggests his own immersed investment as well as a near corporeal effect of his contemplation of computer language as a symbolic sign.

In *The Game* (Fincher, 1997), a psychological thriller about an entertainment company providing fantasy scenarios tailored to the psychological profiles of its clients, everyday life is construed in terms of a theme park logic. The film naturalizes the imbrication of everyday life and simulated reality by eliding the difference between real life and the actual game for its main character, Nicholas Van Orton, and through the use of devices such as point of view shots and restricted knowledge, the spectator experiences the game along with the character.[16] When Van Orton, for example, gets a ride from a cab after his car has broken down, it becomes clear that he has entered another move in the game when the doors are automatically locked, the cab driver abruptly makes his exit, and the vehicle starts to career down a hill toward the San Francisco Bay. Point-of-view shots through the windscreen conflate the spectator's view with Van Orton's view enhancing the spectator's thrill, and the ride, like one in a theme park, culminates in the cab plunging into the water (he escapes). In the film's penultimate scene, physical thrill is implicated in psychic rehearsal when Van Orton jumps from the top of a skyscraper through a glass roof in a suicide attempt only to find that he has unwittingly participated in a special effect in his own game, replete with an inflated cushion to soften his fall. Still alive after his plunge through breaking glass, he has made a spectacular entry into his surprise 48th birthday party, thereby reversing the fate of his father who had committed suicide on the same birthday. Throughout the film, the spectator's knowledge is restricted to that of Van Orton, who never knows when the game has begun, a narrational strategy that produces surprises for the spectator and enhances the "movie ride" effect. Because the marks of the game are erased, moreover, the film represents virtual reality's Ur fantasy of total immersion in a synthetic real.

A visceral sense of immersion is linked to its thematic representation in a number of films. In addition to *Hackers,* with its focus on the relationship between humans and computers, immersion as effect is linked to immersion as theme to describe the relationship between human and human in *Being John Malkovich* (Jonze, 1999), the relationship between personas of the self in *Total Recall* (Verhoeven, 1990), the relationship of humans to history in *The Thirteenth Floor* (Rusnak, 1999), and crucially, the relationship between spectator and screen. In *Hackers,* for example, a character named The Plague, who is the Ellinson Corporation's computer expert, sits in front of a large screened image of the company mainframe as he and a co-worker prepare to trace the hacker. The shots of the men in front of the screen are followed by ones inside the mainframe as the camera careens up and down rectangular shapes that look like skyscrapers and moves along horizontal paths that look like streets. These shots literalize the logic of simulation as an elision of physical reality and virtual worlds by representing computer hardware as a cityscape. The screen of the mainframe, like a film screen, becomes a window on the "world."

The credit sequence in *The Game* also foregrounds the status of immersion as a trope for cinematic spectatorship. The film opens with a series of infinitely receding puzzle pieces that break apart and come out toward the spectator while a digital zoom pulls the spectator's look further into the space of the shot accompanied by the sound of breaking glass.[17] There is a long lineage in U.S. film history of self-reflexive representations of spectatorship invoking the sense of breaking through the cinema screen to recover the real presence in the absent nature of the recorded image (to invoke Metz's analyses of cinema as an "imaginary signifier").[18] Films from *Uncle Josh at the Moving Picture Show* (Edison, 1902) to *The Purple Rose of Cairo* (Allen, 1985) feature characters who step into the film screen and the diegetic world of the film (to varying degrees of success). While the credit sequence in *The Game* appears to rehearse a similar logic of movement into the recorded real, in fact, the film refigures that movement as one toward a virtual real. Erkki Huhtamo describes immersion as a movement from "the immediate physical reality of tangible objects and direct sensory data to *somewhere else*."[19] In *The Game,* the blankness of the puzzle pieces as they tumble outward and the blackness of the interior space toward which the spectator is pulled contribute to the sense of movement toward a non-indexical "somewhere else."

Immersion also often figures in various contemporary media as a way of characterizing the general logic of consumption in a world in which everyday life is mediated through computers. A 1995 cover of a special issue of *Time* magazine entitled, "Welcome to Cyberspace," features a receding image of several blue circuit boards cut open like picture frames. On the left hand side of each frame, the repeated words, "Enter here," enjoin the viewer to enter the image, and the rectangular shapes draw the reader's eye toward a vanishing point marked by a bright white circular dot. This reference to a planet coupled with others that suggest distant stars set against the blue background of the circuit boards invest immersion with the sense of infinity in the association of cyberspace with outer space. The cover from *Time* has intertextual affiliations with the credit sequence in *The Game* as well as a tour through the Orion Nebula and intergalactic space in *Passport to the Universe* (2000), the virtual space show at the Rose Center for Earth and Space, American Museum of Natural History. This blend of advanced entertainment technology and the latest scientific facts ends with a "free fall" movement "headlong through a black hole." A television ad aired during 1999 for Intel Pentium processors harnesses the "somewhere else" of virtuality to commerce by mimicking movement inward into the shot through a tunnel of blue spirals and rectangles until the slogan "inside Pentium processor" is reached. Finally, on *The Tonight Show* (September 30, 1999, NBC), a short feature pictured Jay Leno being sucked into his home computer screen, being transformed into an animated caricature of himself, and then being downloaded by Richard Simmons, sitting in front of his computer. Huhtamo is right to argue that immersion has become a "cultural topos," and it is one that spans different media forms and cultural experiences.[20]

## *Immersed Spectators and Simulation*

Analyzing the implications of immersive strategies in the "movie ride" film and the status of immersion as a trope for spectatorship and consumption in the digital era inevitably involves theoretical assumptions about culture and its consumers. One problematic approach suggests that the uses of technologies are a consequence of their physical characteristics and that technologies evolve in a teleological manner toward the fulfillment of an essential nature (technological determinism). While new media theorists such as Lunenfeld argue instead for modes of analysis that link technological and cultural dimensions through "digital dialectics," technological determinism can still surface like a default position in some discussions. Analyses that suggest a necessary connection between the characteristics of technological forms and their uses and an inevitability in the trajectories of technological development work against more precisely historical assessments of the meanings of technological forms. In early cinema scholarship, for example, studies of the specific nature of exhibition practices, of the particular formal logics of films in particular periods, and of the more general relationship between modernity and early film reception undermine a deterministic view of technologies.[21]

One of the assumptions in this paper is that cultural practices define the meanings of technologies, whose social significance and political consequences are negotiated in public arenas. In order to set the stage for an historical understanding of contemporary strategies of immersion, I turn, initially, to the consumer of such strategies. One context of debate involves a polarized sense of the implications of new media, especially the interactivity of VR and the nonlinear and associative pattern of information retrieval associated with hypertext. On the one hand, a user's ability to shape experience in VR or his/her access to a vastly expanded base of information on the internet is viewed as having an inherently democratizing potential. On the other hand, this interactivity is characterized as a disguised form of hegemony in which choices that appear to be freely made are already circumscribed in ideological and political ways. While a utopianism associated with the former position is problematic because it underestimates the relations of power that circumscribe the parameters of choice, a determinism associated with the later position underestimates the capacity of individuals to use information for their own purposes.

The particular spectator of immersive strategies also enters into public discourse through the back door of a debate in urban and architectural studies about simulated environments epitomized by the theme park. Critics focus both on the negative implications of these places, which are viewed as symptomatic of a decline in the quality of public life, and on their consumers, whose investment in immersion is associated with a lack of critical distance or an inability to negotiate spatial fragmentation in a politically meaningful way. In *The Unreal America: Architecture and Illusion,* for example, Louise Huxtable, former architecture critic for *The New York Times,* assesses the phenomenon of themed environments in which real places are reproduced as simulated versions of themselves, for example, in the reproduction of the original Las Vegas strip, Fremont Street, and in "New York, New York," a hotel and casino complex comprised of a pastiche of famous New York buildings. For Huxtable, "surrogate experience and synthetic settings have become the preferred American way of life."[22] As a consequence, there is a loss of the connoisseurship of original works of art and an erosion of authentic experience. In this argument, the popularity of simulated spaces involves a diminished capacity for critical judgement and a lack of concern to distinguish between simulated and real spaces. An example decried by Huxtable is the equal popularity of the imposing Alamo building made for a film and the smaller and less impressive original Alamo building nearby. To counteract this predisposition toward simulation, Huxtable argues for a return to former cultural logics in which the hierarchy between the original and the reproduction is maintained. She argues, furthermore, that high culture institutions should return to their traditional role as "defenders and keepers of authenticity" in contrast to the masses and to misguided academics who prefer simulation. By contrast, for Walter Benjamin, writing in the 1930s, the technologies of mechanical reproduction such as photography, the phonograph, and cinema embraced by the masses and producing proximity by "enabl[ing] the original to meet the beholder halfway" have a positive effect of shattering the authenticity of the original work of art based on its unique existence. Benjamin aptly makes this point in his famous Artwork Essay: "that which withers in the age of mechanical reproduction is the aura of the work of art." [23] While I am not suggesting that Benjamin's analysis of the implications of proximity associated with mechanical reproduction is directly applicable to technologies of simulation and immersion seventy years later, his essay, which invokes similar terms to those used by Huxtable, is a de facto critique of the presumption that cultural critique should defend the aura of original works of art and that critical distance is the desired mode of consumption.[24]

The more precise question of the logic of spatial relations in simulated environments is taken up by Edward Soja and by Michael Sorkin in their essays in *Variations on a Theme Park*. For Soja, the problem with various simulations in the public spaces of the contemporary exopolis, the city without a center, is that "the disappearance of the real is no longer revealingly concealed." Examples include the University of California campus at Irvine, the city of Costa Mesa and other "scenes from Orange County."[25] For Sorkin, the metropolis, which is associated with modernity, is characterized by an arrangement of geography that involves a clarity of spatial relations, one that also makes social relations legible.[26] This argument assumes a connection between the spatial centeredness of traditional cities such as agoras, piazzas and downtowns and the capacity for public debate engendered by such physical arrangements. In the departicularized contemporary city, by contrast, the lack of a city center along with the fragmentation associated with suburbanization suggest the absence of a sense of place, one that is epitomized by the theme park. For Sorkin, these new spatial arrangements militate against a democratic public realm.[27] While Soja and Sorkin rightly point to the imbrication of real and simulated phenomena in themed places and to a different spatial organization in contemporary cities, they also problematically assume, as does Huxtable, a phenomenological naïveté on the part of the spectator/consumer/citizen.

### Literate Consumers and the Synthetic Real

These assessments produce a critical bind. On the one hand, high cultural models of distinction valorizing critical distance (Huxtable) and critical approaches presuming a clarity with regard to social relations in previous historical periods (Sorkin) keep cultural criticism tied to a past moment by which the commercialism and simulation of the present day will always be wanting. On the other hand, defending the commercialism and simulation of cultural artifacts and practices simply because they are popular inadequately presumes that their popularity is itself the mark of a democratizing potential. Another way of approaching the implications of immersion as a cultural logic is to acknowledge something like a literacy on the part of consumers and spectators when they participate in immersive and simulated environments. In the case of films, one site of literacy is the intertextual reception context that is now part of the way films circulate. Manovich, for example, points to a "new minigenre" of television programs and videos about how special effects are created in the "The Making of . . ." logic of programming.[28] Such texts contribute to the expanding availability of information on the production of special effects for consumers who know how simulated environments are made. More generally, consumer literacy is produced through various kinds of subcultural knowledge of contemporary popular forms. For example, *Jurassic Park*'s status as a "synthetic reality" is supported by a dense network of secondary texts, including articles on how special effects were achieved in popular news magazines such as *Newsweek* and *Time;* periodicals such as *Cinefantastique* geared to specialist film interest groups; a television program such as the "Making of Jurassic Park" for PBS; references to the film in talk shows and cable channels; museum displays that linked the making of the film with educational projects; promotional publicity directly related to the film; a book entitled *The Making of Jurassic Park,* which was on the *New York Times*'s best seller list; and access to information about the film on the Internet as well as chat rooms and subcultural interest groups.[29] While cinephilia in the 1960s was associated with auteur criticism and the New York literati, an important strand in contemporary cinephilia is the amateur's interest in technical detail, and especially the film officiando's gaze at special effects technologies. To be sure, an increased access to such information reinforces the specialized market niching (or segmenting of highly differentiated market groups) that characterizes contemporary consumption in a capitalist post-Fordist economy. But it also makes it hard to be a naive spectator.

The spectator's literacy is also enhanced by the curious status of the digital image, which as already noted, does not share the photograph's indexical relationship to reality. One example is the phenomenon of "synthespians," a copyrighted term by Kleiser-Walczak Co. referring to computer generated characters that replicate dead film and television actors, for example, Fred Astaire and Humphrey Bogart.[30] Other examples are the presence of extinct but moving dinosaurs and combining twentieth-century people with CGIs of prehistoric dinosaurs in *Jurassic Park*. To be sure, many special effects (for example, Dorothy whirling in the tornado in *The Wizard of Oz* [Fleming, 1939]) are apparent as effects, that is, as spectacular images which are the product of extraordinary technical interventions. In the cases, however, of synthespians, which involve moving images of known to be dead actors, or of dinosaurs, which never could have been photographed, the purported reality to which special effects refer is replaced by an explicit absence of an authenticating original. The status of these digital shots as technical effects is more pronounced, and because digital images do not have an obligation to reality in the manner of a photograph, they do not invite the kind of "credulity" associated with the photograph as an indexical sign.

Digital effects challenge the connection between proximity as an aesthetic strategy and naïveté as a spectatorial response due to densely intertextual reception contexts through which knowledge about effects is disseminated and as a result of their status as hybrid signs foregrounding convention. Spatial dislocation, moreover, in the built environment or in cultural forms like "movie ride" films are not equateable with an inability to comprehend or to negotiate them. In the last section of this paper, I extend a notion of literacy beyond a sense of subcultural knowledges and pursue the question of spatial and temporal dislocation in contemporary "movie ride" films in the direction of Kracauer's sense of mass leisure practices as "signs" of their prevailing economic system.

### Mass Ornament / Virtual Ornament

In "The Mass Ornament," Kracauer looks to the phenomenon of body culture, especially the Tiller Girls with their synchronized movements, and gymnastic stadium displays with their "geometric precision" as "inconspicuous surface-level expressions" of the "fundamental substance of the state of things" in an epoch of capitalism associated with the Taylor system.[31] The Taylorism to which Kracauer refers was a time-management approach to work practices stressing efficient use of the body through detailed attention to segmented gestures, an approach associated with the economic regime of Fordism with its regularization of moving assembly lines in the manufacture of Henry Ford's Model T cars in the 1910s. The "inconspicuous" nature of the mass ornaments to which Kracauer refers derives in part from the fact that they are dismissed by the "intellectually privileged," who take "offense" at them and who "judge anything that entertains the crowd to be a distraction of that crowd." These critics are less in touch with the conditions of reality than the mass audience who has "so spontaneously adopted these patterns."[32] More precisely, Kracauer argues that:

> The *aesthetic* pleasure gained from ornamental mass movements is *legitimate*. . . . The masses organized in these movements come from offices and factories; the formal principle according to which they are molded determines them in reality as well. . . . No matter

> how low one gauges the value of the mass ornament, its degree of reality is still higher than that of artistic productions which cultivate outdated noble sentiments in obsolete forms— even if it means nothing more than that.[33]

The legitimacy of the pleasure in the ornamental mass movements to which Kracauer refers derives, in part, from a homology between their formal organization and the conditions shaping the lives of the masses organized by the spectacles ("the formal principle according to which they are molded determines them in reality as well"). The mechanical and geometric patterns produced by the Tiller Girls and stadium displays draw on a logic of rationalization and fragmentation of bodies associated with the experience of work under Taylorism ("the hands in the factory correspond to the legs of the Tiller Girls"). A self-perpetuating and inward logic in these spectacles, which have "no meaning beyond themselves" but are geared simply to "produc[ing] an immense number of parallel lines," also points to the abstract rationality of the capitalist economic system, which evacuates human needs and treats the end point of production as profit and business expansion ("the ornament is an *end in itself*"). In this way, the mass ornament is an "aesthetic reflex of the rationality to which the prevailing economic system aspires."[34] Kracauer is not arguing that the Tiller troupe is therefore a progressive phenomenon or that the masses have a critical purchase on the meaning of the spectacles to which they are drawn. In fact, he explicitly points out that "although the masses give rise to the ornament, they are not involved in thinking it through." The fact of their interest, however, suggests an inchoate response that "at least roughly acknowledges the undisguised facts."[35]

This analysis suggests a way of beginning to understand the cultural significance of what I am calling the virtual ornament or virtual technological spectacles associated with a "movie ride" logic. These spectacles and simulated spaces occupy the domain of the quotidian to which Kracauer devoted his attention, and they are similarly dismissed and misunderstood by critics who defend high cultural forms in a way that "cultivates outdated noble sentiments in obsolete forms." While the philosophical terms of analysis and import of Kracauer's essay go well beyond an identification of parallel structures,[36] I want to start at the point of Kracauer's sense of the connection between the aesthetic level and the productive sphere to suggest a contemporary homology, one that draws on arguments about the specific articulation of capitalism in the contemporary period, especially the differences between Fordism and post-Fordism.[37]

Fordism is generally characterized in terms of a logic of massification in the realm of production, a result of the use of massive industrial machinery, economies of scale in which profit is linked to large numbers of units produced, and the amassing of large bodies of workers in factories as well as standardized mass consumption. Eric Alliez and Michel Feher in "The Luster of Capital" elaborate on this sense of massification and argue that it included an investment in the control over space expressed through "spatial order" and the compartmentalizing of space, for example, in the Fordist factory surrounded by a gate. By contrast in neo-Fordism (the term used in the translation of their article), there is a "blurring of boundaries" of various kinds, for example, between spaces of production and reproduction, between work and leisure, and between person and machine. The dispersal of computers in the home (intensified since the writing of their article with the extensive use of laptop computers) contributes to a temporal and spatial decentralization of work involving the overflow of the workday beyond delimited time periods, which elides the distinction between work and leisure, and the diffusion of the workplace beyond the factory, which erodes the line between home and work.

The kinesthetic effect of "movie ride" scenes can be discussed in relation to this analysis. As distinct from a logic of spatial order, in the virtual ornament there is a blurring of spatial and temporal boundaries expressed in terms of speed (the accelerated movie ride into the computer and through multiple locations in *Hackers*) and in the movement toward indeterminate space (digital space as outer space on the cover of *Time* and in the opening of *The Game*). More generally, the virtual ornament is characterized by a logic of merging. Person merges with the digital image (synthespians, characters in the same scene with dinosaurs in *Jurassic Park*); a loss of identity is effected through an over-identification with technology (VR, *Hackers*); and the spectator's identification with the camera in "movie ride" scenes involves an emplacement in a virtual world (the opening sequence in *The Game;* the use of CGIs in *Jurassic Park*).

Alliez and Feher also assess the difference between Fordism and post-Fordism in terms of workers' subjectivity and the way capital is represented. Fordism involves a sense of "subjection" of the worker related to massification (for example, the worker dwarfed by massive equipment in the Fordist factory or unable to keep up with the moving assembly line). A key factor in the neo-Fordist computerized workplace is the emergence of data processing with the effect that workers and machines are equivalent as "relays" in electronic circuits of information. The broader implication of the shift concerns a mode of workers' subjectivity characterized by incorporation. While spatial order expressed in the "crossing of boundaries" through the Fordist factory gate instantiated a "subjection to capital," in neo-Fordism, the blurring of spatial boundaries contributes to an effect in which "individuals are less subject to than incorporated by capital." The appropriation of time as productive is more central and workers are "led to feel 'responsible' since the profitability of the business . . . is considered to be in the interests of both owners and wage earners alike." Massification as a way of representing capital is replaced by its image as spectacular, ephemeral, and intangible. Developments such as the processing of data as opposed to concrete raw material, the electronic movement of information and money, and the "glitter of telematics" associated with computers in the home suggest this desubstantialized image of capital.[38] For Alliez and Feher, neo-Fordist workers are more intimately bound up with capitalists' interests and are incorporated into an image of "the luster of capital."

There are direct references to these developments in the films discussed in this paper. The equivalence between worker and machine is expressed in *Hackers* in Joey's relationship to Lucy, his computer, and the representation of capital as ephemeral is suggested in the image of The Plague seated in front of the mainframe as a virtual technological spectacle and in the mise-en-scène of algorithms in Joey's contemplation of hacker success. These examples also point to a general principle of organization in the virtual ornament. In the mass ornament, the loss of integrity of individual elements involves their reduction to "mere building blocks and nothing more," making individuals participating in the mass ornament "fractions of a figure" as opposed to "individuals who believe themselves to be formed from within."[39] In the virtual ornament, rationalization involves a substitution of individual terms, frequently expressed as an exchange of equivalent realities. Virtual space becomes a cityscape (*Hackers*), virtual history becomes archaeology (*Jurassic Park*), and the virtual person stands in for a human being (synthespians).[40]

My point is that an incorporative mode of worker subjectivity in post-Fordism finds a homologous logic in immersion in the virtual ornament. This mode of immersion characterizes both the representation of spectatorship in contemporary media and formal strategies drawing spectators into the diegetic worlds of "movie ride" films. When these worlds are virtual, they suggest an investment not only in a synthetic reality but in an ephemeral spectacle.

In recent work, there is an impulse to find historical precedents for new media technologies. The connection between "movie ride" films and post-Fordism, however, suggests there should be more hesitation in drawing long historical continuities between commercial entertainments of different eras. Huhtamo, for example, argues that nineteenth-century lantern shows and early films that feature a camera mounted on the front of a train to approximate a purported spectator's viewpoint (phantom rides) are precursors to contemporary immersive strategies in Cinerama and Imax. From the perspective of relating aesthetic and productive realms, this logic makes phantom rides too familiar and movie rides not historical enough. Alliez and Feher's characterization of neo-Fordism, moreover, suggestively resonates with Charles Baudelaire's characterization of nineteenth century modernity as ephemeral.[41] If one takes the point, however, that incorporation into "the luster of capital" invokes a particular organization of capitalist production then similar experiences will have different implications in vastly different historical periods. Finally, the suggestion in this paper is that the popularity of the virtual ornament relates to an oblique recognition on the part of contemporary audiences of the changes that affect them in work and everyday life in a post-Fordist economy. As opposed to critics who turn away from immersion and simulation, cultural criticism should acknowledge the popularity of virtual ornaments as an index of their more substantial cultural meaning.

## Acknowledgments

Versions of this paper were given as talks at the "Media-in-Transition" Conference, MIT, Cambridge, Massachusetts, October 1999, and at the "Moving Images: Technologies, Transitions, Historiographies" conference, Stockholm University, Stockholm, Sweden, December 2000.

## Notes

1. Cameron is quoted in Paula Parisi, "The New Hollywood Silicon Star," *Wired* (December 1995): 144. Paul Karon in *Variety* echoes a similarly apocalyptic view: "The digital effects revolution is the most profound change to hit the film industry since the movie camera: it's a completely new way of getting images onto celluloid." See Paul Karon, "H'wood Dreads Tech Wreck: Summer Pix Stalled by F/X Costs, Glitches," *Variety* (April 6–12, 1998): 1–2. On computer generated insects, see Ellen Wolff, "Insect Armies lead Global Animation Revolution," *Kemps* (Supplement to *Variety*) (December 21–27, 1998): 16–17. On the effects in *Independence Day*, see Ron Magrid, "The End of the World As We Know It: Traditional Models and Miniatures Are Mixed with Digital Wizardry to Tell *Independence Day's* Tale of Alien Aggression," *Variety* 77, no. 7 (July 1996): 43–49 and Rex Weiner, "'ID4' F/X hit the road: Mobile 'Mother Ship' Runs 'Independence Day' Post-Production," *Variety* (June 17–23, 1996): 48. On digital film repair work, see Bob Fisher, "'Digital Cinematography:' A Phrase of the Future?" (part 1) *American Cinematographer* 74, no. 4 (April 1993): 50–53 and Bob Fisher, "'Digital Cinematography': A Phrase of the Future?" (part 2) *American Cinematographer* 74, no. 5 (May 1993): 31–32. On the ways in which computer generated images are replacing special effects techniques associated with optical processes, matte paintings and miniatures, see Ron

Magrid, "CGI Spearheads Brave New World of Special Effects: Okay, CGI Leads the Revolution. Where Will It Lead?" *American Cinematographer* (December 1993): 26–27, 28, 30, and 32. Other useful articles on computer special effects in films include Christopher Probst, "Future Shock: Director James Cameron and Director of Photography Russell Carpenter, AZC Are Joined by a team of Experts to Tap the Third Dimension in *Terminator 2* 3-D," *American Cinematographer* 77, no. 8 (August 1996): 38–42; Ron Magi, "Digitizing the Third Dimension: Digital Domain Assaults Audiences with an Array of 3-D Effects Methods," *American Cinematographer* 77, no. 8 (August 1996): 45–46, 48–49; and Bob Fisher, "Meteor Man Gets His Digital Wings: Digital Special Effects Take Another Step Towards Fulfilling Their Vast Potential, in Service of a Goofy Superego with a Message," *American Cinematographer* 74, no. 4 (April 1993): 42–44, and 46.

2. See André Bazin, *What Is Cinema?* 1, trans. Hugh Gray (Berkeley: University of California Press, 1967), and Christian Metz, "The Imaginary Signifier," in *Narrative, Apparatus, Ideology: A Film Theory Reader,* ed. Philip Rosen (New York: Columbia University Press, 1986), 244–278 (excerpt) and Christian Metz, *Psychoanalysis and Cinema: The Imaginary Signifier,* trans. Celia Britton, Annwyl Williams, Ben Brewster and Alfred Guzzetti (London: Macmillan Press, 1983).

3. Often cited examples of indexical signs are a weathervane, which points in the direction caused by the wind pushing it, or a fingerprint (Bazin's famous image for cinema), which is a sign that points to a person who once was the source of the print. Photographs are indexical signs in the sense that the film stock with its light sensitive emulsion coating registers the presence of real objects or people who were once literally in the scene and who blocked sections of light going into the camera lens thereby producing negative images that are later developed into positive images. Digital computer images, by contrast, are symbolic signs whose relationship to their referents is conventional not causal involving the numerical language of a binary code based on the symbols or digits of 0 and 1. Computer images as a digital medium, moreover, also involve a numerical translation or conversion of information stored as "formal relationships in abstract structures" (Binkley, 96) as opposed to the analogue medium of photography, which involves a transcription of information from one physical arrangement of material to another analogous arrangement. See Timothy Binkley, "Refiguring Culture," in *Future Visions: New Technologies of the Screen,* ed. Philip Hayward and Tana Wollen (London: British Film Institute, 1993) and Tony Feldman, *Introduction to Digital Media* (London: Routledge, 1997). For a useful discussion of iconic, indexical, and symbolic signs as they were initially theorized by Charles Sanders Peirce and as they pertain to a cinema semiotics before the digital divide, see Kaja Silverman, *The Subject of Semiotics* (New York: Oxford University Press, 1983), 14–25.

4. Lev Manovich, "What Is Digital Cinema?" in *The Digital Dialectic: New Essays on New Media,* ed. Peter Lunenfeld (Cambridge, MA: MIT Press, 1999), 175, and Stephen Prince, "True Lies: Perceptual Realism, Digital Images, and Film Theory," *Film Quarterly* 49, no. 3 (Spring 1996): 35. Also see Lev Manovich, "The Paradoxes of Digital Photography" in *Photography after*

*Photography: Memory and Representation in the Digital Age,* ed. Hubertus V. Amelunxen, Stefan Iglhaut, and Florian Rötzer in collaboration with Alexis Cassel and Nikolaus G. Schneider (New York: Gordon and Breach Arts, 1996), 57–67.

5. Peter Lunenfeld, "Digital Dialectics: A Hybrid Theory of Computer Media," *Afterimage* (November 1993): 5. In this essay, Lunenfeld identifies two key paradigms of the new computer media, namely, immersion associated with virtual reality and extraction associated with hypertext. Also see Peter Lunenfeld, "Introduction—Screen Grabs: The Digital Dialectic and New Media Theory," in *The Digital Dialectic: New Essays on New Media,* ed. Peter Lunenfeld (Cambridge, MA: MIT Press), xiv–xxi. In this introduction, Lunenfeld stresses the implication of a digital dialectic in the fact that "it grounds the insights of theory in the constraints of practice" (xix).

6. In part, because of the broad sense of the implication of immersion in contemporary films in this paper, I extend the category of "movie ride" films to include not only blockbuster special effects films that are more commonly associated with the category, such as *Jurassic Park,* but also films from other genres such as psychological thrillers that include scenes employing these effects and/or that thematize the issue of immersion in terms similar to the logic of "movie ride" films, such as *The Game.*

7. Siegfried Kracauer, "The Mass Ornament," in *The Mass Ornament: Weimar Essays,* ed. and trans. Thomas Y. Levin (Cambridge, MA: Harvard University Press, 1995), 75–86. This essay is one of almost two thousand articles Kracauer wrote for the daily newspaper *Die Frankfurter Zeitung* during the 1920s and 1930s. These early writings represent a philosophical and sociological form of cultural criticism, and as Thomas Y. Levin points out, *Die Frankfurter Zeitung* was known for its feuilleton journalism associated with "substantive sociocritical reflection" (4). See Thomas Y. Levin, "Introduction," in Siegfried Kracauer, *The Mass Ornament: Weimar Essays,* trans. and ed. Thomas Y. Levin (Cambridge, MA: Harvard University Press, 1995), 1–30.

8. Brenda Laurel is quoted by Lunenfeld in "Digital Dialectics," 6.

9. Of course there is a history of experiments with more visceral forms of spectating including 3-D films during the 1950s and their reincarnation in the contemporary period.

10. See Frank Beacham, "Digital Artists: Reinventing Electronic Media: MIT Media Lab Symposium Looks to the Future of Entertainment and Expression," *American Cinematographer* 76, no. 3 (March 1995): 59–61, and Frank Beacham, "Movies of the Future: Storytelling with Computers," *American Cinematographer* 76, no. 4 (April 1995): 36–44, 46, 47–48.

11. The *New York Times* heralds 3-D films as the latest major development in filmmaking. See Matthew Gurewitsch, "The Next Wave? 3-D Could Bring on a Sea Change," *New York Times* (January 2, 2000): 11, 28.

12. Henry Jenkins, "Comparative Media: An Emerging Discipline," Introductory Session, "Media-in-Transition" Conference, MIT, Cambridge, Massachusetts, October 8–10, 1999.

13. There was a planned theme park in Osaka using the animated T-Rex from the film and "Jurassic Park: The Ride" opened at Universal Studios, Hollywood, a water ride that takes a raft through a jungle filled with dinosaurs and ends with the raft going down a steep eight story slide. "Jurassic Park: The Ride" is one of several film based rides at Universal. There are others at Disneyland, Universal Studios in Florida, and Six Flags America. These rides point to a general shift in the theme park industry from "real-estate intensive rides" to "electronic or special-effects intensive entertainment," which means that rides also now draw more directly on "movie ride" sequences in films. See Ray Bennett, "Theme Parks Fix on F/X from Pix," *Variety* (June 14, 1993): 10.

14. Bruce Handy, "Hold on to Your Popcorn," *Vogue* (June 1993): 76.

15. On the importance of *Star Wars* as the first instance of the "movie ride" film, see Handy, "Hold on to Your Popcorn."

16. For a useful discussion of restricted knowledge as a narrational strategy in which spectator's knowledge is limited to character's knowledge as distinct from an overall omniscient understanding of plot events, see David Bordwell, "Classical Hollywood Cinema: Narrational Principles and Procedures," in *Narrative, Apparatus, Ideology: A Film Theory Reader,* ed. Philip Rosen (New York: Columbia University Press, 1986), 17–34.

17. Erkki Huhtamo's description of a trend of such shots in films nicely portrays this opening credit scene in *The Game,* namely, there is a "proliferation of 'subjective' steady-cam shots, computer-generated 'virtual zooms' and 'ride' sequences along the depth axis of the image—often combined with their 'counter-tropes,' objects 'flying' *towards* the spectator," giving a "sensation of plunging through the screen into the diegetic world of the film." See Erkki Huhtamo, "Encapsulated Bodies in Motion: Simulators and the Quest for Total Immersion," in *Critical Issues in Electronic Media,* ed. Simon Penny (Albany: State University of New York, 1995), 160. On this point Huhtamo draws on and quotes from a conference paper delivered by Margaret Morse entitled "Television Graphics and the Body: Words on the Move" (Society for Cinema Studies, Montreal, 1987), in which she characterizes a new language of cinema that is similarly appropriate to *The Game.* She notes that "'the spectator is out of balance, grabbing his/her fellow spectator in fear. The camera has to absorb him/her all the time. This is a novelty'" (160).

18. Christian Metz's sense of the cinema as "an imaginary signifier" develops from an assessment of a paradox in the film image over the fact that it involves a presence and an absence. The full perceptual presence of the film image for the spectator stems from the fact that it employs various sensory registers and its absent quality comes from the fact that it is a recorded image, one whose represented reality is not physically there. See Metz, "The Imaginary Signifier."

19. Huhtamo, "Encapsulated Bodies in Motion," 159.

20. Huhtamo, "Encapsulated Bodies in Motion," 160. Also see *Time* 145, no. 12, (special issue, spring 1995). According to the Web page for the new Hayden Planetarium, Rose Center for

Earth and Space, American Museum of Natural History, this show is produced by "the largest and most powerful virtual reality simulator in the world, one that is matched only by the supercomputers used by the National Aeronautics and Space Administration or the largest of military research facilities." *Passport to the Universe* (Executive Producer, American Museum of Natural History in conjunction with Batwin and Robins Productions) premiered at the Rose Center on February 19, 2000 and is narrated by Tom Hanks. For the quote about the show, further details and a brief clip, see <http:/amnh.org/rose>.

21. For critiques of technological determinism in film studies see Steve Neale, *Cinema and Technology: Image, Sound, Colour* (London: British Film Institute, 1985), and Robert C. Allen and Douglas Gomery, *Film History: Theory and Practice* (Boston: McGraw-Hill, Inc., 1985), especially 109–128. For work in early cinema that points to specific exhibition practices, see Charles Musser, *The Emergence of Cinema: The American Screen to 1907* (New York: Charles Scribner's Sons, 1990); on the specificity of the early period, see Tom Gunning, "The Cinema of Attraction: Early Film, Its Spectator and the Avant-Garde," *Wide Angle* 8, nos. 3/4 (1986): 63–70, and David Bordwell, Janet Staiger, and Kristin Thompson, *The Classical Hollywood Cinema: Film Style and Mode of Production to 1960* (New York: Columbia University Press, 1985); and on the relationship between cinema and modernity, see Tom Gunning, "An Aesthetic of Astonishment: Early Film and the (In)credulous Spectator," *Art and Text* 34 (1989): 31–45, and Miriam Hansen, *Babel and Babylon: Spectatorship in American Silent Film* (Cambridge, MA: Harvard University Press, 1991).

22. Ada Louise Huxtable, "Living with the Fake, and Liking It," *New York Times* (March 30, 1997), sec. 2, 1. Huxtable's article is an excerpted chapter from her book, *The Unreal America: Architecture and Illusion* (New York: The New Press, 1997).

23. Walter Benjamin, "The Work of Art in the Age of Mechanical Reproduction," in *Illuminations: Essays and Reflections,* ed. Hannah Arendt, trans. Harry Zohn (New York: Schocken Books, 1969), 220, 221.

24. Benjamin reconsiders the implications of aura in Walter Benjamin, *Charles Baudelaire: A Lyric Poet in the Era of High Capitalism,* trans. Harry Zohn (London: New Left Books, 1973).

25. Edward Soja, "Inside Exopolis: Scenes from Orange County," in *Variations on a Theme Park: The New American City and the End of Public Space,* ed. Michael Sorkin (New York: The Noonday Press, 1992), 121.

26. Michael Sorkin, "Introduction: Variations on a Theme Park," in *Variations on a Theme Park: The New American City and the End of Public Space,* ed. Michael Sorkin (New York: The Noonday Press, 1992). The film *Metropolis* (Lang, 1926), in which there is an underground city of workers who provide the infrastructure for the above-the-ground city of the bourgeoisie, is an example of the spatial clarity Sorkin describes.

27. As both Rosalyn Deutsche and Nancy Fraser suggest, however, nostalgic constructions of past public spheres are problematic because they mask the exclusions of social groups,

including women, in those spheres. See Deutsche in "Agoraphobia," in Rosalyn Deutsche, *Evictions: Art and Spatial Politics* (Cambridge, MA, 1996), 269–327; and Nancy Fraser in "Rethinking the Public Sphere: A Contribution to the Critique of Actually Existing Democracy," in *The Phantom Public Sphere,* ed. Bruce Robbins for the Social Text Collective (Minneapolis: University of Minnesota Press, 1993), 1–32.

28.  Manovich, "What Is Digital Cinema," 178.

29.  There are a large number of Web sites on the films in the *"Jurassic Park* trilogy" on scientific issues suggested by the films, mailboxes where fans can discuss the films, etc. For example, <http://www.jurassicpark.com> is the Universal Studio Web site that includes a message board for viewer comments, and <www.geocities.com> also has a chat room; <http://www.paleo.de> features the jurassic reef park and includes scientific information on underwater reefs; <http://www.hometown.aol.com> has a study guide for a science class on the issues raised by *Jurassic Park;* <www.math.rice.edu> talks about *Jurassic Park* and fractals; <http://www.dinosaur.org> looks at the science and "non-science" of the films; and <www.sdnhm.org> gives information on frequently asked questions about the science of *Jurassic Park* and is sponsored by the San Diego Natural History Museum of Paleontology; finally, <http://www.bigwaste.com> is place where viewers can talk about the factual mistakes in the films.

30.  See Katherine Stalter, "Mirage Making Magic: Firm's Synthespians Searching for a Niche in L. A.," *Variety* (January 20–26, 1997): 43; Katherine Stalter and Ted Johnson, "H'wood Cyber Dweebs Are Raising the Dead," *Variety* (November 4–10, 1996): 1, 103; Chris Jones, "Who Owns Your Face?" *Sight and Sound* 6, no. 3 (March 1996): 33; and Kirby Carmichael, "Beyond *Jurassic Park,*" *Popular Mechanics* (March 1994): 35–37. There are interesting legal and insurance issues regarding ownership of such images. As of 1996, there were various lawsuits over the necessity of obtaining permission from the estates of deceased stars. Statler and Johnson also speculate on whether film insurance companies will make performers have themselves digitally scanned in the event of their death during the filming of a project, an issue raised by the death of Brandon Lee during the filming of *The Crow.*

31.  Kracauer, "The Mass Ornament," 75.

32.  Ibid., 79, 85.

33.  Ibid., 79.

34.  Ibid., 76, 78 and 79.

35.  Ibid., 77, 85.

36.  Kracauer pursues the homology between the Tiller Girls and stadium displays and Taylorism in a way that illuminates the paradoxical status of the mass ornament. In "The Mass Ornament," he characterizes the abstract rationality of capitalism as a "murky reason" because it does not take account of human needs: "*It does not encompass man*" (Kracauer, 81). He

contrasts this to a sense of reason that is more progressive because it has a potential to liberate mankind from the forces of nature. The mass ornament in its thorough-going rationalization of individuals exposes this difference between capitalist "*Ratio*" and reason. Kracauer ends his essay by suggesting that the form of reason that would take account of man is to be found in a process that does not turn away from the mass ornament, but in one that "leads directly through the center of the mass ornament" (Kracauer, 86).

Kracauer's work has been undergoing a significant revision in film studies where he was formerly characterized problematically as a naive realist. For recent work that illuminates the philosophical underpinnings and historical specificity of Kracauer's writings and the shifts in his thinking during the mid-1920s that inform "The Mass Ornament" essay, see Thomas Y. Levin, "Introduction," in *The Mass Ornament;* Miriam Bratu Hansen, "America, Paris, the Alps: Kracauer (and Benjamin) on Cinema and Modernity," in *Cinema and the Invention of Modern Life,* ed. Leo Charney and Vanessa R. Schwartz (Berkeley: University of California Press, 1995), 362–402; and Gertrud Koch, *Siegfried Kracauer: An Introduction,* trans. Jeremy Gaines (Princeton: Princeton University Press, 2000). For my purpose in this paper, Kracauer's identification of a homology suggests a way of understanding the popularity of an entertainment form that does not reduce it to an expression of bad faith on the part of the audience. Moreover, in the context of a tendency in contemporary criticism to divorce the realm of consumption from the realm of production, Kracauer's identification of such homologies is both striking and salutary.

37.  Among economists, urban planners, and cultural theorists on the left, there is a debate over the extent of continuity between the capitalist economic regime characterizing the present era of post-Fordism and Fordism. David Harvey, for example, uses the term "flexible accumulation" rather than post-Fordism to characterize a new "regime of accumulation" and modes of social regulation since 1973, but he argues that they also exhibit continuities with Fordism. For Alliez and Feher, as I discuss below, the contemporary period is marked by a rupture with Fordism. In the translation of Alliez and Feher's essay, the term "neo-Fordism" is used. In this paper, when I refer to their argument I use the term "neo-Fordism;" however, when I refer to debates more generally, I use the more commonly used term of post-Fordism. See David Harvey, *The Condition of Postmodernity* (Cambridge, MA: Blackwell Publishers, 1990), and Eric Alliez and Michel Feher, "The Luster of Capital," trans. Alyson Waters, *Zone* 1 and 2 (1987): 315–359. I also draw on Alliez and Feher's analysis in an extended discussion of the imbricated relationship between post-Fordist economics and the representation of economics in *Jurassic Park.* See Constance Balides, "Jurassic Post-Fordism: Tall Tales of Economics in the Theme Park," *Screen* 41.2 (Summer 2000): 139–160. For other useful discussions of post-Fordism, see Robin Murray, "Life After Henry (Ford)," *Marxism Today* (October 1988), and Stuart Hall and Martin Jacques, eds., *New Times: The Changing Face of Politics in the 1910s* (London: Verso, 1990). On the left, post-Fordist does not mean post-capitalist. For a problematic conservative assessment of "post-Fordist" developments in the context of an argument

that capitalism has been superseded, see Peter F. Drucker, in *Post-Capitalist Society* (New York: Harper Business, 1994).

38. Alliez and Feher, "The Luster of Capital," 347, 339, 446.

39. Kracauer, "The Mass Ornament," 76.

40. Two recently released films are even better examples of this last point, *Lara-Croft—Tomb Raider,* (Simon West, 2001) in which a human actress plays a computer game heroine, and *Final Fantasy* (Sakaguchi, 2001) which features digital characters and scenery.

41. See Charles Baudelaire, *The Painter of Modern Life and Other Essays,* ed. and trans. Jonathan Mayne (London: Phaidon Press, 1964).

# 20 *The Virtual Window*

Anne Friedberg

**The Virtual Window**

*Just as water, gas, and electricity are brought into our houses from far off to satisfy our needs in response to a minimal effort,* **so we shall be supplied with visual and auditory images,** *which will appear and disappear at the simple movement of the hand, hardly more than a sign. . . . I don't know if a philosopher has ever dreamed of a company engaged in the home delivery of Sensory Reality.*[1]
—Paul Valéry "The Conquest of Ubiquity" 1928

Paul Valéry's forecast is a stunning augury of contemporary telecommunications: images and sounds are a utility, delivering "sensory reality" to the home at "the simple movement of the hand." As the twentieth century ended, new systems of circulation and transmission began to replace the projection screen, and to link the screens of the computer and television with the dialogic interactivity of the telephone. This paper—part of a larger project called *The Virtual Window: A Cultural History of Windows and Screens*—is, in many ways, both pre-quel and sequel to my book *Window Shopping*. It means to expand an account of the emergence of a mobilized and virtual visuality backward, in a thicker history of the framed visuality of the window, and forward, to the window's ever more virtual functions.[2] Along the way, we will reconsider a history of what used to be called "spectatorship": because, I will argue, the very term "spectatorship" has lost its theoretical pinions, as screens have changed, as has our relation to them.[3]

Here, I consider the screen—the film screen, the TV screen, the computer screen—as a component piece of architecture, a "virtual window" which renders the wall permeable to light and "ventilation" and which has dramatically changed the materiality (and—perhaps more-radically—the temporality) of built space. The window has a deep cultural history as a figurative trope for the framing and mediating of the pictorial image. The architectural role of the window changed, I will argue, with the development of its virtual analogs. And, as twentieth-century images were projected and transmitted, the window became an equally compelling metaphor for the screen.

## The Architectural Window and the Virtual Window

In the film treatment of his 1933 novel, *The Shape of Things to Come,* H. G. Wells describes a scene from the year 2054, a scene that is realized (see fig. 20.2) in the 1936 William Cameron Menzies film adaptation. In a room with austerely streamlined decor, a young girl stands in front of a framed screen supported almost invisibly by plexi-glass. She declares, albeit somewhat leadenly: "I love history and I love history pictures! It's so exciting to see how the world has changed." A picture of the New York skyline appears on the screen:

> "What a funny place New York was," she shrieks, "all sticking up and full of windows!"
> Ralph Richardson, her wizened great-grandfather, attempts to supply an explanatory caption to the view:
> "They opened and shut those windows to let in the wind and the wet and the cold. I don't know how to describe these windows to you but perhaps there are pictures. . . . The age of windows," he goes on to explain, "lasted four centuries."

In H. G. Wells's fictional imaginary, the buildings of the future did not have windows, but had instead the virtual windows of tele-screens. As the above "picture" illustrates—doubling here for the double function of the "history picture" in *Things to Come*—

Figure 20.2    "The age of windows lasted four centuries"—from the film *Things to Come* (William Cameron Menzies, 1936) based on H. G. Wells's 1933 novel *The Shape of Things to Come*.

"pictures" render "history" through their evidentiary power. The picture of the New York skyline provides the only record of the architectural window and this "history picture" also serves as a window—as the architectural window is replaced by the screen, its virtual substitute.

If we conduct a rough historical calculation: Large sheets of cast glass, rolled and poured, were available as a building material in the mid seventeenth century. With this as a starting point, four centuries of windows would conclude in the middle of the twenty-first century, a moment in the not-so-far-off future.

### A Brief History of Fenestration

A brief history of this "the age of windows" will demonstrate how the window as an architectural opening for light and ventilation ceded its priorities to the modern function of the window: to frame a view. The window began as an opening slit for light and ventilation (a clostra) and developed in Roman times as glazing was introduced. Representations of windows appear in wall paintings in Egypt and in reliefs from Assyria. In early Christian and Byzantine churches, small pieces of glass were inserted into a masonry frame. But it was not until the twelfth and thirteenth centuries that the technique of using different colors of glass—stained glass—was deployed to produce detailed ornamental patterns. In the Middle Ages, as glazing improved, windows grew larger and more transparent.[4]

Glass properties were altered by changing ingredients: soda lime instead of lead alkali materials made a glass of greater transparency and strength.[5] The technologies for glass production were highly guarded secrets between the fifteenth and seventeenth century when the Venetian glassmakers dominated the European glass industry. In Lewis Mumford's account, glass played a determinant role in the scientific transformation of the modern world. "Without the use of glass for spectacles, mirrors, microscopes, telescopes, windows and containers," Mumford writes, "the modern world as realized by physics and chemistry could scarcely have been conceived."[6]

As the Germans and English began to discover and refine their own methods in the nineteenth century, glass remained a luxury, used for public buildings and optical instruments. Between 1696 and 1851 property tax in England was assessed, not by the square footage of property; but by the number of windows, enforcing both the measure of glass as a taxable luxury and the number of windows as a measure of privilege. The British taxing of windows set the precedent for the French door and window tax between 1798 and 1917. Windows were a measure of property and wealth, indicating the ideology and privilege of those possessing a window-view.[7]

The window served as the membrane between inside and outside, and light was the material that modulated this relation. In the late eighteenth century—and into the nineteenth century—middle and upper class residences demonstrated an ambivalence toward the invasion of light into the domestic interior; crystal clear window panes were heavily curtained openings, as if to enact the separation between private and public space. Improvements in cast iron architecture—the rolled wrought iron sash bar and section— meant that complete glass structures like the Crystal Palace (Joseph Paxton, 1851) and the glazed roofs of train stations (Kings Cross Station, 1851), market halls (*Les Halles*/Victor Baltard, 1853–1858) and department stores (*Bon Marche*/ *Boileau* and *Eiffel,* 1869–1887) could be built. All of these structures allowed blazing light into an uncurtained, undraped, and hence well-lit interior space.[8]

As the window grew in relation to the wall—shedding its mullions and posts—it became more and more of a permeable interface, its transparency enforced a two-way model of visuality: by framing a private view outward—the "picture" window—and by framing a public view inward—the "display" window. The shop window was a consequence of improved glass technology and the commercial exploitation of its visual display, framing the gaze of passing *flâneurs* and *flâneuses* at commodities seductively displayed. The pane of the shop window enacted the *entre libre* principle of the department store, where the consumptive mode of "just looking" had its own price not in the obligation—but in the desire—for purchase. "Show windows lead to larger openings in the wall," Siegfried Gideon writes, "It was from these store windows that we first learned how to use large glass areas in dwelling houses."[9]

The window became a display frame and, as the architectural use of the horizontal or ribbon window demonstrated, the window could also become a wall.[10] As a material, glass offered both transparency and protection; could keep the outside out and at the same time bring it in. "Fully apprehending the outside from within, yet feeling neither cold nor wind nor moisture, is a modern sensation," argues Richard Sennett, which produced " a complete visibility without exposure of the other senses."[11] This association of visibility with isolation developed, Sennett maintains, as air-conditioning and thermal glass were perfected a half a century later; culminating in the paradigmatic modernist "glass box."

The modern house became not only a "dwelling machine" but also a "viewing machine." As Frank Lloyd Wright asserted:

> Had the ancients been able to enclose interior space with the facility we enjoy because of glass, I suppose the history of architecture would have been radically different, although it is surprising how little this material has yet modified our sense of architecture beyond the show-windows the shop keeper demands and gets . . . The machine has given to architects, in glass, a new material with which to work. Were glass eliminated now from buildings, it would be, so far as our buildings have gone, only like putting our eyes out. We could not see or see into the building. We have gone so far with it as to make it the eyes of the building.[12]

The materials of glass and its properties of transparency led Wright to this optical metaphor. Windows become the "eyes of the building," prosthetic organs for looking out and for looking in. The window is a visual metaphor with a literal analog; an architectural figure and a philosophical paradigm.

## The Window and Perspective

The history of the window is inextricably linked with the history of perspective. As a representational system, perspective was a technique for re-producing the spatial coordinates of vision on the flat plane of a virtual representation.[13] The perspectival image, organized to provide the viewer with a centered position in relation to the picture, was embodied in Leon Battista Alberti's descriptive metaphor for the painting (*pictura*) as a "an open window *(aperta finestra)* through which the subject to be painted is seen."[14] Leonardo daVinci also described techniques of perspective by imagining a "pane of glass, quite transparent, on the surface of which the objects behind that glass are drawn."[15]

In Dürer's famed illustration for his 1525 treatise on perspective, *The Painter's Manual,* the artist sits in front of a window-like grid through which he measures his subject. As Dürer explained it: "Perspectiva is a Latin word which means 'seeing through.'[16] Dürer's image with the artist, male; the subject, voluptuous, reclining and female—has often been used to indicate the gendered difference between the holder of focal point perspective and the massive 3D subject of this perspective. The grid-system—itself a prototype for dividing an image into its picture elements, or pixels, for 3D—imaging—aided the artist in transforming the three-dimensional natural world onto the two-dimensional plane of representation.

The window frame of perspectival positioning implied a subjective distance, a separation through representation. The viewer of this "windowed," monocular view of space has been commonly conflated with Descarte's description of a subject who stood outside of the world and represented its reality to him/herself. As Heidegger would posit in "The Age of the World Picture" (1938): "The fundamental event of the modern age is the conquest of the world as picture."[17] To Heidegger, the transformation of the world into "picture" (*Bild*) was coincident with the Descartes' seventeenth-century meditations on the subjectum who represents the world through thought—*ego cogito (ergo) sum.*"[18] Heidegger asserts: "That the world becomes picture is one and the same event with the event of man's becoming subjectum in the midst of that which is."[19]

### The Virtual Window and the Screen

At which point does the history of the window begin to converge with its virtual substitutes? The virtual grail of representation had a history rooted in all forms of "picture-making" but was most dramatically achieved with photography's indexical record. Let's begin with the earliest extant photograph: Nicéphore Niépce's view from his window, a view that he fixed on pewter plate in 1826. For Niépce's eight-hour exposure, the window was convenient as a site, and its view is held static and fixed in virtual fashion (see fig. 20.3).

## The Cinema Screen

The moving image expanded the photograph's virtuality by adding mobility, altering but not contradicting its perspectival positioning. But if the cinema provided a virtual mobility for its spectators it did so within the confines of a frame. Early panoramic films, for example, illustrate how the panorama—once a large-scale form that could be viewed by a spectator placed in the center, turning one's head—became reduced to framed images recorded by a moving ("panning") camera. Some historians of early cinema describe this early fascination with movement as a fascination with spectacle and sensation—the cinema of attractions.[20] But let's reframe that assumption thinking about the virtuality of such movement: i.e., the spectator is not really moving; his or her head and body is relatively immobile. The visuality here is compensatory—along the lines of the paradox,

Figure 20.3    Joseph Nicéphore Niépce, view from his window at Gras, 1826.

which I'll repeat: as the mobilized gaze became more virtual, it grew to involve less physical mobility, and became located within the confines of a framed visuality. Even today's "blockbuster," "shit blows up" special effects films illustrate a limit-case fascination with explosive high-speed motion in a confined frame. In this way, the cultural force of the cinematic and televisual has produced an ingrained virtuality of the senses, removing our experience of space, time and the real to the plane representation, but in form of delimited vision, in a frame. The cinema screen transfered the sensual isolation produced by the plate-glass window onto a virtual register. A virtual window is reliant not on its transparency but on its opacity; its highly mediated modulation of light provides an aperture—not to a reality—but to a delimited virtuality.

In the critique of Jean Louis Baudry and other 1970s film theorists, it was the film frame and the perspectival monocularity of its limited window that organized the spectator's vision. Following Alberti and the spatial codes of Renaissance perspective, the film frame imbricated—interpellated—the spectator into its philosophical program and ideological consequences.[21] Stephen Heath described the relay between Quattrocento codes of perspective—from seen to scene—from camera to frame to screen:

> It may well be that classical cinema acquires "the mobility of the eye" while preserving the contained and delimited visual field on which "correct" perspectives depend . . . the eye in the cinema is the perfect eye, the steady and ubiquitous control of the scene passed from director to spectator by virtue of the cinematic apparatus.[22]

As a key component of the "basic cinematic apparatus"—consisting of the film, the film projector, the screen and spectator in a fixed relation—"apparatus theory" cast the film screen as a conflationary substitute for the film frame.[23] Apparatus theory may have been dismantled by feminist (and other) correctives to its ahistoric generalizations and disregard for oppositional strategies of style or exhibition and yet—importantly—it described the screen itself as the locus of fascination, the site of enfolding psychic space onto physical space.[24]

### The Television Screen

Much of the early competition between film and television centered around screen size; the 10–12" television screen was tailored to the domestic scale of the home. Movie producers and exhibitors competed by differentiating their offerings with color, 3D and wider screen formats. Drive-in "roofless" theaters or "ozoners" catered to the mobility and domestic encapsulation of the automotive spectator; "four-walled" or "hardtop" theaters introduced Widescreen and Cinerama formats to compensate for what the small black and white screens of television could not supply.

And, as television scholars are quick to note, the placement of televisions in the home significantly alters the function of such spectatorship. Lynn Spigel, for example, likens the television's screen—a form of "home theater"—to the 1950s architectural use of the picture window, a "window-wall" designed to bring the outside in.[25] Some exhibitors tried to attract television viewers outside the home, as late 1940s experiments with "theater television" illustrate. Although both the content and the form of television competed with the film industry for viewers, television also became a delivery system for motion pictures—first in broadcast and syndicated format and later in basic and premium cable movie channels. As films were shown on television, the changes in cinema screen sizes/aspect ratios meant that films were either panned and scanned or more appropriately letter-boxed to fit in the 3X4 rectangular format of the television screen. The television "viewer" could now view films in a space that was, as Roland Barthes described it, "familiar, organized, tamed."[26] The VCR was the first technology to begin to erode the historical differences between television and film, altering as it has, the terms of electronic and cinematic viewing.[27]

Large screen televisions and high-resolution flat-screen wall displays illustrate how screens have gotten big enough and flat enough to substitute for real windows. In 1995, the *New York Times* described the wall-sized screens in Bill Gates's $30 million home in Seattle: "Instead of travelling the world to collect great art for his nooks and sky-lighted reception rooms," cyber-baron Gates "bought the electronic rights to art from museums like the National Gallery in London. With the press of a switch, the bathroom walls will become Rembrandts."[28] (If masterpieces can hang in your bathroom in electronically reproduced form; one can easily imagine a subscription service that would display the originals—a true Masterpiece theatre.) As flat-screen technology improves and screens replace real windows with a kind of "inhabited TV," a "windows environment" may give way to virtual "window-walls," an image not far from the shape of H. G. Wells's *Things to Come.*

### The Computer Screen

The scale and domestic place of the television prepared us for the screens of the "personal" computer. But computer "users" are not spectators, not viewers. The "interface" may retain some immobility (with focussed attention on a cathode ray screen) but the computer "user" interacts with the framed image on a small screen, "using" a device—keyboard, mouse, or (in the case of touch-screens) the finger—to manipulate what is contained within the parameter of the screen.[29] Software designers have worked to model "interface" to emulate the associative patterns of human thought, as we become dyadic partners in a cyber-metaphysical relationship.[30] But as complaints about the awkwardness of this relationship are surfacing, one critic has proclaimed: "Using computers is like going to the movie theater and having to watch the projector instead of the film."[31]

But it is not only a new "interface" that has changed our relation to the screen. Perhaps more importantly, the computer has produced a further metaphysical challenge in our relation to the screen. The "integral realism" of the camera image meets its most subversive challenge: the digital image takes the assaults to concepts of aura and originality produced by photography and film to new extremes; it radically subverts the photograph's evidentiary power. Digital "information" can be manipulated easily and rapidly by computer, and hence is more susceptible to alteration. As films like *Forrest Gump* and *Wag the Dog* broadly illustrate, if digitally altered images are "history pictures"—to return to H. G. Wells's term—"history" is easily revised, corrected to fit any "counter-factual" (ideological) agenda.

Beyond just the future of imaging, digital technology also transforms delivery and display. Turning Marshall McLuhan's assertion "the medium is the massage" on its head, Nicholas Negroponte asserts the "mediumlessness" of the digital: "The medium is not the message in the digital world, " he writes. "It is an embodiment of it. A message might have several embodiments automatically derivable from the same data."[32] Friedrich Kittler had proclaimed this in 1986 when he wrote:

> Something is coming to an end. The general digitalization of information and channels erases the difference between individual media. Sound and image, voice and text have become mere effects on the surface or, to put it better, the interface for the consumer. Sense and the sense become mere glitter.[33]

The movie screen, the TV screen, the computer screen may still occupy separate spaces (their very location changes our concept of spectatorship—the place of the computer in the home or in the workplace is quite different from the domestic lodging of the TV set), but the types of images one sees on each of them are losing their medium-based specificity. Images have become a utility; each household has a supply that enters the home via broadcast signals, cable wires, satellite reception, or telephone modem hook-ups—supplied to the virtual windows that ventilate domestic space.

## Microscreen (Microsoft) Windows

Yet the metaphor of the window has retained a predominant role in the technological re-framings of our visual field. The computer "window" is only a portion of the computer screen, scalable in size. Pioneered by Douglas Englebart at the Stanford Institute, who developed a prototype of multiple-window screens and mice in the 1950s and 60s, "windows" became a key component of the graphical interface developed at Xerox PARC known as the (yes) WIMP interface—Windows, Icons, Mouse, Pull-down Menus—and was featured on all original 1984 Apple MacIntosh systems. The "windows" *environment* makes the screen smaller and allows for simultaneous applications. When Microsoft trademarked its second-generation software as Windows they emphasized the metaphoric nature of much of our computer usage: "mice" which scurry under our fingers at the fluid command of wrist and palm and "desktops" which defy gravity and transform the horizontal desk into a vertical surface with an array of possible colors and digital textures. As an "interface," Windows extends screen space by overlapping screens of various sizes; each "window" can run a different application; you can arrange windows on your screen in stacked or overlapping formations or decorate your windows (with wall-papers, textured patterns.) Microsoft launched its PC-based Windows (version 1.0) in 1985 and as the media-saturated campaign for Windows '95 emphasized, Windows became (and has remained) the most widely used operating system.[34]

The "Windows" trope in computer software has become emblematic of the collapse of the single viewpoint, relying on the model of a window that we can't see through; windows that overlap, obscure. Windows are re-sizable, movable. Windows make multitasking possible.[35] A 1998 *New York Times* article reported this statistic: "Microsoft says the average office user of Windows '95 has more than three programs running at a time. At home, more than 10 million American households now have a television and a personal computer in the same room."[36] Multitasking makes it possible to combine work with leisure—watching TV while checking e-mail—and hence serves to equate productivity with a fractured subjectivity.

Quattrocento perspective and its concomittant symbolic system has been challenged on many fronts: by changes in perspective in modern painting; by modern architecture's revision to the role of the window—replacing the "perspectival" window with the horizontal window, the "picture" window or the "picture" wall, and by moving image technologies which provide a temporal exponent to spatial perspectivalism. But while architectural changes in the window were coincident with changes in perspective in modern painting early in the twentieth century, the media of film and television retained a perspectival frame through the "modern" period. The moving image offered multiple perspectives through the sequential shifts of montage and editing; yet, aside from a few historical anomalies, it has only been with the advent of digital imaging technologies and new technologies of display in the 1990s that the media "window" began to include multiple perspectives within a single frame.[37]

Now, a variety of screens—long and wide and square, large and small, composed of grains, composed of pixels—compete for our attention without any (convincing) arguments about hegemony. As screens have multiplied and divided, so has subjectivity. As we spend more and more of our time staring into the frames of television, computer, and hand-held screens—windows full of text, icons, 3-D graphics, streaming-images, streaming audio—a new post-perspectival, post-Cartesian subjectivity has emerged. The multi-screen, windowed visuality of Windows software has become an apt figurative trope for this new subjectivity. As the beholder of multiple windows, we receive images—still and moving, large and small, artwork and commodity—in fractured spatial and temporal frames. With this new "windowed" multiplicity of perspectives we can be at two (or more) places at once, in two (or more) time frames in a fractured post-Cartesian cyber-time.

Just as the instrumental base for the moving image—retinal retention of successive virtual images—produced a new experience of temporality, the instrumental (digital) base for multi-screen multi-tasking poses some new questions about the experience of temporality. For a computer to multi-task, the computer does not do tasks simultaneously but serially and yet at a high speed. Digital optics produce the illusion of simultaneity at a much faster speed than moving image technologies did. In the terms of Paul Virilio:

> The aim is to make the computer screen the ultimate window, but a window which would not so much allow you to receive data as to view the horizon of globalization, the space of its accelerated virtualization.[38]

Virtual images radically transformed the twentieth-century understanding of reality, and yet most virtual images were seen in frames and through frames. Which technologies will break through the frame and have us climb through the metaphoric window? Or will we stay fixed—nose to the glass (or as the French say about window-shopping, *leche les vitrines/* licking the windows) fixed in front of the windows, caught in the hold of an image, framed in display? Or perhaps, as films like *Existenz, The Matrix, Strange Days* predict, the screen will dissolve; images and data will be "uploaded" directly, bypassing the eye and the optics of vision. This new circuitry takes the subject beyond and through the window; this defenestration has new risks and pleasures. Is the "age of windows"—and by extension, the age of screens—reaching, as H. G. Wells predicted, its end?

## Notes

1. Paul Valéry, "The Conquest of Ubiquity," *Aesthetics,* trans. Ralph Manheim (New York: Pantheon Books, 1964) "*La Conquete de l'ubiquite*" was first published in *De la Musique avant toute chose* (Editions du Tambourinaire, 1928); in *Pieces sur l'art* (1934) and in *Oeuvres II* (Pleiade, 1960).

2. In *Window Shopping,* I argued that the moving image emerged as a culmination of 19th-century machines of mobility (trains, steamships, bicycles, elevators, escalators, moving walkways— apparatuses that changed the relation of sight to bodily movement, producing a mobilized visuality) and of 19th-century contrivances for producing a virtual visuality (evidenced by developments in painterly realism, scale, and spectatorial involvement in devices like the panorama and the diorama but most dramatically produced by photography's indexical record). The cinema, I argued, emerged as an apparatus that combined these mobilized and virtual visualities, producing the illusion of transport not only to other places but, significantly, to other times. See Anne Friedberg, *Window Shopping: Cinema and the Postmodern* (Berkeley: University of California Press, 1993).

3. The theorization of "spectatorship"—in terms of either an ideological, psychoanalytic, phenomenological "subject position" or a historically and culturally inflected viewer of a particular race, gender, age etc.—has been at the center of Film and Media Studies debate since the 1970s. For an excellent summary account of these debates see Judith Mayne, *Cinema and Spectatorship* (New York: Routledge, 1993).

4. In a 1929 lecture, Le Corbusier described the "history of architecture" as a "history of windows throughout the ages." The changing forms and functions of windows are emblematic of a historical era: "In the Middle Ages," he wrote "they glazed all they could, using all the resources of wood," while in the Renaissance architects used, "stone mullions in a window that was made as big as possible." See Le Corbusier, *Precisions: On the Present State of Architecture and City Planning* (1930), trans. Edith Schreiber Aujame (Cambridge, MA: MIT Press, 1991), 52.

5. Frances Rogers and Alice Beard, *5000 Years of Glass* (New York, J. B. Lippincott Company, 1937); Ada Polak. *Glass: Its Makers and Its Public* (London: Weidenfield & Nicholson, 1975); R. W. Douglas and Susan Frank, *A History of Glassmaking* (Henley-on-Thames, Oxfordshire: G. T. Foulis & Co. Ltd., 1972).

6. Lewis Mumford, *Technics and Civilization* (New York: Harcourt, Brace and Company, 1934): this quote serves as a caption to an illustration plate between 180–181.

7. Daniel Boorstin, "Walls Become Windows" in *The Americans: The Democratic Experience* (New York: Random House, 1973), 336–345.

8. By the early 1900s, handmade methods were replaced by mechanized sheet glass production, ribbons of molten glass were poured from a furnace onto rollers. See Georg Kohlmaier and Barna von Sartory, *Houses of Glass: A Nineteenth Century Building Type,* trans. John C. Harvey (Cambridge, MA: MIT Press, 1986); also Richard Sennett's discussion of glass in *The Conscience of the Eye* (New York: Alfred A. Knopf, 1990), 106–114.

9. Siegfried Gideon, *Space, Time, and Architecture* (Cambridge, MA: Harvard University Press, 1991), 195.

10. Le Corbusier wished to "de-vignolize" architecture—to challenge its verticality. Le Corbusier's horizontal ribbon window was designed to give more light than vertical window. See Le Corbusier, *Precisions: On the Present State of Architecture and City Planning,* trans. Edith Schreiber Aujame (Cambridge, MA: MIT Press, 1991).

11. Richard Sennett, *The Conscience of the Eye,* 108. "Sight," Sennett writes, "is routinely insulated from sound and touch and other human beings" (109).

12. Frank Lloyd Wright, "The Meaning of Materials—Glass"(1928), *In the Cause of Architecture,* ed. Frederick Gutheim (New York: Architectural Record, 1975) 197–8.

13. The origins, practices and traditions of perspective have been the subject of voluminous scholarly treatises and remain at the center of many ongoing controversies about visual representation itself. Perspective, it is argued, is practical formula (Kemp, Edgerton, Greyson), an epistemological metaphor (Elkins), a transhistorical "symbolic form" (Panofsky), a visual system unique to Italy and distinct from the more aggregate system of visual representation relied upon by Northern Dutch painters (Alpers); the dominant visual system in Western culture or one of several (Jay); a technique for painters (perspectiva artificialis) as evidenced in the writings of Alberti or for architects *(costruzione legittima)* as evidenced in the experiments of Brunelleschi (Damisch, Pérez-Gomez and Pelletier). See Martin Kemp, *The Science of Art: Optical Themes in Western Art from Brunelleschi to Seurat* (New Haven: Yale University Press, 1990); Samuel Edgerton, *Renaissance Rediscovery of Linear Perspective Perspective* (New York: Basic Books, 1975); James Elkins, *The Poetics of Perspective* (Ithaca: Cornell University Press, 1994); Erwin Panofsky, *Perspective as Symbolic Form,* trans. Christopher S. Wood (New York: Zone Books, 1991); Svetlana Alpers, *The Art of Describing: Dutch Art in the Seventeenth Century* (Chicago: University of Chicago Press, 1983); Martin Jay. "Scopic Regimes of Modernity," in *Vision and Visuality,* ed. Hal Foster (Seattle: Bay Press, 1988), 3–23.; Hubert Damisch, *The Origin of Perspective,* trans. John Goodman (Cambridge, MA: MIT Press, 1995) and Alberto Pérez-Gómez and Louise Pelletier. *Architectural Representation and the Perspective Hinge* (Cambridge, MA: MIT Press, 1997).

14. Leon Battista Alberti, *On Painting and On Sculpture: The Latin Texts of "De Pictura" and "De Statua,"* trans. Cecil Grayson (London: 1972), 55. This quote is taken from section I.19 of the 1435 Latin text: *quod quidem mihi pro aperta finestra est ex qua historia contueatur.*

15. J. P. Richter (ed.), *The Literary Works of Leonardo da Vinci,* vol. 1 (London: Oxford University Press, 1939), 150.

16. Indeed this is the first sentence of Erwin Panovksy's *Perspective as Symbolic Form* (1924–1925): "*Item Perspectiva ist ein lateinisch Wort, bedeutt ein Durchsehung.*"

17. Martin Heidegger, "The Age of the World Picture" (1938) published in *The Question Concerning Technology and Other Essays,* trans. William Lovitt (New York: Harper and Row, 1977), 115–154. "The Age of the World Picture" was Heidegger's published version of the lecture entitled "The Establishing by Metaphysics of the Modern World Picture" given on June 9, 1938. Many of its concepts were revised, repeated in four lectures given in Bremen in 1949/1950—"Das Ding" ("The Thing"), "Das Ge-stell" ("Enframing"), "Die Gefahr" ("The Danger"), "Die Kehre" ("The Turning")—and in the lecture "Die Frage nach der Technik" given in Munich on November 18, 1955. The German text to "The Age of the World Picture" appears in *Holzwege* (Frankfurt am Main: Vittorio Klostermann, 1950) 69–104. The German text to "Die Frage nach der Technik" appears in *Vorträge und Aufsätze* (Pfullingen: Günther Neske Verlag, 1954), 13–44.

18. René Descartes, *Meditations on First Philosophy with Selections and Objections and Replies,* trans. J. Cottingham (Cambridge: Cambridge University Press, 1986).

19. The "interweaving" of these two events—"that the world is transformed into picture and man into subiectum"—became the "decisive" determinant of the modern age. "Age of the World Picture," 132. In a long appendix on Descartes, Heidegger expands upon the relation between thought and representation: "Thinking is representing, setting-before, is a representing relation to what is represented."

20. Tom Gunning, "The Cinema of Attractions," in *Early Cinema: Space, Frame, Narrative,* ed. Thomas Elsaesser (London: BFI, 1991).

21. "Apparatus" film theorists of the 1970s (Baudry, Heath, Comolli) traced a continuity between the camera obscura and photography and cinema; while more recent accounts of "vision and visuality" (Crary, Jay) have insisted on the discontinuities/ruptures in geneologies which trace a continuous link between Renaissance perspective/camera obscura and photography/cinema. See Jean Louis Baudry, "Ideological Effects of the Basic Cinematographic Apparatus" (1970), in *Narrative, Apparatus, Ideology,* ed. Philip Rosen (New York: Columbia University Press, 1986), 286–299; Jean Louis Baudry, "The Apparatus: Metapsychological Approaches to the Impression of Reality in Cinema" (1975), in *Narrative, Apparatus, Ideology,* ed. Philip Rosen (New York: Columbia University Press, 1986), 299–318; Heath, Stephen. "On Screen, in Frame: Film and Ideology," in *Questions of Cinema* (London: Macmillan, 1981), 1–18; Heath, Stephen. "Narrative Space," *Screen* 17, no.3 (Autumn 1976): 68–112; Jean

Comolli, "Machines of the Visible," in *The Cinematic Apparatus,* ed. Teresa de Lauretis and Stephen Heath (New York: St. Martin's Press, 1980), 121–133.

22. Stephen Heath, "Narrative Space," *Screen* 17, no. 3 (Autumn 1976): 31–32.

23. In fact, it was the uniformity of film frame size—its aspect ratio as distinct from the variable sizes of frames in painting—that Stephen Heath used to argue as crucial for setting the conditions of spectatorship. The film frame remained, in Heath's account, in the 1.33:1 aspect ratio or was limited to a very few ratios. Stephen Heath, "On Screen, in Frame: Film and Ideology," in *Questions of Cinema* (London: Macmillan, 1981), 10. Also see Heath on the window frame in "Narrative Space Questions of Cinema: 34. Vivian Sobchack provides a critique of film theory's use of the metaphor of the frame and the metaphor of the window and the metaphor of the mirror along phenomenological lines. See: Vivian Sobchack, *The Address of the Eye: Phenomenology and the Film Experience* (Princeton: Princeton University Press, 1992).

24. "Apparatus" here refers to work on the cinema which considers the "cinematic apparatus" as *dispositif,* a more general sense of device and arrangement which includes the metapsychological effects on the spectator and is not simply the "apparatus" as *appareil,* the machine. Unfortunately, "apparatus" has been used as the English-language translation of the French word *dispositif*—a device or arrangement that includes the metapsychological effects on the spectator—and this translation elides the difference between the *dispositif* as arrangement and the *appareil* as machine. See Joan Copjec, "The Anxiety of the Influencing Machine," *October* 23 (1982): 43–59; Constance Penley, "Feminism, Film Theory and the Bachelor Machines," *m/f* 10 (1985): 39–59 and Judith Mayne, *Cinema and Spectatorship* (New York: Routledge, 1993), 47.

25. Lynn Spigel, *Make Room for TV: Television and the Family Ideal in Postwar America* (Chicago: University of Chicago Press, 1992), 102.

26. Roland Barthes' short piece "En sortant du cinema" compares the "urban darkness" of the movie theatre where the "body's freedoms luxuriate" to the space of the television viewer. "En sortant du cinema," was first published in the famous issue of *Communications,* "Psychoanalyse et cinema," Christian Metz, Raymond Bellour, Thierry Kunzel, ed., no. 23 (1975) and translated by Bertrand Augst and Susan White, "Upon Leaving the Movie Theater" in *Cinematographic Apparatus: Selected Writings,* ed. Theresa Hak Kung Cha (New York: Tanam Press, 1980), 1–4.

27. For a lengthier discussion of the slow erosion of differences between film and television see: Anne Friedberg, "The End of Cinema: Multimedia and Technological Change," in *Reinventing Film Studies,* ed. Linda Williams and Christine Gledhill (London: Arnold Publications, 1999): 438–452.

28. Timothy Egan, "It Takes Time to Build a Xanadu for Citizen Gates." *New York Times* (i.e: 12 Jan. 1995): B1.

29. A paradox begins to emerge: The more the image becomes digital, the more the interface tries to compensate for its departure from reality-based representation by adopting the metaphors of familiar objects in space.

30. Sherry Turkle pursues the "interface" in her book *Life on the Screen: Identity in the Age of the Internet* (New York: Simon and Schuster, 1995); also see Vannevar Bush, "As We May Think," *Atlantic Monthly,* July 1945.

31. Brenda Laurel, quoted in David Kline, "The Embedded Internet," *Wired 4.10* (October 1996): 101.

32. Nicholas Negroponte, *Being Digital* (New York: Alfred Knopf, 1995).

33. Friedrich Kittler, *Gramophone, Film, Typewriter* (Berlin: Brinkmann & Bose, 1986); "Gramophone, Film Typewriter," *October* 41 (1986): 102.

34. In retrospect, many accounts of the development of the GUI interface refer to inset "windows" but it is unclear when the term "window" was first used to refer to the inset screen. See William Gates, *The Road Ahead* (New York: Viking, 1995); Paul E. Ceruzzi, *A History of Modern Computing* (Cambridge, MA: MIT Press, 1998); Michael Hiltzik, *Dealers of Lightning: Xerox Parc and the Dawn of the Computer Age* (New York: HarperBusiness, 1999); Paul Freiberger and Michael Swaine, *Fire in the Valley: The Making of the Personal Computer* (New York: McGraw Hill, 2000).

35. Computers don't actually do these things simultaneously, but serially and yet really really fast. ("Even a slow computer with 100 megahertz processor can execute a million instructions between each pair of keystrokes.") Computers can switch faster than humans can, don't have the same psychological toll or residues.

36. Amy Harmon, "Talk, Type, Read E-Mail," *New York Times,* July 23, 1998, G, 1.

37. The multiple-screen experiments of filmmakers from Abel Gance (*Napoleon,* 1927) to the multi-media work of Charles and Ray Eames suggest a few cinematic precursors to multiple-image computer screens.

38. Paul Virilio, *The Information Bomb,* trans. Chris Turner (London: Verso, 2000), 16.

# 21 Architectures of the Senses: Neo-Baroque Entertainment Spectacles

Angela Ndalianis

---

It was sometime in November 2000. I was walking along an Arabian street, taking in the rhythms of the arabesque decorations and the spectacular, multi-colored buildings; being entertained by the exotic street musicians; and occasionally being lured into various bazaars that offered the temptations of products ranging from Persian rugs and glassware, to Versace gowns and DKNY accessories. At one point, I found myself at a pier. I looked up at the sky and, while soft, fluffy clouds punctured its blue (yet somewhat solid) surface, it seemed like it was going to be a beautiful day. But what do I know? No sooner had I thought this than the rumbling sounds of thunder vibrated through the air and flashes of lightning lit up the now-transformed dark and ominous clouds. And the rain came pouring down, creating restless ripples in the previously still waters near the pier. So I left Arabia and walked across the road to Lake Como, where I took in the sights of the palazzo Bellagio as it stood majestically in the background. Initially, the enormous lake reflected the palazzo in its tranquil waters, then thousands of small tubes began to puncture its surface, and the first bars of music suddenly filled this vast space. I recognized the tune—Frank Sinatra's "Lady Luck"—and it was, indeed, a toe-tapper. As hundreds flocked around balconies overlooking the lake, the lake's water began to magically take on a life of its own: spurts of water swayed left and right, back and forth in perfect unison with the rhythms of Sinatra's crooning. And the audience continued to look on, mesmerized by the spectacle they witnessed, astounded by the rhythmic motions of water, which included stretches of up to fifty meters erupting to heights that exceeded one hundred meters.

Confronted by such wonder, I found it very difficult to wipe the smile off my face. And just as the smile began to subside, it would reemerge making the muscles in my face hurt. Why? This was Las Vegas and in this space so much was within my reach. Cities: Arabia (at the Desert Passage/Aladdin), New York (at the New York, New York), Ancient Rome (at Caesar's Palace), Venice (at the Venetian), Egypt (at the Luxor), and Lake Como (at the Bellagio). Technologically produced spectacles: the digitally created storms that erupt from the trompe l'oeil ceilings at the Desert Passage, the computer generated dancing water displays at the Bellagio, the animatronic (robotic) fight of the gods for Atlantis at Caesar's. Blockbuster art exhibitions: the Philips art collection at the Bellagio, and the planned Guggenheim collection soon to grace the interior of the Venetian. 3-D simulation rides: the Race for Atlantis at Caesar's, the Search for the Obelisk at the Luxor, and the multitude of game arcades (which include simulation rides) that are now a prerequisite for all hotel/casinos. And if this variety of visual stimulation wasn't enough, it was always possible to catch a film at the mega- and multi-screen Cineplex next to the MGM Grand.

As a spectacle city—a Spectopolis[1]—Las Vegas (since the dominance of 1980s multimedia conglomerates) stands as a paragon to the ways in which our city environments are transforming, reflecting our era's fascination with visuality and sensory encounters that have become interwoven with entertainment experiences.

In the last two decades entertainment media and our leisure spaces have undergone dramatic transformations. The movement that describes these changes is one concerned with the traversal of boundaries—a traversal that shares a concern with the spectacular possibilities of entertainment forms. Effects such as the water display at the Bellagio, the animatronic Fall of Atlantis at Caesar's, and the interior storm in the Desert Passage are constructed by effects crews that traditionally belonged to the realm of the cinema. In the film *The Matrix*, film technology combines with computer technology in order to construct the highly kinetic effects that were integral to the film's success. The Jurassic Park films, Terminator films and the Spiderman comic books find new media environments in the theme park attractions Terminator 2: 3-D Battle Across Time, and The Amazing Adventures of Spiderman (all three at Universal Studios, Los Angeles and Orlando). Computer and console games like the Tomb Raider and Final Fantasy series cross their game borders by incorporating film styles, genres, and human-like forms into their digital spaces. In turn, these games are reborn as cinematic spectacles. Furthermore, these potent visual entertainment forms invade our cultural spaces, shaping and informing the structures of our cinema complexes, shopping malls, casino complexes, and museum and gallery spaces. We are living in a time when our entertainment spectacles insert themselves into our urbanscapes in spatially invasive ways.

We tend to view the digitally reliant visual effects that populate our social arenas as products that are particular to our postmodern age and, indeed, they are. However, a great deal is to be learned about our contemporary fascination with spectacle by relating it to the history of media cultures. It isn't contemporary media alone that are competing and interacting with one another on the level of spectacle. This fascination with and saturation of the visual is a phenomenon that has older historical roots. Specifically, this essay investigates ways in which late twentieth-early twenty-first-century entertainment spectacles have witnessed a re-emergence of baroque form, reflecting the baroque's metamorphosis into a more technologically driven method of expression of the neo-baroque.

In recent years, a number of theorists and historians, including Calabrese, Deleuze, Perniola and Maravall, have explored the formal, social, and historical constituents of the baroque and neo-baroque. Deleuze understood the baroque in its broadest terms "as radiating through histories, cultures and worlds of knowledge" including areas as diverse as art, science, costume design, mathematics, and philosophy (Conley in Deleuze 1993, xi). Likewise, in his historical and cultural study of the seventeenth-century Spanish baroque, Antonio Maravall has observed that it is possible to establish certain relations between external, purely formal elements of the baroque in seventeenth-century Europe and elements present in very different historical epochs in unrelated cultural areas . . . [Therefore] it is also possible [to] speak of a baroque at any given time, in any field of human endeavour (1983, 4–5).

Concerned with the seventeenth-century, Maravall's interest is in the baroque as a cultural phenomenon that emerges from the specific historical situation of that century. However, Maravall also privileges a sense of the baroque that escapes chronological confines. His approach is a productive one. While exploring eras that are separated by over two hundred years—and which have cultural phenomena particular to their specific historical situations—it is, nevertheless, possible to identify and describe a certain morphology of the baroque that dominates in both eras.

In his book *The Life of Forms in Art*—originally published in 1934—Henri Focillon makes a significant observation with regard to the formal properties of art. Despite his strictly formalist concerns, significantly, Focillon understood form in art as an entity that was not necessarily limited to the constraints of time or specific historical periods. Quoting a political tract from Balzac, he stated that "everything is form and life itself is form" (1992, 33). For Focillon, formal patterns in art are in perpetual states of movement, being specific to temporal confines but also spanning across them. He states:

> Form may, it is true, become formula and canon; in other words, it may be abruptly frozen into a normative type. But form is primarily a mobile life in a changing world. Its metamorphoses endlessly begin anew, and it is by the principle of style that they are above all coordinated and stabilized. (1992, 44)

While the historical baroque has traditionally been contained within the rough temporal limits of the seventeenth century, to paraphrase Focillon, I suggest that baroque form still continued to have a life – one that recurred throughout history, but which existed beyond the limits of a canon. The seventeenth and late twentieth/twenty-first-century nurtured cultural climates that permitted the baroque to "become formula and canon": both epochs reflect wide-scale baroque sensibilities that, while being the product of specific socio-historical and temporal conditions, reflect similar patterns and concerns on formal and aesthetic levels. Both epochs underwent radical cultural, perceptual, and technological shifts that manifested themselves in similar aesthetic forms. While specific historical conditions differ radically, a similar overall formal effect was achieved. Social crisis and change "created a climate from which the baroque emerged and nourished itself" (Maravall 1983, 53). While the cultural transformations are beyond the scope of this essay, through a comparison with seventeenth-century examples of the baroque, I will explore aspects of the neo-baroque aesthetic that are manifested in contemporary media spaces. In particular, I will introduce a central feature of the baroque and neo-baroque in the context of a seventeenth and late twentieth/early twenty-first-century shared fascination with spectacle, illusionism, and the formal principle of the collapse of the frame[2]: specifically, the (neo)baroque architecture of vision.

## Classical and Baroque Form

Deleuze's analysis of baroque vision is an appropriate interpretative tool here. He suggests that the baroque offers an "architecture of vision" that situates the viewer in a spatial relationship to the representation (Deleuze 1993, 21). The spatially invasive nature of (neo)baroque spaces instigates participatory spectatorial positions through dynamic compositional arrangements. With borders continually being rewritten, (neo)baroque vision provides models of perception that suggest worlds of infinity that lose the sense of a center that is traditionally associated with classically ordered space. Rather, the center is to be found in the position of the spectator, with the representational centre changing depending on the spectator's focus. Given that (neo)baroque spectacle provides polycentric and multiple shifting centers, the spectator, in a sense, remains the only element in the image/viewer scenario that remains centered and stable. It is the audience's perception and active engagement with the image that orders the illusion. Rather than providing a statically ordered perspectival arrangement, the 'center' continually shifts, the result being the articulation of complex spatial conditions. The notion of the 'passive spectator' as voyeur collapses when media experiences immerse the viewer in spectacles that aim at perceptually removing the presence of the frame.[3]

Classical systems are characterized by closure. Such closed systems—which have traditionally been associated with the Renaissance—remain centered, ensuring narrative clarity and symmetry of organization. Raphael's mural decoration of the School of Athens (1509–11) reflects such a classical attitude to narrative and visual form.[4] The architectural arrangement recedes into the background, centering the two key figures—Aristotle and Plato—while a series of other philosophers flank them on either side. The fresco is dedicated to Philosophy and, while each of the other philosophers—including Socrates, Pythagoras, Ptolemy, Heraclitus, Diogenes—are depicted in unified groups, "each group is tied to the whole by some detail that serves as a hyphen that relates the details, through compositional arrangement" to the central narrative concern focused around the figures of Aristotle and Plato (Murray 1986, 41). Aided by the use of one-point perspective, the representation aims at perceptually extending the two-dimensional wall space through architectural and figural arrangements that lead the gaze of the spectator into the depth of the composition. The overriding sensation of the compositional and narrative arrangement is of the framing of the main protagonists within a closed and focused narrative and representational scenario, a feat achieved by the rigid, painted architectural framework.

Reflecting the capacity to "rationalize vision through mathematics" Raphael put into practice the Renaissance classical system that was earlier theorized by Alberti in his Della Pittura of 1435.[5] The mathematical clarity of perspective was employed to "produce the illusion of a three-dimensional world on a two-dimensional surface" (Ackerman 1991, 60). According to Ackerman, perspective, in combination with lighting and color, became "the paradigmatic invention of the Renaissance, in that it literally brought all perceived space under rational control" (Ackerman 1991, 61). The effect is one of a representational reality that is contained within the frame. Depicting a represented reality that effaces its construction through rational means, the spectator looks into this space as if looking through a window beyond which another world exists.

It is worth noting the parallels that film theorists and historians have established between the categories of Renaissance art and the classical Hollywood paradigm. Combining Renaissance art's reliance on one-point perspective with the more powerful mimetic system of photographic realism, classical Hollywood cinema has also been viewed as producing a representational space that similarly attempts to be transparent "like a window onto the real" (Bazin 1967, 29). Andre Bazin, for example, viewed the photographic realism of the cinema as containing the "characteristics of the ripeness of a classical art." In particular, Bazin focused on classical form and themes that were also highlighted by Alberti in his Della Pittura: an art that has perfect balance, narratives that stress dramatic and moral themes, and a realism that is self-effacing.[6] As will be discussed below, contemporary effects films and related entertainment media complicate classical form by imposing a baroque logic upon it.

According to Martin Jay, the "baroque ocular regime" is one often associated with a delight in visual spectacle.[7] The baroque is an order that calls upon systems of classical or Renaissance perspective in order to overturn, investigate, or complicate their rational, self-contained visual and narrative spaces. The baroque example of Pietro da Cortona's ceiling painting of The Glorification of Urban VIII (Rome, 1633–1639) in the Palazzo Barberini is, in many respects, a paragon of baroque attitudes to spectacle and illusionism—to the baroque ocular regime. The single, immobile viewpoint of the classical spectator is transformed into a dynamic process that changes as a result of its three-dimensional capacity to actively engage the spectator in spatial terms. The Renaissance ideal of a perspectively guided representation (evident in Raphael's School of Athens) is replaced by a baroque concern with complex, dynamic motion and multiple perspectives that are dependent on the position of the viewer in relation to the work.

Henri Focillon views classical forms as remaining encased in a space that "keeps them intact." Baroque forms, however,

> pass into an undulating continuity where both beginning and end are carefully hidden. . . . [The baroque reveals] "the system of the series"—a system composed of discontinuous elements sharply outlined, strongly rhythmical and . . . [that] eventually becomes "the system of the labyrinth," which, by means of mobile synthesis, stretches itself out in a realm of glittering movement and color. (Focillon 1992, 67)

The baroque's difference from classical systems lies in the refusal to respect the limits of the frame. Instead it "tend[s] to invade space in every direction, to perforate it, to become as one with all its possibilities" (Focillon 1992, 58). The lack of respect for the limits of the frame is manifest with intense visual directness in baroque attitudes towards spectacle. The impact and meaning of Cortona's ceiling painting depends on the interaction and combination of multiple, shifting viewpoints and narrative perspectives—all of which operate to collapse the classical function of the frame. The frame is present so that its function can be undermined. Open systems typical of the baroque permit a greater flow between the inside and outside, and operate according to a polycentric logic.

Rather than reflecting a classical concern for the static, closed and centralized, the baroque system is dependent upon dynamic forces that expand, and often rupture borders (Calabrese 1992, 66). Differentiation, polycentrism and rhythm are central to baroque storytelling strategies and, as will be argued below, neo-baroque entertainment media of the late twentieth / early twenty-first-century also introduce "a taste for elliptical form provided with real centres and multiple potentials" (Calabrese 1992, 44).

Cortona's ceiling painting reveals precisely such a polycentric organization. Whereas Raphael contains his narrative by framing it within a hemispherical border that rigidly encloses the composition, Cortona uses the frame in order to escape its limits. In a sense, by multiplying and layering classical form, Cortona has divided the vault of the ceiling into five parts, each dealing with separate narratives that are demarcated by painted stucco frames. A personification of Divine Providence floats in the central panel offering support for Pope Urban VIII's worthiness of immortality (Wittkower 1985, 252–253).[8] Despite the seemingly distinct narrative segments, Cortona is not concerned with a narrative limit such as that present in Raphael's painting. In the cornice that intersects with Minerva and the Giants, for example, numerous figures and swirling clouds tumble and float in front of and behind the painted stucco frames with the result that the narrative from one panel literally spills into the narrative of another. In addition, the impression is such that, in order to spill into the next visual and narrative space, the figures and objects perceptually appear to enter our own space within the Palazzo Barberini. A strictly classically aligned composition would, instead, have enclosed and kept discrete the separate narrative borders.

While the scene in the center of the vault depicting the glorification of Urban VIII is important, the viewer is also invited to follow serial paths that lead to other representational centers. The depiction of each narrative suggests a dynamic space and open attitude, one that aims at and produces "an unlimited space continuum" (Wittkower 1985, 252). Indeed, baroque spectacle often serves a dual function. It operates on the principle of co-extensive space—a space that illusionistically connects with and infinitely extends from our own (as seen in the central panel of the Barberini ceiling where the solidity of the vault appears to be punctured and perceptually extends to the heavens), and it constructs a labyrinthine space that produces an expansive network of spatial formations that appear to connect with our own (as witnessed by the figures who threaten to tumble into the space of the spectator). It therefore draws the gaze of the spectator "deep into the enigmatic depths and the infinite" (Perniola 1995, 93) while also rhythmically recalling what Focillon labels the "system of the labyrinth."

### Neo-Baroque Architectures of Vision

Our own neo-baroque spectacles similarly reflect Deleuze's articulation of the architectural dimension of baroque vision. Two recent examples suggest the extent to which this dual articulation of the "architecture of vision" embodied by the infinite and the labyrinth has become ingrained in Hollywood effects cinema, primarily as a result of computer generated special effects.

The opening scene of *Contact* (Zemeckis, 1997) literally (at least, in visual terms) makes the spectator become "lost in space." Computer effects create the illusion of the longest zoom-out shot in the history of the cinema as the camera appears to travel ever outwards through infinite space, continually relocating its center, from planet to planet, solar system to solar system. We are confronted by an infinite vision, one that ultimately deceives us as it shifts from outer space to inner space—while placing equal emphasis on the infinite.

*Event Horizon* (Anderson, 1997) again plunges the audience's vision into an infinite zoom-out. In one sequence, the camera (or the computer effect mimicking a camera motion) centers on the view of a figure through a window. The figure appears to be hanging upside down but, as the camera pulls out it also rotates and recenters the spectator's view to one that encompasses a larger view of a space station which includes further figures seen through windows situated at different angles to the original figure. Again, the camera zooms out and, as it rotates, provides an even longer shot of the station. So it continues, until this dizzying 'architecture of vision' reveals the massive polycentric and labyrinthine structure that is the space station, which is itself situated within a boundless space. All the while, the spectator's vision becomes the locus for multi-centered viewpoints.

A neo-baroque logic pervades both scenes, one that turns traditional monodirectional perspective on its head. In the construction of a co-extensive and labyrinthine space, "a" center is no longer present. The continual and multiplication of relocation of the center creates a spatial disorientation that emphasizes kinetic motion. In these instances, via the camera (and computer that produces the digital effects) our vision often appears to be violently thrust into the space and representation on the screen. In *Event Horizon* and *Contact* the combination of film and computer technology create a spectacle of kinetic motion, one that intensifies the seventeenth-century baroque's fascination with movement and the "turning-eye" (Kemp 1990, 212). Once the frame illusionistically collapses, traditional perspective, which relies on the frame and a static viewpoint also collapses. An illusion of infinity itself is placed before the spectator and an invitation is extended to engage with the spectacle in spatially and architecturally disorienting terms.[9]

In her discussion of contemporary science fiction cinema, Vivian Sobchack suggests that Jameson's articulation of postmodernist space finds expression in post-1977 science fiction films. Special effects spaces present themselves as "total spaces" that "stand for, and replace all other space"; the special effects environments of science fiction cinema also "celebrate hybrid expression, complexity, eclecticism, and 'variable space with surprises'" (Sobchack 1987, 255).[10] The special effects spaces of science fiction cinema—and, I would add, effects-driven cinema, theme park attractions, and spectacle cities like Las Vegas—play on precisely such complexities and spaces that surprise, calling upon the (neo)baroque concept of the great theatre of the world where the world and theatre, reality and performance blur. Contemporary entertainment spectacles greatly expand upon techniques of co-extensive space that drive the illusionistic traditions that dominate in the seventeenth-century baroque—where the fictive and the real appear to merge. The art that emerges, then and now, is concerned with perceptually (and sometimes literally) escaping the limitations of two-dimensional space.

It is theme park rides like Star Tours at Disneyland, the Back to the Future and Terminator 2: 3-D attractions at Universal Studios, and the recent Amazing Adventures of Spiderman 3-D roller coaster at Universal's Islands of Adventure in Florida, that further expand the potential for realizing a neo-baroque complexity of space. Theme park attractions evoke a spatial indeterminacy that thrives on kineticism and intense sensory engagement. Often using hydraulically powered motion simulators combined with film and digital technology, the participatory and invasive nature of these spectacles produce such an intense sense of the architectural dimension of sight that many an audience member literally suffers the effects in the form of nausea.

This is the realm of baroque spectacle as theatre of the world: once invited beyond the proscenium, and beyond the frame, the frame perceptually disintegrates embroiling the viewer in a series of baroque "folds," to use Deleuze's term, that present the possibility of a limitless scope of vision. The outside becomes inside and the inside out (Deleuze 1993, 34). The baroque phenomenon of border-crossing is best expressed by Deleuze:

> If the Baroque establishes a total art or a unity of the arts, it does so first of all in extension, each art tending to be prolonged and even to be prolonged into the next art, which exceeds the one before. We have remarked that the Baroque often confines painting to retables, but it does so because the painting exceeds its frame and is realized in polychrome marble

sculpture; and sculpture goes beyond itself by being achieved in architecture; and in turn, architecture discovers a frame in a façade, but the frame itself becomes detached from the inside, and establishes relations with the surroundings. . . . We witness the prodigious development of a continuity in the arts, in breadth or in extension: an interlocking of frames of which each is exceeded by a matter that moves through it (1993, 123).

Theme park attractions (which stand at the center of the most "cutting edge" developments in the entertainment industry) take to new limits the baroque "unity of the arts." While played out overtly in contemporary effects films and the entertainment spaces of Las Vegas, the polycentrism and spatial ambiguity inherent in neo-baroque architectures of vision finds its most intense form of expression in contemporary theme park attractions. Where effects cinema interweaves the represented frames of computer-generated, filmic and architectural realities, theme park attractions often take the ambiguity of the frame further still. Insides and outsides are continually rewritten, and multiple media and lived realities are continually reframed. The proscenium that demarcates audience space from the performance is blurred, and the audience becomes a participant in an enveloping entertainment spectacle.

## The Amazing Adventures of Spiderman and the Unity of the Arts

The Amazing Adventures of Spiderman, a multi-media attraction at Universal Studios' Islands of Adventure, Florida, is typical of the unity of the arts that populates current entertainment forms. Screen action using computer, video and film technology combines with live action in the form of a roller coaster to produce an exhilarating, participatory entertainment experience.

In the Marvel Superhero Island—one of the lands of the Islands of Adventure[11]—the groups of adventurers enter the Daily Bugle, the newspaper complex that is the workplace of Peter Parker, alias Spiderman. Once inside, and as we pass through the room that displays a portrait of J. Jonah Jameson (the Bugle Boss) we walk through the 'bowels' of the newsroom. The offices of Peter Parker and other reporters are experienced both as architectural environment and as sculptural space where objects like desks, newspapers, computer terminals, photographs, discarded food, and clothing appear as if frozen in time as a three-dimensional realization of a comic book world. With the exception of the attraction-adventurers who file through the offices, the workstations are abandoned and television screens overhead provide the clue as to the en masse exit: reporters (in animation form) inform us of the catastrophic events that have occurred in New York City.

Dr. Octopus—Spiderman's archenemy—and his group of villainous accomplices are wreaking havoc on the city and have stolen the Statue of Liberty, holding it for ransom.

We're thus primed for the next space, a larger auditorium where Jameson himself greets us—as mediated through a large screen. Jameson informs us that Dr. Octopus and his group of hoons, including Electro, Mysterio, and Hobgoblin (all of whom we're introduced to onscreen), are at large. It's our job, says JJJ, to act as stand-in reporters and bare witness to the chaotic events occurring in the city. With our mission clear, we move into the next room, a "subway station" where we enter a "scoop"—a roller coaster buggy—and head off on our reporting job.

Armed with our protective goggles (3-D glasses), our journey in the scoop takes us through the streets of New York (á la Marvel Universe) which appear as architecture, painted sets, and sculptured environments. As we plummet through the city—at times being swirled around in multiple 360-degree spins (a fact that disturbs the centered vision associated with classical form)—at various intervals we're strategically placed in front of 3-D-filmed images projected onto domed and wide screens. These larger-than-life filmed animations place us further in the middle of the action. Spiderman, for example, introduces himself by "leaping" onto our scoop car—causing our car to rock—then somersaulting back into one of the film screens. Informing us he will be our protector, he nevertheless fails to spare us the shocking sensations of being electrocuted by Electro or torched by Dr. Octopus. Likewise, he's nowhere in sight when our scoop-mobile plunges downwards at a 45-degree angle and we appear to fall from skyscraper-height and into an IMAX-constructed illusion of a New York pavement as it speedily approaches us. Admittedly, Spidey does save us from the fate that awaits us by setting up one of his trademark webs below us, but this only sends us rocketing back upwards. With barely enough time to check out the status of our innards we continue on our ride, witnessing the Statue of Liberty being hoisted above us (in sculptural form) and experiencing numerous other 3-D villain attacks (in 3-D animated, widescreen form) until, finally, Spiderman saves the day by battling the supervillains and trapping them in his web.

In this attraction, the reality of the audience's presence within Universal's Islands of Adventure melds with the fiction of the Spiderman comic book universe. Like many of the effects films and attractions that preceded It, the Spiderman attraction has pushed film technology and amusement park rides to new limits by unifying previously self-contained media forms. Likewise, operating according to the logic of the "unity of the arts" rides such as Spiderman not only draw upon the formal aspects of other media, they actually incorporate multiple media formats into their structure—in the process, engaging with as many senses as possible in order to heighten the illusion of the collapsing frame. Superheroes and supervillains are now placed within a 3-D context, and the illusionistic outcome is not only technologically groundbreaking but phenomenologically new.[12] All the while, audience members sit in their seats, their emotions vacillating between a child-like joy and a state of wonder at how these illusions are possible.

Neo-baroque entertainment spectacles like Spiderman may provide alternate techno-logical and multi-media dimensions to audience encounters, but the essence of this ex-perience relies on familiar media forms. As the song goes: "Everything old is new again." In their book *Remediation: Understanding New Media,* Jay Bolter and Richard Grusin sug-gest that all media, no matter how "new," rely on a media historicity. New media always retain a connection with the past in an effort to continually remediate, redefine and revi-talize their own form by drawing upon other media. They state: "Both new and old me-dia are invoking the twin logics of immediacy and hypermediacy in their efforts to remake themselves and each other" (1999, 5). Like the traditions of painting, architecture and sculpture, which have a longer history to draw upon, contemporary media forms such as the cinema and theme park attractions "remediate" or refashion other media forms, adapting them to their media-specific, formal and cultural needs. In short, "No medium today, and certainly no single media event, seems to do its cultural work in isolation from other media" (1999, 15). The fascinating morphological and experiential facets of many contemporary media examples, however, are found in the way they remediate and merge media forms, the outcome being the production of a neo-baroque aesthetic.

Entertainment forms like the Spiderman theme park attraction engage in such a com-plex and excessive level of interaction and remediation that it becomes increasingly diffi-cult to untangle one media form from another. Does Spiderman, for example, belong to the realm of the cinema, television, computer technology, sculpture, architecture, the theatre, the comic book, the animated cartoon, or the theme park attraction? A neo-baroque "fold" informs the logic of these remediated spectacles: all of these multimedia 'realities' intermingle with and fold into one another; characters from within the screen appear to enter the space of the audience; and the space of the audience appears to be-come one with the space of the screen. 3-D images, theatrical effects, computer graph-ics, animation, widescreen technologies, digital sound, and roller coaster engineering combine to construct the illusion of a breakdown of spatial boundaries that separate the audience's reality from the representation: the end result is that—while immersed in the exhilarating kinetics and illusions of the ride—it becomes difficult to fix the boundaries that frame the illusion and distinguish it from the space of reality.

The total unity of the arts that Deleuze discusses occurs through extension, invoking the motion of the fold: like the fluid media and figural transformations of Cortona's Barberini ceiling, one space extends into another, one medium into the next, the spectator into the spectacle, and the spectacle into the spectator. However, extending the baroque spatial dimension of sight, such neo-baroque attractions employ multi-media technologies to produce virtual trompe l'oeil effects. Introducing motion, sound, and other sensorial encounters to spectacle, the neo-baroque articulates the perceptual collapse of the frame more powerfully, and in ways not witnessed before.

Adding the "new" to the "old" media experiences, this multiplication of remediated forms—which stand as paragon to the baroque unity of the arts—also serves to heighten the greater emphasis that the neo-baroque places on the involvement of multiple senses. The combined effort of all of these innovative effects makes the experience seem and feel 'real'. For example, when the animated version of Dr. Octopus blasts the audience with fire, the animated fire ruptures its film boundary and enters the architectural interior that we inhabit, appearing as 'real' fire whose heat we feel and whose smoke effects we smell—and even taste. Additionally, the surround sound systems that wide screen cinema first introduced as a five-speaker format in the 1950s (and which were given new life with the release of *Star Wars* in 1977 and in the era of surround-sound entertainment cinema that followed) are now replaced with new digital audio effects by the Soundelux Entertainment Group that comprise over two hundred audio tracks and hundreds of speakers that are littered throughout the attraction, thus providing an auditory illusion that matches the visual.

State of the art digital effects, the digital sound system, roller coaster technology, revamped widescreen and 3-D cinema formats combine with the theatrical effects such as fire and smoke to produce an immersive and sensorially entertaining experience that engages all our senses—from the haptic, gustatory and the olfactory, to the auditory and the visual.[13] Revealing the dynamic nature of form, our own era has taken baroque games of perception to new limits. This fact necessitates a rearticulation of Gilles Deleuze's concept of a baroque "architecture of vision" and Martin Jay's "baroque ocular regime." When discussing the neo-baroque we also need to consider an architecture and regime that engages the sensorium.

## Remediations and Neo-Baroque Virtuosity

A central feature of contemporary effects films and theme park attractions lies in the spectator's state of uncertainty while in the midst of these games of perception. A neo-baroque ambivalence lies beneath the spectacle. The special effects illusions—whether it be the maniacal Dr. Octopus torching our car, or the perception of our scoop plunging down a New York skyscraper—impinge upon the audience in the way they invite us to experience the fantastic in such 'real' terms. The tricks have always been there, but the technology has now changed. Contemporary entertainment forms employ a variety of technological means to achieve this shift in perception. In the process, current effects cinema and theme park attractions also perform and compete with prior effects traditions, continually attempting to technically out-perform previous effects technology—and, along with it, the perceptions of reality these technologies delivered. Indeed, underlying Bolter and Grusin's statement regarding the concerns for immediacy and hypermediacy lies the possibility for a baroque logic: in "their efforts to remake themselves," current entertainment media often display a baroque obsession with virtuosity and the grand theatricality of illusionism. By seeking to remove the proscenium arch current entertainment spectacles like *The Amazing Adventures of Spiderman* also insist on the eventual revelation of the process of mediation.

*The Amazing Adventures of Spiderman* reflects the inherent virtuosity embedded in many contemporary entertainment media. The attraction lures the audience into various layers of 'reality' by displaying a variety of technologically conjured effects—in the process, setting itself up as a new kind of techno-spatial experience. A condition of the audience embracing the immediacy of the illusion as perceptually real is that we also (eventually) recognize and applaud the complexities involved in its construction. Indeed, by remediating 3-D cinema, animated cartoons, comic books, television, and the roller coaster, Spiderman also stakes its claim for out-performing these media. The result is that an interplay occurs between old and new traditions, one that suggests that the remediation of prior forms in Spiderman, the ride, has "improved" or "advanced" the audience's encounter with older media experiences.

Framing itself within its own historicity, therefore, underlying Spiderman is a virtuoso concern, one that results from its flawless articulation of an illusion that invades the audience's space in such deceptively real and immediately experiential ways. Throughout the entire attraction, the spectacle maintains an undeniable sense that this convincingly real representational space is also being displayed in order that the audience may admire it as a multi-technological feat of illusionism.[14] The visual and sensory games that entertainment technologies articulate flaunt their capacity for making a reality out of an illusion—or, rather, for making the fantastic enter our world in such immediate and sensorially invasive ways.

Increasingly, and through their own media-specific methods, entertainment media strive to obliterate the frame that demarcates a distance between reality and fantasy. The cinema relies on widescreen formats, computer-generated special effects, and surround sound experiences. The entertainments of Las Vegas rely on fantastic architecture and effects splendors. Theme park attractions draw upon a variety of methods including Imax and Omnimax screen formats, widescreen images, 3-D, simulation rides, and theatrical experiences. The future journeys that neo-baroque spectacles will take us on will be limited only by the technologies that drive them. Where these journeys will take us, one can only guess. However, one thing is certain: I will definitely go a long for the ride.

## Notes

1. I am indebted to Alison Inglis for devising the term "spectopolis." Given the visual assault our senses were exposed to during our research adventures in this sensorial city, we decided that the invention of a new term was required—one that could adequately convey the sensations evoked in these astounding spaces.

2. The negative ideological implications of spectacle in the contexts of the seventeenth and late twentieth/early twenty-first-century cultures have been issues of debate for numerous historians and theorists. Perniola, for example, cites the post-68 'society of spectacle' popularized by Guy Debord as instrumental in assuming that postmodern spectacle is riddled with "deception and secrets" (Perniola 1995). Baroque spectacle of the seventeenth-century faced a similar fate: the function of spectacle has been understood to function as optical persuasion that serves an ideological purpose. While not denying the ideological function underlying (neo)baroque spectacle, symptomatic interpretations dealing with the ideological function of spectacle offer but one perspective on the nature of audience/media relations. On the ideological implications of seventeenth-century spectacle, see Beldon Scott (1991), Martin (1965), and Wittkower (1985). For the ideological function of spectacle in Hollywood cinema see Britton (1986), Collins (1995), and Corrigan (1991). For accounts of the historical development of such theoretical traditions dealing with the function of spectacle see Best and Kellner (1991), Jay (1994), and Stafford (1994, 1996).

3. Such a position radically alters the psychoanalytic spectatorship models that were the basis on film theory in the 1970s and 1980s. In the Althusserian/Lacanian tradition of film spectatorship theory the spectator remains in a passive and static relationship to an image on the screen. The spectator is placed in the position of voyeur and driven by unconscious psychic and ideological processes. The world beyond the frame or world reflected back by the screen as mirror, in turn, framed the spectator: it framed their understanding of gender relations, their place within patriarchy, and the construction of their subjective selves. For detailed accounts of the psychoanalytic tradition of film spectatorship see Baudry (1981a, b), Heath (1981), Metz (1974), Mulvey (1975). For overviews and critiques of this tradition, see Carroll (1988) and Mayne (1993).

4. The fresco is part of a series of paintings that Raphael was commissioned to paint in the Stanza della Segnatura, Vatican. See Levey (1975), 51–53.

5. Raphael's painting adheres closely to Leon Battista Alberti's treatise Della Pittura (1435–1436). Here Alberti stresses the significance of "istoria," a term that carries with it notions of history and story. Reflecting concerns that were later remanifested in discussions of the classical Hollywood paradigm, Alberti stresses the importance of a centerd pictorial composition that supports clarity of narrative presentation. Above all, Alberti emphasises the need to "avoid excesses" (John R. Spencer in Alberti 1966, 23).

6. Expanding on a model first applied to Hollywood cinema by André Bazin, in the seminal study *The Classical Hollywood Cinema*, Bordwell, Staiger, and Thompson (1985) defined Hollywood cinema of the pre-1960s according to classical forms related to the Renaissance model. They state that classical aesthetic norms dominated the industry of this period, norms that reflect a closed attitude to form through centred framing, narrative progression and resolution; the visual and auditory style remains at the service of narrative unity, refusing to exceed the purposes required of story action. The causal narrative structure and centerd compositions create the effect of an enclosed story world, one that rationally frames a visual, auditory, and narrative representation that the spectator passively observes. The effect of this classical ordering has traditionally been viewed as one that "effaced itself before reality" (Lapsley and Westlake 1988, 160).

7. Jay (1994) argues that the baroque scopic regime has co-existed with two other visual systems. The first, that aligned with the Renaissance tradition, depends on Cartesian perspectivalism, and a "monocular static point of beholding" (1994, 60). This tradition also demands narrative clarity and order which impacts upon the visual articulation of narrative events. The second regime is that of the tradition of 'empirical descriptivism' and is characterised by the Dutch painting tradition which emphasizes a world of description "mapped in two dimensions" (Wollen 1993, 9). While all three regimes can co-exist, during different points in history, one ocular regime may dominate others. Periods dominated by a baroque order of vision interrogate "the privileged scopic regime of the modern era" that is dominated by "Cartesian perspectivalism aligned with Renaissance spatial order" (Jay 1994, 60).

8. The four other scenes on the vault are allegories that reflect on the Pope's attributes and works: the first, depicting Minerva Destroying Insolence and Pride in the Form of Giants, symbolizes Urban's battle against heresy; in Silenus and the Satyrs, Urban's piety is seen as overcoming "lust and intemperance"; Hercules driving out the Harpies allegorizes Urban's justice; and in The Temple of Janus his prudence ensures peace (Wittkower 1985, 252).

9. The shifting perceptions of the baroque are well expressed by the seventeenth-century philosopher Leibniz whose writings reflect the dissipation of the privileged omniscient view point that ordered classical systems as a view controlled by a single view point and a self-contained universe (Crary 1994, 50). Leibniz's baroque perception of the world suggested that the central, omniscient viewpoint was replaced by a world of multiple viewpoints. "The

monad became for Leibniz an expression of a fragmented and decenterd world, of the absence of an omniscient point of view, of the fact that every position implied a fundamental relativity that was never a problem for Descartes" (Crary 1994, 50).

10. Also see Jameson 1984.

11. The other lands are: Toon Lagoon, Jurassic Park, Lost Continent, and Seuss Landing.

12. The classical paradigm associated with pre-60s Hollywood cinema, and its associations with narrativity and the 'passive' spectator (a model that persists to this day in film theory in relation to contemporary cinema), no longer seems viable given new entertainment experiences concerned with spectacle, multimedia formations, and active audience address and participation. Spectacle engulfs the audience in invasive, spatial, and theatrical terms, producing participatory and sensorially engaging experiences. Indeed, film theorists such as Noel Carroll (1988), Jim Collins (1995), Judith Mayne (1993), and Vivian Sobchack (1992) have queried whether the "passive spectator" model was ever viable.

13. Las Vegas's Luxor Hotel/Casino is another case in point. Not only does this space offer visual and auditory experiences in the form of architectural spectalces that reconstruct ancient Egypt, or IMAX and simulation rides by Douglas Trumbull that digitally transport us back and forth in time, but on opening the doors to the hotel, the visitors'smell and taste is bombarded with the aromatic aromas of herbs and spices.

14. For an analysis of a similar virtuoso performance in relation to the *Terminator 2:* 3-D attraction at Universal Studios, see Ndalianis 2000.

## References

Ackerman, James S. 1991. *Distance Points: Essays in Theory and Renaissance Art and Architecture.* Cambridge, MA: MIT Press.

Alberti, Leon Battista. 1966. *On Painting* (introduction John R. Spencer). New Haven: Yale University Press.

Baudry, Jean-Louis. 1981 "The Apparatus." In *Apparatus,* ed. Theresa Hak Kyung Cha. New York: Tanam Press, 41–62.

————.1981b. "Ideological Effects of the Basic Cinematographic Apparatus." *Apparatus,* ed. Theresa Hak Kyung Cha. New York: Tanam Press, 25–40.

Bazin, Andre. 1967. *What Is Cinema?* Berkeley: University of California Press. Vol. 1.

————1971. *What Is Cinema?* Berkeley: University of California Press. Vol. 2.

Beldon Scott, John. 1991. *Images of Nepotism: the Painted Ceilings of Palazzo Barberini.* Princeton: Princeton University Press.

Belton, John. 1992. *Widescreen Cinema*. New York: Columbia University Press.

Best, Steven, and Douglas Kellner. 1991. *Postmodern Theory: Critical Interrogations*. London: Macmillan.

Bolter, Jay David, and Richard Grusin. 1999. *Remediation: Understanding New Media*. Cambridge, MA: MIT Press.

Bordwell, David, Janet Staiger, and Kristin Thompson. 1985. *The Classical Hollywood Cinema: Film Style and Mode of Production to 1960*. London: Routledge.

Britton, Andrew. 1986. "Blissing Out: the Politics of Reaganite Entertainment," *Movie* 31–32 (Winter): 2–42.

Calabrese, Omar. 1992. *Neo-Baroque: a Sign of the Times*. Princeton University Press, (originally published 1987).

Carroll, Noel. 1988. *Mystifying Movies: Fads and Fallacies in Contemporary Film Theory*. New York: Columbia University Press.

Collins, Jim. 1995. *Architectures of Excess: Cultural Life in the Information Age*. New York: Routledge.

Corrigan, Timothy. 1991. *A Cinema without Walls: Movies and Culture after Vietnam*. London: Routledge.

Crary, Jonathan. 1994. *Techniques of the Observer: On Vision and Modernity in the Nineteenth Century*. Cambridge, MA: MIT Press.

Debord, Guy. 1970. *The Society of Spectacle*. Detroit: Black and Red.

Deleuze, Gilles. *The Fold: Leibniz and the Baroque*. Trans. Tom Conley. Minneapolis: University of Minneapolis Press (originally published 1988).

Focillon, Henri. 1992. *The Life of Forms in Art*. London: Zone Books. (Originally published in 1934).

Heath, Stephen. 1981. *Questions of Cinema*. Bloomington: Indiana University Press.

Jameson, Fredric. 1984. "Postmodernism: the Cultural Logic of Late Capitalism," in *New Left Review* 146: 53–93.

Jay, Martin. 1994. *Downcast Eyes: the Denigration of Vision in Twentieth-Century French Thought*. Berkeley: University of California Press.

Kemp, Martin. 1990. *The Science of Art: Optical Themes in Western Art from Brunelleschi to Seurat*. New Haven: Yale University Press.

Lapsley, Robert, and Michael Westlake. 1988. *Film Theory: An Introduction*. Manchester: Manchester University Press.

Levey, Michael. 1975. *High Renaissance*. Middlesex: Penguin.

Maravall, Jose Antonio. 1983. *Culture of the Baroque: Analysis of a Historical Structure*. Trans. Terry Cochran. Minneapolis: University of Minnesota Press. (Originally published 1975).

Martin, John Rupert. 1965. *The Farnese Gallery*. Princeton: Princeton University Press.

Martin, John Rupert. 1977. *Baroque*. London: Penguin.

Mayne, Judith. 1993. *Cinema and Spectatorship*. New York: Routledge.

Metz, Christian. 1974. *Film Language: a Semiotics of the Cinema*. London: Oxford University Press.

Mulvey, Laura. 1975. "Visual Pleasure and Narrative Cinema," *Screen* 16: 6–18.

Murray, Linda. 1986. *The High Renaissance and Mannerism*. London: Thames and Hudson.

Ndalianis, Angela. 2000. "Special Effects, Morphing Magic and the 1990s Cinema of Attractions." In *Meta-morphing: Visual Transformation and the Culture of Quick Change*. ed. Vivian Sobchack. Minneapolis: University of Minnesota Press, 251–271.

Perniola, Mario. 1995. *Enigmas: the Egyptian Movement in Society and Art*. Trans. Christopher Woodall. New York: Verso. (Originally published 1990).

Sobchack, Vivian. 1987. *Screening Space: the American Science Fiction Film*. New York: Ungar.

Sobchack, Vivian. 1992. *The Address of the Eye: A Phenomenology of Film Experience*. Princeton: Princeton University Press.

Stafford, Barbara Maria. 1994. *Artful Science: Enlightenment Entertainment and the Eclipse of the Visual Education*. Cambridge, MA: MIT Press.

————. 1996. *Good Looking: Essays on the Virtue of Images*. Cambridge, MA: MIT Press.

Wittkower, Rudolf. 1985. *Art and Architecture in Italy 1600–1750*. Middlesex: Penguin (originally published 1958).

Wollen, Peter. 1993. "Baroque and Neo-Baroque in the Age of Spectacle," *Point of Contact* 3 (April 3): 9–21.

# 22 Media Technology and Museum Display: A Century of Accommodation and Conflict

Alison Griffiths

*We must have integrity of content and integrity of presentation, for we are in the business of education, not indoctrination and not entertainment.*
—Kenneth Starr, 1990[1]

Since the mid-1980s, electronic media have assumed an ever-greater presence in museums of science, technology, natural history, and art.[2] For the most part, museum directors and curators have embraced new interactive technologies for their promise to democratize knowledge, to offer contextual information on exhibits, and to boost museum attendance. Corporate sponsors and donors of museum technology are interested in new media for their own reasons; with their logos emblazoned on interactive kiosks and published gallery guides, corporate patrons have been increasingly active in sponsoring special exhibitions, branding specific gallery spaces, or donating equipment.[3] Museum visitors, especially children and young adults,[4] have responded enthusiastically to interactive exhibits, even coming to expect them as an integral part of the museum experience.[5] Curators supporting the new technology argue that multimedia platforms offer innovative solutions to the problem of representing complex ideas and processes; as Kathleen McLean argues: "They can activate an otherwise static exhibition with sound and moving images; provide a variety of view points; engage visitors in multi-layered activities; and encourage and support interaction among people in an exhibition."[6]

Digital technologies have found a home in the modern museum in the forms of interactive touch-screen kiosks, CD-ROMs, computer games, large-screen installations and videowalls with multiple images, digital orientation centers, "smart badge" information systems, 3-D animation, virtual reality, and sophisticated museum Web sites.[7] Such technologies have changed the physical character of the museum, frequently creating striking juxtapositions between nineteenth-century monumental architecture and the electronic glow of the twenty-first-century computer screen. Via the World Wide Web, the museum now transcends the fixities of time and place, allowing virtual visitors to wander through its perpetually deserted galleries and interact with represented objects in ways previously unimagined.[8] Even at this early state of the on-line museum, there are emerging parallels between the experience of virtual and actual museum-going; as exhibit developer Stephen Botysewicz notes, "browsing through a CD-ROM or Web site is strikingly similar to the 'grazing' behavior that museum visitors engage in—moving from attractor to attractor, not always adhering to the programmed march exhibit designers intend for them."[9]

Despite its embrace by many museum professionals and visitors alike, the growing prominence of digital media in exhibition design has also provoked a sustained and sharp debate within museum circles. This debate concerns the effect of electronic media upon traditional notions of authenticity and ownership of the museum artifact, and upon contemporary practices of museum access and professional ethics, as well as the role of new media in relation to traditional sources of knowledge in museums such as labels, docents (explainers), and printed guidebooks. Some observers worry that digital technology is blurring the line between the traditional public museum and the commercial theme park and retail complex, such as NikeTown in New York City, into generic spaces of "edutainment."[10] As Michael Welch, Manager of Nike Global Retail and Design argues, "More and more we're all using similar systems—in retail, theme parks, and museums."[11]

Three recurring themes have dominated these discussions: the role of digital media in what is seen as a "third evolution" in methods of museum exhibition (following those at the turn of the last century and in the 1950s and 1960s); the nature and effects of interactivity in contemporary museum exhibit design; and the tension between the museum as a site of uplift and rational learning as opposed to one of amusement and spectacle. While a great deal of research is yet to be done on the implications of digital media on museums, a striking feature of contemporary debates is the sense of déjà vu found in the historically widely separated reactions to issues of modernization, interactivity, and the tension between education and entertainment. For example, current cautions about the "Disneyfication"[12] of natural history museums echo concerns voiced by turn-of-the-century critics who argued that the use of popular display methods such as habitat groups, lantern slides, and motion pictures required careful supervision, lest their associations with popular culture contaminate the scientific seriousness of the exhibit and institution.[13] The discursive oppositions between science and spectacle, information and entertainment, and passive and interactive spectators first articulated in relation to these visual technologies one hundred years ago have repeatedly resurfaced in contemporary debates over multi-media exhibits in public museums.

My aim in this essay is to trace the roots of current museological debates over the adoption of digital media to efforts a century ago to make museums more accessible to the general public through the adoption of then-new visual technologies and display techniques. As the first generation of professional curators began dismantling (both-literally and figuratively) the "storehouse of curiosities" model of traditional nineteenth-century museums, many of them worried that the shift towards more popular exhibit techniques risked blurring the boundaries between the museum as an institution of moral and social uplift and other less reputable cultural sites, including the nickelodeon and the sensationalist dime museum.

Clues for understanding contemporary museum attitudes toward new media technologies can therefore be found in a number of experimental exhibits proposed (if not always installed) in American and European museums at the beginning of the twentieth century. At one extreme, French scientist Félix-Louis Regnault's turn-of-the-century plan for an encyclopedic ethnographic archive strikingly anticipates contemporary visions of the multi-media museum and Web site. In Regnault's imagined ethnographic museum, anthropologists and members of the general public could retrieve written texts, sound recordings, and still and moving images of indigenous peoples at the flick of a switch.[14] In a more prosaic fashion, the Metropolitan Museum of Art in New York City experimented with interactive exhibits in 1901, when it designed an installation that allowed visitors to turn the pages of an art book by inserting their hands into the side of the display case.[15] Contributors to such professional museum journals as the *British Museums Journal* (1901–) and the *American Museum News* (1924–) as well as popular journals such as *The World's Work, The Outlook, The Independent,* and *Popular Science Monthly* debated the suitability of various methods of visual display for museums highly conscious of their social function in a culture experiencing the stresses of rapid industrialization, urbanization, and immigration. Responding to what was widely perceived as the shrinking attention span of the urban museum-goer, late nineteenth-century curators charged with the task of making exhibits more accessible turned to novel methods of exhibit design in search of suitable prototypes for the modern museum. These prototypes will form the basis of my discussion in part one of this essay, where I examine efforts undertaken by turn-of-the-century curators to formulate new paradigms of museum collection and display. In part two, I consider how these modernization efforts were greeted by museum professionals of the time, some of whom were skeptical of "gimmicks" that might lead the museum spectator to think that "he is in a raree show," in the words of one curator, rather than an institution of scientific or aesthetic enlightenment.[16] Interspersed throughout this discussion will be contemporary examples of how these issues continue to challenge curators and designers.

### *"Drifts about a Mental Derelict": Reforming the Museum Visitor*

At the "Museums as Places of Popular Culture" conference held in Mannheim, Germany in 1903, Dr. Lichtwark envisioned a "great revolution in the equipment and methods of museums."[17] One of the aims of the conference was to consider ways in which museums could make themselves more accessible to working people (the upper classes, it was argued, were "above instruction") through the media of photography and magic lantern slides.[18] Curators at the conference also discussed the need for exhibits to be designed around a coherent idea rather than function as "overcrowded storehouses of material, purposelessly heaped together."[19] According to British Museums Association President Francis Arthur Bather, the physical crowding of museum galleries and display cases provoked a "crowding relative to the mind of the visitor," brought about by gazing at endless rows of identical objects.[20] Speaking at the Museums Association's 1903 Aberdeen Conference, Norwegian curator Dr. Thiis argued that "nothing is more wearisome to the eye, less advantageous for the individual objects, than those long stretches of cases, all to one pattern, covered with black velvet, that are so often seen in museums."[21] In 1907, American Museum of Natural History (AMNH) President H. C. Bumpus complained that the average museum visitor, overwhelmed by the sheer number of display cases, "became quite lost in the maze of exhibited material, and losing alike both points of the compass and sequence of theme, drifts about a mental derelict."[22] Despite repeated proclamations of the demise of the overcrowded museum since the turn of the last century, criticisms that curators continue to cram too many artifacts into the limited space of exhibit halls persist within museum circles. For example, museum scholar George E. Hein recently called upon curators to display fewer objects in museums, arguing that collections should be distributed between exhibition and study areas rather than crammed into the exhibit halls.[23] To obviate the feared sensory overload of museum-goers, contemporary designers have deliberately included empty or negative spaces in galleries to allow visitor's eyes to rest.[24]

Many nineteenth-century museum observers also criticized display cases for shoddy construction and for their frequently awkward or ostentatious design, which, it was thought, competed with the objects on display for spectator attention.[25] Henry Crowther, curator at the Leeds Museum in the north of England, urged curators to consider the inherent limitations of the display case, arguing that an over-stuffed, over-labeled exhibit couldn't possibly convey the "mind-thought of the curator or assistant curator who put them up."[26] The most radical suggestion for the re-design of cases and labels was offered by George Browne Goode, Director of the National Museum at the Smithsonian, and influential spokesman on museum design in the early part of this century, who advocated "a collection of well expressed, terse labels, illustrated by a few well-selected subjects."[27] Indeed, the design and function of labels were controversial topics within the turn-of-the-century museological world, with critics taking up positions along a continuum. Dr. E. Hecht, for example, argued that detailed labeling as proposed by Goode was unlikely to have much impact on visitor interest and comprehension: "Certainly we can multiply and amplify the labels . . . we can have, or ought to have, guide-books with their illustrations" Hecht opined, "but labels are not always read,[28] and guide-books, if purchased, seldom read."[29]

As early twentieth-century museum professionals debated trends in exhibit design, they increasingly wrote of the need to contextualize the objects on display, a shift in philosophy that in many ways prefigures the use of interactive technologies in contemporary museums. For example, in 1903, Bather argued that "even when there is nothing strikingly incongruous or offensive in the manner of exhibition, the mere removal of objects from their natural environment places them at a disadvantage."[30] Implicitly recognizing the discursive implications of exhibiting artifacts, what Ivan Karp and Stephen D. Levine call the "poetics and politics of museum display,"[31] in 1903 Dr. Hecht recommended the use of "stopping points" in galleries, which he defined as displays relating to the primary exhibit but "chosen in order to arouse, from time to time, the interest of the public, to lead their mind from the view of a single animal to larger ideas, to a general conception."[32] Hecht's "stopping points" anticipate one major role for computer installations in contemporary exhibition design, inviting visitors to pause in order to draw connections between an exhibited object and its uses and contexts.

While the recent proliferation of interactive technologies points to an emerging model of museum spectatorship in which context and interactivity play increasingly important roles in structuring the museum experience, it is striking that such ideas were first articulated a hundred years ago. As one curator noted in 1905, "an hour's worth of teaching would not get so much information into the mind of the child as he would get by finding out the information for himself."[33] One early attempt to make the museum display case more accessible to visitors was the Rotary Cabinet, designed by the Reverend S. J. Ford in 1907, which allowed objects to be viewed at will by the museum spectator, who, by turning a driving handle on the side of the cabinet could rotate for display each drawer in turn. The appeal of this device was that all of the specimens could be brought to the top of the display case for inspection without the "cabinet being opened or the specimens disturbed." Advocating its use in museums, schools, and homes, Reverend Ford claimed that its simple design and mechanism meant that "even a blind-folded child could work it."[34] If keeping objects out of the hands of museum-goers (and ensuring their security) was one of the implicit goals of the Rotary Cabinet, there were other critics who were equally ardent about letting museum goers, especially children, roll up their sleeves and touch as much as they liked.

Proposals for hands-on exhibits within museums were made by a number of early commentators, many of whom were, interestingly, women. In 1901, Kate M. Hall, curator at the 48-foot by 32-foot Whitechapel Museum in London, stated that when school groups visited the tiny museum, the objects they wanted to study "should, whenever possible, be taken out of their cases."[35] Hall was also a firm believer in making connections between living specimens and the dead ones in the cases in order "not to give a child facts, but to entangle him or her in an interest and love of living things" in order that they "not think the study of natural history a study of dead things only."[36] Present in this discourse on hands-on displays is recognition of the tactile pleasures involved in handling exhibits, an acknowledgment that anticipates the popularity of Discovery Rooms and Hands-On Centers in contemporary museums. Writing at the time, AMNH President H. C. Bumpus went so far as to criticize the "impounding of specimens in cases," arguing that in some instances, displays should be out in the open, such as the 1906 Elk Group at the AMNH. According to Bumpus, curators should be sensitive to the "touch sense" of their visitors and attempt to overcome the feelings of remoteness visitors experienced when they viewed objects behind glass.[37] (It is interesting to note that the haptical pleasures of the exhibition gallery—the fact that people respond to the textural surfaces of the objects on visual display—is factored into contemporary exhibition design and can be heightened for the museum-goer through the use of different textures on the floors, gallery seating, display panels, and so on).[38] If Bumpus's plan for liberating his exhibits from their glass enclosures created logistical and security problems for museum personnel, his vision for the twentieth-century natural history museum is nevertheless remarkably sympathetic to modern pronouncements on the educational aims of museums and the role that digital technologies can play in furthering these ends. But there were inherent risks involved in popularizing exhibits, as we shall see in the next section.

## *Treading a Difficult Path: A Changing Landscape of Popular Techniques*

The task of preserving a balance between civic uplift and economic viability has never been easy for museums, and while contemporary museums increasingly appropriate the protocols and values of business into their operations, retail and leisure complexes look to museums for models on how to integrate digital media into their attractions. Retail stores with interactive kiosks more and more resemble museums, and museums with flight simulators, IMAX screens, and corporate logos increasingly resemble theme parks, while companies such as Discovery Zone, a Chicago-based corporation offering for-profit play centers for children, compete aggressively with public children's museums for patronage.[39] In this context, it is worth considering how curators responded to the education versus entertainment challenge a hundred years ago.

In some ways, little has changed over the course of the twentieth century. Curators were as cognizant of the need to make the learning experience pleasurable at the turn-of-the-century as they are today. The real challenge lay in reconciling crowd-pleasing exhibition techniques with the philosophical remit of the institution. Writing in the Architectural Record in 1900, L. A. Gratacap viewed the relationship between high and low culture in uncomplicated terms: "The Popular [sic] system of the scientific Museum is the system of the Dime Museum greatly elevated, dignified, and replenished with culture."[40] AMNH President H. C. Bumpus expressed the ambivalence of many museum professionals concerning the balance between scientific accuracy and respectability versus public accessibility: "For purposes of popular exhibition and profitable instruction we no longer seek the exhaustive collections of 'every known species'; we look askance at extraordinary and monstrous types; we view with some misgivings the elaborately technical schemes of classification . . . and we become thoughtful when we witness the visitor's vacuity of expression as he passes before cases devoted to the phylogeny of the arachnids."[41] Bumpus's disapproval of the freak-show display of "extraordinary and monstrous types," was echoed by other curators at the beginning of the twentieth century. Frank Woolnaugh wrote in the *Museums Journal* in 1904 that: "The old curiosity shop days of the museum are over. The misguided lamb with two heads, and the pig with two tails, are relegated to a back closet, if they have not already found a resting place in the sphere of the dust-bin. There is so much that is beautiful in nature to preserve that we have neither time, space, nor inclination to perpetuate her freaks and errors."[42] However, at the same time as some critics bemoaned the sensationalist leanings of turn-of-the-century exhibits, others maintained that museums were inaccessible to the general public due to their overly scholarly preoccupations; as Lisa C. Roberts has noted, Goode himself, expressed this ambivalence toward museums by criticizing them for being "both vulgar sideshows and elitist enclaves."[43]

The conflicting demands of scientific rigor and popular appeal remains a pervasive theme in contemporary museum criticism, and it is telling that it became part of the discourse on museum exhibitory at such an early stage. One hundred years ago, advanced technology seemed to many observers to solve the challenge of balancing the demands of science and spectacle. Discussing the importance of free daily lectures for attracting audiences to museums in 1904, Dr. Ant Fritsch was one of the first curators to recommend the use of phonograph recordings in installations. "The time may not be far distant," Fritsch declared, "when we shall be able, by dropping a cent into a phonograph by the side of interesting objects in the museum, secure the pleasure of a short discourse on the exhibit."[44] Fritsch's idea of using the phonograph to provide contextual information on an exhibit—one of the key objectives of contemporary interactive technologies—had already been adopted in the display techniques of world's fairs and expositions, where a great many of the modern methods of exhibition were pioneered. It was at such expositions, one commentator pointed out, that "what you could not see for yourself you could read, for lecturetts were posted conveniently on each side of the case." That these methods were considered radical for their time, in the same way that computer installations were once cutting edge, is suggested by the observer's remark that "here was canned science with the can-opener handy!"[45] But we can also detect an undertone of disapproval here, a sense, perhaps, that in making exhibits more accessible to the public, curators risked compromising or over-simplifying scientific ideas.

At the same time, some curators, as they began to reconfigure exhibition spaces for a generation of museum-goers trained in the viewing protocols of modern urban culture at the end of nineteenth century, came to believe that traditional display methods would continue to dominate. That is, technology might help museums compete with popular amusements for audiences and offer museum-goers opportunities for greater understanding of scientific principles, but technology would never usurp the artifact, which curators realized, was the primary reason people visited museums. Not surprisingly, skepticism over the suitability of museum exhibits heavily dependent on technology as a mediating device has repeatedly surfaced throughout a century of debates on museum design, including a report from the

American Association of Museum Task Force on Education in 1991, as digital media and interactive kiosks were increasingly adopted by museums: "The key to the realization of the higher value of museums lies in the receptivity of those responsible for objects to new interpretations of their roles. It does not lie in new technologies of presentation."[46]

Contextualizing museum objects within realistic settings was another technique curators used to make display cases more aesthetically pleasing and more effective in conveying intended object-lessons; even to this day, habitat groups and period rooms, despite the expense and space they demand, remain popular with the public, since the impact of a re-created space can evoke the sensory experience of immersion and time travel.[47] Habitat groups (displaying the flora and fauna of a particular region) and life groups (illusionistic displays representing indigenous people against diorama backdrops) were among the most popular, and costly, display methods used at the turn-of-the-century.[48] One English commentator remarked that this effort toward realistic exhibits "recognizes the fact that we shall never succeed in infusing into the minds of those who have it not a love of nature, until we get as near as possible to nature herself."[49] But this view was not shared by all curators; one dissenter at the Museums Association 1906 conference argued that museums "had of late gone a step too far in what might be called 'bringing the scent of the hay over the footlight,'" a prophetic statement when we consider the use of virtual reality installations or simulators in some contemporary museums. According to this critic: "Slabs of nature were transported bodily into museum cases and their lessons rendered so obvious that people found it easier to stroll into a museum to learn the habits of animals than to lie in wait for them in their native fields . . . Thus instead of creating naturalists, our museum helped people to lose the naturalist's chief faculty—observation."[50] The claim here is that the habitat and life groups' privileging of sight as the source of scientific knowledge would make spectators lazy and, paradoxically, diminish the skills of visual acuity and patient observation. Some turn-of-the-century curators feared that if spectators consumed natural history in the distracted and passive manner in which they consumed the pervasive advertising imagery within the urban landscape, then spectators' interest in seeking out the natural world for themselves would be diminished. Moreover, the fear was that overt theatricality and voyeurism of realistic displays, along with their tendency toward sensationalism, would leave the museum visitor with little work to do beyond absorbing the spectacle. If the habitat group's reconstruction of picturesque (and sometimes violent) vignettes of wildlife vivified nature and created a memorable exhibit for museum-goers, for some critics, the installation's hyper-verisimilitude underscored its own artificiality, drawing audience attention to its construction and trompe-l'oeil effects:[51]

The charge of early critics that habitat groups and other illusionistic exhibits might generate a sense of wonder in the spectator without offering much in the way of scientific explication is echoed today by skeptics of the use of interactive technologies. Chandler Screven, for example, has argued that "the three-dimensionality of exhibits and their novelty, gadgetry, and manipulatory aspects can have intrinsic interest and generate attention but distract viewers from the main ideas, distinctions, or story line."[52] Subscribing to a similar view, Lisa C. Roberts feels that evocative display settings and high-tech equipment may in fact end up "overshadow[ing] the objects they were designed to set off. Not only do these innovations compete for attention, they compete for space: every new device represents a reduction in display area."[53] There is also little empirical evidence that interactive exhibits have any lasting effect on visitor comprehension of exhibit themes or whether they are effective in altering misconceptions; as Tim Caulton has noted, "the educational arguments in favor of interactive exhibitions may be compelling, but the evidence to date is patchy and largely anecdotal. Interactive exhibitions remain a largely untapped laboratory for systematic research to investigate how people learn in an informal environment."[54] What is clear, though, from the few studies that have been conducted, is that visitors enjoy using interactive exhibits and that electronic media and digital technologies have been secured a home in the twenty-first-century museum.[55]

There is, then, a definite sense of *déjá vu* pervading contemporary debates about the uses of digital technology in museums, with curators facing many of the same challenges that their predecessors faced. With revenue-generating attractions such as Imax screens as an increasingly regular feature in most natural history and science museums, curators may feel they have little alternative other than to look to the spectacular, the popular, and the profitable as a three-pronged approach to fiscal health and customer satisfaction. As curators ponder the ontological status and pedagogical value of technology-dependent exhibits within the twenty-first-century museum, they might do well to consider what lessons can be learned from the enduring debates of the past.

### Notes

1. Kenneth Starr, "MER at Twenty: Some Observations on Museum Education," *Journal of Museum Education* 15, no. 1 (Winter 1990): 18 reprinted in *Patterns in Practice: Selections from the Journal of Museum Education* (Washington, DC: Museum Education Roundtable, 1992), 67.

2. See *Museum Practice,* 3, no. 3 (1998) for a special issue on museums and multi-media.

3. There are inevitable trade-offs, however, in relying upon external funding, since some sponsors are only interested in "blockbuster shows" (those with large budgets and likely to attract huge audiences), expect their logo to be highly visible, and may even want a say in the creative process. See Kathleen McLean, *Planning for People in Museums* (Washington DC: Association for Science-Technology Centers, 1993), 152.

4. In a survey of existing studies of the impact of gender on the use of computer interactives, Lynn D. Dierking and John H. Falk suggest that there is conflicting opinion over whether men or women are more or less likely to use the technology. In an early study conducted at the National Museum of Natural History, 65 percent of interactive kiosk users were male whereas in a summative evaluation of the "Spirit of the Motherland" exhibition at the Virginia Museum of Fine Arts, users were predominantly female. Dierking and Falk, "Audience and Accessibility," in Selma Thomas and Ann Mintz, ed., *The Virtual and the Real: Media in the Museum* (Washington, DC: American Association of Museums, 1998), 65. E. Sharpe, Touch Screen Computers: An Experimental Orientation Device at the National Museum of American History (Washington, DC: National Museum of American History, Smithsonian Institution) and Dierking, Falk, and C. Abrams, Summative Evaluation of 'Liberation 1945,' US Holocaust Museum (Annapolis, MD: Science Learning Inc., forthcoming). Other studies on gender and new technology cited by Dierking and Falk include K. Morrissey, "Visitor Behavior and Interactive Video," *Curator* 34, no. 2 (1991): 109–118 and J. Pawlukiewicz, K. Bohling, and Z. Doering, "The Caribou Connection. Will People Stop, Look and Question?" Paper presented at the American Association of Museums, Mar. 15, 1989, Washington, DC.

5. Dierking and Falk point out "while media is only one option for interactivity, visitors to science museums and science centers are increasingly expecting to encounter some type of media experience at a museum (IMAX film, computer interactive, or a videodisk)." "Audience and Accessibility," 66.

6. McLean, *Planning for People,* 29.

7. At the Smithsonian Institution's International Gallery, a show entitled "Microbes: Invisible Invaders, Amazing Allies," allowed combined hands-on activities with high-tech computer software; according to the *Washington Post,* visitors could "look through microscopes, play video games, participate in quiz shows and much more." Catherine O'Neill Grace, "Have you ever met a microbe?" *Washington Post,* June 1, 1999, 18.

8. Within days of being launched, the British "24-Hour Museum," which offers a "cyberspace gateway to hundreds of UK collections," ran into controversy as a result of its endowment by culture secretary Chris Smith as "the UK's thirteenth official national collection." According to Smith, the 24-Hour Museum created for the first time a "single unified national collection" and because of its status as a "national museum of the Web," it was designated a national museum. According to Julie Nightingale, museum directors, volunteers, campaigners, and members of the press criticized the endowment arguing that it "undermined

the importance of the status of national museums for the sake of publicity." The site was co-developed by the Campaign for Museum and mda (Museum Documentation Association). Nightingale, "Museums go on-line," *Museums Journal* [hereafter abbreviated to *MJ*] 99, no. 6 (June 1999): 7. For an editorial comment on the 24-Hour Museum, see "Virtual Reality" in the same issue, 16. As Ruth Perlin explains, "works of arts, their contexts, and their display arrangements are being electronically transported out of exhibit spaces to be examined and visited in homes and other settings by individuals who may never enter the art museum." Ruth R. Perlin, "Media, Art Museums, and Distant Audiences," in *The Virtual and the Real,* ed. Thomas and Mintz, 84.

9. Stephen Botysewicz, "Networked Media: The Experience is Closer than you Think," in *The Virtual and the Real,* ed. Thomas and Mintz, 114.

10. This term comes from the title of Ann Mintz's article, "That's Edutainment," *Museum News* 73, no. 6 (1994): 32–35. I discuss her argument and its relevance for the concerns of this paper later in the essay.

11. Michael Welch, quoted in Cynthia Wisehart, "Multimedia Merchandising," *Textile World* (January 1999), n.p.

12. Lisa C. Roberts refers to these critiques in *From Knowledge to Narrative: Educators and the Changing Museum* (Washington, DC: Smithsonian Institution Press, 1997), 69.

13. For a discussion of institutional responses to the uses of motion pictures at the AMNH from 1903 through the late teens, see chapter six of my book *Wondrous Difference: Cinema, Anthropology, and Turn-of-the-Century Visual Culture* (New York: Columbia University Press, 2002).

14. For a brief discussion of Regnault's proposal, see Peter Bloom, "Pottery, Chronophotography, and the French Colonial Archive," unpublished paper presented to Screen Studies Conference, Glasgow, Scotland, June 1993.

15. F. A. Bather, "The Museums of New York State," *MJ* 1, no. 3 (September 1901): 73.

16. F. Jeffrey Bell, "On 'Good Form' in Natural History Museums," *MJ* 3, no. 5 (November 1903): 160.

17. Dr. Litchwark cited in Anon. "The Mannheim Conference on Museums as Places of Popular Culture," *MJ* 3, no. 4 (October 1903): 105.

18. Ibid., 107.

19. Prof. Dr. Ant. Fritsch, "The Museum Question in Europe and America," *MJ* 3, no. 8 (February 1904): 252.

20. Francis Arthur Bather, "Museum's Association Aberdeen Conference, 1903," *MJ* 3, no. 3 (September 1903): 80.

21. Dr. Thiis, "Arbog of the Nordenfjeldske Kunstindustrimuseum, 1898–1901," p. 121, cited in F. A. Bather, "The Aberdeen Conference, 1903, Address by the President," *MJ* 3, no. 4 (October 1904): 119

22. H. C. Bumpus, "A Contribution to the Discussion on Museum Cases," *MJ* 6, no. 9 (March 1907): 299.

23. George E. Hein, *Learning in the Museum* (London: Routledge, 1998), 44.

24. McLean, *Planning for People,* 128.

25. A. B. Meyer, "The Structure, Position, and Illumination of Museum Cases," *MJ* 6, no. 7 (January 1907): 237.

26. Henry Crowther, "The Museum as Teacher of Nature-Study," *MJ* 5, no.1 (July 1905): 8.

27. George Browne Goode cited in Frank Collins Baker, "The Descriptive Arrangement," *MJ* 7, no. 4 (October 1902): 108. One should point out that curating as an occupation was undergoing professionalization throughout this period; influential museum spokesman Sir William Flower—President of the British Zoological Society of London before becoming Director of the Natural History Museum in 1884—argued in 1889 that "What a museum really depends on for its success and usefulness is not its buildings, not its cases, not even its specimens, but its curator. . . . He and his staff are the life and soul of the institution, upon whom its whole value depends," in "Discussion," 61. In lyrico-poetic terms, F. A. Bather described the successful curator as "a man of enthusiasm, of ideas, of strictest honor, of sincerity, with the grip and devotion of a specialist, yet with the wisdom born of wide experience, with an eye for the most meticulous detail, but with a heart and mind responsive to all things of life, art, and nature" ("The Man as Museum-Curator," *MJ* 1, no. 7 [January 1902]: 188).

28. Contemporary studies on the effect of labeling on visitor interest and retention of information suggest that combining labels with photographs, drawings, objects, and other sensory elements can make a difference. McLean, *Planning for People,* 106. The recent supplement to the April 1999 issue of *Museums Journal* (vol. 99, no. 4) included step-by-step guidelines on label-making (font, size, position, etc.) suggesting perhaps that almost a hundred years on from these discussions, museum professionals can still benefit from detailed instruction in label design and manufacture. For a discussion of the challenges of knowing with certainty how visitors respond to labels (and the findings of a fascinating study of visitor interaction with exhibit texts at the British Museum [Natural History]) see Paulette M. McManus, "Oh Yes, They Do: How Museum Visitors Read Labels and Interact with Exhibit Texts," *Curator* 32, no. 3 (1989). 174–189.

29. Dr. E. Hecht, "How to Make Small Natural History Museums Interesting," *MJ,* 3, no. 6 (December 1903): 188.

30. Bather, "Museum's Association," 81.

31. Ivan Karp and Steven D. Levine, ed., *Exhibiting Cultures: The Poetics and Politics of Museum Display* (Washington, DC: Smithsonian Institution Press, 1991).

32. Hecht, "How to Make," 189.

33. "Discussion," *MJ* 5, no. 4 (October 1905): 118.

34. Rev. S. J. Ford, "A Rotary Cabinet for Museum Specimens," *MJ* 6, no. 9 (March 1907): 304–305.

35. Kate M. Hall, "The Smallest Museum," *MJ* 1, no. 2 (August 1901): 42.

36. Ibid.

37. H. C. Bumpus, "A Contribution," 298.

38. McLean, *Planning for People,* 135–136.

39. Mintz, "That's Edutainment," 32.

40. L. A. Gratacap, "The Making of a Museum," *Architectural Record,* no. 9 (April 1900): 399.

41. Ibid., 301.

42. Frank Woolnaugh, "Museums and Nature Study," *MJ* 4, no. 8 (February 1905): 265.

43. Roberts, *From Knowledge to Narrative,* 22.

44. Fritsch, "The Museum Question," 255.

45. Anon., "The Spectator," *The Outlook* (May 29, 1909): 274.

46. "Excellence and Equity: Education and the Public Dimension of Museums," *Journal of Museum Education* 16, no. 3 (fall 1991): 92. American Association of Museums Task Force on Museum Education.

47. McLean, *Planning for People,* 23.

48. An editorial in the *Museums Journal* entitled "The Question of Groups" stated that habitat groups could only be "properly executed by institutions having at their command considerable sums of money and a large and efficient corps of workers." *MJ* 8, no. 12 (June 1909): 446.

49. Alderman W. R. Barker, "The Bristol Museum and Art Gallery," MJ 6, no. 2 (1906): 78–79.

50. "Discussion on the Papers on Museum Cases Read at the Bristol Conference, 1906," *MJ* 6, no. 12 (June 1907): 405.

51. For more on debates occasioned by the hyper-illusionism of museum group exhibits see chapter two of my book *Wondrous Difference: Cinema, Anthropology, and Turn-of-the-Century Visual Culture* (New York: Columbia University Press, 2002).

52. Chandler Screven, cited in Roberts, *From Knowledge to Narrative,* 19.

53. Roberts, *From Knowledge to Narrative,* 86.

54. Tim Caulton, *Hands-on Exhibitions: Managing Interactive Museums and Science Centers* (London: Routledge, 1998), 2. A study conducted by John Stevenson in 1991 on the long-term impact of interactives found that six months after a visit to Launch Pad, an interactive exhibit at the Science Museum in London, people were able to talk about the exhibits in detail and recalled that their experience had been enjoyable. Stevenson, "The Long-term Impact of Interactive Exhibits," *International Journal of Science Education* 13, no. 5 (1991): 521–531.

55. According to one study, the presence of a computer interactive in an exhibit enhanced the experience for visitors by encouraging them to spend more time in the gallery and to work cooperatively around the computer. D. D. Hilke, "The Impact of Interactive Computer Software on Visitor's Experiences: A Case Study," *ILVS Review* 1, no. 1 (1988): 34–49.

# Contributors

*Luis Arata* is chairperson of the Department of Fine Arts, Languages, and Philosophy at Quinnipiac University in Hamden, Conn. He has written on theatre, film, and cultural issues and has been awarded a visiting faculty fellowship at Yale University's Digital Media Center for the Arts.

*Constance Balides* is an associate professor in the Department of Communication at Tulane University. Her forthcoming book on women and the silent film era is entitled *Making Dust in the Archives.*

*William Boddy* is the author of *Fifties Television: The Industry and Its Critics* and has published on media history in *Screen, Cinema Journal, Media, Culture, and Society,* and the *International Journal of Cultural Studies* as well as in numerous anthologies. He is a professor at Baruch College and the Graduate Center of the City University of New York.

*Gregory Crane* is the author of *The Ancient Simplicity: Thucydides and the Limits of Political Realism* and *The Blinded Eye: Thucydides and the New Written Word.* He is Winnick Family Chair in Technology and Entrepreneurship and a professor of classics at Tufts University, and editor-in-chief of the Perseus Project, an online humanities library.

*Sharon Cumberland* is an associate professor of English at Seattle University and is working on a book about fan fiction and emerging genres of narrative on the Internet. Her articles on fan culture and critical theory appear in *Reload: Rethinking Women + Cyberculture* and an anthology about Walter J. Ong, forthcoming from Hampton Press.

*Peter S. Donaldson* is head of the literature section at the Massachusetts Institute of Technology, the author of *Machiavelli and Mystery of State* and *Shakespearean Films / Shakespearean Directors,* and director of the Shakespeare Electronic Archive.

*Paul Erickson* is completing his dissertation on sensational urban fiction in antebellum America at the University of Texas, Austin.

*Oz Frankel* is an assistant professor of history at the New School University. He recently completed a book manuscript based on his UC–Berkeley dissertation titled *States of Inquiry: The Politics, Rituals, and Texts of Social Investigations in 19th-Century Britain and the US.*

*Anne Friedberg* is the author of *Window Shopping: Cinema and the Postmodern* and co-editor of *Close Up 1927–1933: Cinema and Modernism.* She is an associate professor of film and visual studies at the University of California, Irvine.

*Lisa Gitelman* is an associate professor of English and media studies at Catholic University. She is the author of *Scripts, Grooves, and Writing Machines: Representing Technology in the Edison Era* and coeditor of *New Media, 1740–1915.*

*Alison Griffiths* is an assistant professor in the Department of Communication Studies at Baruch College, the City University of New York. The author of *Wondrous Difference: Cinema, Anthropology, and Turn-of-the-Century Visual Culture,* Griffiths is now writing a book on museums, technology, and the emergence of the spectacular view.

*Tom Gunning* is the author of *D. W. Griffith and the Origins of American Narrative Film* and *The Films of Fritz Lang: Allegories of Vision and Modernity* as well as many articles on early film. He is a professor in the Department of Art History and the Committee on Cinema and Media at the University of Chicago.

*Shelley Jackson* is the author of the hypertext novel *Patchwork Girl.* She has written and illustrated several children's books, and soon will publish her first collection of stories, *The Melancholy of Anatomy.*

*Henry Jenkins* is the John E. Burchard Professor of Humanities and director of the Program in Comparative Media Studies at MIT, where he writes a monthly column on media and culture, "Digital Renaissance," for *Technology Review.* His books include *Textual Poachers: Television Fans & Participatory Culture* and *The Children's Culture Reader.*

*Michael Joyce* is the author of *Moral Tales and Meditations: Technological Parables and Refractions* and a collection of essays, *Othermindedness: The Emergence of Network Culture.* He is an associate professor of English at Vassar College.

*William Mitchell* is professor of architecture and media arts and sciences and dean of the School of Architecture and Planning at MIT. His publications include *City of Bits: Space, Place, and the Infobahn* and *The Reconfigured Eye: Visual Truth in the Post-Photographic Era.*

*Priscilla Coit Murphy* holds a Ph.D. in media history from the School of Journalism and Mass Communication at the University of North Carolina at Chapel Hill, as well as degrees from American University and Swarthmore College. Her research interest concerns the role of books in the twentieth-century media system.

*Angela Ndalianis* teaches cinema and new media in the Cinema Studies Program at the University of Melbourne, Australia. Her research explores the overlaps among such media as film, computer games, comic books, and theme-park attractions.

*Daniel Thorburn* teaches history and social science at National University in California.

*David Thorburn* is a professor of literature at MIT and director of the MIT Communications Forum. He is the author of *Conrad's Romanticism* and many essays and reviews on literary, cultural, and media topics and was the founding editor of an earlier book series, *Media and Popular Culture.*

*William Uricchio* is a professor in the Program in Comparative Media Studies at MIT. He has authored, coauthored, and coedited several books, including *The Many Lives of Batman* and *Reframing Culture,* and is completing projects on the early Hollywood Western, cyber-history, and television in the Third Reich.

# Index